{ advance praise } for *Rose Reisman's Family Favorites*

Some of Rose's family's favorite recipes are on their way to becoming classics in mine too. There is so much to learn from this book—most of all the love of family and the transmission of knowledge that happens in families.

—RICARDO, HOST OF *RICARDO AND FRIENDS* ON FOOD NETWORK CANADA

Rose Reisman's Family Favorites is a complete package—great nutritional information, bright, appetizing pictures and recipes that the whole family will enjoy.

—CHRISTINE CUSHING, HOST OF *FEARLESS IN THE KITCHEN* ON THE W NETWORK

The recipes are ingenious yet simple, and the photos are inspiring. But the part I like best is Rose Reisman's valuable reminder about the absolute importance of family time spent around the dinner table. Use this book, and those dinners are guaranteed to be delicious!

—SENATOR LINDA FRUM

Rose Reisman's Family Favorites is a must-read for anyone who eats, cooks and wants to stay healthy. It's chock-full of current food wisdom and practical tips, along with recipes true to Reisman's easy, family-friendly touch. My advice? Read a section while baking her potato wedges sprinkled with olive oil and spices—the aroma and taste will revolutionize your idea of comfort food.

—ELLIE TESHER, AUTHOR AND SYNDICATED ADVICE COLUMNIST

Rose has that magical "mom" quality—she educates without being preachy, and makes difficult concepts easy to grasp. Her ideas about the dinner table are profoundly important to young families today. She's an original, and this book is akin to sitting down with her and picking her brain for a few hours. All you need to know is right there.

—RON JOHNSON, POST CITY MAGAZINES

Rose Reisman has always been focused on the family. When it comes to mealtime, we all know studies state that sitting down with the family at dinner is one of the biggest gifts you can give your kids. Now we have a book that can help us eat nutritiously, spend less time in the kitchen and more time with our family. Not to mention the recipes are delicious!

—MARILYN DENIS, MORNING COHOST, 104.5 CHUM FM (TORONTO)

Rose Reisman's Family Favorites will be dog-eared in no time. It's a time-tested collection of home cooking and homespun wisdom, as well as a handy reference for healthy living. Rose's approach goes beyond great-tasting recipes that are good for you. She cuts out the stress and chaos around meal plans and preparation. Rose puts the "comfort" in food because her key ingredient is family at the dinner table.

—DAVE TRAFFORD, NEWSTALK 1010 (TORONTO)

Healthy food habits start at home, and introducing your family to good shopping and eating practices is the foundation of Rose Reisman's message in her newest book, *Rose Reisman's Family Favorites*. In it, Reisman stresses the importance of scheduled meals, with tips on how to cut out the calories and control weight, and meal-planning instructions that are easy to understand and implement. The second part of the book is dedicated to a stunning array of beautifully photographed recipes—from breakfasts and appetizers to main dishes and desserts—that are rich on taste without compromising nutrition. From Mexican- and Italian-inspired staples like her shrimp quesadillas with cheese and avocado and her layered tortilla lasagna with chickpeas to the classic children's favorite mac 'n cheese, Reisman's recipe creations span old and new favorites that are lighter on the waistline than their traditional counterparts.

—ANN-MARIE COLACINO, STYLE AND FOOD EDITOR, METRO ENGLISH CANADA

ROSE REISMAN'S
Family Favorites

ROSE REISMAN'S
Family Favorites

whitecap

Whitecap Books is known for its expertise in the cookbook market, and has produced some of the most innovative and familiar titles found in kitchens across North America. Visit our website at www.whitecap.ca.

RECIPES EDITED BY Theresa Best
INTRODUCTION EDITED BY Melva McLean
DESIGN BY Mauve Pagé
FOOD PHOTOGRAPHY BY Ryan Szulc, except page 153 (© iStockphoto.com/Trawick Images) and page 285 (© iStockphoto.com/jcaunedo)
FOOD STYLING BY Nancy Midwicki
PROP STYLING BY Madeleine Johari

Printed in China

LIBRARY AND ARCHIVES CANADA CATALOGUING IN PUBLICATION

Reisman, Rose
Rose Reisman's family favorites.

Includes index.
ISBN 978-1-77050-006-8

1. Cookery. 2. Nutrition.
I. Title. II. Title: Family favorites.

TX714.R45 2010 641.5'63 C2009-906417-0

The publisher acknowledges the financial support of the Government of Canada through the Canada Book Fund (CBF) and the Province of British Columbia through the Book Publishing Tax Credit.

10 11 12 13 14 5 4 3 2 1

{ contents }

{ foreword } by dr. david macklin

As a trained family physician, I focus my practice exclusively on helping people learn how to eat well, lose weight, exercise and manage stress. Naturally, nutrition is one of my main concerns. In medical school I became obsessed with how poor eating was ruining the health of so many of my patients. Food—and its role in human health—has always been important to me. And I'm certain it has to do with having been raised in a home where healthy home-cooked meals were the rule and not the exception.

Eating healthy meals at home—Rose has written a book based on this simple premise. I think this book will strike an important chord with all families. She has created an exciting resource that I can see improving, perhaps even turning around, the health of any family.

People are eating dinner at home less and less every year. In the 1970s, 74% of people ate dinner at home; today only 36% do. Over the exact same time span our weights have spiraled up uncontrollably. Also shocking is *what* those eating dinner at home are usually eating: processed foods, foods high in fat, foods high in sugar. Sadly, this is not very different from when we eat out.

So why is it important to avoid exposing our children and families to this unhealthy food? Simply said, these foods lead to overeating and weight gain. Firstly, processed foods obliterate our ability to feel full—the actual center in our brain that senses fullness gets blocked. Secondly, overeating foods high in fat and added sugars can create a serious addiction. Eating has evolved to feel rewarding, to support the biological imperative of calorie intake. This natural and subtle reward circuitry is simply overwhelmed and overstimulated by processed foods. And this "hyper-reward" leads to "hypereating." (It's the same process that leads some of us to become addicted to drugs, alcohol, cigarettes, sex, gambling and shopping.) Family meals based on poor nutrition have created a generation of children and adults who have lost the natural capacity to feel full and who look to the dinner table for their next "fix."

This book is all about how to avoid having yourself and your family fall into this trap. Rose manages this expertly. I have eaten dinner at Rose's and marveled at how easily she prepares delicious, healthy, natural foods for her guests and family. Using these recipes will provide a framework for getting healthy—through delicious family dinners that everyone will love. And I speak from firsthand experience. Over the last two years the majority of the dinners I have eaten at home have been recipes Rose has collected for this book, as well as recipes from her past books. And I have never been healthier and more energized. I have Rose to thank, and so can you.

By the way, if you do want to thank her, she reads all her email and often replies at five in the morning when she is up starting her day. She answers email, exercises, and obviously plans the family meal! She is always making sure her family stays healthy.

It's a true inspiration for her readers. Enjoy.

Dr. David Macklin
December 2009

{ message }

from the president and CEO of Breakfast for Learning

Rose, over her career, has had a huge impact on the way we think, eat and act—she's transformed our ideas about food consumption and our attitudes toward exercise and healthy living. And as a mother of four, Rose understands the importance that nutrition plays in the healthy development of our children and youth. She knows that starting each day with a good nutritious breakfast is one of the best things we can do for our children and ourselves. It isn't just what research tells us, but something she's gained from life experience. Not only does a good breakfast improve concentration and increase energy levels, but it improves overall performance in school. And it improves one's quality of life. But we are living in a world where far too many children and youth go to school hungry: Nearly one-third of elementary school children and a shocking two-thirds of secondary school children in Canada still go to school each morning without eating breakfast. We can do better!

Building on Rose's long-standing practice of giving back to the community, she has partnered with our organization, Breakfast for Learning (BFL). We are proud to announce that she's recently become our spokesperson. BFL's mission is to help local communities start and sustain programs that provide breakfast, lunch and snacks to students. Who better than Rose to represent us and spread our message?

Rose's latest book deals with one essential ingredient to good health—taking the time to dine together as a family. Families live healthier and more satisfying lives this way, and it's a key element in the development of our children. We are thoroughly delighted and honored to welcome Rose. We thank her for her unwavering support of our cause and for her contribution to our organization. When it comes to child nutrition, Rose Reisman is truly a dedicated champion!

Wendy Wong
December 2009

{ dedication }

The same dedication book after book! My passion, energy and love for what I do comes directly from my incredible husband and four children. Life becomes richer each day with them in my life.

SAM—As always, my number one supporter. I'll love you forever.

NATALIE—Your enthusiasm for life affects all around you. Hugs to Ricky, my future son-in-law!

DAVID—You are a sensitive, kind, charming and personable young man. And might I add, so good looking! (Only your mother can say that.)

LAURA—Finding your passion of teaching young children has been an inspiration to your family. It's a joy watching you mature into a poised and intuitive young woman.

ADAM—You will always be my "baby." You're leaving the nest this fall to go to university. Your perseverance and determination have been a role model for us all.

MY ANIMAL CLAN—To the wonderful and loving animals in my home that give me tranquillity on the busiest of days. My German shepherds, Aspen and Rocky, and two Ragdoll cats, Misty and Ozzie!

AND TO MARY FINSON, my mother who loved me unconditionally.

{ preface } in praise of family dinners

This book supports Breakfast for Learning, an organization that recognizes the benefits of basic nutrition for children. Our future generation's health is, indeed, dependent on a healthy breakfast. While this is its namesake and focused mission, its broader mandate is to support families in ensuring their children are not negatively impacted by a nutrition deficiency.

We are daily bombarded with information about how our poor diets and lack of exercise threaten our well-being. It is indeed a paradox that despite more compelling evidence about how we can prevent disease simply by eating better and moving more, our children's generation are still likely to be less healthy than ours. What we eat and the way we eat have become a lethal threat to our well-being, translating to increased blood pressure, high cholesterol levels, a dramatic increase in type 2 diabetes, obesity, heart and stroke disease, as well as various cancers and other chronic diseases. While these statistics may especially apply to those who are obese, it can also apply to those of normal weight but still asymptomatic.

It's become pretty clear that one of the challenges in improving our diets is not lack of information. We "know" too much already! I firmly believe the answer is in *doing*. Let's talk less about health and nutrition and—believe it or not—*eat more*. Let's focus our efforts on the practice of preparing simple, delicious, balanced, nutritious meals. And let's enjoy those meals with our family around the kitchen table.

Spending mealtime with the family is shown to improve a child's emotional, intellectual and physical health. Studies show that frequent family meals may actually reduce the chances that your child will use drugs or drink or smoke later on. Let this book help you make your kitchen a valuable resource for your entire family. My recipes take only minutes to prepare but can add years to your children's lives. And remember, it's not all or nothing. Even one night a week can have a positive impact on your family's well-being.

We don't need more information—we need action. We can't change the health of our nation simply by providing more facts. The change must come from individuals like yourselves, one kitchen at a time. Together we can change our population's diets and health forever!

So, welcome to my 18th book. Whether it's my best one or not will be for you to judge (although I hope you think so!). Bringing families back to the table is my newest initiative, but spreading the message of eating well and eating delicious meals has been my mission for the past 15 years. What I am certain of is that it's my most important work. This book is intended as a "recipe" for family harmony and health. Follow it and your life will be the better for it. Enjoy!

Rose Reisman

Laura

{ introduction } keeping your family healthy

My last book, *The Art of Living Well*, discussed the state of our country's health. It wasn't such a pretty picture. Heart attacks, strokes, obesity, cancer, type 2 diabetes, high cholesterol and high blood pressure were ruining our health. That book was written in 2004. We're starting to improve our lifestyle, but not soon enough. Today, North Americans spend more on health care than do any other people in the world. We won't be able to afford to be sick, so the best thing to do is to start living healthier lifestyles now!

If you want your children to grow up with healthy eating habits, it's of course best to start from day one, but it's really never too late to introduce good shopping and eating habits to your family. Here are some key principles:

» Lean toward a whole foods diet consisting of whole grains, fruits and vegetables, lean protein and lower-fat dairy products.
» Eat fewer processed and packaged foods.
» Drink more water, 100% fruit juice (in moderation) and lower-fat milk products.
» Choose to bake/roast/grill, not fry, foods. In fact, if you have a deep-fryer at home, get rid of it!

{ canada's food guide }

One tool to help you get started toward healthy eating is Canada's Food Guide (www.healthcanada.gc.ca/foodguide). Updated in 2007, the Guide now gives serving amounts for children, teens and adults and breaks down servings for males and females. In addition, the Guide is now available in 12 different languages, and takes into account various cultures and their food preferences.

The Guide is a great education in what to eat, how much to eat and when to eat it. It's easy to follow, and I consider the Guide to be the "magic bullet" to maintaining your weight and meeting your needs for nutrients that help prevent serious and chronic diseases.

The Guide advises you on choosing the healthiest foods in each of the food groups; the types of fat best consumed; the most nutritious fruits and vegetables; various whole-grain products; lower-fat dairy products; and lean choices of meat or other sources of protein such as beans, lentils and tofu. It emphasizes lowering the amount of fat, sugar and calories in your diet (while maintaining that you can still enjoy all foods in moderation).

{ THE FOOD GROUPS

Canada's Food Guide recommends the number of servings people of various ages should eat daily from the four groups. The servings break down something like this:

- Vegetables and fruits: 4 to 10 servings
- Grain products: 3 to 8 servings
- Milk and alternatives: 2 to 4 servings
- Meat and alternatives: 1 to 3 servings

So how do you combine these groups to get the most nutrition as well as maintain your weight? The key is to include something from at least three and preferably four of the major food groups in each main meal and at least two food groups in each snack. Combining three or four of the food groups in each meal will keep you satisfied before your next snack or meal. For example, breakfast might consist of yogurt, fruit and whole-grain toast. Lunch could be a salad with protein and a side roll or a whole-grain sandwich with turkey and vegetables. Just add a yogurt or milk and you've covered all four food groups. That's how easy it is. Snacks can consist of fruit and ½ oz (12 g) cheese, ¼ cup (60 mL) of nuts, or crackers with 1 Tbsp (15 mL) of peanut butter.

It's best to go through the Guide with your family doctor or a nutritionist to learn more about how to interpret the Guide and prepare a plan for each member of your family based on their metabolic rate and activity level. But let's take a moment to look at what the Guide has to say about the four food groups, supplements, oils and fats, and water.

Vegetables and fruits

You can never eat enough fruits and vegetables. These superfoods are low in fat and calories and provide nutrients, which include carbohydrates, vitamins A and C, potassium, magnesium and some B vitamins. Depending on age and gender, the Guide recommends that you eat four to ten servings from this group daily. One serving might be an apple or banana, 1 cup (250 mL) of green salad or ½ cup (125 mL) of juice. Choose at least one dark green and one orange vegetable daily because they are rich in folate and beta-carotene, which the body converts to vitamin A. Enjoy vegetables steamed, baked or stir-fried instead of deep-fried. Frozen or canned vegetables and fruit are a healthy, convenient option, but avoid fruits packed in heavy syrup and vegetables packed in oil and excess salt.

Grain products

Grains, specifically whole grains, are a source of fiber, which helps you feel full and satisfied, and assists in weight maintenance. Never follow any diet that excludes these complex carbohydrates. According to the Dietitians of Canada (www.dietitians.ca), fiber has been shown to lower LDL (bad cholesterol), prevent bowel problems, reduce the risk of colon cancer, help control type 2 diabetes and aid weight loss. New studies indicate that with every 10-gram increase in fiber, the risk of heart attack may decrease by 20%. Most North Americans consume only about 11 grams of fiber daily. The National Cancer Institute of Canada recommends eating between 25 and 35 grams of fiber every day (The Canadian Breast Cancer Network, www.cbcn.ca).

There are two types of fiber: soluble and insoluble. Soluble fiber is found in oats, barley, vegetables, fruit, brown rice and oat bran, among other foods. This type of fiber decreases bad cholesterol, thereby possibly decreasing the risk of heart disease. Insoluble fiber is found in wheat and corn bran, fruits and vegetables and nuts and seeds. This type of fiber helps promote regularity, which may decrease the risk of colon cancer.

Grains are complex carbohydrates that provide B vitamins, iron, zinc and magnesium. Depending on age and gender, Canada's Food Guide recommends that you eat three to eight servings *daily*. One serving might be a slice of toast, ¾ cup (185 mL) of cereal, half a small bagel or ½ cup (125 mL) of pasta or rice. At least half of your grain products should be labeled "whole" or "whole-grain." Some examples of whole grains are bulgur, millet, pot barley (less processed than pearl barley), quinoa, spelt, large rolled oats (also known as "old-fashioned"), buckwheat and wild rice. Foods that are high in fiber have at least 4 grams of fiber per serving.

THE GLYCEMIC INDEX

There has been a lot of buzz in recent years about the glycemic index (GI). This index ranks carbohydrate foods based on their immediate effect on blood glucose levels. Carbohydrates that break down quickly during digestion have a high glycemic index and raise your blood sugar quickly. The result is that you quickly get hungry, and you tend to snack more often, which may cause your weight to increase. High-glycemic foods include pastries, sugar cereals, white flour products and white potatoes.

Carbohydrates that break down slowly during digestion raise blood sugar slowly and keep you feeling full longer. Lowering blood glucose levels is a major means of minimizing the complications associated with type 2 diabetes. Low-glycemic foods include high-fiber fruits and vegetables, bran cereals, legumes and beans. Although the GI is a helpful tool in choosing your carbohydrates, don't base everything on the GI. Note that the effect of the whole meal is more important than the GI of each individual food.

Milk and alternatives

This food group provides calcium, vitamins A, D and B12, zinc, magnesium, potassium, protein and fat. These nutrients help develop strong bones and decrease the risk of osteoporosis. Canada's Food Guide recommends two to four servings daily, depending on age and gender. One serving might be two slices of packaged cheese, ¾ cup (80 mL) of yogurt, 1 cup (250 mL) milk or 1 cup (250 mL) soy beverage. Choose skim, 1% or 2% milk products and consume fortified soy beverages if you do not drink milk.

Meat and alternatives

The meat-and-alternatives food group supplies you with protein. Your body needs protein to build and maintain muscle tissue and repair cells. Protein strengthens bones, produces enzymes to help digest your food and allows your brain to see, hear and think. Protein also boosts your metabolism and fills your stomach so you won't feel hungry. This group also provides you with iron, zinc, magnesium, B vitamins (including B6 and B12) and fat.

Canada's Food Guide recommends that you eat one to three servings daily, depending on your age and gender. Other forms of protein include eggs, fish, legumes, meat, nuts and seeds and tofu. Try to include a few more "vegetarian days" rather than meat-based meals, to reduce the saturated fat in your diet. One serving might be 2½ oz (75 g) meat, fish or chicken, ¾ cup (185 mL) beans, 2 Tbsp (30 mL) peanut butter or ¾ cup (185 mL) of tofu. Eat at least two servings of (sustainable) fish each week. Select lean meat and alternatives. Trim visible fat from meat and remove skin from poultry. Roast, bake or poach poultry and fish rather than frying them.

{ SUPPLEMENTS

Remember that a pill cannot supply all the necessary vitamins, minerals and other nutrients you need to strengthen your immune system—only a healthy diet can do that. The key is maintaining a diet rich in fruits, vegetables, grains, lean protein and lower-fat dairy products. You can obtain the majority of your nutrients from these foods in order to fight disease and strengthen your immune system. Vitamins and minerals are necessary for proper metabolic functioning. They can help prevent malnutrition, heart disease and certain cancers. They also improve the quality of hair, nails and skin. The body can't produce all the needed vitamins and minerals, so we obtain them from food, and the fresher the foods, the more nutrients they supply to your body.

Vitamins

There are 13 essential vitamins, divided into two groups: fat-soluble and water-soluble. The fat-soluble vitamins are stored in your body and include vitamins A, E, D and K. Because you can store these vitamins, you don't need to get a daily supply of them. The exception is vitamin D. The lack of this vitamin is now associated with a risk of cancer, heart disease, diabetes and autoimmune diseases. In terms of supplements, check with your doctor on the correct amount. And look for fortified foods such as dairy and cereals. Fatty fish also contain vitamin D.

The water-soluble vitamins dissolve in water, so any extra is carried out of your body, and you need to get a fresh supply every day. Water-soluble vitamins include C and all the B vitamins.

Minerals

Your body needs calcium, chloride, magnesium, phosphorus, potassium, sodium, sulfur and other minerals, in very small amounts,

MULTIVITAMIN SUPPLEMENTS

A daily multivitamin acts as a "safety net" in your day when it may not always be possible to eat a balanced diet. You should look for a multivitamin that supplies 100% to 300% of your RDA (recommended daily allowance). It should contain beta-carotene; vitamins A, D, B1, B2, B6, B12 and B9 (folic acid); and iron, zinc, copper, magnesium, iodine, selenium and chromium.

CHOLESTEROL

There are two types of cholesterol, often called "good" and "bad." Good HDL helps your body get rid of the cholesterol in your blood; the higher the number, the better off you are. A level of less than 0.9 is considered low and increases your risk for heart disease. Bad LDL is the cholesterol that builds up in the walls of your arteries. The higher this number, the greater the risk for heart disease. A desirable LDL is less than 3.4.

for normal growth and general health, and to regulate metabolism.

OILS AND FATS

We are a fat-phobic society, yet certain fats are necessary for good health. Fats play an important role in hormone production, red blood cell formation, joint lubrication and proper insulin function. They supply essential fats that help our bodies absorb vitamins A, D, E and K. It's best to consume monounsaturated fats, which include peanut, olive and grapeseed oil.

The polyunsaturated fats include non-hydrogenated margarine, soybean, sunflower, safflower, canola and corn oil. These oils are less likely to increase your cholesterol or lead to heart disease.

Reduce the amount of saturated fat such as butter, lard and animal fat, which can clog your arteries, leading to heart disease or stroke.

Eating the right fats in moderation will not cause you to gain excess fat. A healthy diet should consist of a daily intake of between 25% and 30% fat. However, the typical North American diet, which consists of 40% or more fat, exceeds that considerably.

WATER

The body needs water for the transportation and absorption of nutrients, for digestion, for circulation, for the regulation of body temperature and for flushing our systems, and it is essential to drink at least eight glasses of water every day. Although you can get some water through fruits and vegetables and other beverages, water is still the best fluid for ensuring that the body functions correctly. Only one question remains: What type of water is the best? We've been led to believe that bottled water is healthier for us than tap water. But then we hear that bottled water is only as good as the source. Let's look at some of the various types of water we can consume.

TAP WATER This water, which originally comes from lakes, rivers or reservoirs, has been treated to remove contaminants. Your local government is supposed to check the safety of your water supply for contamination, and you should check the health records of your city to be sure that this is monitored effectively. If you get your water from a private well, it is your responsibility to have the water checked. Installing a filtration system is a good way to guard against contaminants.

BOTTLED WATER There are two types of bottled water: filtered water, from which the minerals have been filtered out, and mineral water, which has minerals and comes from a natural spring.

BISPHENOL A IN PLASTIC

The chemical Bisphenol A (BPA) is a chemical monomer used primarily in the production of polycarbonate plastic and epoxy resins. Polycarbonate is used in food contact materials such as beverage bottles, infant feeding bottles, food containers and processing equipment. (Polycarbonate containers that contain BPA usually have a #7 on the bottom.) Epoxy resins are used in protective linings for a variety of canned foods and beverages, including infant formula. One reason people are concerned about BPA is that human exposure to BPA is widespread. A recent National Health and Nutrition Examination Survey conducted by the Centers for Disease Control and Prevention (CDC) found detectable levels of BPA in 95% of a sample of people tested in the USA. These data are considered representative of exposures in the United States. In Canada, some animal studies report harmful effects in fetuses and newborns exposed to BPA (Health Canada, www.hc-sc.gc.ca). Here are some recommendations:

» Don't microwave polycarbonate plastic food containers.
» Reduce your use of canned foods.
» When possible, opt for glass, porcelain or stainless steel containers, particularly for hot food or liquids.
» Use baby bottles that are BPA free.

Bottled water is not necessarily safer than tap water. Bottled water can have a higher bacterial count than tap water and can be sold even if it does not meet regional standards for tap water. You can always check with the International Bottled Water Association (www.bottledwater.org) and see what they have to say about your bottled water manufacturer.

In general, watch out for trendy marketing ploys making bottled water sound healthier than it is.

DISTILLED WATER Distilled water is the purest of waters. It contains no sodium and no solid materials. Unlike mineral water, which tastes of the minerals it contains, distilled water has no taste at all.

HOME-DISTILLED WATER For between $100 and $500 you can get a countertop distiller that boils water and condenses the vapor. Distilling reduces levels of chemicals in the water and can kill microorganisms and remove chlorine and fluoride. Be sure your toothpaste contains fluoride if you drink distilled water.

HOME-FILTERED WATER To improve the taste of your water, a filtering pitcher will do just fine. Inexpensive home water filters might make tap water taste better, but they don't make it healthier. If you're trying to remove contaminants, you could consider installing a permanent water filter, although at a cost of more than $1,000, it is an expensive alternative.

VITAMIN WATER Sometimes called "fitness water," this water is distilled and combined with vitamins, herbs and flavors. The concept sounds great, but most North Americans are not vitamin deficient, except for vitamin E, and vitamin water is high in sugar—approximately 2 Tbsp (30 mL) of fructose (simple sugar) per bottle. Don't waste your money.

OXYGENATED WATER There's very little reliable evidence to show that oxygenated (or oxygenized) water has any significant effect on exercise performance, energy levels or recovery. This water isn't going to hurt you, but there's no reason to believe it's going to help you substantially.

{ the best foods for your family }

According to the Guide, the perfectly balanced plate consists of 50% nonstarchy vegetables, 25% protein and 25% grains or starchy vegetables.

You and your family should be eating three meals a day and two nutritious snacks, limit high-sugar and high-fat foods and increase the amount of fruits and vegetables, lean meats and low-fat dairy products, including three servings of milk, cheese or yogurt to meet their calcium needs. To avoid giving unnecessary supplements, here are the foods that your family should be consuming.

High-fiber foods	fruits, vegetables, legumes (peas and beans), breads and cereals
Protein-rich foods	milk, soy milk, eggs, yogurt, peanut butter, lean meats, fish and poultry, beans, tofu
Iron-rich foods	red meats, seafood (salmon, tuna), beans, iron-fortified grains
Calcium-rich foods	milk, yogurt, salmon, tofu, spinach
Whole foods	fruits, vegetables, legumes, nuts and seeds, whole grains, milk, meat
Foods high in vitamin C	red pepper, strawberries, citrus fruits, broccoli, kiwis
Potassium-rich foods	tomatoes, nuts and seeds, raisins, prunes, potatoes, bananas, deep yellow vegetables

{ ADULTS AND SENIORS

As we age, eating properly becomes an even more important issue. Many seniors live alone and find it an effort to cook and to eat healthily, especially in the winter months. Because caloric needs decline as we age, obesity can become an issue, one that leads to more serious chronic diseases. A balanced diet can prevent certain age-related conditions such as heart and stroke, cancer, cataracts and neurological disorders, as well as disorders of the joints and osteoporosis. The 2007 Canada's Food Guide inclusion of nutritional information for people over 50 is further indication of the importance of good nutrition throughout our lives. In addition, this handy nutritional guide will help you plan meals around the daily requirements for men and women over 19.

One general rule regarding the appropriate number of calories per serving: 40 calories is low, 100 calories is moderate and 400 calories or more is high (FDA U.S. Food and Drug Administration, www.fda.gov/Food/).

	WOMEN AGED 25–50	WOMEN OVER 50	MEN OVER 24
Calories	2,000	2,000 or less	2,700
Protein	50 g	50 g or less	63 g
Fat	65 g or less	65 g or less	88 g or less
Saturated fat	20 g or less	20 g or less	27 g or less
Carbohydrates	304 g	304 g	410 g
Fiber	25–35 g	25–35 g	25–35 g
Cholesterol	300 mg or less	300 mg or less	300 mg or less
Iron	18 mg	8 mg	8 mg
Sodium	2,300 mg or less	1,500 mg or less	2,300 mg or less
Calcium	1,000 mg	1,200 mg	1,000 mg

Adapted from Center for Food Safety & Applied Nutrition (www.fda.com/Food/) and Cooking Light Magazine *(www.cookinglight.com)*

{TO BE OR NOT TO BE VEGETARIAN

Vegetarianism has been accepted as part of the norm of healthy eating for the past few decades. No longer considered a fad, vegetarianism involves changing the way you think about food, and doesn't have to be an all-or-nothing type of diet. A vegetarian regime is liable to be very healthful, because in its emphasis on whole grains, legumes, vegetables and dairy or soy products, it results in a higher intake of plant-based products that contain more antioxidants, vitamins and minerals. A well-balanced vegetarian diet, which is low in cholesterol and high in fiber, can help combat conditions and diseases that may be connected to a diet high in fat, such as obesity, heart disease, high blood pressure, high cholesterol, diabetes, gallstones and cancers.

Careful planning is necessary to ensure that vegetarians get all of the required vitamins and minerals. Vegans have to be particularly cautious and make sure that they get enough calcium and vitamin B12.

FRUITARIANS avoid all animal products and processed foods.

VEGANS avoid all animal products.

LACTO-VEGETARIANS eat dairy products but not eggs.

LACTO-OVO-VEGETARIANS eat both dairy products and eggs.

SEMIVEGETARIANS eat fish and/or chicken but no red meat. They are not officially classed as vegetarians.

FLEXITARIANS enjoy meatless meals on a regular basis.

There's been a rise in vegetarianism in children and teens. Statistics suggest that about one in 200 children avoids eating meat. Other surveys suggest the rate could be four to six times that among older teens, who have more control over what they eat than do young children.

There is nothing to worry about if your child wants to try being a vegetarian—whether it's because they want to be healthier or because they are concerned about animal welfare—but keep in mind that growing children have to get sufficient amounts of protein, vitamin B12 and vitamin D, iron, calcium and other important nutrients that most people get from meat, eggs and dairy.

It's always better to get these nutrients from food rather than supplements, so here's a chart that can help you make sure your young vegetarians are eating the right foods.

Vitamin B12	nutritional yeast, seaweed, miso-fortified soy beverages, cereals
Vitamin D	fortified dairy, soy beverages, cereals, fatty fish, sunshine
Calcium	calcium-processed tofu, broccoli, seeds, nuts, kale, bok choy, legumes (peas and beans), greens, lime-processed corn tortillas, soy beverages, grain products, orange juice enriched with calcium
Iron	legumes, tofu, leafy green vegetables, dried fruit, whole grains, iron-fortified cereals and breads (especially whole wheat). Note that absorption is improved by vitamin C, found in citrus fruits and juices, tomatoes, strawberries, broccoli, peppers, leafy dark-green vegetables and potato skins.
Zinc	whole grains (especially the germ and bran), whole wheat bread, legumes, nuts, tofu
Protein	tofu and other soy-based products, legumes, seeds, nuts, grains, vegetables

THE IMMUNE SYSTEM

The stronger your immune system, the less you are prone to diseases in general. Following Canada's Food Guide, eating well and exercising regularly keeps your immune system strong. Here are some tips to improve your immune system.

» Moderate consumption of caffeine.
» Minimize alcohol.
» Avoid extreme dieting, especially those that omit entire food groups.
» Eat half a clove of garlic each day.
» Use freshly grated ginger in tea or foods.
» Eat dark chocolate (with 70% or more cocoa content), in moderation. It contains antioxidants that fight disease.
» Make chicken soup. The compound in it called *cystine* has a decongestant quality.
» Take probiotic supplements or eat more yogurt or kefir.
» Eat vitamin C foods daily (bell peppers, strawberries, grapefruit).
» Eat foods rich in vitamin A daily (yellow and green vegetables).
» Eat vitamin E foods (nuts, seeds, grains, vegetables).
» Eat foods rich in zinc (seafood, red meat, yogurt, enriched cereals).

{ making meals a family affair }

The family dinner table is still one of the best places for family to get together and bond, to talk about our days and our problems and to share the latest gossip about our friends and acquaintances and the latest news about the world. In my family, we try to sit down at least four times a week for family meals. It's a great ritual to reacquaint yourself with your family.

{ OBSTACLES

It takes time to change old habits and behaviors. You have to overcome a lot of obstacles on the road to healthy family dinners. Knowing what they are can help you prepare a proactive strategy.

Too much fast food

There's no question why McDonald's and other heavily marketed fast-food outlets have been so successful. It's hard to compete against delicious-tasting, salty and fatty food served quickly, in a fun and exciting place that gives you toys to boot.

Too much processed and junk foods

Processed and preserved foods are abundant in our supermarkets. Many have labels that are either misleading or difficult to understand. And junk food is everywhere, even finding its way in schools, which should not be in the business of promoting foods and beverages that are high in calories and fat and low in nutrition. Yet many schools and universities still have vending machines filled with food that is poor in nutrients since this is an excellent source of revenue.

Too little time

Working parents and children's after-school activities make it difficult to sit down together as a family.

{ KICK-START SUGGESTIONS

Although it may take time for you to get your family eating together, have patience. The benefits of eating at home are numerous. "Breaking bread" with your family will improve family relationships, give you the opportunity to serve and educate your family on healthier and tastier meals, improve your family's health by offering healthier meals and, ultimately, save you money. Here are seven suggestions to help kick-start family dinners.

Start with two days a week

In the beginning, don't worry about eating together every day. Consider having one of the family meals on the weekend when family members have more time. If you can't find one or two nights a week to eat together, carefully look at your family's activities and try to cut back on them.

Involve children in food preparation

Children improve their reading and math skills while cooking, and they're more likely to eat a meal they had a role in preparing.

Find age-appropriate ways for them to help cook, clean up and safely store food. Be sure they're having fun—be creative and not just instructional.

Use themes

The same old dinners week after week give children a good excuse for not being at the table. Have a Mexican, Asian or Italian night. Let them choose the theme! It's an opportunity for everyone in the family to learn about other cultures and their food.

Keep meals simple

Preparing gourmet-style meals is an option once you've established the family-dinner habit, if you are so inclined. In the beginning, keep the meals simple.

Keep dinner conversations fun

Dinnertime ought to be a fun and positive time for the family—it's not the time to discipline your children, complain about their grades or friends or argue with your spouse about money issues.

Invite friends over

Occasionally having friends for dinner adds a different and positive aspect to your dinners. Let your children do it too. Everyone behaves better when a guest is at the table, and I find children are more willing to try new foods.

Turn off the TV

During the dinner hour, make it a rule to turn off the television, the cell phone and the BlackBerry.

COOKBOOKS FOR KIDS

Cooking Rocks! Rachael Ray's 30-Minute Meals for Kids, by Rachael Ray (Lake Isle Press, 2004)
This book is filled with drawings, great photos and recipes that are age specific. For ages 4 to 10.

Cooking with Children, by Marion Cunningham (Knopf, 1995)
Both adults and children learn culinary skills, as well as the importance of quality family time, through cooking. For ages 7 and up.

Emeril's There's a Chef in My Soup, by Emeril Lagasse (HarperCollins, 2005)
Over 75 recipes like "Grill-It-Up-a-Notch Ham and Cheese Sandwich," "Baby Bam Burgers" and "Oh-Yeah-Baby Glazed Carrots." For ages 12 and up.

Pretend Soup and Other Real Recipes: A Cookbook for Preschoolers and Up, by Mollie Katzen and Ann L. Henderson (Tricycle Press, 2004)
The child is the main focus, and attention is paid to her physical abilities. The process is more relevant here than the product. For ages 5 to 8.

Kitchen for Kids: 100 Amazing Recipes Your Children Can Really Make, by Jennifer Low (Whitecap Books, 2004)
Great photographs accompany recipes like "Paddy Thai Noodles" (an oven-baked take on Pad Thai), "Baby Lemon Meringue Pies" and "Strawberry Fudge Striped Cake." For ages 9 to 12.

Fanny at Chez Panisse: A Child's Restaurant Adventures with 46 Recipes, by Alice Waters (William Morrow Cookbooks, 1997)
This delightful book tells the story about how food gets from the garden to the kitchen of a famous restaurant. For ages 9 to 12.

{ PLANNING MEALS

So you've got them back to the table a few more times a week. Now it's time to start eating healthier meals. First, you have to start planning meals. Most of us fall into the trap of getting home at the dinner hour only to realize that we're missing the ingredients we want to make a certain dish. Here are some tips to help you.

Plan a week ahead

Organize your shopping around a weekly menu. Order in your groceries if you don't have time to shop. You can cut down on the cost of online or telephone shopping by ordering large quantities. If cooking on the spot is not your forte, prepare some meals on the weekend that you can package, refrigerate or freeze for the week ahead.

Plan with family favorites

Know what your family's favorites are. If your family loves meat and potatoes, just try serving a smaller portion but accompanied with whole grains and vegetables. Create new family favorites! There will always be nights when one member of the family won't like the choice. You can make a bowl of pasta and tomato sauce as a backup plan.

Plan based on your pantry

The foods you store are those you know your family likes. First do a careful label check to see if these foods fit into your new healthier lifestyle. Look at the calories, fat, sodium and cholesterol per serving to see how it measures up to what you need to maintain a healthy body weight.

Plan based on supermarket deals

Check your grocery store ads to see what's on sale and plan meals around those items. You can also stock up on good buys and freeze them, well wrapped and with the date marked, to help you with future meals.

Plan using balance

Don't be too concerned with perfectly balancing each day's nutrients. Try instead to balance nutrients, calories and fat intake over several days. Balance for temperature: A mix of hot and cold foods makes a more interesting meal. Also balance for texture: Combine soft foods with crunchy ones.

Plan using color

The more color on the plate, the better balanced the meal. Really! Plus a colorful plate is a treat for the eyes.

{ David Reisman (Rose's son) }

{ three meals a day }

In an ideal world, we would all sit down to eat together three times a day, but it's not an ideal world. Still, you can try. There's no rule saying that one of the two meals a week you start with has to be dinner. Whatever meal it is, make it as healthy as you can.

{ BREAKFAST

New research reiterates what Mom said every morning: "Eat your breakfast!" In general, the research shows that breakfast—

» kick-starts metabolism after a night's sleep.
» reduces hormones that increase carbohydrate craving.
» significantly increases your daily dietary intake of fiber, vitamins and minerals.
» increases a student's math grades and reading scores (American Diabetes Association, via www.healthcastle.com).
» reduces a child's risk of being overweight as an adolescent (American Diabetes Association, via www.healthcastle.com).

A good breakfast should consist of some combination of protein and fiber that keeps you full until lunch or midmorning snack time. Some examples:

» Cereal (or oatmeal) and milk
» Eggs and toast
» Peanut butter and whole-grain bread
» Yogurt and fruit

Cereals

When we're in a rush, breakfast cereals are the easiest and quickest way to get out the door. But there's a big difference in the nutritional value of cereals. Many may sound nutritious, but when you read the labels you'll see sugar is one of the first ingredients. Breakfast cereals are heavily marketed to children. Yet many adults are consuming these sugary cereals as well.

The word *sugar* has become so negative that manufacturers have removed the word from their names and replaced them with other adjectives, such as honey or golden crisp, but they still contain the same amounts of sugar. Some cereals have reduced the sugar, but if you carefully read the nutrition label, you'll see even more calories because they've added fat to replace the flavor of the missing sugar.

Even if they read the nutritional labels, most people usually end up eating up to 50% more cereal than a regular portion, thus increasing sugar intake that much more. One large bowl of a sugary cereal can give you over half your recommended sugar intake for the day. Three quick tips:

» Choose a cereal with less sugar and serve it with milk and fruit.
» Use smaller bowls or half the serving size.
» Mix your kids' favorite sugary cereal with a healthier one.

Preferred cereals: lower in sugar *(6–7 g per serving)* and higher in fiber *(2–8 g per serving)*	Less preferred cereals: higher in sugar *(11–14 g per serving)* and lower in fiber *(≤ 1 g per serving)*
» MultiGrain Cheerios	» Nestlé Lion cereal
» Nature's Path EnviroKidz™ Penguin Puffs	» Kellogg's® Frosties Turbos®
» Post's LiveActive Nut Harvest Crunch	» Nestlé Cookie Crisp

Oatmeal

If your excuse for not eating breakfast is that it's always cold, say no more! Oatmeal or hot cereal is a great source of whole grains, fiber, selected vitamins and minerals. It's low in calories and can lower your cholesterol. But you have to be careful. There is a difference between quick-cooking and large rolled oats (also known as "old-fashioned oats")—the longer-cooking large rolled oats contain the most nutrients. For more flavor you can cook the oats in milk, or add almonds and a little bit of honey with fresh fruit.

Eggs

Eggs provide our bodies with protein, iron and vitamin A, but they do contain saturated fat and cholesterol. The fat and cholesterol is found in the egg yolks, not the whites, and one egg can have over 250 mg of cholesterol, which is close to your recommended daily intake of 320 mg. If you want to minimize the calories, fat and cholesterol from eggs, try just egg whites or the egg substitutes that are made primarily from egg whites. They still have a natural yellow color and creamy consistency because some eggs yolks are included.

Whole-grain bread

A grain is considered whole when all three parts—bran, germ and endosperm—are present. Whole grains are a good source of B vitamins, vitamin E, magnesium, iron and fiber as well as other valuable antioxidants not found in some fruits and vegetables. Most of the antioxidants and vitamins are found in the germ and the bran of a grain. Cheese or peanut butter on 100% whole-grain bread is a good start to your day.

Yogurt and fruit

Having some plain yogurt and fresh fruit makes for a healthy breakfast. It's better to stay away from the artificially sweetened yogurts and use a low-fat plain yogurt, adding fresh fruit and honey if desired.

{ LUNCH

If you have a good breakfast, a small mid-morning snack is all you should need to keep you satisfied until lunch. A healthy, nutritious lunch, followed by a midafternoon snack, will keep your energy and focus up for the afternoon and keep you from binge eating before the dinner hour.

Children, especially, need a good lunch to keep them focused for the rest of the day and to prevent a drop in blood sugar that can cause low energy and fatigue. Don't depend on school for nutritious lunches. Most schools don't have the budget to provide fresh seasonal foods. They depend on prepacked, frozen, fried, high-sugar and fast foods. It's better to make your children a healthy lunch consisting of fiber and protein. Start by incorporating the four food groups from Canada's Food Guide. Here are some suggestions:

» Prepare a roast turkey sandwich with vegetables and milk or yogurt. That's four food groups right there.
» Select whole grains, deep-colored fruits and vegetables, low-fat dairy products and lean protein to make up the backbone of your lunch.
» Save sweets and fatty foods for an occasional treat, not every day. The more sugar and fat a child eats, the more he wants to eat.
» Don't let children have diet beverages on a daily basis. Limit the amount of juice they drink because it will fill them up and replace necessary foods. Water is always the best drink.

PICKY EATERS

There's one in every family! Actually, out of my four, I have two picky eaters. Every meal served gets complaints.

You won't win by fighting, punishing or trying to be rational. Patience is what is needed when handling picky eaters. Do not give in and become a short-order cook. Try the following instead:

» Try to get your picky eater to the table hungry. They must avoid unhealthy snacks a couple of hours before dinner.
» Lower your expectations. You may never have a child with an international palate. Keep the meals simple, healthy, tasty and fun.
» Add color, shape, texture and aroma to foods to entice them.
» Slowly introduce new foods at the table and encourage them to try a taste.
» Watch their intake of beverages, which will fill them quickly and add excess, unnecessary calories to their meals. Leave the milk and juice for snacks and just have water with meals.
» Ask them to participate in the preparation and encourage them to eat their own creations.

{ DINNER

Most children and teens seem to love the taste of fast food. Until they get into the habit of eating healthy meals, it's key not to force them to eliminate these foods, but rather to teach them to enjoy them in moderation. At home, make healthier versions of their favorite fast foods. Some examples:

» **PIZZA** Make whole wheat, thin-crust pizzas with a variety of vegetables, and cheese kept to a moderate amount.
» **MACARONI AND CHEESE** Use whole-grain pasta and use low-fat milk and low-fat or lighter cheese.
» **FRENCH FRIES** Homemade, baked french fry wedges are delicious. Brush with some olive oil and seasonings.

{ DESSERTS

Homemade lower-fat desserts will satisfy their sweet tooth and keep them away from the store-bought processed desserts with their high amounts of sugar and fat. Check out the Desserts chapter as well as the muffins and loaves recipes in the Breakfast & Brunch chapter. These sweets can be enjoyed daily, in moderation.

{ SNACKS

Midmorning and midafternoon snacks and a light one in the evening often prevent hunger and binge eating. One of the reasons we have obesity problems is that we go long hours without food and then overeat high-calorie and high-fat foods. I believe that it's best to give yourself "fuel" every two to three hours. Here are some examples of good snacks that combine at least two of Canada's Food Guide groups:

» A small portion of nuts
» Fruit and low-fat yogurt
» Vegetables and low-fat dip
» Cheese and whole-grain crackers
» Peanut butter and bread or crackers

ENERGY BARS

I personally have never been a fan of these bars—I still find whole foods have more natural nutrients and satisfy you more. But, I do think these bars have their place. When you just can't find nutritious food, an energy bar will give you nutrients and prevent the hunger that may cause binge eating.

Be sure to read the labels for the protein, carbohydrates and sugar amounts. Avoid any containing hydrogenated vegetable oils, such as coconut or palm kernel oil; these are trans fats. If you're having the bar as a meal, look for one that's higher in protein—about 10 to 15 grams. As a snack, choose one that has 3 grams of fiber or more.

{ Laura and Natalie Reisman (Rose's daughters) }

{ meal planning to control weight }

When childhood obesity is a concern, think fewer calories and less fat, and portion control. For example, many beverages are now sold in 32 oz (1 L) bottles, but a single serving is just 8 oz (250 mL). By drinking the larger bottle, children get four times the calories of one serving.

One caution though: Some food items are sold in a single package or container, but that doesn't mean that they really are just a single serving. Read the label for what constitutes one serving. It's important that children eat three meals a day with snacks in an age-appropriate portion size:

» A toddler's portion should equal to about a quarter of an adult's portion.
» Children from the age of about four to eight years old should have portions that are about a third of an adult's.
» Older children and teens can have portions that are equivalent to adult portion sizes provided they're active and still growing.

100-CALORIE PORTIONS

Manufacturers are attempting to respond to the obesity epidemic by offering 100-calorie snack packs. They have become incredibly popular.

In moderation these snacks are great for a quick fix for your dessert cravings. But depending on them as your daily snacks is a mistake. The key is eating from the four food groups throughout the day and leaving these snack packs for the occasional treat.

If you compare the price for the 100-calorie snacks with the price of a whole package with the same food, you'll find that per ounce you are paying much more. But consumers like to have someone control their portions and this is definitely one way. One economical solution is to buy the regular package size and divide it into smaller portions. This does take self-control.

{ WAYS TO CUT FAT IN HOME COOKING

One of the reasons I love to cook at home is that I'm in control of the amount of fat, calories and sodium I add to the meals. I can always experiment with improving the healthiness of a meal by altering the ingredients, for instance by using herbs instead of salt and milk instead of cream. Here are some tips to cut the fat:

» Use nonstick cooking spray instead of adding excess butter or oil.
» Use monounsaturated heart-healthy oils, such as canola, olive, peanut and grapeseed.
» Minimize saturated fats and trans fats.
» If using margarine, pick a soft tub variety with no hydrogenated oils. (See the sidebar "Butter or Margarine?" on page 42.)
» Choose extra-lean meat and skinless chicken breasts and thighs.
» Trim the fat from meats before cooking and drain excess fat after.
» Avoid heavily marbled meat such as pork back ribs, bacon, brisket and deli meats.
» Avoid deep-frying and sautéing in excess oil. It's best to bake, braise, sauté (with a small amount of oil), steam, poach, stir-fry, grill, slow-cook and microwave foods.
» Cut back 50% of the meat in a recipe such as chili, meatloaf or burgers by using a ground soy substitute, mashed/whole canned beans or a cooked grain such as bulgur.
» Coat chicken and fish in breadcrumbs

rather than batter, and opt to bake instead of fry.

- In your favorite egg dishes or cakes, where each serving usually consists of two eggs, instead use one egg and two egg whites; or cut fat and cholesterol completely by using egg substitutes that contain 80% egg whites and 20% egg yolks. They are delicious and contain very little fat or cholesterol, and few calories.
- Substitute two fish or vegetarian meals each week for meat dishes.
- Use lower-sodium chicken broth or low-fat milk, sour cream or low-fat plain yogurt in mashed potatoes, soups, gravies and stews, instead of butter or cream.
- Try 2% evaporated milk or light coconut milk in creamy soups and casseroles instead of heavy cream or butter.
- Use phyllo dough for pastries rather than pastry dough. Spray sheets with vegetable oil instead of brushing them with melted butter.
- Cut potatoes into wedges and oven-fry them instead of making or buying french fries. Brush them with olive oil and sprinkle on a variety of spices, limiting the amount of salt. (See the recipe for Potato Wedges on page 351.)
- Experiment with herbs, spices, fruits and salsas to flavor your food instead of excess oil, mayonnaise or salt.
- Use low-fat cheeses and reduce the amount you use. If using full-fat cheese for flavor, cut the amount in half.
- Cut fat in a dessert by as much as 50% with substitute ingredients such as applesauce, crushed pineapple, low-fat plain yogurt or low-fat sour cream, ripe bananas and purée of cooked dates or prunes.

{ Adam Reisman (Rose's son) }

{ eating in restaurants }

In times of recession, the restaurant business suffers, unless the food offered is inexpensive and substantial. The more people try to cut back on expenses, the more they head to fast-food restaurants. It's a purely economical decision. The problem is that these inexpensive meals are probably the worst for you in terms of nutrition. There are healthier choices in these restaurants, but a lot of people don't choose them. They are thinking short term instead of long term—thinking about their pocketbook or their schedule instead of their health.

Supersizing has also made a comeback. You might win in the dollar department but you definitely lose in the health arena. Supersizing increases the price modestly, but substantially increases calorie, sodium, cholesterol and fat. Manufacturers call this value marketing—they provide more food for less money. This tactic greatly profits food companies, but for the average person it contributes to overeating and future disease.

{ FAST-FOOD RESTAURANTS

Restaurants do offer healthier dishes, but these healthier dishes often cost more. What you can do is order a regular or small portion of fast food in the restaurant and then, when you get home, eat a snack that has more nutrition. You can also ask restaurants for nutritional information so you can compare and choose the least of all evils.

California became the first U.S. state to require fast-food restaurant chains to list calories on their menus. Similar calorie information regulations went into effect in New York City in 2008, and the pack is following. In the United States, as of July 1, 2009, fast-food chains with more than 20 outlets are required to offer diners a list detailing calorie counts and nutritional information for their menus. From January 1, 2011, they will have to list this information on their menus and menu boards. In Canada, although there are no requirements to provide nutritional information for food at restaurants, many establishments provide this information on a voluntary basis.

{ SIT-DOWN RESTAURANTS

Sit-down restaurant meals often contain more calories than fast-food meals because they have bigger portions and offer more variety. A single meal at one of these restaurants could actually contain more calories than most of us should eat in a whole day. People tend to eat more at sit-down restaurants than the smaller portions offered at the fast-food alternatives. Sit-down meals often start with a basket of bread, appetizers and free refills on beverages.

On the positive side, when you leave a sit-down restaurant you are usually full and eat less during the day, as opposed to the fast-food consumer who has eaten less and gets hungry sooner. The best advice is to eat more frequently at home and save eating out for either special occasions or when you're confident you're going to make a healthy choice. Your safest bet is to have at least three meals weekly at home. When you are in control, you can ensure your food has more nutrition, fewer calories and less fat.

Myths about eating in restaurants

People are very confused when they step out to eat. They read the latest headlines about what's good and not so good for their health. Let's clarify some of the most common myths.

"Chicken and fish dishes are always good choices for dieters"

Both are lower in calories, fat and saturated fat than red meat, but fried or battered fish always has excess calories. So do chicken and fish served with butter, cream or cheese sauces.

"Red meat dishes are not good choices for health-conscious diners"

Most red meat dishes contain more fat than chicken or fish, but if you select lean cuts with visible fat trimmed away, you can enjoy 3 to 4 oz (90 to 125 g) at your meals—even on a *daily* basis. The problem is that in most restaurants, portions are fattier cuts, which are cheaper and at least double this size. One thing you can do is share an entrée or take half home. Another is to start your meal with a salad or a soup that's not cream based. Either will fill you up enough so that 4 oz (125 g) of beef will suffice.

"Vegetarian dishes are always healthy"

We all know we should be consuming more vegetables and fruits, but vegetarianism is not always the answer. Many meatless dishes contain loads of fat, cheese, oil or nuts, and they can be very high in calories, fat and even saturated fat.

"It's impossible to eat healthily at fast-food restaurants"

Most fast-food restaurants today offer healthy options. Ask the server for those items.

{ at the supermarket }

Healthy eating starts with informed shopping. The food industry has been implicated in the obesity epidemic. Remember that supermarkets are in the business of making money, and food costs have been consistently rising over the past few years. There are many reasons for this rise in cost, including the following:

- There has been a record number of droughts and floods.
- Energy costs are skyrocketing.
- The middle class in China and India are flourishing—and they've developed a taste for grain-fed beef, pork and chicken.
- Wheat, corn and soy are now put into everything from bread to animal feed, fast food and biofuels and are available to the highest bidder.
- Farmers have reduced the amount of cropland reserved for wheat and soybeans and given it to corn to supply the ethanol industry, which is more profitable for farmers.

With rising food costs, and our slumping economy, families are going back to inexpensive fast-food choices that are usually high in calories, fat and sodium and that lack nutritional benefits.

Even though food costs are higher, we can't rely on cheap unhealthy fast foods because all we'll do is raise a generation of unhealthy children. I believe we can definitely still eat healthily and keep our grocery bills in check. Here are some of my quick tips:

- Choose the supermarket that has the best buys even if it's a mile farther away than your local market.
- Avoid buying general groceries at specialty food shops.
- Make a practical list of food items for weekly meals and stick to it—don't shop on autopilot.
- Avoid impulse buys of items you don't need, unless they are a better quality.
- Avoid prepared foods that are usually more expensive and contain excess or harmful preservatives.
- A good rule of thumb when at the supermarket is to avoid the center aisles. You want to stick to the produce, dairy and meat departments and avoid the aisles selling processed food (with its excess fat, salt and calories).
- Don't always buy larger quantities due to

ADVERTISING TO CHILDREN

In the 1970s, our children watched an average of about 20,000 commercials on television. Today they are watching over 50,000 commercials per year.

In 2006, The Institute of Medicine (www.iom.edu) determined that there was compelling evidence to link food advertising on television to increased childhood obesity. According to the IOM, if children watched fewer fast-food advertisements there would be a strong probability that the number of overweight children would be reduced by about 18%. Children gain weight because they insist on the foods advertised and they exercise less.

The most popular fast-food establishments aim their advertising at children. McDonald's, Burger King, Kellogg's, Kraft and others are among the companies spending large amounts on promotion. But consumer response is now affecting how and when these large companies are advertising. There is less or no direct advertising to children under the age of 12, and some of these companies are improving the nutritional value of their products.

the prices. It may be more economical but you tend to toss out a lot of excess food at the end of the week.

» Buy locally grown foods in season, which reduces extreme transportation costs and keeps the nutrients in foods longer.
» Watch value products or store-brand products—cheaper imitations of the real thing are often not good quality, and you may end up using more.
» Fresh produce is affordable when in season, but don't buy more than what you will eat in a few days so you don't waste any due to spoilage.
» Buy a water-filter pitcher instead of expensive individual bottles of water.
» Buy bulk items when they are on sale, as well as canned goods, frozen vegetables, fish and seafood.
» Buy a whole chicken and cut it into pieces at home. This saves a lot of money compared to purchasing separate parts.
» When meats are on sale, buy larger quantities and freeze individual cuts in freezer paper or freezer bags to take advantage of the savings.
» Make your own snacks with mixed nuts, dry cereals, raisins and other ingredients. Divide the snacks into individual portions and keep them in bags, to control calorie intake.
» Look for online coupons, as well as the coupons in newspapers and magazines.

{ORGANIC FOODS: ARE THEY SAFER AND MORE NUTRITIOUS?

A food that is truly organic must carry a sticker on the packaging that says "Certified Organic." Government standards regulate how these foods are grown, handled and processed. I believe everyone would eat organic if they could, but it costs considerably more than eating nonorganic food. The higher prices are due to more expensive farming practices, higher labor costs, stricter government regulations and lower crop yields. The final decision is up to you. If you can afford to,

CONVENTIONAL FARMERS—	ORGANIC FARMERS—
» apply chemical fertilizers to promote plant growth.	» apply natural fertilizers, such as manure or compost, to feed soil and plants.
» spray insecticides to reduce pests and disease.	» use beneficial insects and birds, mating disruption or traps to reduce pests and disease.
» use chemical herbicides to manage weeds.	» rotate crops, till, hand-weed or mulch to manage weeds.
» give animals antibiotics, growth hormones and medications to prevent disease and spur growth.	» give animals organic feed and allow them access to the outdoors. They also use preventive measures—such as rotational grazing, a balanced diet and clean housing—to help minimize disease.

Information from The Mayo Clinic (www. mayoclinic.com)

FARMERS' MARKETS

There are over two million farms in North America. About 80% of those are small family farms. More and more of these farmers are now selling their products directly to the public at farmers' markets, food co-ops, farm stands and other direct marketing channels. Visiting a farmers' market near you is a great opportunity for a change of pace and a chance to pick up some of the freshest, most nutritious foods around. Farmers pick produce at the peak of flavor to preserve the nutritional content. Local produce does not travel as far to get to your table, and the difference in mileage saves fossil fuels. Some farmers grow heirloom produce and raise heritage breeds of cattle and fowl. Foods at farmers' markets will not necessarily be organic; if this is a concern, you will have to ask. There are now several organic grocery delivery programs in major cities, offering customers the opportunity to receive a weekly or monthly basket of produce, flowers, fruits, eggs, milk, meats or any sort of different farm products. The products will vary weekly according to availability and the season.

{ *Sam Reisman (Rose's husband)* }

I would suggest going organic with the foods you consume on a daily basis, such as your fruits, vegetables, milk and protein products (beef, chicken and fish).

Some people are confused about how to read organic labeling. In general, labels will identify the amount of organic product as follows:

» **100% ORGANIC** means the product is completely organic or made of all organic ingredients.
» **ORGANIC** means a product that is at least 95% organic.
» **MADE WITH ORGANIC INGREDIENTS** means products contain at least 70% organic ingredients. The organic seal cannot be used on these packages.

Don't confuse labels like **ALL-NATURAL**, **FREE-RANGE** or **HORMONE-FREE** with the term *organic*.

{ the common culprits }

With all the media coverage about the health of our nation, most North Americans are concerned with their health and wellness. According to "Canadian Food Trends to 2020" (Agriculture and Agri-Food Canada, www.agr.gc.ca), people have been changing their lifestyles by trying a wide range of diet fads or by purchasing those foods with labels like "trans fat free," "low fat," "low sodium" or "no sugar added." This is good news: Most people understand what the healthy alternatives are.

It is becoming more and more common for governments to push suppliers to take steps to counteract obesity and the medical problems associated with it. Most food producers are working voluntarily to eliminate trans fats from their foods, in order to stay competitive. Many fast-food restaurants are adding healthy food options and posting nutritional information either in their outlets or on their websites, so consumers can identify the healthiest choices.

Still, it is up to us to make sure we are as vigilant with the food products we bring into our homes. Some of the culprits to beware of include salt, sugar, high-fructose corn syrup, and trans fats, so let's take a closer look at each.

{ SALT

The good news is that sodium is a mineral that is essential for our health. It helps conduct nerve signals, helps muscles contract and maintains the fluid balance in the body. The bad news is that we are a salt-addicted population. Salt tastes great and preserves food, but excess salt leads to increased blood pressure. A silent killer, high blood pressure can lead to a stroke, which is the fourth highest cause of death in Canada. Excess salt is also linked to heart problems, kidney problems and stomach cancer. Because salt causes the body to lose calcium through urine, salt is correlated with osteoporosis and other bone problems.

It's rare that getting enough salt in our diet is a problem. The average person needs only about 1,500 mg of sodium daily, and shouldn't have more than 2,300 mg (about 1 tsp/5 mL). The average daily amount, however, is a bit over 3,000 mg, which is 100% more than necessary.

Salt is not only what we shake into our foods. It includes baking powder, baking soda, garlic salt, onion salt and other seasonings. Packaged, frozen, dried, processed, smoked, cured, canned and preserved foods usually have large amounts of salt as well.

Other foods to watch out for are processed meats and fish, pickled and marinated products, and fast and preserved foods.

Foods taste better with more salt, but salt also makes soups thicker, reduces dryness in crackers and pretzels, and increases sweetness in cakes and cookies. Salt also helps disguise a metallic or chemical aftertaste in products such as soft drinks.

A GUIDE TO FOOD LABELS

As defined by the U.S. Food and Drug Administration:

- "Reduced sodium" or "Less sodium": At least 25% less sodium than the regular product
- "Low sodium": 140 mg or less per serving
- "Very low sodium": 35 mg or less per serving

KINDS OF SALT

There are various types of salt. By weight, kosher salt, sea salt and table salt all contain the same amount of sodium. But because Kosher salt comes in differently sized crystals, 1 tsp (5 mL) of Kosher salt tastes about half as salty as 1 tsp (5 mL) of table salt, for example.

Table salt contains iodine, which is a nutrient needed by the thyroid (other salts have no additives). *Fleur de sel* ("flower of salt") is a hand-harvested sea salt that dissolves faster than regular salt. It's good for sprinkling onto food just before serving.

Nearly 80% of the salt in North American diets comes from processed and packaged food. Another 10% of our salt intake is the salt that occurs naturally in foods. This means that you only control 10% with the saltshaker—another good reason to reduce your intake of processed and packaged foods.

Some companies have different standards for what they call low sodium. Although programs like The Health Check are helpful, they are not without faults, allowing 480 mg sodium for a 250 mL serving of soup. Read the labels and know what they mean.

It's imperative to take steps to lower your salt intake today. Here are a few suggestions:

» Get rid of the saltshaker on the table and use herbs, spices, fresh garlic, onions, ginger, basil, dill and pepper on your food instead.

» Minimize your consumption of condiments, processed foods, MSG, soy sauce and deli meats.

» Read food labels carefully. Salt can be listed as sodium, sodium benzoate, sodium propionate and sodium bicarbonate.

» Drain and rinse canned foods to remove the brine, which contains large amounts of salt.

» Do not salt the water used to cook pasta, rice or other grains.

» Choose foods labeled "low sodium" or "reduced sodium."

» Select roasted meats instead of smoked or deli meats.

» Eat at home or pack lunch more often so that you can control salt levels. Restaurant, fast-food and packaged meals can contain over two or three times the sodium amount of the same dish prepared from scratch.

{ SUGAR

We all know that too much sugar in our diet is not healthy, but we may not be aware that excess sugar (which also means excess calories) may lead to serious and chronic diseases. Reducing sugar can be a challenge because it's in many prepared foods. Ongoing studies are attempting to prove a correlation between excess sugar in our diet and obesity, heart disease, high blood pressure, rises in triglyceride levels, depression, mood swings, blood-sugar problems, gallstones, kidney problems and diabetes. To date, there is no direct proof that sugar causes these diseases, only that it may precipitate them.

High-fructose corn syrup (HFCS), often listed as "fructose glucose" on labels, is often used in prepared foods because it is inexpensive and acts as a preservative. It is less nutritious than sugar. Some studies show that consuming excess HFCS may increase triglycerides levels, a risk factor for obesity. Anything ending in "-ose" is a form of sugar. Glucose, sucrose, fructose, maltose, lactose, dextrose and monosaccharides are included. Molasses, honey, corn syrup and brown sugar are also forms of sugar, none being more nutritious than another, except for molasses, which contains B vitamins, calcium and potassium.

Some alarming statistics indicate that the average North American consumes about 120 pounds of sugar per year—approximately 40 teaspoons of sugar daily (Ag Marketing Resource Center). All we need is 6 tsp/2 Tbsp (30 mL) daily. This includes what we add to our foods and what is already in our foods. That's the reason we have to be aware when we consume desserts, beverages, sauces or dressings.

That said, you don't have to eliminate sugar from your diet unless you have diabetes or get a reaction from eating excess sugar, such as mood swings, excessive hunger or overeating. Excess sugar stimulates the release of insulin, the hormone responsible for getting energy to our muscles. This causes the body to convert excess calories into fat. To prevent serious side effects from sugar, always combine sugar with foods either high in fiber and/or protein, which will delay the entry of sugar to the bloodstream. This is similar to what diabetics do. They don't have to eliminate sugar altogether from their diets.

Sugar in processed food

We are always hearing about how much sugar we consume on a daily basis. It's not the sugar we add to our coffee or what is only used in our baking, but that which is hidden in so many of the foods we eat. Manufacturers are constantly being attacked on the amount of sugar in their products. Sugar has virtually no nutritional qualities. It does not contain vitamins and minerals and often displaces nutritious foods in your diet. We get full and satisfied on sugar-filled products, and that often prevents us from eating nutritious foods. Sugar promotes obesity that can lead to other serious and chronic diseases. The most commonly consumed sugar products are canned soft drinks, sweetened fruit drinks, sweets and candies, cakes and cookies, dairy desserts such as ice cream or frozen yogurt and breakfast cereals. The biggest controversy is the high amount of sugar in foods for kids.

We have all been reminded that breakfast is the most important meal of the day in order to maintain our energy, make our metabolism more efficient and keep our weight in control. Children especially should be consuming a healthy breakfast if they want to maximize their energy and focus.

In North America, breakfast cereals are the norm. They're easiest to eat and serve. But many breakfast cereals marketed to children are more than half sugar by weight, and many have inadequate nutritional values. One consumer group found that such cereals as Kellogg's® Honey Smacks® carry as much sugar as a glazed donut (Consumer Reports, www.consumerreports.org). Children also tend to pour themselves about 50% more cereal than the recommended serving size, especially when they like the flavor.

Take a look at the sugar and fiber content per serving of some of your favorite breakfast cereals; the chart below lists cereals that aren't the best choices. A healthy cereal is made from whole grains, contains at least 5 grams of fiber and has no more than 8 grams of sugar and 4 grams of fat.

BRAND	SUGAR	FIBER
Kraft, Post Golden Crisp	15 g (more than 50% sugar by weight)	0 g
Kellogg's® Honey Smacks®	15 g (more than 50% sugar by weight)	1 g
Kellogg's® Corn Pops®	13 g	0 g
Kix, Honey Nut Cheerios	6 g	3 g
Banana Nut Cheerios®	9 g	1 g

Sugar substitutes

Having said all this about the negative effects of sugar in our diet, it's true that many manufacturers have created sugar substitutes that are used by millions of people. What used to be known as an "artificial sweetener" is now called a sugar substitute or a low-calorie sweetener, simply because the word "artificial" has a negative connotation.

Artificial sweeteners can be found in chewing gum, yogurt, beverages, cakes, chocolate bars, candies and more. Such sweeteners have been around for decades but still haven't put an end to obesity. One reason may be that people who use artificial sweeteners or eat artificially sweetened foods consume "missing calories" elsewhere, usually by eating foods higher in fat.

There are also studies indicating that sugar substitutes increase your appetite (*American Journal of Clinical Nutrition*, 2007). So, sugar substitutes aren't teaching you how to eat sugar in moderation, which is the key to permanent weight maintenance.

Here are my thoughts on the different substitutes:

Splenda

I would advise using sweeteners only for health reasons, and the best product on the market is Splenda™. It is made from sucralose and to date has not been associated with cancer or other serious diseases. It comes in white and brown variations. Use it like any sugar in measurements.

Aspartame

This sugar substitute is also known as Nutrasweet™ or Equal™ and is 180 times sweeter than sugar. It is one of the most widely used sugar substitutes, but it cannot be used in cooking because it loses its stability when heated. The U.S. Food and Drug Administration (FDA) and the World Health Organization have concluded that this sweetener is safe, but it has been known to cause such side effects as rashes, headaches, nausea and mild depression.

Stevia

This is a herbal extract that has been used as a calorie-free sweetener in South America and Japan. Under the U.S. Dietary Supplement Act of 1994, stevia can be sold as a "dietary supplement" in health food stores, on the Internet or by mail order. It can't be labeled as a "sweetener"—this term can only be applied to approved food additives—or used in commercial food or beverages yet. Stevia can be used for cooking and is 300 times sweeter than sugar unless diluted.

Evaporated cane juice

This is a minimally processed sweetener made from fresh, evaporated cane juice and is used like sugar.

Organic sugar

Organic sugar is harvested, clarified, evaporated and crystallized within 24 hours. The sugar is produced under strict organic standards. It retains most of the nutrients found in cane sugar. Refined sugar, in contrast, loses most of these nutrients during processing. At least 90% of the natural sugar plant is stripped away during the refining process, which removes the fiber and protein of the sugar cane.

The bottom line is that artificial sweeteners used in moderation and not as a major part of your diet are fine. Don't depend on them for weight loss or to eliminate excess calories from beverages, desserts or main meals. It never works, and you will make up those calories by bingeing on other foods. Most foods containing artificial sweeteners are of poor nutritional value. Their only benefit is that they don't cause tooth decay and they offer a sugar alternative to people with diabetes. Incorporating appropriate serving sizes of real sugar into your daily diet may be more satisfying in the end and will teach you to use sugar in moderation.

{THE NEWEST CULPRIT: HIGH-FRUCTOSE CORN SYRUP

High-fructose corn syrup (HFCS) is a common sweetener and preservative and is made by altering the sugar (glucose) in cornstarch to another form of sugar—fructose. The end product is a combination of fructose and glucose. Today you'll find it in products from canned pop to cookies, energy bars, salad dressings, breakfast cereals and other packaged foods where sugar has traditionally been used. Goods with HFCS are high in calories and low in nutritional value. It also has a longer shelf life than sugar, making it even more attractive to food manufacturers.

{FAT AND TRANS FAT

Trans fat is made when manufacturers add hydrogen to vegetable oil. This process is called hydrogenation, and it benefits the manufacturer by increasing shelf life, flavor and the stability of foods containing these fats. You'll find trans fats in vegetable shortenings, some margarines, crackers, cookies, snack foods and other foods made with partially hydrogenated oils. Trans fats are formed when food manufacturers use a heat process to turn liquid oils into solid fats like shortening and hard margarine. Trans fat, like saturated fat and dietary cholesterol, hurts your health by raising the LDL cholesterol that increases your risk for heart disease.

Major food sources of trans fat

The American Heart Association recommends limiting trans fat intake to less than 1% of total daily calories. The average daily trans fat intake for North Americans is 5.8 grams or 2.6% of calories. As you can see in the chart below, processed cakes, cookies, crackers, pie and breads make up a major portion of the amount of trans fats being consumed.

Since January 2006, food manufacturers must list the amount of trans fat in all their products. You will find trans fat listed on packaging, in the Nutrition Facts panel directly under the line for saturated fat.

BROWN SUGAR

The brown sugar sold at grocery stores is actually white granulated sugar with added molasses. Brown sugar contains small amounts of minerals. But unless you eat a gigantic portion of brown sugar every day, the mineral content difference between brown sugar and white sugar is absolutely insignificant. The idea that there's a big difference between brown and white sugar is another common nutrition myth.

BREAKDOWN OF AVERAGE DAILY INTAKE OF TRANS FATS

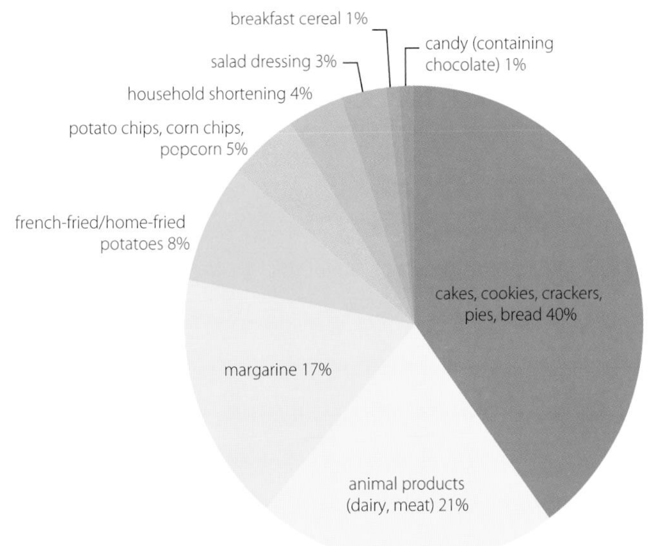

Data based on FDA's economic analysis for the final trans fatty acid labeling rule. "Food Labeling: Trans Fatty Acids in Nutrition Labeling, Nutrient Content Claims, and Health Claims" (July 11, 2003)

Trans fat ban

Many cities in North America and Europe have begun the process of banning trans fat foods from restaurants as well as packaged goods, and many more will join the ranks in due time. The difficulty facing authorities is how to enforce this ban effectively. Time will tell how successful North America will be at eliminating or reducing the amount of trans fats in our foods. These laws are not easy to implement or to monitor, especially outside major restaurant chains and food manufacturers.

BUTTER OR MARGARINE?

Butter is an animal fat that contains both saturated fats and cholesterol. These types of fats can increase our bad blood cholesterol (LDL).

Margarine is the industry's answer to our concerns about the calories and fat content of butter, but brings up other concerns such as taste, trans fats and genetic modification. Virtually all margarines contain mixtures of soybean oil and food additives and nothing from a cow. These products are usually lower in saturated fat and free of lactose and hormones, but can be loaded with additives, emulsifiers, gels, flavors and colors to make them taste and act similar to butter. You'll notice that most good quality margarines are no longer a source of trans fats, but manufacturers are now adding small amounts of modified palm and palm kernel oil to keep the margarine smooth and trans fat free.

Remember that whether you eat butter, margarine, oil or vegetable shortening, they are all fats and contain virtually the same number of calories and amount of fat. Oil differs, however, in that it doesn't contain the same amount of saturated fats. The monounsaturated oils can improve our good cholesterol (HDL), whereas the saturated fats increase our bad cholesterol (LDL).

My personal preference is butter, but in reduced amounts. If you still prefer margarine for health reasons or otherwise, the American Heart Association recommends the following soft nonhydrogenated margarines:

» Becel
» Benecol®
» Blue Bonnet Soft Spread
» Canola Harvest® Canola (Nonhydrogenated)
» I Can't Believe It's Not Butter®
» Promise®
» Smart Balance (Light)

{PROCESSED FOODS

Processed foods may be convenient, but read the labels for those that contain harmful preservatives, hydrogenated vegetable oil, artificial flavorings, food dyes and artificial sweeteners. These ingredients prolong shelf life and enhance flavor but may not represent healthy choices. If I have the choice, I always choose fresh foods over canned, processed or frozen. But at times, depending on where you live, it's difficult and costly to have fresh foods on hand. If selecting canned, frozen or processed foods, read the nutritional labels carefully since they often have excess fat, salt, and preservatives. Products should have less than 15 grams of fat per serving, less than 400 calories per serving, and less than 800 mg of sodium per serving. Here are some facts about processed foods you should know.

Frozen vegetables can be more nutritious than fresh ones, which may take days or even weeks to arrive on your shelves. When food is frozen, the nutrients are more potent, since little time has elapsed between the picking and the freezing.

Canned foods are different. They have fewer nutrients and more salt and other additives to help preserve the food. Having certain canned foods on hand makes cooking easier, more efficient, and less expensive, but the taste of the end result may be inferior. Acceptable canned products are canned tuna packed in water (not oil), canned soups (but avoid those that are cream based or have excess sodium), tomato sauces that contain ripe tomatoes, legumes and fruit packed in its own juice.

{IRRADIATED FOOD

Because more than one-third of Canadians

are suffering from food poisoning each year, the government is considering making irradiation mandatory for an increasing list of foods. Irradiation is a process that exposes food to a controlled amount of energy called "ionizing radiation." This is the same energy used in microwaves.

During irradiation, packaged food arrives in cardboard boxes and is loaded onto a conveyor belt. The food winds its way through a tunnel to an enclosed area where the box is shot with a beam, permeating the contents and killing all living bacteria by breaking its DNA. Other techniques used today to kill bacteria include heating, canning, chemical treatments and steam pasteurization. The difference is that irradiation can also help prevent bacteria from forming. Irradiation can—

» prevent E. coli in ground beef.
» prevent salmonella and Campylobacter bacteria in poultry.
» prevent spoilage and molds.
» increase shelf life by slowing the ripening or sprouting in fresh fruits and vegetables.

Studies show that, over 40 years of testing, no radioactive energy remains in the food after the treatment. In August 2007, the World Health Organization and the Food and Agriculture Organization of the United Nations recognized irradiation as safe for iceberg lettuce and spinach. To date, 39 countries have approved irradiation of over 40 different foods. In Canada, onions, potatoes, flour, spices and seasonings are approved for irradiation. As of 2009, Health Canada is proposing irradiation for fresh and frozen ground beef, poultry, shrimp and mangoes.

Some new research suggests eating irradiated food is unsafe. There is the possibility of a new class of chemicals called cyclobutanones being created during irradiation that have been shown to cause genetic and cellular damage in rats as well as people. Don't be lulled into a false sense of security with irradiated food. Even if these chemicals turn out to be safe, the food can still become contaminated if not stored, handled or packaged properly.

{ FORTIFIED AND ENRICHED FOOD

Fortified means that vitamins or minerals have been added to the food to replace the same nutrients lost during processing. Milk, fortified with vitamin D, has eliminated childhood rickets. This "sunshine vitamin" helps build strong bones and reduces the risk of osteoporosis. Salt is fortified with iodine. Cereals and fruit juices are also fortified, but read the labels carefully for the added sugar, which often cancels out any nutritional benefits.

Foods are sometimes enriched to replace nutrients such as vitamins or minerals that were lost during the refining process. For example, if the food originally had iron, but the iron was lost during the refining process, the food will be "enriched" to add the iron back into it. Flour is enriched with B vitamins and iron.

Don't be fooled by all fortified foods, some of which are high in fat and/or sugar. Again, read the labels!

{ FOOD ADDITIVES

Not all foods added by the food industry are good for us. The topic of food additives can be very confusing to the consumer. Just the word *additive* conjures up negative thoughts. Many foods contain additives, but not all are

FOOD ALLERGENS

Parents of children with allergies have to be extravigilant when it comes to food labels and eating out. Food allergies in our children seem to be on the rise in North America. Many children grow out of allergies to milk, soy and eggs, but allergies to nuts, wheat, fish and shellfish tend to be lifelong. Parents must form the habit of reading food labels carefully and always asking questions. For more information, visit the Allergy/Asthma Information Association website at www.aaia.ca.

{ Adam Reisman }

harmful to our health. Some actually enhance the nutritional quality of our food. Processed foods will always contain the most additives; they are used to enhance shelf life, color and texture. They do not benefit your health. Here are some of the additives you want to avoid or minimize:

Saccharin

This is the oldest artificial sweetener, used in Sweet'N Low and found in many diet foods and sodas. There have been numerous studies linking it to cancer, and in 1977 the FDA proposed banning it. An FDA-mandated label is no longer required, but saccharin is still considered by many to be a possible carcinogen.

Artificial coloring

Many artificially colored foods use synthetic dyes. Over the years, the FDA has banned many dyes while certifying others for use in our baked goods, beverages and candies. Still, some health groups maintain that the approved dyes Blue 1 and 2, Red 3 and Yellow 6 pose cancer risks, and that further research has to be done.

Olestra

The additive olestra is better known by its brand name, Olean, which is used in fat-free Frito Lay potato chips. Despite being approved by the FDA, for many years foods containing olestra were labeled with a warning that the additive may cause abdominal cramping and gastrointestinal problems, as well as inhibit the absorption of essential vitamins.

Sulfites

Sulfites are chemicals that are used to keep cut fruits and vegetables from discoloring. They're also used to prevent bacterial growth and fermentation in wine. Once considered safe, sulfites have been found to cause fatal allergic reactions in some people. In the 1980s, Congress urged the FDA to ban sulfite use on raw fruits and vegetables, and the FDA has been broadening its ban on the additives ever since.

BHA and BHT

These two chemicals slow the rate of oxidation in food, preventing changes in color, smell and taste. Some studies have shown BHA to be carcinogenic. The jury is still out.

Sodium nitrite

Sodium nitrite is most often used as a preservative. Eating meats preserved with it—such as hot dogs, bacon and breakfast sausages—can increase the risk of cancer because nitrite can form carcinogenic compounds when exposed to hot environments, such as in a frying pan, or acidic environments, such as the digestive system.

{ FISH

I get asked so many questions about buying, cooking and storing fish that I have decided to compile this brief "go-to" guide from my experiences as a chef.

Fish is one of the healthiest foods you can consume. Here are some reasons why:

- Fish is a good source of protein and B vitamins (B12, B6 and niacin).
- Fatty fish is a good source of vitamins A and D.
- Soft bones of sardines and smelts and canned bone in fish like salmon are good sources of calcium.
- Fish is low in cholesterol.
- Dark-flesh fish, such as tuna, herring and mackerel, and white-flesh fish are high in omega-3 fatty acids—healthy polyunsaturated fat—and can help in cases of cardiovascular disease by controlling cholesterol and reducing blood pressure.
- Eating fish may increase brain function and lowers rates of depression and dementia.

Buying fish

- In most cases, the freshest fish you can buy has actually been frozen. Fish sold as "fresh" can be from 1 to 14 days out of the water, having been kept on ice until reaching your store.
- For top quality, look for "Frozen at Sea" (FAS)—fish that has been flash frozen at extremely low temperatures. When thawed, it is indistinguishable from fresh.
- Choose a quality fish market—fish should be displayed attractively and surrounded by lots of crushed ice.
- Pick the freshest-looking fish, which should look bright, wet and translucent.
- Fresh fish should have no distinct smell, and frozen fish should have no freezer burn.

Storing fish

- Place fish in a plastic bag; then place that bag inside a Ziploc bag filled with ice.
- Thaw fish in the refrigerator, or place in a sealed plastic bag in a bowl of cold water.
- Refrigerate whole fish up to two days, fillets and steaks for only one day.
- White fish such as cod, swordfish, tilapia, catfish, halibut, sole, snapper, shrimp and squid is good to freeze. But oily fish—salmon and tuna—aren't!
- Keep frozen fish no longer than 6 months.

Fish and toxins

Almost all fish contain low levels of toxins. Mercury, which we're hearing a lot about today, is of great concern. The mercury comes from industrial pollution and affects our bodies of water through rain. Fish absorb these pollutants as they feed off smaller fish. Mercury can seriously affect the central nervous system, kidneys, immune system and brain development.

PCBs are also dangerous compounds that increase the risk of learning disabilities, behavioral problems and poor memory. These toxic chemicals are produced as lubricants and insulators for electrical equipment. They were banned years ago, but the problem is that they don't degrade over time. They are fat soluble and settle in the fatty tissues of fish such as bluefish, wild striped bass and Atlantic salmon. You can reduce the risk of negative effects by trimming the skin and removing visible fat before cooking. Even fish oil pills, which are a good source of nutrients, can contain contaminants. Check with your doctor or dietitian regarding a safe brand.

SAFE FISH

Wild Alaskan salmon (chum, Coho and pink)

Canned pink salmon

Fresh tilapia

Northern (or pink) shrimp (from Canada)

Farmed blue mussels

Farmed bay scallops

Haddock

Rainbow trout

Children and fish

As parents we are always looking for healthier alternatives for children's meals. Fish comes to mind; however, because of the contaminants discussed above, we have to consider warnings that say children (as well as seniors and pregnant women) should either avoid fish or eat smaller servings, or eat the following only once or twice per month, in smaller serving sizes: Atlantic salmon, striped bass, swordfish, shark, bluefish, sea scallops, tuna, sole, halibut, lobster and snapper. For more information on choosing and serving fish to your children, visit KidSafe Seafood's website at www.kidsafeseafood.org.

{ MEAT AND DAIRY

The beef and dairy industries are about big business—increasing production levels and keeping costs down. They foster the production of cheap feed, cause pollution, hire low-wage workers and cut corners on food safety; cows are forced to produce more milk and pack on more pounds.

The modern farm has become a factory. As many as 30,000 head of cattle may be penned in and fed a specially formulated grain mixture.

Often the companies treat the animals poorly—feedlots, batteries and barns are large and dirty, and animals are confined in small spaces for their entire life cycle. At the age of nine months, cattle are sent to the meat factory, where they are vaccinated and injected with growth hormones and antibiotics. The cattle are fed a high-energy grain diet of barley and wheat. It adds up to a system that produces beef in just a fraction of the time it took on "Old MacDonald's Farm."

Grass-fed beef versus corn-fed cattle

Diseases like "Mad Cow," hamburger disease and E. coli have not helped beef sales. Some farmers are reverting to a more traditional means of producing meat: letting cattle graze on grass. Grain-fed beef is lower in saturated fat and cholesterol and higher in omega-3 fatty acids than corn-fed. Grass is a low-starch, high-protein food in comparison to corn and soybeans. Grass is higher in vitamins A and E and contains antioxidants. The downside is that it takes longer to raise these animals, which results in higher prices for their meat. It may be worth the cost, though: Data suggest that meat from grass-fed cattle may help reduce the risk of heart disease, breast cancer, type 2 diabetes and immune deficiency diseases.

{ANTIBIOTICS IN FOOD

Antimicrobials are prescribed and used therapeutically for the treatment of diseases in both humans and animals. Antimicrobials are also added to the feed of food-producing animals to promote growth, to increase feed efficiency and to prevent infections, making for safer and more affordable food products. But due to their overuse, a global crisis in antibiotic resistance threatens human health. We face a rising number of bacterial infections untreatable with antibiotics. Antibiotic resistance in both humans and animals leads to increased vulnerability to disease and infections, such as salmonella. It can also cause a delay in treating these infections, thereby giving them more time to spread. The search for alternate treatments is expensive and puts further stress on an already overburdened health care system. Diseases and infections themselves may become more virulent to humans, thereby prolonging the course of illness.

{ David and Laura Reisman }

{ safety at home }

Our family members are precious to us, so we want to keep them safe at all times. That includes what we feed them, how we cook it and how we store it.

{ HIGH-HEAT COOKING

Many people still do not know that grilling on the barbecue, broiling in the oven or pan-frying on top of the stove can be unhealthy. In 2005, the American Institute for Cancer Research (www.aicr.org) found a possible link between grilling and the risk of colon and stomach cancer. The cancer risk from grilling is real, but it changes dramatically with what you grill and how you do it. Never let your foods burn no matter how you cook them. The effects will be the same as those of grilling. The smoke that interacts with the meat on the grill causes the dripping fat to flare and form polycyclic aromatic hydrocarbons (PAHs), which are deposited back onto the food. The worst offenders are fried chicken and grilled meats. Here are some simple rules to avoid risks associated with high-heat cooking:

- Thaw frozen meat completely so cooking is even.
- Before grilling or broiling, precook meat or poultry in the microwave for two to five minutes and throw away the juice. By discarding this juice, you can reduce PAHs by as much as 90%.
- Marinate your meat and poultry. Marinating for even a few minutes protects the meat against heat. If you use less oil in the marinade, you'll avoid flare-ups.
- Place food on the grill *after* the coals have cooled to embers, or adjust the gas flow and rack height to prevent burning.
- Heat one side of the grill and grill the meat on the side without the heat. Longer to cook, yes, but it's definitely safer.
- Instead of frying meat on top of the stove, roast or stew it at lower temperatures.
- Cut off any blackened beef.
- Use lean cuts of meat and poultry. They produce fewer chemicals because there's less fat to drip on the heating source.
- Try fish or shellfish more often. Most have less fat than meat, take a shorter time to cook and create fewer chemicals.
- Substitute meat with grilled veggies, tofu or veggie hot dogs and burgers and avoid the chemicals entirely.

{ STORING FOOD

After cooking, cover, cool and refrigerate. Do not refrigerate hot foods since they can bring down the temperature of your refrigerator. Cool foods fast—the shallower the container (3 inches/8 cm or less), the faster foods cool. Cool large quantities of warm food in several shallow containers—not one large container.

Refrigeration

Refrigeration slows spoilage but doesn't prevent bacteria from forming. Your refrigerator

Refrigerator and freezer storage chart

		REFRIGERATOR 40°F (4°C)	FREEZER 0°F (−18°C)
Fresh Meat	Beefsteaks, roasts	2–4 days	10–12 months
	Pork chops, roasts	2–4 days	8–12 months
	Lamb chops, roasts	2–4 days	8–12 months
	Veal roasts	3–4 days	8–12 months
	Ground meat	1–2 days	2–3 months
Fresh Poultry	Chicken, turkey whole	2–3 days	1 year
	Chicken, turkey pieces	2–3 days	6 months
Fresh Fish	Lean fish	3–4 days	6 months
	Fatty fish	3–4 days	2 months
	Shellfish	12–24 hours	2–4 months
	Scallop, shrimp, cooked shellfish	1–2 days	2–4 months
Leftovers	Cooked meat, stews, egg or vegetable dishes	3–4 days	2–3 months
	Gravy and meat broth	1–2 days	2–3 months
	Cooked poultry and fish	3–4 days	4–6 months
	Soups	2–3 days	4 months
Eggs	Fresh, in shell	3–4 weeks	Don't freeze
	Fresh yolks and/or whites (out of shell)	2–4 days	4 months
	Hard-cooked	1 week	Doesn't freeze well
	Egg substitute, unopened	10 days	1 year
Dairy Products	Milk, opened	3 days	6 weeks
	Cottage cheese, opened	3 days	Doesn't freeze well
	Yogurt, opened	3 days	1–2 months
	Cheese:		
	Soft	1 week	Doesn't freeze well
	Semisoft	2–3 weeks	8 weeks
	Firm	5 weeks	3 months
	Hard	10 months	Up to 1 year
	Processed cheese	Several months	3 months
	Butter	8 weeks	Salted—1 year Unsalted—3 months
	Butter, opened	3 weeks	Don't freeze
Deli Foods	Deli meat	3–4 days	2–3 months
	Store prepared or homemade salads	3–5 days	Don't freeze
Frozen Vegetables	All types	n/a	10–12 months

(from Canadian Partnership for Consumer Food Safety Education, www.canfightbac.org)

{ *Laura and Rose Reisman* }

should be set below 40°F (4°C), so keep a thermometer in the refrigerator and check it occasionally (see chart on the previous page). Cover food in the refrigerator so that one food doesn't contaminate another. Mark the "expiration" date of food (found on packages) on your containers and consult before cooking.

Freezing

Freezer temperature should be set at 0°F (–17°C) or lower. If it's even 5°F (3°C) warmer, storage time will be cut in half (see chart). It helps to label food with the date prior to freezing it. Always thaw food out thoroughly before cooking.

The pantry

This is the safest way to store dry goods because there's not enough moisture for bacteria to grow; however, food loses flavor over time, so read the expiry dates. Watch that canned foods have no bulging, which could indicate botulism. Toss out any dented cans as well.

Cookware safety

There are so many types of cookware available today that choosing the best for your budget, as well as for your family's health, can be confusing. Materials from some cookware can leach into foods. Most cookware being sold in North America is safe to use for daily meal preparation. Choose good quality pans; I recommend stainless steel with an aluminum conductor, anodized aluminum and cast iron.

{ being active }

Eating well is the first step to living a healthier lifestyle, but fitness is what really completes the equation. Despite our good intentions, this is an area many of us fall short. The usual pattern seems to be being active for a period of time—then life stepping in the way.

Only 31% of North American adults and less than half of North American children are physically active. Our sedentary lifestyle is contributing to an obesity epidemic, not to mention other chronic health issues.

But all you have to do is move! Just moving your body at a pace rapid enough to raise your heart rate counts as exercise. Walking is great if going to the gym or other typical forms of exercise are not your thing. Using a pedometer will help keep you motivated.

The benefits of exercise are numerous, including increased metabolism and energy, decreased stress, better mental functioning and prevention of disease. Anyone can start an exercise routine; and of course it would be ideal if this routine becomes part of your everyday life! You can start slow and increase intensity and duration as you progress. What works for me is scheduling exercise as if it were an appointment, making it harder for me to break the promise to myself.

The essential elements of an exercise routine:

» cardio
» strength training
» core training (abdominal exercises, yoga, Pilates)
» flexibility / stretching

Don't worry about doing all four in one exercise session. You can spread them out over a week.

Most adults need at least 20 minutes of moderate physical activity at least four to five days per week. Ideally, adults and seniors should be doing endurance exercises 20 minutes every day, and weights twice per week. Children and teens should have 60 minutes or more of physical activity each day.

Most important is to get the whole family involved. With you volunteering as a role model, your children are sure to become more motivated.

{ a note about the recipes }

When there are two options listed, the **NUTRITIONAL ANALYSIS** is based on the first ingredient listed, rather than the ingredient in parentheses.

CHOOSE WHOLE GRAINS AND WHOLE WHEAT AS MUCH AS POSSIBLE. This applies to flour tortillas, couscous, rice, pasta and breads (such as English muffins, pita bread, baguettes and pizza crust). The nutritional analysis is based on the plain white version unless specified in the ingredients list.

When a recipe calls for **ROASTED RED PEPPERS**, you can either roast fresh peppers yourself (see page 100 for instructions), or buy them water-packed in a jar. Avoid roasted red peppers that are packed in oil.

Use dry-packed **SUN-DRIED TOMATOES**, and reconstitute them in boiling water. Sun-dried tomatoes packed in oil contain excess calories and fat.

When sautéing, I like to lightly coat the skillet with **COOKING SPRAY** before adding the oil, to reduce the amount of oil needed. Cooking spray is not listed as a separate ingredient in the ingredients list. I also use cooking spray when I bake or roast, and any other time I need a quick nonstick coating (you can even spray scissors before using them to chop up dates!). The brand I like to use is Pam.

I like to use the low-fat versions for all **DAIRY PRODUCTS**:

» low-fat yogurt = 1% M.F.
» low-fat milk = 1% or 2% M.F.
» low-fat evaporated milk = 2% M.F. (you can substitute with 2% milk)
» light buttermilk = 1% M.F.
» light ricotta = 5% M.F.
» light cream cheese = 19% M.F.
» low-fat sour cream = 3%–5% M.F.

I avoid using skim versions, however, as I find this compromises flavor.

You can substitute the **STOCK** of your choice (beef, chicken or vegetable) for the stock suggested.

Be sure to use **100% PURE MAPLE SYRUP**, and not Aunt Jemima.

LEMON and **LIME JUICE** are always freshly squeezed.

{ *breakfast & brunch* }

Baked muffins and loaves can be frozen, but use within 2 weeks for the best quality. Package well to avoid freezer burn • Splenda can replace the sugar with a ratio of 1 to 1 in these recipes. Brown sugar Splenda is also available • The egg dishes are best made fresh. If the egg dishes have a vegetable stuffing, it can be made ahead of time and refrigerated • Egg substitutes can be found in the egg section of your supermarket. Look for those that consist of only eggs, with no preservatives • Smoothies are best made fresh • Quiches (without a phyllo crust) can be prepared up to a day in advance and gently reheated in a 350°F oven for 10 minutes

rose's whole wheat nut 'n fruit granola { *Makes about 4 cups*

2 cups large rolled oats
½ cup whole wheat flour
½ cup packed brown sugar
1 tsp cinnamon
½ tsp ground ginger
3 Tbsp vegetable oil
¼ cup apple juice
3 Tbsp maple syrup
½ cup chopped nuts of your choice
¼ cup chopped dried dates
¼ cup chopped dried cranberries

YOU'LL NEVER WANT TO EAT packaged granola again after you try this. This is the number-one breakfast food in my catering company, and a favorite on the brunch menu at my restaurant, Glow. It also has fewer calories and less fat than other granolas due to a smaller amount of oil and the use of apple juice and maple syrup. Serve with yogurt or milk.

1. Preheat the oven to 300°F. Line a baking sheet with foil and lightly coat with cooking spray.
2. Combine the oats, flour, brown sugar, cinnamon, ginger, oil, apple juice, maple syrup and nuts in a large mixing bowl and stir to combine. Spread the mixture out on the prepared baking sheet and bake for 35 minutes, tossing once to prevent burning.
3. Remove the granola from the oven and let it cool to room temperature. Add the dried fruit and stir. Store in an airtight container.

PER SERVING (⅓ CUP) Calories 194 • Protein 4 g • Carbohydrates 31 g • Fiber 3 g • Total fat 6.2 g • Saturated fat 0.4 g • Cholesterol 0 mg • Sodium 5 mg • **PREP TIME** 15 minutes • **COOK TIME** 35 minutes • **MAKE AHEAD** Bake and store in an airtight container for up to 2 weeks, or freeze for up to 2 months. • **NUTRITION WATCH** Rolled oats are low in saturated fat, and have no cholesterol. They are also a good source of thiamin, riboflavin, niacin, vitamin B6, folate and vitamin B12, and a very good source of manganese.

muesli with strawberries and dried apricots

{ *Makes about 3 cups*

2 cups large rolled oats
⅔ cup low-fat milk
⅔ cup orange juice
1 Tbsp brown sugar
2 Tbsp maple syrup
1 tsp orange zest
½ tsp cinnamon
1 tsp vanilla extract
1 cup low-fat plain yogurt
1 cup sliced strawberries
⅓ cup chopped dried apricots

THIS IS A DELICIOUS cold oat cereal often served in bed-and-breakfast inns. It's filling and nutritious and will keep you going the entire morning.

Combine the oats, milk, orange juice, brown sugar, maple syrup, orange zest, cinnamon and vanilla in a large bowl and stir until well combined. Refrigerate for at least 4 hours or overnight. Add the yogurt, strawberries and apricots and serve.

PER SERVING (½ CUP) Calories 211 • Protein 7.8 g • Carbohydrates 39 g • Fiber 3.8 g • Total fat 2.8 g • Saturated fat 0.6 g • Cholesterol 5 mg • Sodium 40 mg • **PREP TIME** 10 minutes + 4 hours refrigeration • **COOK TIME** None • **MAKE AHEAD** Can be stored in an airtight container and refrigerated for up to 2 days. • **NUTRITION WATCH** Dried fruit does not contain water, and is very high in sugar content. Owing to high calories in dried fruits, it is advisable to consume them in only moderate quantities. Dried apricots are a good source of potassium and a very good source of vitamin A.

strawberry yogurt parfait with granola

{ *Serves 4*

2 cups low-fat strawberry yogurt
2 cups sliced strawberries
½ cup Rose's Whole Wheat Nut 'n Fruit Granola (see page 57)

THIS IS A GREAT BREAKFAST for children and teens because it contains all the elements they need for a healthy breakfast, and it looks attractive. Substitute any flavor of yogurt or fruit you like.

Spoon about ¼ cup yogurt, ¼ cup of strawberries and 1 Tbsp of granola into each of 4 decorative 8 oz glasses. Repeat the layers and serve.

PER SERVING Calories 237 • Protein 7 g • Carbohydrates 44 g • Fiber 3.4 g • Total fat 4.4 g • Saturated fat 0.8 g • Cholesterol 10 mg • Sodium 65 mg • **PREP TIME** 5 minutes • **MAKE AHEAD** Can be assembled a few hours in advance. • **NUTRITION WATCH** Strawberries are a good source of folate and potassium, and a very good source of dietary fiber, vitamin C and manganese.

creamy oatmeal with maple syrup, bananas and dates { *Serves 6*

1⅓ cups large rolled oats
3 cups water (or low-fat milk)
2 Tbsp maple syrup
1 tsp cinnamon
1 banana, sliced
⅓ cup chopped dried dates

PREPACKAGED OATMEAL has little nutrition and excess sugar—there is no comparison to homemade oatmeal. This only takes a few minutes to prepare in the morning.

1. Bring the oats and water to a boil in a medium saucepan. Reduce the heat to low, cover and simmer for 15 to 20 minutes, stirring occasionally, or until the oatmeal is cooked and the liquid has been absorbed.
2. Remove from the heat, add the maple syrup, cinnamon, banana and dates and serve hot.

PER SERVING Calories 136 • Protein 3.1 g • Carbohydrates 29 g • Fiber 3.4 g • Total fat 1.4 g • Saturated fat 0.03 g • Cholesterol 0 mg • Sodium 3 mg • **PREP TIME** 5 minutes • **COOK TIME** 15 minutes • **NUTRITION WATCH** Bananas are a good source of dietary fiber, vitamin C, potassium and manganese, and a very good source of vitamin B6.

pear cinnamon streusel muffins { *Makes 12 muffins*

STREUSEL TOPPING
3 Tbsp packed brown sugar
3 Tbsp large rolled oats
2 Tbsp all-purpose flour
pinch of cinnamon
1½ tsp vegetable oil
1½ tsp water

MUFFINS
¼ cup vegetable oil
1 cup granulated sugar
1 large egg
⅓ cup unsweetened applesauce
3 Tbsp low-fat sour cream
1 cup all-purpose flour
¼ cup whole wheat flour
1 tsp baking powder
½ tsp baking soda
1 tsp cinnamon
pinch of salt
¾ cup peeled and finely diced ripe pears

BOTH THE PEARS and the applesauce keep these muffins moist without using any excess fat. You can try flavored applesauce as long as there's no added sugar. (Pictured on page 63.)

1. Preheat oven to 350°F. Lightly coat a 12-cup muffin tin with cooking spray.
2. To make the streusel topping, combine the brown sugar, oats, flour, cinnamon, oil and water in a bowl. Mix together with a fork and set aside.
3. To make the muffins, combine the oil, sugar, egg, applesauce and sour cream in a large bowl and beat with a whisk or electric mixer until well combined.
4. In another bowl, stir together both flours, baking powder, baking soda, cinnamon and salt. Using a wooden spoon, stir the dry mixture into the applesauce mixture until the dry ingredients are just moistened. Do not overmix. Add the pears and fold in.
5. Divide the batter among the prepared muffin cups and sprinkle the streusel topping evenly over the tops. Bake for about 18 to 20 minutes, or until a tester inserted into the middle of a muffin comes out clean.

PER SERVING (1 MUFFIN) Calories 199 • Protein 3 g • Carbohydrates 34 g • Fiber 1.3 g • Total fat 6.5 g • Saturated fat 0.7 g • Cholesterol 19 mg • Sodium 132 mg • **PREP TIME** 15 minutes • **BAKE TIME** 20 minutes • **MAKE AHEAD** Can be baked a day in advance, or baked and kept frozen for up to 2 weeks. • **NUTRITION WATCH** Pears are a good source of vitamin C and copper. Both of these nutrients can be thought of as antioxidants that help protect cells in the body from oxygen-related damage due to free radicals. The fiber in pears helps prevent constipation and ensure regularity.

banana and date muffins { *Makes 12 muffins*

¼ cup vegetable oil
⅔ cup granulated sugar
1 large ripe banana, mashed (about ½ cup)
1 large egg
⅓ cup low-fat plain yogurt
1 tsp vanilla extract
1 tsp cinnamon
¾ cup all-purpose flour
¼ cup whole wheat flour
1½ tsp baking powder
1 tsp baking soda
pinch of salt
¾ cup chopped dried dates

I LIKE TO USE BANANAS in my baking because they add volume and moisture, which allows me to use far less oil or butter. They also give muffins a deliciously distinct flavor. Buy your dates in bulk and keep them in the freezer . . . forever! Use scissors lightly coated with cooking spray to chop them. (Pictured on page 63.)

1. Preheat oven to 350°F. Lightly coat a 12-cup muffin tin with cooking spray.
2. In a large bowl, combine the oil, sugar, banana, egg, yogurt, vanilla and cinnamon. Whisk together until well combined.
3. In another bowl, combine both flours, baking powder, baking soda, salt and dates. Stir well. Add the dry ingredients to the wet ingredients gradually and stir until the dry ingredients are just moistened.
4. Spoon the batter into the prepared muffin cups and bake for about 14 minutes, or until the tops are firm and a tester inserted in the middle of the muffin comes out clean.

PER SERVING (1 MUFFIN) Calories 176 • Protein 2 g • Carbohydrates 30 g • Fiber 1.6 g • Total fat 5.6 g • Saturated fat 0.6 g • Cholesterol 18 mg • Sodium 209 mg • **PREP TIME** 10 minutes • **BAKE TIME** 14 minutes • **MAKE AHEAD** Bake up to a day in advance or freeze for up to 2 weeks. • **NUTRITION WATCH** Fresh dates are a premium source of vitamin C. They are fat free, cholesterol free and a good source of fiber. Dates have a number of other vitamins including A1, B1, B2, B3 and B5, and more than 20 different amino acids, which help us to digest carbohydrates more easily and control blood-sugar levels and the content of fatty acids in our bodies.

peanut butter and jam muffins { *Makes 12 muffins*

3 Tbsp vegetable oil
¾ cup granulated sugar
1 large ripe banana (about ½ cup)
3 Tbsp smooth natural peanut butter
1 large egg
⅔ cup low-fat sour cream
1 tsp vanilla extract
1 cup all-purpose flour
¼ cup whole wheat flour
1½ tsp baking powder
½ tsp baking soda
1 tsp cinnamon
pinch of salt
3 Tbsp raspberry jam

YOU CAN'T FIND A BETTER combination than peanut butter and jam. Always use natural peanut butter (the kind that contains peanuts only). The other types often contain hydrogenated vegetable oil and icing sugar. If you're baking for someone with a peanut allergy, try using other nut butters or soy butter.

1. Preheat oven to 350°F. Lightly coat a 12-cup muffin tin with cooking spray.
2. Using a whisk or electric beaters, combine the oil, sugar, banana, peanut butter, egg, sour cream and vanilla in a large bowl. Beat until smooth.
3. In another bowl, combine both flours, baking powder, baking soda, cinnamon and salt with a wooden spoon. Add the dry ingredients to the wet ingredients gradually and stir until the dry ingredients are just moistened.
4. Divide the mixture among the prepared muffin cups. Bake for 15 to 18 minutes, or until a tester inserted in the middle of a muffin comes out clean. Press gently in the center of each muffin to make an indent and place a small amount of the jam inside.

PER SERVING (1 MUFFIN) Calories 251 • Protein 3.8 g • Carbohydrates 43 g • Fiber 1.2 g • Total fat 7.5 g • Saturated fat 1.3 g • Cholesterol 22 mg • Sodium 160 mg • **PREP TIME** 15 minutes • **BAKE TIME** 15 minutes • **MAKE AHEAD** Bake up to a day in advance or freeze for up to 2 weeks. • **NUTRITION WATCH** Natural peanut butter (unlike regular peanut butter) does not have hydrogenated oils, colors or preservatives.

CLOCKWISE FROM TOP LEFT *Cranberry, Orange and Applesauce Cake* (page 64), *Peanut Butter and Jam Muffins* (facing page), *Pear Cinnamon Streusel Muffins* (page 60), *Banana and Date Muffins* (page 61) and *Date and Cranberry Oatmeal Squares* (page 377)

cranberry, orange and applesauce cake { *Makes one 8-inch-square cake*

TOPPING
¼ cup large rolled oats
2 Tbsp brown sugar
2 Tbsp all-purpose flour
pinch of cinnamon
2 tsp vegetable oil
1 tsp water

CAKE
⅓ cup unsweetened applesauce
¼ cup vegetable oil
1 cup granulated sugar
1 large egg
1 Tbsp orange zest
2 Tbsp orange juice concentrate
1 tsp vanilla extract
¼ cup low-fat plain yogurt
¾ cup all-purpose flour
⅓ cup whole wheat flour
1 tsp cinnamon
1 tsp baking powder
½ tsp baking soda
¼ tsp nutmeg
pinch of salt
⅔ cup dried cranberries

THIS IS A PERFECT LOAF for breakfast with some fruit, or as a midmorning snack. I use very little oil due to the applesauce, yogurt and added flavorful ingredients. You can also bake this using a loaf pan. (Pictured on previous page.)

1. Preheat oven to 350°F. Lightly coat an 8-inch-square baking pan with cooking spray.
2. To make the topping, in a small bowl, stir together the oats, brown sugar, flour, cinnamon, oil and water. Mix together with a fork and set aside.
3. To make the cake, combine the applesauce, oil, sugar, egg, orange zest, orange juice concentrate, vanilla and yogurt in a large bowl. Whisk together until well combined.
4. In another bowl, stir together both flours, cinnamon, baking powder, baking soda, nutmeg, salt and cranberries. With a wooden spoon, stir the dry mixture into the applesauce mixture until the dry ingredients are just moistened. Pour the mixture into the prepared pan. Sprinkle the topping mixture over the batter.
5. Bake in the center of the oven for about 30 to 35 minutes, or until a tester inserted in the middle of the cake comes out clean. Cut into 16 squares.

PER SERVING (1 SQUARE) Calories 167 • Protein 2 g • Carbohydrates 30 g • Fiber 1.1 g • Total fat 4.7 g • Saturated fat 0.5 g • Cholesterol 14 mg • Sodium 100 mg • **PREP TIME** 15 minutes • **BAKE TIME** 30 minutes • **MAKE AHEAD** Can be baked up to 2 days in advance and frozen for up to 1 month. • **NUTRITION WATCH** Unsweetened applesauce contains no sugar, whereas the sugar in regular applesauce almost doubles the number of calories.

carrot, pineapple and banana loaf { *Makes 1 loaf*

¼ cup vegetable oil
1 cup granulated sugar
2 large eggs
1 large ripe banana, mashed (about ½ cup)
1½ tsp cinnamon
pinch of nutmeg
1 tsp vanilla extract
⅓ cup low-fat plain yogurt
1¼ cups grated carrots
½ cup canned crushed pineapple, drained
½ cup raisins
1⅓ cups all-purpose flour
⅓ cup whole wheat flour
1½ tsp baking powder
1 tsp baking soda

THIS TASTES LIKE A CARROT CAKE but has more flavor, much less fat and fewer calories. You can also try grated zucchini or sweet potato for a change in flavor.

1. Preheat oven to 350°F. Lightly coat an 9- × 5-inch loaf pan with cooking spray.
2. Using a whisk or electric mixer, combine the oil, sugar, eggs, banana, cinnamon, nutmeg, vanilla and yogurt in a large bowl until well combined. Stir in the carrots, pineapple and raisins.
3. In another bowl, combine both flours, baking powder and baking soda. With a wooden spoon, stir the dry mixture into the banana mixture until dry ingredients are just moistened. Pour the mixture into the prepared loaf pan.
4. Bake for 40 to 45 minutes, or until a tester inserted in the middle of the loaf comes out clean. Let the loaf cool in the pan on a wire rack before removing and cutting into 8 slices.

PER SERVING (⅛ SLICE) Calories 163 • Protein 2.5 g • Carbohydrates 29 g • Fiber 1.4 g • Total fat 4.4 g • Saturated fat 0.5 g • Cholesterol 27 mg • Sodium 149 mg • **PREP TIME** 20 minutes • **BAKE TIME** 40 minutes • **MAKE AHEAD** Bake up to 2 days in advance or freeze up to 1 month. • **NUTRITION WATCH** No other vegetable or fruit contains as much carotene as carrots, which the body converts to vitamin A. This is a truly versatile vegetable and an excellent source of vitamins B and C as well as calcium pectate, an extraordinary pectin fiber that has been found to have cholesterol-lowering properties.

banana chocolate chip loaf { *Makes 1 loaf*

1 large ripe banana, mashed (about ½ cup)
¼ cup vegetable oil
¾ cup granulated sugar
1 large egg
1 tsp vanilla extract
¼ cup low-fat sour cream
¾ cup all-purpose flour
2 Tbsp whole wheat flour
1 tsp baking powder
½ tsp baking soda
⅓ cup semisweet chocolate chips

BANANA LOAF is an all-time favorite. The loaves are traditionally made with an excess of oil and chocolate chips. By using more banana and low-fat sour cream I enhance the flavor so I can use fewer chips. This is great as a dessert, breakfast or snack.

1. Preheat oven to 350°F. Lightly coat an 8- × 4-inch loaf pan with cooking spray.
2. Using a whisk or electric mixer, combine the banana, oil, sugar, egg, vanilla and sour cream in a large bowl until smooth.
3. In another bowl, combine both flours, baking powder and baking soda. With a wooden spoon, stir the dry mixture into the banana mixture until the dry ingredients are just moistened. Fold in the chocolate chips.
4. Pour into the prepared pan and bake for about 30 to 35 minutes or until a tester inserted in the middle of the loaf comes out clean. Let the loaf cool in the pan on a wire rack before removing and slicing into 8 slices.

PER SERVING (½ SLICE) Calories 127 • Protein 1.6 g • Carbohydrates 19 g • Fiber 0.8 g • Total fat 5.3 g • Saturated fat 1.2 g • Cholesterol 15 mg • Sodium 81 mg • **PREP TIME** 10 minutes • **BAKE TIME** 30 minutes • **MAKE AHEAD** Bake up to a day in advance and freeze for up to 1 month. • **NUTRITION WATCH** Semisweet chocolate is high in saturated fat, calories and sugar. Use it in moderation to give flavor, but not excess calories.

whole wheat french toast with caramelized bananas { *Serves 4*

½ cup egg substitute (or 2 large eggs)
3 egg whites
⅓ cup low-fat milk
1 tsp cinnamon
1 tsp vanilla extract
4 slices multigrain bread
2 Tbsp maple syrup (more to serve)

BANANAS
1 tsp vegetable oil
2 Tbsp brown sugar
1 large banana, sliced

FRENCH TOAST traditionally is an unhealthy breakfast due to the number of eggs used to dip the bread, the excess oil or butter used to cook the toast and the overload of maple syrup, butter and/or whipped cream served alongside. I'm using an egg substitute that's made primarily with 80% egg whites and 20% egg yolks. This saves calories, fat and cholesterol. One egg-substitute brand is Break Free, which is available in major supermarkets in the egg section.

1. Whisk together the egg substitute, egg whites, milk, cinnamon and vanilla in a shallow bowl until well blended.
2. Lightly coat a large nonstick skillet with cooking spray and place over medium heat.
3. Dip a piece of bread into the egg mixture, making sure both sides are moistened. (Don't leave the bread in the mixture for too long or the bread will fall apart.) Cook 2 pieces at a time, browning each side for about 2 minutes. Repeat with the remaining slices of bread.
4. Meanwhile, in a small nonstick skillet lightly coated with cooking spray, add the oil, brown sugar and banana slices. Sauté for 1 to 2 minutes, or until bananas are just browned and softened. Keep warm. Divide the bananas over warm French toast and serve with maple syrup if desired.

PER SERVING Calories 266 • Protein 12 g • Carbohydrates 44 g • Fiber 3.4 g • Total fat 4.5 g • Saturated fat 0.6 g • Cholesterol 2 mg • Sodium 259 mg • **PREP TIME** 10 minutes • **COOK TIME** 5 minutes • **NUTRITION WATCH** Egg substitute is a good alternative for those who are watching their cholesterol. This product is very low in cholesterol and calories, and high in iron, phosphorous, riboflavin and zinc. It is a very good source of vitamin B5 and selenium.

french strawberry crêpes { *Makes 8 to 10 crêpes*

CRÊPES
⅓ cup all-purpose flour
2 Tbsp whole wheat flour
1½ Tbsp granulated sugar
pinch of salt
¾ cup low-fat milk
2 tsp vegetable oil
¼ cup egg substitute (or 1 large egg)

FILLING
1⅓ cups light ricotta (5%)
¼ cup light cream cheese (about 2 oz), softened
2 Tbsp granulated sugar
1 Tbsp lemon juice
1½ tsp vanilla extract
2 cups sliced strawberries
3 Tbsp maple syrup

PEOPLE MIGHT NOT TEND to make crêpes at home very often because they think it's too much bother, but these crêpes are easy to prepare, and the filling is outstanding.

1. To make the crêpes, combine the flours, sugar and salt in small bowl. Stir well and set aside.
2. Using an electric mixer or a food processor, combine the milk, oil and egg substitute until smooth. Add the flour mixture gradually and beat until well combined. Cover and chill for 30 minutes.
3. Lightly coat an 8-inch nonstick skillet or crêpe pan with cooking spray and set over medium heat. Pour 2 Tbsp batter into pan and tilt pan in all directions so batter covers the pan. Cook for about 1 minute. Lift the edge of the crêpe with a spatula to test; flip when the bottom is lightly browned. Cook for 30 seconds, or until just set. (Note that the first crêpe is often not the best. Feel free to toss it out.) Repeat with remaining batter. Set the crêpes aside.
4. To make the filling, combine the ricotta, cream cheese, sugar, lemon juice and vanilla in a bowl and beat using an electric mixer or a food processor until well combined. Gently fold in 1 cup of the sliced strawberries.
5. To assemble, spread about ¼ cup of the ricotta mixture on each crêpe and roll up. Lightly coat a large skillet with cooking spray and heat over medium heat. Brown the crêpes on all sides, for about 2 minutes. Serve with the remaining 1 cup strawberries and the maple syrup.

PER SERVING (2 CRÊPES) Calories 206 • Protein 8 g • Carbohydrates 32 g • Fiber 2.6 g • Total fat 6.0 g • Saturated fat 2.6 g • Cholesterol 52 mg • Sodium 139 mg • **PREP TIME** 15 minutes • **COOK TIME** 1 to 2 minutes for each crêpe • **MAKE AHEAD** Cook crêpes up to a day in advance; fill and heat just before serving. • **NUTRITION WATCH** Ricotta, which has 5% milk fat, makes a great reduced-fat alternative to heavy cream cheese, which has over 30% fat.

blintz soufflé with blueberry sauce { *Serves 8*

BATTER

2 eggs
¾ cup low-fat milk
1½ Tbsp low-fat sour cream
2½ Tbsp vegetable oil
1 tsp vanilla extract
¾ cup all-purpose flour
2 Tbsp granulated sugar
1 tsp baking powder

FILLING

2 cups light ricotta (5%)
½ cup light cream cheese (about 4 oz), softened
1 egg
⅓ cup granulated sugar
2 tsp lemon zest
1½ Tbsp lemon juice

SAUCE

¼ cup orange juice
¼ cup granulated sugar
1½ tsp cornstarch
2 tsp lemon juice
1 cup fresh or frozen blueberries (thawed)

I LOVE BLINTZES, but making them individually takes time and effort. This baked version is an easy way to prepare this classic dish. The blueberry sauce is sensational.

1. Preheat oven to 350°F. Lightly coat an 8-inch-square baking dish with cooking spray.
2. To make the batter, purée the eggs, milk, sour cream, vegetable oil, vanilla, flour, sugar and baking powder in the bowl of a food processor until smooth. Pour a little less than half the mixture in the bottom of the dish. Bake for 10 minutes.
3. To make the filling, beat the ricotta and cream cheeses, egg, sugar, lemon zest and juice in the bowl of a food processor or with electric beaters until smooth. Pour over baked blintz mixture. Carefully pour the remaining batter over the filling. Bake for 25 to 30 minutes or until mixture is no longer loose and top is puffy.
4. To make the sauce combine the orange juice, sugar and cornstarch in a small skillet over medium heat. Whisk until the cornstarch is dissolved. Bring to a boil, then simmer on low heat for 3 minutes or until mixture is thicker and clear. Add the lemon juice and blueberries and cook for 2 minutes. Serve over the blintz soufflé.

PER SERVING Calories 299 • Protein 11 g • Carbohydrates 36 g • Fiber 0.9 g • Total fat 12 g • Saturated fat 4.4 g • Cholesterol 104 mg • Sodium 230 mg • **PREP TIME** 20 minutes • **BAKE TIME** 35 minutes • **MAKE AHEAD** Prepare sauce up to 2 days in advance. • **NUTRITION WATCH** Blueberries are loaded with antioxidants that provide energy, better brain function and cancer-fighting power.

buttermilk pancakes with caramelized pears { *Makes 8 pancakes*

PANCAKES
½ cup all-purpose flour
1 tsp baking powder
½ tsp baking soda
1 Tbsp granulated sugar
pinch of salt
⅓ cup light buttermilk
¼ cup low-fat milk
¼ cup egg substitute (or 1 large egg)
2 Tbsp vegetable oil

PEARS
1½ tsp vegetable oil
3 Tbsp packed brown sugar
2 cups peeled and thinly sliced pears
pinch of cinnamon

PANCAKES THAT ARE SERVED in restaurants are usually considered unhealthy, but this is only due to the added butter, maple syrup and whipped cream. I add some caramelized pears to enhance the flavor. Add a small amount of maple syrup if you choose.

MAKE YOUR OWN BUTTERMILK SUBSTITUTE

For every ⅓ cup of buttermilk substitute, use ⅓ cup low-fat milk and add 1 tsp of lemon juice. Let stand for 5 minutes before using.

1. Whisk together the flour, baking powder, baking soda, sugar and salt in a large bowl. In a separate bowl, whisk together the buttermilk, milk, egg substitute and oil. Whisk the flour mixture into the buttermilk mixture and let stand for 10 minutes.
2. Lightly coat a large nonstick skillet with cooking spray and set over medium heat. Pour in 3 Tbsp of batter and cook until the pancake is covered with bubbles and the edges turn brown, about 2 minutes. Turn and cook the other side for 2 minutes or until golden brown. Repeat with the remaining batter.
3. Meanwhile, make the caramelized pears by adding the oil and brown sugar to a small nonstick skillet over medium heat. Add the pears and cinnamon and sauté for 2 minutes, or until the pears are just softened and glazed with the sugar. Add maple syrup if desired. Serve overtop pancakes.

PER SERVING (1 PANCAKE) Calories 237 • Protein 6.8 g • Carbohydrates 44 g • Fiber 3.4 g • Total fat 4.4 g • Saturated fat 0.8 g • Cholesterol 10 mg • Sodium 65 mg • **PREP TIME** 10 minutes • **COOK TIME** 6 minutes per batch • **NUTRITION WATCH** Buttermilk is a good source of vitamin B12 and phosphorus, and a very good source of riboflavin and calcium. It's often used as a substitute for sour cream or yogurt. Make sure to buy light buttermilk, which has much less fat than regular buttermilk!

cinnamon waffles with tropical fruit salsa { *Makes three 6- × 6-inch waffles*

¾ cup all-purpose flour
¼ cup whole wheat flour
2 Tbsp granulated sugar
1½ tsp baking powder
½ tsp cinnamon
pinch of salt
1 cup low-fat milk
2 Tbsp vegetable oil
¼ cup egg substitute (or 1 large egg, lightly beaten)

FRUIT SALSA

¾ cup diced mango
¾ cup diced kiwi
3 Tbsp maple syrup

A WAFFLE MACHINE is an inexpensive kitchen appliance that's fun to use when you have a little more time—weekend brunch is perfect. Use different fruits to create your own combination.

1. Combine both flours and the sugar, baking powder, cinnamon and salt in a medium bowl.
2. In another bowl, whisk together the milk, oil and egg substitute. Add the egg mixture to the flour mixture and whisk together until well blended.
3. Preheat a 6-inch waffle iron, and lightly coat it with cooking spray. Spoon one-third of the batter over the waffle pan, covering it completely. Cook for 3 to 4 minutes or until the steaming stops; repeat this procedure with the remaining batter.
4. Combine the mango, kiwis and maple syrup in a bowl and divide over the waffles. Serve with extra maple syrup if desired.

PER SERVING (½ WAFFLE) Calories 276 • Protein 7 g • Carbohydrates 45 g • Fiber 3.1 g • Total fat 8.1 g • Saturated fat 1.4 g • Cholesterol 57 mg • Sodium 214 mg • **PREP TIME** 10 minutes • **COOK TIME** 9 minutes • **NUTRITION WATCH** Mangoes are an excellent source of vitamins C and A, both important antioxidant nutrients. Vitamin C promotes healthy immune function and collagen formation. Vitamin A is important for vision and bone growth.

french baguette casserole with cranberries and cinnamon { *Serves 8*

8 slices whole wheat French baguette (about 1 inch thick and 3 inches in diameter)

BOTTOM LAYER
⅓ cup packed brown sugar
2 Tbsp vegetable oil
2 Tbsp maple syrup
½ cup dried cranberries

TOP LAYER
2 tsp orange zest
½ cup orange juice
½ cup low-fat milk
¼ cup packed brown sugar
½ tsp cinnamon
1 tsp vanilla extract
½ cup egg substitute (2 large eggs)

FRUIT TOPPING
1 cup sliced strawberries

I CAME ACROSS this recipe in a breakfast magazine, but it was made with excess butter, eggs and heavy cream. I played around with it and came out with a delicious healthier version. This is best served hot right from the oven.

1. Lightly coat a 9-inch-square ovenproof casserole dish with cooking spray. Prepare the bottom layer by combining the brown sugar, oil, maple syrup and cranberries in a bowl and spread it across the bottom of the dish. Place the baguette slices over the bottom layer.
2. Make the top layer by whisking together the orange zest, orange juice, milk, brown sugar, cinnamon, vanilla and egg substitute in a large bowl. Pour the mixture over the baguette slices. Cover and refrigerate at least 4 hours or overnight.
3. Preheat the oven to 350°F. Take the casserole dish out of the fridge and turn the baguette slices over in the dish. Let sit at room temperature for 15 minutes. Bake for 25 minutes. Serve immediately with sliced strawberries and the sauce from the bottom of the pan served on top of the casserole.

PER SERVING Calories 323 • Protein 8.3 g • Carbohydrates 58 g • Fiber 2.9 g • Total fat 6.4 g • Saturated fat 1.0 g • Cholesterol 1 mg • Sodium 429 mg • **PREP TIME** 15 minutes • **BAKE TIME** 25 minutes • **NUTRITION WATCH** Maple syrup is an excellent source of manganese, which supports energy production. It is also a good source of zinc, which has been touted as a prostate-cancer fighter and support for male reproductive health. Use maple syrup in moderation, since 1 Tbsp has 50 calories.

egg muffins with sun-dried tomatoes and goat cheese { *Makes 6 egg muffins*

1½ cups egg substitute (or 6 large eggs)
¼ cup chopped rehydrated sun-dried tomatoes
¼ cup crumbled goat cheese (about 1 oz)

THIS IS THE GREATEST CREATION since the McDonald's McMuffin, but much healthier. The egg mixture is baked in a muffin tin and can then be served over an English muffin, toast or bagel.

1. Preheat oven to 350°F. Lightly coat a 6-cup muffin tin with cooking spray.
2. Combine the egg substitute with half of the sun-dried tomatoes (about 2 Tbsp). Divide evenly into the 6 muffin cups. Bake for 15 to 20 minutes or until the eggs are just set.
3. Combine the remaining sun-dried tomatoes with the goat cheese in a small bowl. Top each egg muffin with a little of the tomato and cheese mixture. Carefully remove the eggs with a knife.

PER SERVING Calories 74 • Protein 9 g • Carbohydrates 2 g • Fiber 0.3 g • Total fat 3.4 g • Saturated fat 1.1 g • Cholesterol 3 mg • Sodium 176 mg • **PREP TIME** 10 minutes • **BAKE TIME** 15 minutes • **NUTRITION WATCH** Sun-dried tomatoes are a good source of dietary fiber, thiamin, riboflavin, niacin, iron, magnesium and phosphorus, and a very good source of vitamin C, vitamin K, potassium, copper and manganese. They are, however, high in sodium, so if you are watching your salt intake, eat them in moderation. Use the dry-packed version and soak them yourself in boiling water. Those packed in oil contain excess calories and fat.

scrambled eggs with smoked salmon, capers and dill { *Serves 2*

1 tsp oil
½ cup finely diced red onion
1½ cups egg substitute (or 6 large eggs)
¼ cup diced smoked salmon (about 1 oz)
1 tsp chopped capers
2 Tbsp chopped fresh dill

THE ADDITION OF SMOKED SALMON to scrambled eggs is a real treat. The key is to add the smoked salmon after the eggs have come off the heat so as not to cook the salmon.

Lightly coat a nonstick skillet with cooking spray. Add the oil and warm it over medium heat. Add the onions and sauté for 3 minutes, or until soft. Add the egg substitute and scramble until the eggs are just set. Remove from the heat and add the smoked salmon, capers and dill. Serve immediately.

PER SERVING Calories 221 • Protein 26 g • Carbohydrates 7 g • Fiber 1.0 g • Total fat 9.5 g • Saturated fat 1.6 g • Cholesterol 5 mg • Sodium 452 mg • **PREP TIME** 10 minutes • **COOK TIME** 4 minutes • **NUTRITION WATCH** Salmon is a good source of omega-3 fatty acids, which are "healthy" fats, beneficial because they lower blood pressure, triglyceride (fat in the blood) levels and the risk of blood clots. They are the building blocks of nerve tissue and brain cells. Smoked salmon, however, is high in salt. Eat it in moderation if you are watching your blood pressure.

frittata with sautéed mushrooms and havarti { *Serves 2*

1 tsp vegetable oil
⅓ cup finely chopped onion
½ tsp chopped garlic
¾ cup sliced mushrooms
¼ cup diced red bell pepper
½ cup egg substitute (or 2 large eggs)
3 egg whites
⅓ cup low-fat milk
1 cup fresh baby spinach
½ cup shredded havarti
2 Tbsp chopped parsley

TO ENHANCE THE FLAVOR, use wild mushrooms such as oyster, shiitake or portobello. Button mushrooms work as well, but be sure to sauté on a higher heat so the excess liquid evaporates.

1. Lightly coat a small nonstick skillet with cooking spray. Add the oil and set over medium heat. Add the onion and garlic and sauté for 3 minutes, or until the onion is soft and lightly browned. Add the mushrooms and red pepper and cook for 5 minutes, or until the mushrooms are slightly dried. Set aside.
2. Wipe out the skillet and respray. Combine the egg substitute, egg whites and milk. Cook for 4 minutes over medium heat or until the egg begins to set. Add the onion and mushroom mixture, spinach and cheese. Cover and cook another 2 minutes, or until the cheese melts.
3. Slip the frittata onto a serving platter with a spatula. Cut into wedges, garnish with parsley and serve immediately.

PER SERVING Calories 205 • Protein 19 g • Carbohydrates 8 g • Fiber 1.3 g • Total fat 10.4 g • Saturated fat 4.2 g • Cholesterol 17 mg • Sodium 320 mg • **PREP TIME** 10 minutes • **COOK TIME** 14 minutes • **NUTRITION WATCH** Phytonutrients found in mushrooms have cancer-fighting properties.

poached eggs with cream cheese and smoked salmon on english muffins { *Serves 4*

2 tsp white vinegar
4 large eggs

2 whole wheat English muffins
¼ cup light cream cheese (about 2 oz), softened

2 oz smoked salmon
1 Tbsp chopped fresh dill

I USED TO BE NERVOUS about making poached eggs. I left it for restaurants to do it for me. But once I learned how easy it is, I couldn't stop making them. The key to keeping the eggs intact is vinegar.

1. Add the vinegar to a pot of water and bring to a boil. Gently crack the eggs and drop them carefully into the water. Simmer over low heat for about 3 minutes, or until the white of the egg solidifies around the yolk. Use a large slotted serving spoon to carefully remove the eggs and place them on a plate.
2. Meanwhile, slice and toast the English muffins. Spread them with the cream cheese and divide the smoked salmon equally among the 4 muffins. Top with a poached egg and garnish with the dill.

PER SERVING Calories 191 • Protein 13 g • Carbohydrates 16 g • Fiber 2.3 g • Total fat 8.3 g • Saturated fat 3.5 g • Cholesterol 226 mg • Sodium 463 mg • **PREP TIME** 5 minutes • **COOK TIME** 3 minutes • **NUTRITION WATCH** Whole wheat English muffins have three times more fiber than English muffins made with white flour. Fiber has been shown to protect your heart by lowering bad cholesterol and increasing good cholesterol.

southwest breakfast burrito with black beans and charred corn { *Serves 6*

2 tsp vegetable oil
⅓ cup finely diced onion
⅓ cup canned corn, drained
¼ cup finely diced red bell pepper
¼ cup canned black beans, drained and rinsed
1 tsp finely chopped garlic
1 cup egg substitute (or 4 large eggs)
½ cup medium salsa
3 large whole wheat flour tortillas
½ cup shredded aged cheddar cheese
pinch of salt and pepper

THIS TEX MEX WRAP is loaded with flavor from the sautéed vegetables, salsa and aged cheddar cheese. By using the egg substitute you cut back on all the excess calories, fat and cholesterol.

1. Heat the oil in a nonstick skillet over medium heat. Add the onion and sauté for 3 minutes or until soft. Add the corn and sauté for 5 to 8 minutes, or until the corn begins to char. Add the bell pepper, beans and garlic, and sauté for 2 more minutes. Set aside.
2. Lightly coat a nonstick skillet with cooking spray. Add the egg substitute and scramble over medium heat for 2 minutes or almost set. Fold in the beans and corn mixture and cook for 1 more minute, or until the eggs are set. Keep warm.
3. To assemble the burritos, spread the salsa evenly over the 3 tortillas. Place one-third of the eggs along the center of each tortilla. Sprinkle with cheese and season with salt and pepper. Fold in both sides and roll. Cut in half.
4. If desired, toast the burritos in the oven or toaster oven at 400°F for 5 minutes before serving.

PER SERVING (½ TORTILLA) Calories 104 • Protein 8 g • Carbohydrates 6 g • Fiber 1.1 g • Total fat 5.3 g • Saturated fat 1.8 g • Cholesterol 7 mg • Sodium 248 mg • **PREP TIME** 15 minutes • **COOK TIME** 15 minutes • **NUTRITION WATCH** Black beans are a very good source of cholesterol-lowering fiber, as are most other legumes. In addition to lowering cholesterol, the high fiber content of black beans prevents blood-sugar levels from rising too rapidly after a meal, making these beans an especially good choice for individuals with diabetes, insulin resistance or hypoglycemia.

frittata with baby spinach, caramelized onions and aged cheddar { *Serves 2*

1 tsp vegetable oil
½ cup diced onion
½ tsp finely chopped garlic
½ tsp brown sugar
½ cup egg substitute (or 2 large eggs)
3 egg whites
⅓ cup low-fat milk
⅛ tsp salt
⅛ tsp pepper
½ cup baby spinach
⅓ cup shredded aged cheddar cheese

A FRITTATA is an open-faced omelette with a variety of toppings. This version mixes some sweet flavorings from the caramelized onions with a savory taste from the spinach and aged cheddar.

1. Lightly coat a small nonstick skillet with cooking spray. Add the oil and set over medium heat. Add the onion and garlic and sauté for 3 minutes, or until the onion is soft and lightly browned. Add the brown sugar and sauté on low heat for 3 minutes. Remove from the heat and set aside.
2. Whisk together the egg substitute, egg whites and milk, and season with salt and pepper. Add the onion mixture.
3. Lightly coat a 9-inch skillet with cooking spray. Add the egg mixture and cook over medium-low heat for 4 minutes, or until nearly set. Add the spinach and cheddar cheese, cover and cook until the frittata is set, about 2 minutes. Slip the frittata onto a serving platter with a spatula. Cut into wedges and serve immediately.

PER SERVING Calories 222 • Protein 19 g • Carbohydrates 9.1 g • Fiber 0.9 g • Total fat 12 g • Saturated fat 5.1 g • Cholesterol 21 mg • Sodium 415 mg • **PREP TIME** 10 minutes • **COOK TIME** 9 minutes • **NUTRITION WATCH** Egg whites are great for those who want some of the benefits of eggs without the fat, calories and cholesterol. One egg white has 15 calories, no fat and no cholesterol. One egg has 90 calories, 5 g of fat and over 250 mg of cholesterol.

mexican omelette with black beans, cheddar and salsa { *Serves 2*

1 cup egg substitute (or 4 large eggs, beaten)
¼ cup diced roasted red pepper (about ½ small roasted red pepper) (see page 100)
¼ cup canned black beans, drained and rinsed
¼ cup chopped green onions
¾ cup shredded cheddar cheese
2 Tbsp medium salsa
2 Tbsp chopped cilantro

WHEN YOU'RE IN THE MOOD for a variation on the typical omelette, this is perfect. It has more flavor and more nutrients. You can use any variety of beans or cheese you'd like, and the addition of some guacamole would be delicious.

1. Lightly coat a 9-inch nonstick skillet with cooking spray. Add the egg substitute and cook over medium-low heat for 3 minutes. Add the pepper and beans and cook for another 2 minutes or until the eggs are almost set. Add the green onions, cheddar, salsa and cilantro.
2. Fold one-half of the omelette over the other and cook another minute, or until the cheese melts.

PER SERVING Calories 157 • Protein 23 g • Carbohydrates 8.3 g • Fiber 1.8 g • Total fat 7.7 g • Saturated fat 3 g • Cholesterol 50 mg • Sodium 509 mg • **PREP TIME** 10 minutes • **COOK TIME** 5 minutes • **NUTRITION WATCH** Salsa is a low-fat condiment; 2 Tbsp has only 9 calories and no fat.

mediterranean omelette with black olives, tomatoes and feta { *Serves 2*

1 cup egg substitute (or 4 large eggs)
⅓ cup seeded and diced plum tomatoes
3 Tbsp diced black olives
¼ cup crumbled feta cheese (about 1 oz)
½ tsp dried basil
2 Tbsp chopped fresh basil

THE MEDITERRANEAN WAY of eating has been credited with lowering heart attacks and strokes, reducing the risk of certain cancers and maintaining weight control. We have it all here in one omelette.

1. Lightly coat a 9-inch nonstick skillet with cooking spray. Add the egg substitute and cook over medium-low heat for 4 minutes. Add the tomatoes, olives, feta and dried basil and cook for another 2 minutes, or until the eggs are almost set.
2. Fold one-half over the other and cook for another minute. Garnish with the fresh basil.

PER SERVING Calories 157 • Protein 18 g • Carbohydrates 3.5 g • Fiber 1 g • Total fat 7.8 g • Saturated fat 2.5 g • Cholesterol 6.3 mg • Sodium 509 mg • **PREP TIME** 10 minutes • **COOK TIME** 7 minutes • **NUTRITION WATCH** Feta cheese is a good source of calcium. Light feta contains half the fat and calories of hard cheeses.

potato-crusted quiche with chicken, green bell pepper and aged cheddar { Serves 8

CRUST

- 1 lb Yukon Gold potatoes, peeled and cut into chunks
- 1 Tbsp olive oil
- pinch of salt and pepper
- ½ tsp finely chopped garlic
- 3 Tbsp canned evaporated milk (2%)

FILLING

- 3 oz skinless boneless chicken breast, diced
- 1 Tbsp all-purpose flour
- 2 tsp vegetable oil
- 1 cup diced onion
- 2 tsp vegetable oil
- 1½ tsp finely chopped garlic
- ¾ cup diced green bell pepper
- 2 eggs
- ¼ cup egg substitute
- ¾ cup canned evaporated milk (2%)
- ⅔ cup shredded aged white cheddar cheese
- 3 Tbsp grated Parmesan cheese
- pinch of salt and pepper

ANOTHER VERSION OF A QUICHE, using a mashed-potato crust instead of a traditional butter or lard crust. This cuts the fat and calories tremendously. Feel free to replace the green bell pepper and cheese with varieties of your choice.

1. Preheat oven to 375°F. Lightly coat a 9-inch pie pan with cooking spray.
2. Cover the potatoes with water and bring to a boil. Cook for 15 minutes or until potatoes are just cooked. Drain, mash and add the remaining ingredients for crust. Pat into the bottom and sides of the pie pan and bake for 25 minutes. Remove from the oven and reduce the heat to 350°F.
3. Meanwhile, lightly coat a skillet with cooking spray. Dust the chicken with flour and add half of the oil to the pan. Sauté the chicken for 5 minutes or until no longer pink. Set aside.
4. Wipe out the pan and respray. Sauté the onion with the remaining oil and the garlic for 3 minutes. Add the bell pepper and sauté for 3 minutes. Return the chicken to the pan.
5. In a small bowl, mix the eggs, egg substitute, milk, cheeses and salt and pepper. Add to the chicken mixture and pour into the potato crust. Bake for 25 to 30 minutes or until quiche is just set.

PER SERVING Calories 213 • Protein 12 g • Carbohydrates 19 g • Fiber 1.3 g • Total fat 10 g • Saturated fat 3.5 g • Cholesterol 73 mg • Sodium 180 mg • **PREP TIME** 20 minutes • **BAKE TIME** 50 minutes • **MAKE AHEAD** Bake the potato crust up to a day in advance. • **NUTRITION WATCH** Olive oil is a good source of monounsaturated (good) fatty acids, which are excellent for the heart. The best quality is extra virgin olive oil.

phyllo quiche with broccoli and red bell pepper { Serves 8

2 tsp vegetable oil
1 cup diced onion
1 tsp finely chopped garlic
1 cup diced red bell pepper
1 cup diced steamed broccoli
2 eggs
⅔ cup canned evaporated milk (2%)
¾ cup shredded aged cheddar cheese
pinch of salt and pepper
6 sheets phyllo pastry

I LOVE TO WORK WITH PHYLLO, and it makes the best-tasting crust for this healthy quiche filling. Quiche traditionally is high in calories and fat due to the crust, which is usually made with butter or vegetable shortening. This phyllo allows for great texture and flavor without the excess calories. The broccoli called for is steamed before being put in the quiche. Cook the broccoli in a small amount of water or in the microwave for about 2 minutes or until it just turns bright green; then drain.

1. Preheat oven to 350°F. Lightly coat a 9-inch pie pan with cooking spray.
2. In a large skillet lightly coated with cooking spray, add the oil and sauté the onion and garlic for 3 minutes. Add the red pepper and sauté for 3 minutes. Add the steamed broccoli.
3. In a small bowl, combine the eggs, evaporated milk, cheese, salt and pepper. Combine with the vegetable mixture.
4. Place 2 sheets of phyllo overlapping in the pie pan. Lightly coat with cooking spray. Repeat with the remaining 4 sheets and lightly coating every second sheet with spray. Add the filling. Enclose the quiche by folding the phyllo over the filling and bake for 30 to 35 minutes until the phyllo is golden.

PER SERVING Calories 150 • Protein 8 g • Carbohydrates 15 g • Fiber 1.1 g • Total fat 6.2 g • Saturated fat 2.8 g • Cholesterol 50 mg • Sodium 246 mg • **PREP TIME** 20 minutes • **BAKE TIME** 30 minutes • **MAKE AHEAD** Prepare the entire filling up to a day in advance, but place in the phyllo and bake just before serving. • **NUTRITION WATCH** Phyllo is lower in fat and calories than traditional high-fat pastries. Per 1 oz, phyllo has 85 calories and 1.7 g of fat, whereas regular pie crust has 146 calories and 9 g of fat.

raspberry, banana and orange smoothie { *Serves 4*

½ cup low-fat milk (or soy milk)
½ cup low-fat raspberry yogurt
1 small ripe banana, sliced
1 cup frozen or fresh raspberries
½ cup orange juice
1 Tbsp honey

SMOOTHIES ARE A QUICK, easy and nutritious way to start your morning. You can use a yogurt that has a sugar substitute but I'd be aware of the amount of sugar substitutes you're consuming. A yogurt with sugar may be better in the long run. Any fruit yogurt can be used.

Combine the milk, yogurt, banana, raspberries, orange juice and honey in a blender, and purée. Serve immediately.

PER SERVING Calories 104 • Protein 3 g • Carbohydrates 18 g • Fiber 1.6 g • Total fat 1g • Saturated fat 0.4 g • Cholesterol 3.7 mg • Sodium 34 mg • **PREP TIME** 10 minutes • **NUTRITION WATCH** Raspberries are a rich source of manganese and vitamin C, two critical antioxidant nutrients that help protect the body's tissue from oxygen-related damage. Raspberries may even contain potential cancer-fighting agents.

peach smoothie { *Serves 6*

1 cup low-fat milk
½ cup low-fat plain yogurt
1 small ripe banana, sliced
3 cups sliced fresh or frozen peaches
2 Tbsp honey
1 tsp vanilla extract

YOU CAN FIND frozen peaches all year round in the supermarket. You can always substitute another fruit of your choice such as plums, nectarines or mangoes.

Combine the milk, yogurt, banana, peaches, honey and vanilla in a blender, and purée. Serve immediately.

PER SERVING Calories 105 • Protein 3 g • Carbohydrates 21 g • Fiber 1.7 g • Total fat 1.4 g • Saturated fat 0.8 g • Cholesterol 5 mg • Sodium 32 mg • **PREP TIME** 5 minutes • **NUTRITION WATCH** Peaches are a good source of dietary fiber, vitamin A, niacin and potassium, and a very good source of vitamin C.

creamy cappuccino and banana smoothie { *Serves 6*

1 cup cold chocolate milk (1%) (or soy milk)
1 cup low-fat coffee-flavored yogurt
1 medium-size ripe banana, sliced
2 Tbsp honey
1 Tbsp cocoa powder

I'M A CHOCOHOLIC and I have discovered that 1% chocolate milk (made with cocoa) is the best treat I can have either for breakfast or a snack. Adding chocolate milk to this smoothie satisfies your chocolate cravings and makes it taste like a chocolate milkshake, but without the calories and fat.

Combine the milk, yogurt, banana, honey and cocoa powder in a blender, and purée. Serve immediately.

PER SERVING Calories 108 • Protein 4 g • Carbohydrates 22 g • Fiber 1.1 g • Total fat 1.0 g • Saturated fat 0.6 g • Cholesterol 4 mg • Sodium 54 mg • **PREP TIME** 5 minutes • **NUTRITION WATCH** Honey contains a variety of flavonoids and phenolic acids, which act as antioxidants, scavenging and eliminating free radicals. Generally, darker honeys have a higher antioxidant content than lighter honeys.

{ *appetizers* }

The best olives for these recipes are kalamata olives packed in oil. Although they are higher in calories and fat than the canned ones packed in water, the taste is superior. If calories are a concern, use the canned version • A variety of lighter cheeses reduce the calories, fat and cholesterol of these recipes. If you prefer the intense flavor of full-fat cheese, use it in small amounts • Use low-sodium soy sauce to reduce the sodium by 50%

mediterranean platter { *Serves 6*

3 canned artichoke hearts, drained and cut into quarters
2 red bell peppers, cored and sliced into quarters
2 small zucchini, each sliced lengthwise into 3 pieces
1 large onion, sliced into wedges
3 portobello mushrooms, cut into quarters
1 small head of garlic
8 large kalamata olives
8 rehydrated sun-dried tomatoes

DRESSING

2 Tbsp olive oil
1½ tsp balsamic vinegar

TO SERVE

3 Tbsp chopped fresh basil or parsley
½ cup hummus
2 large pitas, sliced into wedges and warmed

THIS IS SIMILAR TO THE ANTIPASTO PLATTERS you enjoy in Italian restaurants, where the vegetables are usually sitting in excess oil, dramatically increasing the fat and calories. Instead I prepare these roasted vegetables with a small amount of olive oil and balsamic vinegar and serve them with some hummus, which gives great flavor without the extra calories from excess oil.

1. Preheat the oven to 425°F.
2. Lightly coat a baking sheet with cooking spray. Arrange the artichoke hearts, peppers, zucchini, onions, and mushrooms onto the baking sheet. Lightly coat the vegetables with more cooking spray. Slice the top off the head of garlic and wrap it in foil. Place it on the baking sheet. Bake everything for about 25 minutes. Turn the vegetables over and bake for another 20 minutes or until the vegetables are just beginning to brown. Add more time if needed, or remove the vegetables before they burn.
3. Remove the skin from the peppers. Squeeze out the garlic from the cloves. Cut the zucchini pieces in half. Arrange all the grilled veggies on the platter along with the olives and sun-dried tomatoes. Combine the oil and vinegar in a small bowl and drizzle over the vegetables. Garnish with basil, and serve with hummus and pitas.

PER SERVING (VEGETABLES ONLY) Calories 213 • Protein 6.5 g • Carbohydrates 27 g • Fiber 5.2 g • Total fat 9.7 g • Saturated fat 1.2 g • Cholesterol 0 mg • Sodium 340 mg • **PREP TIME** 10 minutes • **BAKE TIME** 45 minutes • **MAKE AHEAD** Cook the vegetables up to a day before. Reheat in a 350°F oven for 10 minutes, or until warmed through. • **NUTRITION WATCH** Adding a large artichoke to the daily diet adds 6 g of dietary fiber to your daily fiber intake. Artichokes are also a good source of vitamin C, folate and magnesium. Use the canned versus those packed in oil.

pesto pizza with artichoke, feta and roasted pepper { *Serves 8*

one 12-inch-round store-bought thin pizza crust
¼ cup pesto (see page 244)
3 canned artichokes, drained and diced
¼ cup crumbled feta cheese (about 1 oz)
¾ cup shredded mozzarella cheese
½ cup diced roasted red pepper (about 1 small roasted red pepper) (see page 100)
¼ cup diced black olives

THE HEALTHIEST WAY to enjoy pizza is using a thin crust and refraining from deli meats and excess cheese. This pizza has a lot of flavor from the vegetables and feta cheese. Use a pizza stone to create a crispier crust.

1. Preheat the oven to 400°F. Line a baking sheet with foil.
2. Place the pizza crust on the baking sheet, and spread the pesto evenly over the crust. Top with the artichokes, feta and mozzarella cheeses, roasted pepper and olives.
3. Bake for 20 minutes, or until the pizza crust gets crisp and lightly browned. Cut into 8 wedges.

PER SERVING Calories 204 • Protein 10 g • Carbohydrates 27 g • Fiber 1.8 g • Total fat 7 g • Saturated fat 2.1 g • Cholesterol 8 mg • Sodium 516 mg • **PREP TIME** 10 minutes • **BAKE TIME** 20 minutes • **MAKE AHEAD** Prepare earlier in the day, but bake just before serving. • **NUTRITION WATCH** One slice of whole wheat crust has about three times the fiber of white flour crust.

shrimp skewers with hoisin-apricot sauce

{ *Makes 16 skewers*

16 medium shrimp (about 12 oz), peeled and deveined
16 wooden skewers (about 6 inches long)
¼ cup apricot jam
1 Tbsp oyster sauce
3 Tbsp hoisin sauce
3 Tbsp chopped fresh basil

THE COMBINATION OF SHRIMP, hoisin and apricot flavors is wonderful. This would also be delicious with scallops or thin strips of boneless chicken breast.

1. Thread shrimp on skewers.
2. Combine the apricot jam, oyster and hoisin sauce in a small bowl. Set aside half of the sauce. Brush the other half over the shrimp.
3. In a grill pan or a skillet lightly coated with cooking spray, sauté the shrimp, just until they are no longer pink, about 5 minutes. Serve with the remaining sauce and garnish with basil.

PER SERVING (1 SKEWER) Calories 35 • Protein 4 g • Carbohydrates 5 g • Fiber 0.1 g • Total fat 0.3 g • Saturated fat 0.1 g • Cholesterol 32 mg • Sodium 94 mg • **PREP TIME** 15 minutes • **COOK TIME** 5 minutes • **MAKE AHEAD** Prepare the skewers early in the day. • **NUTRITION WATCH** Shrimp is a good source of niacin, iron, phosphorus and zinc, and a very good source of protein, vitamin B12 and selenium.

CLOCKWISE FROM LEFT *Shrimp Skewers with Hoisin-Apricot Sauce* (facing page), *Chicken Satays with Peanut Coconut Sauce* (page 94) and *Beef Kebobs with Soy Ginger Sauce* (page 96)

smoked salmon and avocado sushi rolls { *Makes 16 pieces*

RICE
1 cup sushi rice
1 cup water
2 Tbsp rice vinegar
1 tsp granulated sugar

ROLLS
2 nori sheets
¼ cup light mayonnaise
1½ tsp wasabi paste (for mayonnaise)
1 Tbsp sesame seeds
6 oz sliced smoked salmon
1 tsp wasabi paste (for assembly)
8 strips of thinly sliced cucumber (about 4 × ¼ inch)
8 strips of thinly sliced red bell pepper (about 4 × ¼ inch)
8 strips of thinly sliced avocado (about 4 × ¼ inch)

TO SERVE
2 Tbsp low-sodium soy sauce

PREPARING SUSHI AT HOME never seems to be worth the effort or time. But these rolls are so easy and economical and you'll take great pride in serving them.

1. Bring the rice and water to a boil in a large pot. Cover and simmer over the lowest heat for 10 minutes. Remove from the heat, and let sit, covered, for 10 more minutes. Add the rice vinegar and sugar and mix well. Place on large plate and let the rice cool a little; it should still be warm to the touch, but not hot.
2. Place 1 nori sheet on a wooden sushi mat. With wet hands, spread half of the rice evenly over the nori, about ½ inch from each edge. Combine the mayonnaise with the wasabi and spread 1 Tbsp of it over the rice with your fingers. Sprinkle with half of the sesame seeds.
3. Lay out half the smoked salmon on top of the rice until covered. Press the salmon firmly on the rice. Pick up the nori sheet by the ends and gently flip the whole layer over. Spread 1 Tbsp of the wasabi mixture along the long edge of the nori sheet. Place half the cucumber, bell pepper and avocado slices at the same end of the sheet. Using the sushi mat to keep everything in place, roll tightly, with the rice on the outside of the roll, making sure that the salmon clings to the rice. Repeat the procedure with other nori sheet.
4. Wrap the rolls tightly with plastic wrap and chill until ready to serve. Cut each roll into 8 pieces. Serve with soy sauce.

PER SERVING (1 PIECE) Calories 46 • Protein 3 g • Carbohydrates 7 g • Fiber 0.5 g • Total fat 0.9 g • Saturated fat 0.1 g • Cholesterol 2 mg • Sodium 156 mg • **PREP TIME** 15 minutes • **COOK TIME** 20 minutes • **MAKE AHEAD** Prepare early in the day and keep refrigerated. • **NUTRITION WATCH** Avocados contain 81 mcg of the carotenoid lutein, which some studies suggest may help maintain healthy eyes. They also have a high mono- and polyunsaturated fat content, and are a healthy substitute for foods rich in saturated fat.

smoked trout, avocado and cheese tortilla slices { *Serves 8*

⅔ cup light ricotta (5%)
¼ cup light cream cheese (about 2 oz), softened
1½ Tbsp light mayonnaise (or low-fat sour cream)
1½ Tbsp lemon juice
½ tsp Dijon mustard
pinch of pepper
2 Tbsp chopped fresh dill (or ½ tsp dried dill)
4 large flour tortillas
1 cup baby spinach
⅓ cup diced avocado
½ cup finely diced red bell pepper
¼ cup finely diced red onion
4 oz smoked trout, flaked

THESE ARE GREAT APPETIZERS to serve at a dinner party. Smoked trout is usually available in the fish section of your supermarket. If it's unavailable, use smoked salmon or another smoked fish.

1. Beat the ricotta, cream cheese, mayonnaise, lemon juice, mustard and pepper together in a food processor, or in a bowl using an electric mixer, until smooth. Stir in the dill.
2. Divide and spread the mixture evenly over the 4 tortillas. Sprinkle each one evenly with spinach, avocado, red pepper, onion and trout. Roll up tightly.
3. Wrap rolls in plastic wrap and chill until just cold. Cut each tortilla on the diagonal, into 6 pieces.

PER SERVING (3 PIECES) Calories 274 • Protein 11 g • Carbohydrates 34 g • Fiber 2.9 g • Total fat 10 g • Saturated fat 2.7 g • Cholesterol 29 mg • Sodium 445 mg • **PREP TIME** 15 minutes • **MAKE AHEAD** Prepare early in the day and keep refrigerated. • **NUTRITION WATCH** Spinach may protect you from osteoporosis, heart disease, colon cancer and arthritis.

shrimp and cheese eggrolls { *Makes 10 eggrolls*

2 tsp vegetable oil
½ cup finely chopped onion
1½ tsp finely chopped garlic
½ cup diced carrots
½ cup diced green bell pepper
6 oz medium shrimp, peeled, deveined and finely chopped
1 cup tomato sauce (see page 334) or store-bought spaghetti sauce
¾ cup shredded havarti (about 2 oz)
2 Tbsp grated Parmesan cheese
10 large eggroll wrappers (5½ inches in diameter)

TRADITIONAL EGGROLLS ARE TASTY because they are deep fried. The fillings tend to be boring, the only flavor coming from the oil they've been deep fried in. The flavor of these eggrolls is delicious, from the variety of sautéed vegetables, shrimp, tomato sauce and cheese. No reason to deep fry.

1. Preheat the oven to 425°F. Lightly coat a baking sheet with cooking spray.
2. In a nonstick skillet, heat the oil over medium heat. Sauté the onions and garlic for 3 minutes. Add the carrots and pepper, and sauté over medium heat for 4 minutes. Add the shrimp and sauté for 2 minutes, or until the shrimp just turns pink. Remove from the heat. Stir in the tomato sauce and havarti and Parmesan cheeses.
3. Put 1 wrapper on a work surface with 1 corner pointing toward you. Keep the rest of wrappers covered with a damp cloth to prevent them from drying out. Put 2 Tbsp of the filling in the center of the wrapper. Fold the lower corner up over the filling, fold in the 2 sides and roll the bundle away from you. Arrange onto the prepared baking sheet. Repeat with the remaining wrappers.
4. Bake for 15 to 18 minutes, or until golden, turning the rolls halfway through baking.

PER SERVING (1 EGGROLL) Calories 132 • Protein 8 g • Carbohydrates 18 g • Fiber 1.3 g • Total fat 3.7 g • Saturated fat 1.6 g • Cholesterol 31 mg • Sodium 250 mg • **PREP TIME** 15 minutes • **COOK TIME** 25 minutes • **MAKE AHEAD** Prepare up to a day ahead and refrigerate. • **NUTRITION WATCH** Baked eggrolls are lower in calories and fat than fried eggrolls. One baked eggroll has less than 4 g of fat versus 8 g for fried, and only 130 calories versus 200 for fried.

seafood potstickers with hoisin sauce { *Makes 28 potstickers*

SAUCE

3 Tbsp hoisin sauce
2 Tbsp low-sodium soy sauce
2 Tbsp rice vinegar
1½ Tbsp brown sugar
1 tsp sesame oil
1 tsp finely chopped garlic
½ tsp finely chopped ginger

FILLING

8 oz raw shrimp, peeled, deveined and diced
1 clove garlic, finely chopped
1 green onion, chopped
2 Tbsp chopped cilantro
28 small eggroll wrappers (about 3 inches square) (or wonton wrappers)
½ cup seafood (or chicken) stock
3 Tbsp chopped cilantro

WHEN I GO FOR DIM SUM I enjoy potstickers. But, as with eggrolls, I often find the fillings boring, and tasty only with the dipping sauce. My version of potstickers has a delicious filling and they're easy to prepare. For a thinner wrapper, use wontons.

1. To make the sauce, combine the hoisin sauce, soy sauce, rice vinegar, brown sugar, sesame oil, garlic and ginger in a small bowl. Set aside about 2 Tbsp of the sauce.
2. To make the filling, combine the shrimp, garlic, green onion, and cilantro in the bowl of a food processor. Add the 2 Tbsp of reserved sauce, and pulse on and off until the filling is finely and evenly chopped and everything is well combined.
3. Place 2 tsp of the filling in the center of each wrapper. Pull the edges up to make a small bundle, pleating and bunching. Press the edges together to seal.
4. In a large nonstick skillet lightly coated with cooking spray, cook the potstickers, flat side down, over medium-high heat for 3 minutes, or until they are golden brown on the bottom.
5. Add the stock and reduce the heat to low. Cover and cook for 2 minutes or until cooked though. Remove from the pan; discard any remaining stock. Serve with the remaining sauce. Garnish with the cilantro.

PER SERVING (1 POTSTICKER) Calories 81 • Protein 4 g • Carbohydrates 15 g • Fiber 0.6 g • Total fat 0.6 g • Saturated fat 0.1 g • Cholesterol 12 mg • Sodium 230 mg • **PREP TIME** 20 minutes • **COOK TIME** 5 minutes • **MAKE AHEAD** Prepare early in the day and keep refrigerated. Cook just before serving. • **NUTRITION WATCH** The majority of Asian sauces, including hoisin, are high in sodium. Consume in moderation.

chicken satays with peanut coconut sauce { *Makes 18 satays*

12 oz skinless boneless chicken breasts (about 3 breasts)
18 wooden skewers (about 6 inches long)

SAUCE
¼ cup light coconut milk
2 Tbsp natural peanut butter
2 tsp low-sodium soy sauce
2 tsp sesame oil
2 tsp rice vinegar
1 tsp honey
1 tsp finely chopped garlic
½ tsp finely chopped ginger
½ tsp hot chili sauce

GARNISH
3 Tbsp chopped cilantro
1 tsp sesame seeds

THESE DELICIOUS SATAYS can be served as an appetizer or a main course with a side dish of rice or rice noodles. Be sure to use a natural peanut butter to avoid trans fats and added sugar. Light coconut milk is readily available and much healthier than the regular version. It only has 3 grams of fat per ¼ cup, compared to 10 grams for the regular. (Pictured on page 89.)

1. Cut the chicken into strips about 4 inches long and 2 inches wide. Thread the strips of chicken onto the skewers.
2. In a bowl whisk together the coconut milk, peanut butter, soy sauce, sesame oil, rice vinegar, honey, garlic, ginger and chili sauce. Reserve half of the sauce; brush the other half over the chicken satays.
3. In a nonstick skillet, or a grill pan lightly coated with cooking spray, cook the chicken for 5 minutes or just until no longer pink. Serve with the remaining sauce and garnish with cilantro and sesame seeds.

PER SERVING (1 SKEWER) Calories 42 • Protein 4 g • Carbohydrates 1 g • Fiber 0.1 g • Total fat 2.2 g • Saturated fat 0.3 g • Cholesterol 10 mg • Sodium 34 mg • **PREP TIME** 15 minutes • **COOK TIME** 5 minutes • **MAKE AHEAD** Prepare up to a day in advance and refrigerate. Cook just before serving. • **NUTRITION WATCH** Coconut milk, especially regular coconut milk, is very high in saturated fat. Try a light coconut milk instead. Coconut milk is a good source of manganese that promotes optimal function of your thyroid gland and keeps your bones strong and healthy.

mini meatballs with black bean sauce { *Serves 6*

SAUCE

3 Tbsp packed brown sugar
⅓ cup ketchup
¼ cup black bean sauce
1½ Tbsp rice vinegar
1 tsp sesame oil
1½ tsp finely chopped garlic
1½ tsp finely chopped ginger

MEATBALLS

½ lb lean ground beef
3 Tbsp seasoned dry breadcrumbs
1 tsp finely chopped garlic
1 egg
2 Tbsp finely chopped green onions

GARNISH

1 tsp sesame seeds
2 Tbsp chopped cilantro or parsley

GREAT AS AN APPETIZER or a main meal served over rice or rice noodles. The black bean sauce is readily available in the Asian section of your supermarket.

1. Preheat the oven to 375°F. Lightly coat a baking sheet with cooking spray.
2. For the sauce, combine the brown sugar, ketchup, black bean sauce, rice vinegar, sesame oil, garlic and ginger in a bowl. Set aside.
3. For the meatballs, combine the beef, breadcrumbs, garlic, egg and green onions in a large bowl. Add 3 Tbsp of the reserved sauce. Mix well. Form into 20 to 24 small meatballs, about 1 inch in diameter. Place on baking sheet and bake for 10 minutes, turning halfway through the baking time.
4. In large skillet, add the cooked meatballs and remaining sauce. Cover and simmer on low heat for 4 minutes or just until hot.
5. Garnish with sesame seeds and cilantro or parsley.

PER SERVING Calories 133 • Protein 9 g • Carbohydrates 13 g • Fiber 0.5 g • Total fat 5 g • Saturated fat 1.1 g • Cholesterol 56 mg • Sodium 227 mg • **PREP TIME** 20 minutes • **COOK TIME** 15 minutes • **MAKE AHEAD** Bake meatballs up to a day in advance. • **NUTRITION WATCH** Black bean sauce is high in sodium. You can always use half water or stock and half black bean sauce to reduce the sodium.

beef kebobs with soy ginger sauce { *Makes 12 kebobs*

12 oz lean steak, cut into 1-inch cubes
12 wooden skewers (about 6 inches long)

SAUCE
¼ cup packed brown sugar
2 Tbsp low-sodium soy sauce
1½ Tbsp rice vinegar
1 Tbsp water
2 tsp sesame oil
1½ tsp cornstarch
1 tsp finely chopped garlic
½ tsp finely chopped ginger

GARNISH
1 tsp sesame seeds
3 Tbsp finely chopped green onions

USE A GOOD QUALITY OF STEAK THAT DOESN'T HAVE TO BE MARINATED. I like rib eye or sirloin. Feel free to substitute the beef with boneless chicken breast or shelled shrimp. (Pictured on page 89.)

1. Place 2 beef cubes on each skewer.
2. Whisk together the brown sugar, soy sauce, rice vinegar, water, sesame oil, cornstarch, garlic and ginger in a small saucepan until the cornstarch is dissolved. Simmer for 2 minutes or just until thickened. Brush half of the sauce on the kebobs.
3. In either a nonstick grill pan or skillet lightly coated with cooking spray, sauté the kebobs just until cooked to your preference. Garnish with sesame seeds, green onions and the remaining sauce.

PER SERVING (1 KEBOB) Calories 64 • Protein 6 g • Carbohydrates 4 g • Fiber 0.1 g • Total fat 2.7 g • Saturated fat 0.8 g • Cholesterol 11 mg • Sodium 102 mg • **PREP TIME** 15 minutes • **COOK TIME** 5 minutes • **MAKE AHEAD** Prepare the kebobs and sauce up to a day in advance. Cook just before serving. • **NUTRITION WATCH** Lean beef is lower in calories and fat than regular-cut beef such as a rib roast. A 3 oz serving of lean beef has 175 calories and 9 g of fat. A rib roast has 300 calories and 18 g of fat.

spiced bagel garlic toasts { *Serves 4*

2 medium whole-grain bagels
2 Tbsp olive oil
¼ tsp onion powder
¼ tsp garlic powder
pinch of chili powder
2 Tbsp grated Parmesan cheese
1 Tbsp chopped parsley

THESE ARE AS TASTY as garlic bread, but don't have all the calories and fat. Use any herbs and spices you like best.

1. Preheat the oven to 400°F. Line a baking sheet with foil and lightly coat with cooking spray.
2. Slice each bagel into 5 or 6 very thin slices. Place the slices on the prepared baking sheet.
3. Combine the olive oil with the onion, garlic and chili powders in a small bowl and lightly brush the bagel slices with this mixture. Sprinkle with the Parmesan. Bake for 8 minutes or until crisp. Sprinkle with parsley.

PER SERVING (ABOUT 3 SLICES) Calories 154 • Protein 4 g • Carbohydrates 16 g • Fiber 2.7 g • Total fat 9 g • Saturated fat 1.7 g • Cholesterol 2 mg • Sodium 151 mg • **PREP TIME** 10 minutes • **BAKE TIME** 8 minutes • **NUTRITION WATCH** Parsley is great for your heart and contains more vitamin C than any other vegetable. The iron content is exceptional, and this herb is a good source of manganese and calcium.

seasoned baked "pita chips" { *Serves 4*

3 large flour tortillas
3 Tbsp finely grated Parmesan cheese
pinch of salt and pepper
pinch of paprika
pinch of garlic powder
pinch of onion powder

STORE-BOUGHT PITA CHIPS are deep fried, which increases their calories and fat content. The spices in this recipe add flavor instead of oil. Feel free to substitute spices of your choice. Try a variety of different colored and flavored tortillas. The whole wheat version has more fiber and nutrients. (Pictured on page 99.)

1. Preheat the oven to 350°F. Line a large baking sheet (or 2 medium baking sheets) with foil.
2. Slice each tortilla into 8 wedges. Arrange the wedges on the baking sheet, not overlapping. Lightly coat with cooking spray.
3. Combine the Parmesan, salt, pepper, paprika and garlic and onion powders in a small bowl. Sprinkle the seasoning evenly over the tortillas and bake for 12 minutes, or just until lightly browned.

PER SERVING (ABOUT 6 CHIPS) Calories 191 • Protein 6.5 g • Carbohydrates 28 g • Fiber 2.5 g • Total fat 5.6 g • Saturated fat 1.9 g • Cholesterol 4 mg • Sodium 419 mg • **PREP TIME** 5 minutes • **BAKE TIME** 12 minutes • **MAKE AHEAD** Can be made ahead and stored in an airtight container for up to 1 week. • **NUTRITION WATCH** Paprika is a powerhouse spice. It has vitamin A, vitamin C, vitamin E (alpha tocopherol), vitamin K, riboflavin, niacin, vitamin B6, iron and potassium.

black olive tahini spread { *Makes 1⅓ cups / Serves 6*

1 cup canned chickpeas, drained and rinsed
¼ cup tahini
3 Tbsp water
2 Tbsp olive oil
2 Tbsp lemon juice
1 tsp finely chopped garlic
½ tsp hot chili sauce
⅓ cup finely diced canned black olives
2 Tbsp chopped fresh basil or parsley

THIS IS SIMILAR TO A HUMMUS DIP, but with black olives added. To cut back the calories and fat you can use canned sliced olives that are packed in water, not oil, but if you want more flavor, use those packed in oil and pitted. Tahini is sesame seed paste, found in the ethnic section of your supermarket.

1. Combine the chickpeas, tahini, water, olive oil, lemon juice, garlic and chili sauce in the bowl of a food processor. Purée until smooth.
2. Stir in the olives and garnish with basil or parsley.

PER SERVING Calories 157 • Protein 4 g • Carbohydrates 11 g • Fiber 2.4 g • Total fat 11 g • Saturated fat 1.5 g • Cholesterol 0 mg • Sodium 93 mg • **PREP TIME** 5 minutes • **MAKE AHEAD** Prepare up to a day in advance. • **NUTRITION WATCH** Chickpeas have iron for energy and are a good source of protein if you are looking for a vegetarian protein alternative.

white bean and artichoke hummus { *Serves 8*

1 cup canned white kidney beans, drained and rinsed
4 canned artichoke hearts, drained and chopped
2 Tbsp tahini
1½ Tbsp olive oil
2 Tbsp lemon juice
1½ tsp finely chopped garlic
¼ tsp ground cumin
pinch of salt and freshly ground black pepper
¼ cup chopped cilantro

ANOTHER TWIST on traditional hummus. The addition of white beans and artichoke hearts is outstanding.

1. Combine the beans, artichokes, tahini, olive oil, lemon juice, garlic, cumin, salt and pepper in the bowl of a food processor. Purée until smooth.
2. Add the chopped cilantro and stir to combine.

PER SERVING Calories 79 • Protein 2 g • Carbohydrates 6 g • Fiber 1.7 g • Total fat 5 g • Saturated fat 0.7 g • Cholesterol 0 mg • Sodium 91 mg • **PREP TIME** 5 minutes • **MAKE AHEAD** Prepare up to a day in advance. • **NUTRITION WATCH** Kidney beans are a good source of thiamin, which can help memory function.

CLOCKWISE FROM TOP LEFT *Black Olive Tahini Spread* (facing page), *Red Bell Pepper Hummus* (page 100), *White Bean and Artichoke Hummus* (facing page) and *Seasoned Baked "Pita Chips"* (page 97)

red bell pepper hummus { *Serves 8 / Makes ¾ cup*

½ cup canned chickpeas, drained and rinsed
¼ cup roasted red pepper (about ½ small roasted red pepper) (see left)
1½ Tbsp tahini (sesame seed paste)
1 Tbsp lemon juice
1 Tbsp olive oil
2 tsp water
½ tsp finely chopped garlic
½ tsp hot chili sauce
2 Tbsp chopped parsley

ROASTED RED PEPPERS

To roast red peppers, cut the pepper in half lengthwise and remove ribs and seeds. Lay on a foil-covered baking sheet and roast at 425°F for 25 minutes, or just until browned on all sides. Place bell peppers in a covered bowl and let sit for 10 minutes before peeling off the skin. Store in the fridge for up to 3 days.

THE ADDITION OF ROASTED BELL PEPPER to a hummus dip creates a new flavor and color. This is not only great as a dip but also as a spread for sandwiches or tortillas. (Pictured on page 99.)

1. In the bowl of a small food processor, combine the chickpeas, roasted red pepper, tahini, lemon juice, oil, water, garlic and chili sauce.
2. Purée until smooth. Garnish with parsley.

PER SERVING Calories 53 • Protein 1.5 g • Carbohydrates 4 g • Fiber 0.9 g • Total fat 3.5 g • Saturated fat 0.5 g • Cholesterol 0 mg • Sodium 29 mg • **PREP TIME** 5 minutes • **MAKE AHEAD** Prepare up to a day in advance. • **NUTRITION WATCH** The sesame seeds in tahini have a cholesterol-lowering effect.

hummus bake with feta and kalamata olives { *Serves 6*

1 can (19 oz) chickpeas, drained and rinsed
1 clove of garlic
½ cup vegetable (or chicken) stock
3 Tbsp tahini (sesame seed paste)
3 Tbsp lemon juice
2 Tbsp olive oil
½ tsp hot chili sauce
pinch of pepper
¼ tsp ground cumin
⅓ cup crumbled feta cheese (about 1½ oz)
3 Tbsp finely chopped kalamata olives
2 Tbsp chopped cilantro

THIS HEATED VERSION OF HUMMUS, with a sprinkling of feta and olives, is perfect for dipping with crackers or lavash (a thin, flat Armenian bread).

1. Preheat the oven to 400°F.
2. Place the chickpeas, garlic, stock, tahini, lemon juice, oil, chili sauce, pepper and cumin in the bowl of a food processor. Purée until smooth and transfer to a mixing bowl.
3. Add ¼ cup of the feta (leaving the remaining feta for the topping) and the olives and stir to combine.
4. Place the mixture in a small ovenproof baking dish lightly coated with cooking spray and sprinkle with the remaining feta. Bake for 12 minutes, or just until heated through and the top is slightly browned.
5. Garnish with cilantro and serve with pita wedges or crackers.

PER SERVING Calories 212 • Protein 8 g • Carbohydrates 19 g • Fiber 3.9 g • Total fat 12 g • Saturated fat 1.9 g • Cholesterol 2 mg • Sodium 269 mg • **PREP TIME** 10 minutes • **BAKE TIME** 12 minutes • **NUTRITION WATCH** Store-bought regular stock is high in sodium, so it's better to make stock at home, since you are the one who controls the amount of sodium in your pot. If you are buying stock, select low-sodium stock more often.

{ *salads* }

Use fresh, crisp vegetables for salads • If cooking vegetables such as snow peas, asparagus or broccoli, cook only until tender-crisp by steaming, boiling or microwaving. To prevent discoloration, drain and rinse with cold water until no longer warm • Use fresh herbs—they have more flavor than dried herbs. But if you have to use dried herbs, the ratio is 3 to 1: If a recipe calls for 1 Tbsp of fresh parsley, use 1 tsp dried parsley • Try a variety of greens for salad, such as Boston lettuce, Bibb lettuce, radicchio, red leaf lettuce and endive. Avoid iceberg lettuce, which has few nutrients and little flavor • If excess liquid is a problem when you use fresh tomatoes, either deseed them or use plum tomatoes • Prepare a salad up to 4 hours before serving, then cover and refrigerate. If prepared any earlier, the vegetables will lose their crispness • Prepare dressing early in the day or up to 2 days ahead. Keep covered and refrigerate. Do not dress and toss the salad until ready to serve • Use extra virgin olive oil for the best flavor • Use fresh lemon or lime juice, not the bottled version • Use light mayonnaise, which has 50% less fat and calories than regular mayonnaise • Rinse canned beans well to eliminate excess sodium • If preparing avocado beforehand, prevent discoloration by soaking in a mixture of water and lemon juice (3 parts water to 1 part juice)

fresh corn salad { *Serves 4*

SALAD

3 fresh cobs of corn

½ cup diced red onion

½ cup diced roasted red pepper (about 1 small roasted red pepper) (see page 100)

½ cup chopped fresh basil

DRESSING

2 Tbsp olive oil

1 Tbsp apple cider vinegar

1½ tsp finely chopped jalapeño pepper

1 tsp finely chopped garlic

pinch of salt and pepper

THIS IS THE SALAD TO MAKE when corn is at its ripest. I always look for small white and yellow kernels on cobs that have been picked that day if possible. You'll have to go to a local farmers' market. It's well worth the trip. If you want to make this salad year round, buy canned or frozen corn niblets and sauté about 2 cups in a skillet just until browned. (Pictured on page 277.)

1. Lightly coat a grill pan with cooking spray and set over medium-high heat, or heat your barbecue to medium-high heat. Grill the corncobs for about 5 minutes, or until the corn begins to brown. Using a sharp knife, slice the niblets off of the cobs and place in a bowl.
2. Add the red onion, roasted red pepper and basil to the corn and stir to combine.
3. To prepare the dressing, whisk together the olive oil, cider vinegar, jalapeño, garlic, salt and pepper. Pour the dressing over the salad and toss to combine.

PER SERVING Calories 159 • Protein 4 g • Carbohydrates 17 g • Fiber 2.9 g • Total fat 9 g • Saturated fat 1 g • Cholesterol 0 mg • Sodium 168 mg • **PREP TIME** 5 minutes • **COOK TIME** 5 minutes • **MAKE AHEAD** Can be prepared early in the day and kept refrigerated. • **NUTRITION WATCH** Corn is a good source of many nutrients, including thiamin (vitamin B1) for memory, pantothenic acid (vitamin B5) for energy, folate for cardiovascular health, dietary fiber, vitamin C, phosphorus and manganese.

green mango salad { *Serves 4*

SALAD

1 large green (unripe) mango, thinly sliced
¾ cup thinly sliced red bell pepper
⅓ cup thinly sliced red onion
¼ cup chopped fresh mint
¼ cup chopped cilantro

DRESSING

1 Tbsp low-sodium soy sauce
1 Tbsp lime or lemon juice
2 tsp sesame oil
1½ tsp fish (or oyster) sauce
2 tsp brown sugar
1 tsp finely chopped jalapeño pepper
½ tsp finely chopped garlic
½ tsp finely chopped ginger

GARNISH

¼ cup chopped toasted cashews

THAI MENUS ALWAYS FEATURE THIS SWEET AND SAVORY SALAD. The key is finding an unripe mango, one that's still firm. This salad is perfect to serve before a rice-noodle type of dish such as pad Thai.

1. Place the mango, red pepper, onion, mint and cilantro in a serving bowl.
2. Whisk together the soy sauce, lime juice, sesame oil, fish sauce and brown sugar in a small bowl. Stir in the jalapeños, garlic and ginger.
3. Pour the dressing over the salad and toss. Garnish with the chopped cashews.

PER SERVING Calories 132 • Protein 3 g • Carbohydrates 17 g • Fiber 2.5 g • Total fat 7 g • Saturated fat 1.3 g • Cholesterol 0 mg • Sodium 316 mg • **PREP TIME** 15 minutes • **MAKE AHEAD** Prepare earlier in the day but dress just before serving. • **NUTRITION WATCH** Jalapeños strengthen the digestive system since they have antibiotic and antiviral properties.

tomato salad with bocconcini cheese and olives { *Serves 4*

SALAD
2 tsp vegetable oil
½ large sweet white onion, thinly sliced
1 tsp brown sugar
2 large field tomatoes, cut into ¼-inch slices
4 plum tomatoes, each cut into 4 wedges
1½ cups cherry or grape tomatoes, cut in half
2 oz bocconcini cheese, thinly sliced
¼ cup halved kalamata olives

DRESSING
2 Tbsp olive oil
1 Tbsp low-fat sour cream
1 Tbsp light mayonnaise
1½ tsp balsamic vinegar
½ tsp honey
½ tsp finely chopped garlic

GARNISH
3 Tbsp chopped fresh basil

A FAVORITE SALAD often served in Italian restaurants. I usually find that there's too much cheese for this salad. You can now purchase mini bocconcini, which suits the salad better in terms of nutrition.

1. Lightly coat a small skillet with cooking spray and add the oil. Sauté the onion slices over medium heat for 10 minutes, or until tender and lightly browned. Add the sugar and sauté another 5 minutes. Set aside.
2. Arrange the tomatoes, bocconcini cheese and olives on a serving platter. Place the caramelized onions on top.
3. Prepare the dressing by whisking together the oil, sour cream, mayonnaise, balsamic vinegar, honey and garlic until well blended. Pour the dressing evenly over the salad and toss. Garnish with basil and serve.

PER SERVING Calories 247 • Protein 5 g • Carbohydrates 14 g • Fiber 3 g • Total fat 15 g • Saturated fat 3.9 g • Cholesterol 12 mg • Sodium 320 mg • **PREP TIME** 15 minutes • **COOK TIME** 15 minutes • **MAKE AHEAD** Prepare the salad early in the day and refrigerate until ready to serve. Dress at the last minute. • **NUTRITION WATCH** Lycopene, which is an antioxidant in tomatoes, may have cancer-fighting properties.

spinach salad with cinnamon almonds, strawberries and goat cheese { *Serves 8*

CINNAMON ALMONDS
¼ cup whole almonds
⅓ cup packed brown sugar
½ tsp cinnamon
¼ tsp nutmeg
¼ tsp ground ginger

SALAD
8 cups baby spinach
1 cup thinly sliced red bell pepper
1 cup sliced strawberries
½ cup crumbled goat cheese (about 2 oz)

DRESSING
1½ Tbsp apple cider vinegar
1 Tbsp olive oil
1 Tbsp apple juice concentrate
1 tsp brown sugar
½ tsp chopped garlic
½ tsp Dijon mustard

6 oz grilled sliced chicken or shrimp (optional)

THIS SALAD IS PERFECT for entertaining with all its vibrant colors, flavors and textures. The combination of spinach, spiced nuts, strawberries and goat cheese gives it loads of character. Prepare the almonds in larger quantities and keep in an airtight container for up to 2 weeks.

1. Preheat the oven to 350°F. Line a baking sheet with foil and lightly coat with cooking spray.
2. Rinse the almonds with cold water. Drain but do not let them dry. Place them in a bowl and add the brown sugar, cinnamon, nutmeg and ground ginger. Toss to coat. Spread out on the prepared baking sheet and bake for 15 minutes, tossing once. Let cool, then remove from the baking sheet and chop coarsely.
3. Place the baby spinach, red pepper, strawberries and goat cheese in a large serving bowl.
4. Prepare the dressing by whisking together the apple cider vinegar, olive oil, apple juice concentrate, brown sugar, garlic and mustard in a small bowl. Pour the dressing over the salad and toss. Top with the chopped almonds. Serve topped with grilled chicken or shrimp, if desired.

PER SERVING (WITHOUT MEAT) Calories 104 • Protein 3.2 g • Carbohydrates 11 g • Fiber 2.3 g • Total fat 5.6 g • Saturated fat 1.3 g • Cholesterol 3 mg • Sodium 120 mg • **PREP TIME** 15 minutes • **BAKE TIME** 15 minutes • **MAKE AHEAD** Prepare the salad early in the day but dress just before serving. • **NUTRITION WATCH** Almonds are great source of essential fatty acids, which can increase your good cholesterol (HDL).

spinach salad with caramelized pears { *Serves 4*

CARAMELIZED PEARS

1 medium pear, peeled and cut into 1-inch wedges

1 Tbsp brown sugar

½ tsp cinnamon

SALAD

6 cups baby spinach

½ cup crumbled goat cheese (about 2 oz)

⅓ cup dried cranberries

1 cup thinly sliced red bell pepper

⅓ cup toasted sliced almonds

DRESSING

1 Tbsp orange juice concentrate

1 Tbsp olive oil

1 Tbsp apple cider

1 tsp honey

½ tsp Dijon mustard

½ tsp finely chopped garlic

THE BABY SPINACH VARIETY has a sweet and tender texture that goes well in any salad. The caramelized pears highlight this salad and go well with the goat cheese, dried cranberries and orange dressing.

1. Lightly coat a small nonstick skillet with cooking spray. Add the pear wedges and sauté for 1 minute. Add the sugar and cinnamon and sauté for 2 minutes or just until the pears begin to soften. Remove from the heat and set aside.
2. Place the baby spinach, goat cheese, cranberries, red pepper and almonds in a large serving bowl.
3. Prepare the dressing by whisking together the orange juice concentrate, oil, apple cider, honey, mustard and garlic in a small bowl. Pour the dressing over the salad and toss. Garnish with the pear wedges and serve.

PER SERVING Calories 224 • Protein 6 g • Carbohydrates 29 g • Fiber 5.5 g • Total fat 11 g • Saturated fat 2.9 g • Cholesterol 7 mg • Sodium 175 mg • **PREP TIME** 15 minutes • **COOK TIME** 3 minutes • **MAKE AHEAD** Prepare the salad early in the day but dress just before serving. • **NUTRITION WATCH** Spinach may reduce the risk of osteoporosis, heart disease, colon cancer, arthritis and other diseases.

warm spinach salad with asiago cheese and oyster mushrooms { *Serves 4*

SALAD

3 cups oyster mushrooms, sliced in half
8 cups baby spinach
½ cup shredded Asiago (or Parmesan) cheese

DRESSING

2 Tbsp olive oil
1 Tbsp balsamic vinegar
1 Tbsp light mayonnaise
2 tsp honey
½ tsp finely chopped garlic
½ tsp Dijon mustard
pinch of salt and pepper

THIS SALAD has to be served warm so the cheese softens over the warmed mushrooms. Use any variety of mushroom you like. The key is to cook the mushrooms on a medium-high heat until all the moisture evaporates so the mushrooms aren't wet.

1. Lightly coat a nonstick skillet with cooking spray and sauté the mushrooms over medium heat for about 8 minutes, or just until they are no longer wet and are slightly browned. Keep warm.
2. Prepare the dressing by whisking together the olive oil, balsamic vinegar, mayonnaise, honey, garlic, mustard, salt and pepper.
3. Place the spinach, sautéed mushrooms and Asiago in a large serving bowl. Pour the dressing over the salad and toss. Serve immediately.

PER SERVING Calories 178 • Protein 6 g • Carbohydrates 11 g • Fiber 3.1 g • Total fat 13 g • Saturated fat 3.5 g • Cholesterol 14 mg • Sodium 328 mg • **PREP TIME** 10 minutes • **COOK TIME** 8 minutes • **MAKE AHEAD** Prepare the salad early in the day without dressing and reheat the mushrooms just before serving. • **NUTRITION WATCH** The protein quality of oyster mushrooms is nearly equal to that of animal-derived protein—great for vegetarians. They contain fiber, vitamins B1 and B2 and iron.

coleslaw with sautéed pears and cranberries { *Serves 4*

SALAD

1 cup peeled and sliced ripe pear
2 tsp brown sugar
¼ tsp cinnamon
1½ cups thinly sliced green cabbage
1½ cups thinly sliced red cabbage
1 medium carrot, grated (about 1 cup)
¾ cup thinly sliced red or green bell pepper
⅓ cup thinly sliced red onion
2 green onions, finely chopped

DRESSING

¼ cup light mayonnaise
2 Tbsp low-fat plain yogurt
2 Tbsp lemon juice
2 tsp honey
½ tsp Dijon mustard
pinch of salt and pepper

GARNISH

3 Tbsp chopped parsley

FORGET THE OLD-FASHIONED, heavy mayonnaise coleslaws. This lighter version, using caramelized pears and lemony light mayonnaise, is perfect as a side salad or an accompaniment.

1. Lightly coat a small nonstick skillet with cooking spray and set over medium heat. Add the sliced pear, brown sugar and cinnamon. Sauté for 2 minutes, or just until the pear begins to caramelize. Remove from heat and set aside.
2. Place the cabbage, carrot, bell pepper, red and green onions and pears in a large serving bowl.
3. To prepare the dressing, whisk together the mayonnaise, yogurt, lemon juice, honey, mustard, salt and pepper in a small bowl. Pour the dressing over the salad and toss gently. Garnish with parsley and serve.

PER SERVING Calories 133 • Protein 2 g • Carbohydrates 22 g • Fiber 4.1 g • Total fat 5.5 g • Saturated fat 0.1 g • Cholesterol 5 mg • Sodium 238 mg • **PREP TIME** 15 minutes • **COOK TIME** 2 minutes • **MAKE AHEAD** Prepare the salad early in the day and dress an hour before serving. • **NUTRITION WATCH** Phytonutrients in cruciferous vegetables, such as red and green cabbage, have cancer-fighting properties and aid in digestion. The vitamin C in red cabbage may be protective against Alzheimer's disease.

mediterranean bean, olive and artichoke salad { *Serves 6*

1½ cups canned chickpeas, drained and rinsed
1½ cups canned red kidney beans, drained and rinsed
½ cup diced red bell pepper
3 canned artichokes, drained and chopped
12 large marinated olives, quartered (about ¼ cup)
⅓ cup crumbled feta cheese (about 1½ oz)

DRESSING
2 Tbsp olive oil
2 Tbsp lemon juice
1½ tsp lemon zest
1 tsp finely chopped garlic
1½ tsp finely chopped jalapeño pepper (or ½ tsp hot chili sauce)
½ tsp dried basil
¼ tsp dried oregano
pinch of pepper

GARNISH
⅓ cup chopped fresh basil

THIS CAN BE A FILLING, stand-alone salad. The beans, artichokes, cheese, and lemon olive oil dressing are perfectly matched. Use any variety of beans or cheese you prefer.

1. In a large serving bowl, combine the chickpeas, kidney beans, red pepper, artichokes, olives and feta.
2. To prepare the dressing, whisk together the olive oil, lemon juice, lemon zest, garlic, jalapeño, basil, oregano and pepper in a small bowl. Pour the dressing over the salad and toss. Garnish with fresh basil and serve.

PER SERVING Calories 229 • Protein 10 g • Carbohydrates 29 g • Fiber 9 g • Total fat 8 g • Saturated fat 1.4 g • Cholesterol 3 mg • Sodium 450 mg • **PREP TIME** 15 minutes • **MAKE AHEAD** Can be made early in the day with dressing and allowed to marinate. • **NUTRITION WATCH** Chickpeas are a good source of protein and a very good source of folic acid, fiber and manganese. The fiber can help lower cholesterol and improve blood-sugar levels.

edamame and black bean salad with tahini dressing { *Serves 6*

SALAD

1½ cups frozen shelled edamame
1½ cups canned black beans, drained and rinsed
¾ cup chopped red bell pepper
⅓ cup chopped green onions

DRESSING

¼ cup light ricotta (5%)
1½ Tbsp tahini (sesame seed paste)
1½ Tbsp light mayonnaise
1½ Tbsp lemon juice
1 Tbsp olive oil
1 Tbsp low-sodium soy sauce
1 tsp finely chopped garlic
1 tsp finely chopped jalapeño pepper (or hot chili sauce)
¼ tsp ground cumin
⅓ cup chopped cilantro or parsley

BOTH SHELLED EDAMAME and those left in the pod are now available in most supermarkets in the frozen vegetable section. They are delicious on their own, in a salad such as this or as an accompaniment to a main course.

1. Bring a pot of water to the boil and add the edamame. Boil for 1 minute, then drain and rinse with cold water. Place in a serving bowl and add the black beans, red pepper and onions.
2. To prepare the dressing, combine the ricotta, tahini, mayonnaise, lemon juice, olive oil, soy sauce, garlic, jalapeño and cumin in the smaller bowl of a food processor or blender. Blend until smooth. Pour the dressing over the salad and garnish with cilantro or parsley.

PER SERVING Calories 173 • Protein 10 g • Carbohydrates 17 g • Fiber 3.4 g • Total fat 8 g • Saturated fat 0.9 g • Cholesterol 4 mg • Sodium 280 mg • **PREP TIME** 15 minutes • **COOK TIME** 1 minute • **MAKE AHEAD** Can be prepared early in the day, with the dressing. Keep refrigerated. • **NUTRITION WATCH** The soy protein found in edamame contains isoflavones, which may have cholesterol-lowering effects.

tabbouleh with tomatoes, feta and lemon dressing { *Serves 8*

SALAD

- 1 cup chicken (or vegetable) stock
- 1 cup bulgur
- ½ cup finely chopped red onion
- 1 cup finely chopped cucumber
- 1 cup finely chopped plum tomatoes
- ⅓ cup thinly sliced green onions
- ⅓ cup finely chopped black olives
- ½ cup crumbled light feta cheese (about 2 oz)
- ⅓ cup chopped fresh basil
- ⅓ cup chopped fresh mint

DRESSING

- 2 Tbsp lemon juice
- 3 Tbsp olive oil
- 1 tsp finely chopped garlic
- 1 tsp finely chopped jalapeño pepper (or hot chili sauce)
- pinch of black pepper

TABBOULEH IS A CLASSIC MIDDLE EASTERN dish made primarily with bulgur and loads of fresh herbs. I've combined the basic elements with Mediterranean flavors.

1. Bring the stock to a boil. Add the bulgur, cover and remove from the heat. Let the bulgur sit for about 15 minutes. Fluff with a fork, place in a serving bowl and set aside to cool.
2. When the bulgur is cool, add the red onion, cucumber, tomatoes, green onions, olives, feta, basil and mint.
3. To prepare the dressing, whisk together the lemon juice, olive oil, garlic, jalapeño and pepper and pour over the bulgur mixture. Toss well and serve. This salad can be served at room temperature or chilled.

PER SERVING Calories 150 • Protein 5 g • Carbohydrates 18 g • Fiber 4.9 g • Total fat 6.5 g • Saturated fat 1.8 g • Cholesterol 3 mg • Sodium 273 mg • **PREP TIME** 15 minutes • **COOK TIME** 15 minutes • **MAKE AHEAD** Can be prepared early in the day with dressing. • **NUTRITION WATCH** Mint is well known for its ability to soothe the digestive tract and reduce the severity and length of stomachaches.

apricot quinoa salad { *Serves 6*

SALAD

2 cups vegetable (or chicken) stock
1 cup quinoa
⅓ cup chopped snow peas
⅓ cup finely chopped red bell pepper
¼ cup finely chopped red onion
¼ cup raisins
¼ cup finely chopped dried apricots
¼ cup toasted slivered almonds
¼ cup chopped basil or parsley

DRESSING

5 tsp raspberry vinegar
5 tsp orange juice concentrate
4 tsp honey
1 Tbsp olive oil
½ tsp finely chopped garlic

QUINOA, PRONOUNCED "KEEN-WAH," is one of the most nutritious grains you can eat. It's a complete protein and high in calcium and iron. You can now find it in most supermarkets or bulk food stores. I always freeze the uncooked grain to keep it fresh.

1. Bring the stock to boil. Add the quinoa, cover and simmer over low heat for about 15 minutes or until there is no longer any liquid. Remove from the heat and let sit for about 10 minutes. Fluff with a fork, let cool and place in a serving bowl.
2. Add the snow peas, red bell pepper, onion, raisins, apricots, almonds and basil or parsley.
3. To prepare the dressing, whisk together the raspberry vinegar, orange juice concentrate, honey, olive oil and garlic. Pour the dressing over the quinoa mixture and stir to combine.

PER SERVING Calories 225 • Protein 7 g • Carbohydrates 38 g • Fiber 3.3 g • Total fat 6.4 g • Saturated fat 0.7 g • Cholesterol 0 mg • Sodium 196 mg • **PREP TIME** 15 minutes • **COOK TIME** 15 minutes • **MAKE AHEAD** Can be prepared and dressed early on the day of serving. • **NUTRITION WATCH** Eating whole grains, such as quinoa, has been linked to protection against heart disease and strokes, diabetes, insulin resistance, obesity and premature death. Quinoa is an ancient grain that is known as a nutritional powerhouse.

quinoa salad with tuna, green beans and tomatoes { *Serves 6*

SALAD
2 cups chicken (or vegetable) stock
1 cup quinoa
1 cup sliced green beans
1 cup cherry tomatoes, cut in half
1 cup finely chopped English cucumber (unpeeled)
1 can (6 oz) flaked white tuna (packed in water), drained
4 anchovy fillets, finely chopped
¼ cup sliced black olives
¼ cup finely chopped red onion
¼ cup chopped fresh dill
¼ cup chopped parsley

DRESSING
2 Tbsp lemon juice
3 Tbsp olive oil
1 Tbsp balsamic vinegar
1 tsp Dijon mustard
1 tsp finely chopped garlic
¼ tsp pepper

THIS IS MY VERSION OF TUNA NIÇOISE SALAD, using quinoa as the base. If you want to make this more sophisticated, replace the canned tuna by searing fresh tuna—arrange slices of it over the top of the salad.

1. To prepare the salad, bring the stock to a boil in a saucepan. Stir in the quinoa. Reduce the heat to low, cover, and cook for about 15 minutes, or until the liquid has evaporated. Transfer the quinoa to a large bowl and allow it to cool to room temperature. You can also place it in the refrigerator to cool more quickly.
2. Meanwhile, bring a pot of water to a boil and cook the beans for 2 minutes or until tender-crisp. Drain and rinse with cold water. Add the beans, tomatoes, cucumber, tuna, anchovies, olives, onion, dill and parsley to the quinoa. Stir to combine.
3. To prepare the dressing, whisk together the lemon juice, olive oil, balsamic vinegar, mustard, garlic and pepper. Pour the dressing over the quinoa mixture and toss well.

PER SERVING Calories 221 • Protein 12 g • Carbohydrates 26 g • Fiber 3.3 g • Total fat 8 g • Saturated fat 1.2 g • Cholesterol 11 mg • Sodium 625 mg • **PREP TIME** 20 minutes • **COOK TIME** 15 minutes • **MAKE AHEAD** Prepare early in the day and dress just before serving. • **NUTRITION WATCH** If you are watching your calories, use tuna canned in water rather than oil. Tuna in water has 1 gram of fat per 4 oz serving, whereas the oil-packed version has over 9 g of fat.

fresh tuna salad niçoise with roasted vegetables { Serves 4

SALAD

- 6 fingerling potatoes, sliced in half lengthwise, or 1 Yukon Gold potato, quartered
- 12 grape tomatoes
- 3 large slices red onion, about ¼ inch thick
- 8 asparagus spears, trimmed
- 12 oz raw tuna (or canned flaked white tuna packed in water)
- 4 cups baby spinach
- ¾ cup diced cucumber
- 10 kalamata olives

DRESSING

- 2 Tbsp olive oil
- 2 Tbsp lemon juice
- 4 anchovy fillets, finely chopped
- 1 tsp finely chopped garlic
- ½ tsp Dijon mustard
- pinch of salt and pepper

GARNISH

- 3 Tbsp chopped fresh dill

THIS IS MY ALL-TIME FAVORITE SALAD. It's a perfect main course and best with good-quality raw tuna. You can substitute canned tuna packed in water if you prefer.

1. Preheat oven to 425°F. Line a baking sheet with foil and lightly coat it with cooking spray.
2. Place the potatoes, tomatoes, onions and asparagus on the baking sheet. Lightly coat the vegetables with cooking spray and bake for 10 minutes. Turn the tomatoes and asparagus after 5 minutes, and remove the tomatoes and asparagus from the oven after 10 minutes. Continue cooking the red onion for another 5 minutes, then remove from the oven. Continue cooking the potatoes for another 15 minutes, turning halfway through, or until tender.
3. Meanwhile, preheat a nonstick grill pan lightly coated with cooking spray over medium-high heat, or preheat your barbecue to medium-high heat. Sear the tuna on each side for about 1 to 2 minutes, or until the outside of the fish is just cooked but the inside of the fish is rare. Take the tuna off the heat immediately. To stop the cooking process, place in the refrigerator immediately.
4. Arrange the spinach, cucumber and olives on a large serving platter. Top with the roasted vegetables.
5. To prepare the dressing, whisk together the olive oil, lemon juice, anchovies, garlic, mustard, salt and pepper. Pour the dressing over the salad and top with the dill. Slice the tuna thinly and arrange it on top of the salad.

PER SERVING Calories 314 • Protein 24 g • Carbohydrates 29 g • Fiber 4.7 g • Total fat 11 g • Saturated fat 1.7 g • Cholesterol 43 mg • Sodium 455 mg • **PREP TIME** 15 minutes • **COOK TIME** 30 minutes • **MAKE AHEAD** Prepare entire salad early in the day and dress just before serving. • **NUTRITION WATCH** Asparagus is a good source of potassium and is high in vitamin K and folate, which may prevent birth defects.

shrimp salad with charred corn guacamole { *Serves 4*

SALAD

8 oz raw shrimp, peeled and deveined

⅓ cup diced red onion

DRESSING

3 Tbsp light mayonnaise

1 Tbsp lemon juice

1 tsp Dijon mustard

1 tsp finely chopped garlic

3 Tbsp chopped cilantro

pinch of salt and pepper

GUACAMOLE

½ cup canned corn, drained

1 avocado, mashed

¼ cup finely chopped roasted red pepper (about ½ small roasted red pepper) (see page 100)

1 tsp finely chopped garlic

½ tsp finely chopped jalapeño pepper

pinch of ground cumin

1 Tbsp lemon juice

GARNISH

2 Tbsp chopped cilantro

SAUTÉED SHRIMP, avocado and charred corn were meant to be eaten together. It's best to prepare the guacamole as close to serving time as possible so the avocado doesn't darken. If you can't, always sprinkle lemon juice over your avocado to delay browning.

1. Lightly coat a nonstick skillet with cooking spray and place over medium heat. Sauté the shrimp until it just turns pink, about 4 minutes. Cool before chopping it. Place in a large bowl with the red onion.
2. To prepare the dressing, whisk together the mayonnaise, lemon juice, mustard, garlic, cilantro, salt and pepper. Add to the shrimp and red onion and mix well.
3. To prepare the guacamole, lightly coat a small skillet with cooking spray and set over medium-high heat. Sauté the corn for about 5 minutes, or until lightly browned. Place the corn in a bowl and add the avocado, roasted red pepper, garlic, jalapeño, cumin and lemon juice.
4. Divide the shrimp among 4 plates and top with a dollop of guacamole. Garnish with cilantro and serve.

PER SERVING Calories 207 • Protein 11 g • Carbohydrates 14 g • Fiber 4.9 g • Total fat 12 g • Saturated fat 1.2 g • Cholesterol 88 mg • Sodium 332 mg • **PREP TIME** 20 minutes • **COOK TIME** 5 minutes • **MAKE AHEAD** Prepare the shrimp salad early in the day and keep refrigerated. • **NUTRITION WATCH** Light mayonnaise has about 50% fewer calories and less fat than regular mayonnaise.

california sushi salad with smoked salmon { *Serves 6*

SALAD
1½ cups sushi rice
1½ cups water
¼ cup rice vinegar
2 tsp granulated sugar
4 oz diced smoked salmon
1 cup finely chopped cucumbers
1 cup finely chopped red bell pepper
½ cup finely chopped carrots
⅓ cup finely chopped green onions
½ cup chopped avocado
½ sheet nori, cut into very thin strips

DRESSING
¼ cup light mayonnaise
¼ cup low-fat sour cream
½ tsp wasabi paste
4 tsp low-sodium soy sauce
2 tsp toasted sesame oil

GARNISH
1 tsp toasted sesame seeds

IF YOU LIKE SUSHI but can't be bothered making it at home, try this fabulous sushi salad using smoked salmon. The combination of the sushi rice, crisp nori sheets, avocado and smoked salmon is perfect. You can prepare the sushi rice a few hours earlier if you place it on a baking sheet and cover it with a wet towel or keep it airtight in a large Ziploc bag.

1. To prepare the salad, bring the rice and water to a boil. Reduce the heat to low, cover the rice and cook for 12 minutes. Remove the pan from the heat and let the rice stand, covered, for 10 minutes.
2. While the rice is hot, add the rice vinegar and sugar and stir well. Place the rice mixture in a serving bowl to cool until the rice is still warm, but not hot.
3. Stir in the smoked salmon, cucumber, red pepper, carrots, green onions, avocado and nori.
4. To prepare the dressing, whisk together the mayonnaise, sour cream, wasabi, soy sauce and sesame oil in a small bowl. Pour the dressing over the rice mixture and toss to coat. Top with the sesame seeds and serve.

PER SERVING Calories 145 • Protein 8.2 g • Carbohydrates 14.3 g • Fiber 1.9 g • Total fat 6.1 g • Saturated fat 1.5 g • Cholesterol 26.9 mg • Sodium 327 mg • **PREP TIME** 15 minutes • **COOK TIME** 12 minutes • **MAKE AHEAD** Prepare and dress early in the day. Mix well before serving. • **NUTRITION WATCH** Sushi rice is a gluten-free alternative to other grains that contain wheat.

nouvelle cobb salad { *Serves 4*

SALAD
4 oz skinless boneless chicken breast (about 1 breast), pounded flat
2 plum tomatoes, each cut into 8 wedges
4 thick slices Vidalia onion (½ inch thick)
1 fresh cob of corn, cut into 4 pieces
3 cups baby spinach
3 cups chopped romaine lettuce
¼ cup crumbled blue cheese (about 1 oz)
½ avocado, thinly sliced

DRESSING
3 Tbsp light mayonnaise
¼ cup light buttermilk
½ tsp Dijon mustard
2 tsp lemon juice
pinch of salt and pepper

TRADITIONAL COBB SALAD is loaded with blue cheese, hard-boiled eggs, bacon, chicken and a heavy dressing. I've lightened it up by using some grilled vegetables and a buttermilk dressing to replace some of the higher-fat ingredients. You can always prepare a buttermilk substitute—see the sidebar on page 70. When corn is out of season use canned or frozen niblets. Sauté 1 cup in a nonstick pan for 5 minutes just until browned.

1. Lightly coat a nonstick grill pan with cooking spray and set over medium-high heat. Or preheat your barbecue to medium-high heat. Grill the pounded chicken breast for about 3 minutes on each side, or until the chicken is cooked throughout and no longer pink. Slice in thin strips.
2. Respray the same pan and grill the tomatoes, onions and corn on the cob for 5 to 8 minutes, or just until the corn is charred.
3. Arrange the spinach, romaine, blue cheese and avocado, with the tomatoes, onions and corn, on a large serving platter. Top with the strips of grilled chicken.
4. To prepare the dressing, whisk together the mayonnaise, buttermilk, mustard, lemon juice, salt and pepper. Pour the dressing evenly over the salad and serve.

PER SERVING Calories 226 • Protein 15 g • Carbohydrates 17 g • Fiber 4.9 g • Total fat 12 g • Saturated fat 2.3 g • Cholesterol 33 mg • Sodium 347 mg • **PREP TIME** 15 minutes • **COOK TIME** 20 minutes • **MAKE AHEAD** Prepare salad early in the day and dress just before serving. • **NUTRITION WATCH** Vidalia onions, like most onions, may prevent cardiovascular disease and reduce the risk of blood clots. Onions can improve lung function, especially in asthmatics.

grilled calamari salad with grape tomatoes, roasted red pepper and olives { *Serves 4*

12 oz cleaned calamari
¾ cup sliced grape tomatoes
⅓ cup diced red onion
⅓ cup roasted red pepper (see page 100)
⅓ cup diced black olives
2 Tbsp olive oil
1 Tbsp lemon juice
1 tsp finely chopped garlic
1 tsp capers
¼ cup crumbled feta cheese (about 1 oz)
pinch of salt and pepper

GARNISH
2 Tbsp chopped parsley

GRILLED IS THE BEST WAY to serve calamari. I urge you to enjoy the deep-fried version of this delicacy only on an occasional basis. This salad features lightly grilled calamari, which goes great with the tomatoes, bell pepper, olives and lemon–olive oil dressing.

1. Lightly coat a nonstick grill pan with cooking spray and set over medium-high heat. Or preheat your barbecue to medium-high heat. Grill the calamari for 5 minutes, turning halfway, just until charred and no longer translucent. Let cool for 5 minutes. Dice.
2. In a bowl, add the tomatoes, red onion, bell pepper, olives, olive oil, lemon juice, garlic, capers, feta, salt and pepper and calamari. Place on a serving plate and garnish with parsley.

PER SERVING Calories 192 • Protein 15 g • Carbohydrates 8.2 g • Fiber 1.6 g • Total fat 11 g • Saturated fat 2 g • Cholesterol 201 mg • Sodium 394 mg • **PREP TIME** 15 minutes • **COOK TIME** 5 minutes • **MAKE AHEAD** Can be prepared and dressed a few hours before serving. • **NUTRITION WATCH** Calamari is one of the leanest kinds of seafood. A 3 oz serving contains only 78 calories and 1 gram of fat, and is an excellent source of selenium and B12.

{ *soups & chilis* }

Leftover vegetables are perfect for soups • It's always tastier to use homemade soup stock or even the organic stock sold in Tetra Paks, but that's not often practical. Use powdered stock with a ratio of 1 tsp to 1 cup boiling water. You can now find powdered stock, bouillon cubes and packaged stock all without MSG and added preservatives. Two brands I recommend are Imagine and Harvest Sun. Low-sodium stocks are also available • Spray your pan with cooking spray and also use the amount of oil called for in the recipe. If your vegetables begin to stick, add more vegetable spray • Cook your soups covered over medium-low heat to avoid excess evaporation • When puréeing, process in batches to achieve an even, smooth texture. I prefer to use a food processor over a handheld blender or a countertop blender • If you find the soup is too thick while reheating it, add more stock. This will always happen with recipes containing rice or pasta • Chop carrots more finely than you do other vegetables since they take longer to cook • Canned evaporated 2% milk gives the texture and flavor of cream without the excess calories and fat • Always add fresh herbs just before serving for the best flavor and texture • Add 1 Tbsp of low-fat sour cream or yogurt once the soup is in bowls, then sprinkle with chopped fresh herbs

sweet potato and molasses soup with cinnamon pecans { *Serves 6*

CINNAMON PECANS

⅓ cup pecan halves
3 Tbsp icing sugar
¼ tsp cinnamon
pinch of allspice
pinch of nutmeg

SOUP

2 tsp vegetable oil
1½ tsp finely chopped garlic
1½ cups chopped onions
5 cups peeled and diced sweet potatoes
5 cups chicken stock
1 tsp cinnamon
½ tsp ground ginger
pinch of salt and freshly ground black pepper
2 Tbsp molasses
1 Tbsp honey

SWEET POTATO SOUP is creamy and rich. Molasses gives it a darker color and deeper flavor, and the baked cinnamon pecans are the perfect garnish. Perfect for the fall or winter season. The nuts can be made in advance and stored in an airtight container for up to 2 weeks.

1. Preheat the oven to 350°F. Lightly coat a baking sheet with cooking spray.
2. Rinse the pecans with cold water. Drain, but do not let them dry. Combine the icing sugar, cinnamon, allspice and nutmeg in a small bowl. Dip the pecans in the sugar mixture, coating them well. Spread on the prepared baking sheet.
3. Bake for 15 minutes in the center of the oven. Remove and cool. When they're cool enough to handle, chop coarsely.
4. Lightly coat a large pot with cooking spray, add the vegetable oil and place over medium-low heat. Stir in the garlic and onions. Sauté for 5 minutes or just until softened.
5. Stir in the potatoes, stock, cinnamon, ginger, salt and pepper. Bring to a boil, then reduce the heat to medium-low. Cover and cook for 15 to 20 minutes or until the potatoes are tender. Add the molasses and honey.
6. Transfer the soup to a food processor or blender. Purée until smooth, working in batches if necessary.
7. Ladle into individual bowls and garnish with the pecans.

PER SERVING Calories 239 • Protein 6.1 g • Carbohydrates 40 g • Fiber 4.8 g • Total fat 6.6 g • Saturated fat 0.9 g • Cholesterol 4 mg • Sodium 550 mg • **PREP TIME** 15 minutes • **COOK TIME** 20 minutes (prepare the nuts while cooking the soup) • **MAKE AHEAD** Prepare up to a day ahead and reheat gently. • **NUTRITION WATCH** Sweet potato is a "superfood." This vegetable has almost twice the recommended daily allowance for vitamin A, 42% of the recommended daily allowance for vitamin C and four times the RDA for beta-carotene. When eaten with the skin, sweet potatoes have more fiber than oatmeal. All these benefits, with only about 130 to 160 calories!

wild mushroom soup { *Serves 8*

2 tsp vegetable oil
8 cups chopped mixed wild mushrooms (about 1⅓ lb)
1 cup chopped onion
2 tsp finely chopped garlic
½ cup diced carrots
4 cups chicken (or vegetable) stock
1 cup peeled and diced potato
½ tsp dried rosemary
¼ tsp salt
¼ tsp ground pepper
½ cup canned evaporated milk (2%)
3 Tbsp grated Parmesan cheese
3 Tbsp chopped parsley

EVERYONE LOVES a delicious mushroom soup, but most are filled with cream and butter. This soup gets its flavor from mixed mushrooms and evaporated milk.

1. In a large, nonstick pot lightly coated with cooking spray, add 1 tsp of the oil and the mushrooms. Sauté for 15 minutes on medium-high heat or until the mushrooms are no longer wet. Remove and save ½ cup for garnish. Add the remaining oil to the pan.
2. Add the onions and garlic and sauté on medium heat for 5 minutes. Add the carrots and sauté for 3 minutes. Add all but ½ cup of the cooked mushrooms and the stock, potato, rosemary, salt and pepper. Bring to a boil, cover and simmer for 15 minutes or until the potato is tender.
3. Purée in a food processor until smooth. Pour back into the saucepan and add the milk, Parmesan and the remaining cooked mushrooms and heat gently and serve.

PER SERVING Calories 126 • Protein 8.9 g • Carbohydrates 15 g • Fiber 2.2 g • Total fat 3.8 g • Saturated fat 1.4 g • Cholesterol 8 mg • Sodium 560 mg • **PREP TIME** 15 minutes • **COOK TIME** 40 minutes • **MAKE AHEAD** Prepare up to a day in advance and reheat gently. • **NUTRITION WATCH** Evaporated milk is high in calcium, but it is also higher in sugar and saturated fat than regular milk. You can use 2% or skim milk to save calories and fat.

red pepper soup with pesto { *Serves 6*

4 red bell peppers, cored and cut in half
2 tsp vegetable oil
1½ cups chopped onion
2 tsp finely chopped garlic
1½ cups chopped carrots
1½ cups peeled and diced potato
3¼ cups chicken (or vegetable) stock
pinch of salt and pepper
½ cup canned evaporated milk (2%)
2 Tbsp pesto (see page 244)

ROASTED RED PEPPERS are sweet and have a great texture and flavor when puréed in this soup. Try the yellow or orange variety for a change as well. The dollop of pesto adds the savory component. I like to make my own pesto in larger batches and freeze it. (See page 244.)

1. Preheat oven to 425°F. Follow the instructions on page 100 on how to roast red peppers. Cool them slightly, then peel and dice them. Set aside.
2. Lightly coat a large, nonstick pot with cooking spray, then add the oil and set over medium heat. Add the onion and garlic and sauté for 5 minutes or until just softened. Add the carrots, potato, stock, diced roasted red peppers, salt and pepper. Bring to a boil, then reduce the heat and simmer, covered, for 20 to 25 minutes or until the carrots and potato are tender.
3. Purée the soup in a blender or food processor in batches. Return the soup to the saucepan and add the milk. Heat through. Serve the soup in bowls, and garnish each with 1 tsp of pesto.

PER SERVING Calories 143 • Protein 6 g • Carbohydrates 23 g • Fiber 3.9 g • Total fat 3.6 g • Saturated fat 0.6 g • Cholesterol 2 mg • Sodium 423 mg • **PREP TIME** 15 minutes • **COOK TIME** 20 minutes • **MAKE AHEAD** Roast the peppers and refrigerate for up to 3 days or freeze for up to 4 months. Prepare soup up to a day in advance and reheat gently. • **NUTRITION WATCH** Red bell peppers are a good source of vitamin C, thiamin, vitamin B6, beta-carotene, and folic acid. Bell peppers also contain a large number of phytochemicals, which help to protect against cancer and heart disease.

thai butternut squash and coconut soup { *Serves 6*

2 tsp vegetable oil
1 cup diced onion
2 tsp finely chopped garlic
1 tsp finely chopped ginger
6 cups cubed butternut squash (about 1¾ lb)
2 cups chicken stock
1½ tsp hot chili sauce
½ tsp fish sauce
pinch of salt
1 cup light coconut milk
1 tsp honey
¼ cup chopped fresh cilantro or basil

THE LIGHT COCONUT MILK MAKES THIS SOUP healthy yet still creamy. Regular coconut milk is what's typically used in Thai restaurants and has three times the fat and calories. Fish sauce is located in the Asian section of your supermarket or specialty store. If you can't find it, feel free to substitute with soy sauce, but double the amount.

1. Lightly coat a large, nonstick pot with cooking spray. Add the oil and set over medium heat. Sauté the onion, garlic and ginger for 5 minutes or until the onions are just softened.
2. Add the squash, stock, chili sauce, fish sauce and salt. Bring to a boil, then reduce the heat to low. Cover and simmer for about 20 minutes or until the squash is tender.
3. Purée the soup in a blender or food processor in batches. Return the soup to the saucepan and add the coconut milk and honey. Heat through. Serve the soup in bowls, and garnish with cilantro or basil.

PER SERVING Calories 120 • Protein 3 g • Carbohydrates 18 g • Fiber 3.9 g • Total fat 5.2 g • Saturated fat 0.2 g • Cholesterol 0 mg • Sodium 480 mg • **PREP TIME** 10 minutes • **COOK TIME** 20 minutes • **MAKE AHEAD** Prepare soup up to a day in advance. Reheat gently until warm. • **NUTRITION WATCH** Butternut squash is a winter squash that has more beta-carotene and more B vitamins than summer squash. It may help in the fight against cancer, heart disease and cataracts.

artichoke and leek soup with blue cheese { *Serves 4*

2 tsp vegetable oil
1½ cups sliced leeks
2 tsp chopped garlic
3½ cups chicken (or vegetable) stock
6 canned artichoke hearts, drained and diced
1 cup peeled and diced potato
⅓ cup canned evaporated milk (2%)
pinch of salt and pepper
¼ cup crumbled blue cheese (about 1 oz)
3 Tbsp chopped parsley

CANNED ARTICHOKES GO WELL with a hint of blue cheese. This soup is creamy due to the potato and evaporated milk. Substitute another cheese if desired.

1. Lightly coat a large, nonstick pot with cooking spray. Add the oil and set over medium heat. Add the leeks and garlic and sauté for 5 minutes or until leeks are just softened.
2. Add the stock, artichokes and potato. Bring to a boil, then reduce the heat to low and simmer, covered, for 15 to 20 minutes or until the potato is just tender. Purée the soup in a blender or food processor in batches. Return the soup to the saucepan and add milk, salt and pepper. Heat through. Serve the soup in bowls, and garnish with blue cheese and parsley.

PER SERVING Calories 148 • Protein 7 g • Carbohydrates 18 g • Fiber 1.9 g • Total fat 5.2 g • Saturated fat 1.8 g • Cholesterol 7 mg • Sodium 650 mg • **PREP TIME** 10 minutes • **COOK TIME** 15 minutes • **MAKE AHEAD** Prepare up to a day in advance and reheat gently. • **NUTRITION WATCH** Leeks have beneficial flavonoids that may be protective against ovarian cancer.

onion soup with toasted swiss and mozzarella baguette { *Serves 6*

- 2 tsp vegetable oil
- 6 cups sliced Spanish onions, cut into ¼-inch rings
- 2 tsp finely chopped garlic
- 2 tsp brown sugar
- 4½ cups chicken (or beef) stock
- ½ cup dry red wine
- ½ tsp dried thyme or 1 Tbsp fresh
- pinch of salt and pepper
- 1 tsp Worcestershire sauce
- 6 slices whole wheat baguette, cut ½ inch thick
- 3 Tbsp shredded Swiss cheese
- 3 Tbsp shredded mozzarella cheese
- 3 Tbsp chopped parsley

EVERYONE LOVES ONION SOUP with all that thick melted cheese spilling over the bowl—but when made like that, it's not a healthy choice. This soup has delicious caramelized onions and a small sliced baguette with a tablespoon of cheese melted on top. You'll find this is the perfect amount of cheese to satisfy your appetite.

1. Lightly coat a large, nonstick pot with cooking spray, add the oil and set over medium heat. Add the onions and sauté for 10 minutes, stirring constantly, until softened but not browned. Stir in the garlic and sugar and continue cooking over low heat for 20 minutes, stirring often or until the onions are golden brown.
2. Preheat the oven to 425°F.
3. Stir in the stock, wine, thyme, salt and pepper and Worcestershire sauce. Bring to a boil, then reduce the heat to low and simmer, covered, for about 12 minutes.
4. Meanwhile, lightly coat the baguette slices on both sides with cooking spray, and place them on a baking sheet. Bake for 8 to 10 minutes or until golden on top. Turn the slices over and sprinkle the toasted side with the 2 cheeses. Turn the oven to broil, and broil the toasts for about 30 seconds or until the cheese melts.
5. Serve the soup in bowls with 1 cheese toast placed on top, and garnish with parsley.

PER SERVING Calories 210 • Protein 8 g • Carbohydrates 31 g • Fiber 2.7 g • Total fat 2.7 g • Saturated fat 0.8 g • Cholesterol 7 mg • Sodium 635 mg • **PREP TIME** 10 minutes • **COOK TIME** 42 minutes • **MAKE AHEAD** Prepare up to a day in advance and reheat gently. Broil toasts just before serving. • **NUTRITION WATCH** Spanish onions are packed with antioxidants that have cancer-fighting properties.

hummus soup with feta and black olives { *Serves 6*

2 tsp vegetable oil
1 cup chopped onion
2 tsp chopped garlic
½ cup finely chopped carrots
4 cups chicken (or vegetable) stock
3 cups canned chickpeas, drained and rinsed
1 cup peeled and diced potato
3 Tbsp tahini (sesame seed paste)
½ tsp ground cumin
1 tsp lemon juice
1 tsp hot chili sauce
pinch of salt and pepper
3 Tbsp chopped cilantro
2 Tbsp crumbled feta cheese
2 Tbsp finely diced black olives

THE TRANSFORMATION FROM HUMMUS DIP to a soup is unexpected, and the results are outstanding—smooth and delicate in flavor. The garnish of feta and olives completes the soup.

1. Lightly coat a large, nonstick pot with cooking spray. Add the oil and set over medium heat. Add the onion and garlic and sauté for 5 minutes. Add the carrots and cook for 3 minutes.
2. Add the stock, 2½ cups of the chickpeas, potato, tahini, cumin, lemon juice, chili sauce, salt and pepper. Bring to a boil, then reduce the heat and simmer, covered, for 15 minutes or until the potato is just tender.
3. Purée the soup in a blender or food processor in batches. Return the soup to the saucepan and heat through. Serve the soup in bowls, and garnish with the remaining ½ cup chickpeas and the cilantro, feta and black olives.

PER SERVING Calories 254 • Protein 12 g • Carbohydrates 35 g • Fiber 6.6 g • Total fat 7.4 g • Saturated fat 1.1 g • Cholesterol 3 mg • Sodium 680 mg • **PREP TIME** 15 minutes • **COOK TIME** 23 minutes • **MAKE AHEAD** Prepare up to a day in advance and reheat gently. Add the garnish just before serving. • **NUTRITION WATCH** Cumin is a source of iron, which increases your energy and immune function.

potato corn chowder { *Serves 4*

2 cups corn niblets (canned or fresh)
1½ tsp vegetable oil
1 cup chopped onion
1½ tsp finely chopped garlic
½ cup chopped red bell pepper
1 cup peeled and diced potato
2½ cups chicken stock
½ tsp hot chili sauce (or finely chopped jalapeño pepper)
2 tsp all-purpose flour
1 cup canned evaporated milk (2%)
pinch of salt and pepper
3 Tbsp chopped parsley

TRADITIONAL CORN CHOWDER is usually prepared with excess cream and butter. My version uses evaporated milk, and you'll be surprised at how creamy and rich the soup tastes. Charring the corn gives the soup a fresher flavor.

1. Lightly coat a nonstick skillet with cooking spray and set over medium heat. Sauté the corn for about 8 minutes, stirring often or just until lightly browned. Purée half of the corn in a small food processor. Combine the puréed corn with the whole corn in a small bowl and set aside.
2. Add the oil to a large, nonstick pot and set over medium heat. Add the onion and garlic and sauté for about 4 minutes. Add the red pepper and sauté for another 2 minutes. Add the potato, stock, chili sauce and corn mixture. Bring to a boil, then reduce the heat to low and simmer, covered, for about 15 minutes or until the potato is tender.
3. Whisk together the flour and milk in a small bowl and gradually add to the soup. Add the salt and pepper. Simmer, stirring occasionally for 3 minutes or until slightly thickened and heated through. Serve in bowls, and garnish with parsley.

PER SERVING Calories 211 • Protein 10 g • Carbohydrates 35 g • Fiber 3.9 g • Total fat 3.7 g • Saturated fat 0.9 g • Cholesterol 5 mg • Sodium 565 mg • **PREP TIME** 15 minutes • **COOK TIME** 30 minutes • **MAKE AHEAD** Prepare up to a day in advance and reheat gently. • **NUTRITION WATCH** Corn is a good source of pantothenic acid. This B vitamin is necessary for the metabolism of carbohydrates, protein and lipids. This is great for when you are stressed.

carrot and parsnip soup { *Serves 6*

2 tsp vegetable oil
2 tsp finely chopped garlic
1 cup chopped onion
4 cups chicken stock
1½ cups diced carrots
1½ cups diced parsnips
1 cup peeled and diced potato
½ tsp cinnamon
pinch of salt and pepper
⅓ cup canned evaporated milk (2%)
2 tsp honey
2 Tbsp low-fat sour cream

PARSNIPS HAVE COME BACK to our kitchens. They have a wonderfully sweet flavor and are perfect in a soup. This is a great soup during the Thanksgiving or Christmas holiday seasons.

1. Lightly coat a nonstick pot with cooking spray, add the vegetable oil and set over medium heat. Add the garlic and onion and sauté for 5 minutes or until they are just softened.
2. Add the stock, carrots, parsnips, potato, cinnamon, salt and pepper. Bring to a boil, then reduce the heat to low and simmer, covered, for 20 minutes or until the parsnips are tender.
3. Purée the soup in a blender or food processor in batches. Return the soup to the saucepan and stir in the milk and honey. Heat through. Serve the soup in bowls, and garnish with a dollop of sour cream.

PER SERVING Calories 129 • Protein 5 g • Carbohydrates 22 g • Fiber 301 g • Total fat 2.7 g • Saturated fat 0.6 g • Cholesterol 3 mg • Sodium 586 mg • **PREP TIME** 15 minutes • **COOK TIME** 25 minutes • **MAKE AHEAD** Prepare up to a day in advance and reheat gently. • **NUTRITION WATCH** Parsnips have heart-friendly potassium and folic acid, for the creation of healthy cells.

carrot and cauliflower soup { *Serves 6*

2 tsp vegetable oil
1 cup chopped onion
2 tsp finely chopped garlic
2 cups chopped carrots
2 cups chopped cauliflower
1 cup peeled and diced potato
3½ cups chicken (or vegetable) stock
½ tsp cinnamon
pinch of ground cloves
pinch of salt and pepper
2 tsp honey
½ cup canned evaporated milk (2%)
3 Tbsp low-fat sour cream
3 Tbsp chopped fresh mint

THE COMBINATION OF CARROTS and cauliflower makes this soup more savory than sweet. The fresh mint is perfect for a garnish. Feel free to substitute fresh basil or cilantro.

1. Lightly coat a large, nonstick pot with cooking spray, add the oil and set over medium heat. Add the onions and garlic and sauté for 5 minutes or until the onions are just softened.
2. Add the carrots, cauliflower, potato, stock, cinnamon, cloves, salt and pepper. Bring to a boil, then reduce the heat to low and simmer, covered, for 15 minutes or until the vegetables are just tender.
3. Purée the soup in a blender or food processor in batches. Return the soup to the saucepan and add the honey and milk. Heat through. Serve the soup in bowls, and garnish with sour cream and fresh mint.

PER SERVING Calories 125 • Protein 6 g • Carbohydrates 19 g • Fiber 3.0 g • Total fat 3.1 g • Saturated fat 0.8 g • Cholesterol 4 mg • Sodium 579 mg • **PREP TIME** 15 minutes • **COOK TIME** 20 minutes • **MAKE AHEAD** Prepare early in the day and reheat gently before serving. • **NUTRITION WATCH** Carrots are an excellent source of antioxidant compounds, and the richest vegetable source of the vitamin A carotenes. Carrots' antioxidants protect against cardiovascular disease and cancer and promote good vision, especially night vision.

vegetable minestrone with cherry tomatoes and tortellini { *Serves 4*

2 tsp vegetable oil
1 cup chopped onion
2 tsp finely chopped garlic
½ cup chopped carrots
½ cup chopped parsnips
4 cups vegetable (or chicken) stock
2 Tbsp tomato paste
1 tsp dried basil
pinch of salt
¼ tsp pepper
1½ cups cherry tomatoes, sliced in half
1 cup frozen cheese tortellini
¼ cup grated Parmesan cheese
2 cups baby spinach leaves

THE ADDITION OF HALVED CHERRY TOMATOES and tortellini makes this minestrone unique. It's a full-bodied soup, and could be your main course when served with a green salad.

1. Lightly coat a large, nonstick pot with cooking spray, add the oil and set over medium-high heat. Add the onion and garlic and sauté for 4 minutes or until the onion is just softened.
2. Add the carrots, parsnips, stock, tomato paste, basil, salt and pepper. Bring to a boil, then reduce the heat to medium and cook for 12 minutes or until the vegetables are just tender.
3. Stir in the cherry tomatoes, tortellini and half (about 2 Tbsp) of the Parmesan cheese. Cover and cook for 5 minutes over medium heat or until the tortellini is heated through and the vegetables are tender. Add the spinach and cook for 1 minute. Serve in bowls, and garnish with the remaining Parmesan.

PER SERVING Calories 217 • Protein 12 g • Carbohydrates 28 g • Fiber 3.9 g • Total fat 6.7 g • Saturated fat 2.4 g • Cholesterol 16 mg • Sodium 693 mg • **PREP TIME** 15 minutes • **COOK TIME** 22 minutes • **MAKE AHEAD** Prepare up to a day in advance, but add the tortellini just before serving. • **NUTRITION WATCH** Tomato paste is a by-product of tomatoes. Tomatoes, due to their lycopene, have been shown to be helpful in reducing the risk of prostate cancer.

old-fashioned split pea and barley soup { *Serves 6*

¼ cup pearl barley
2 cups water (or vegetable or chicken stock)
2 tsp vegetable oil
1 cup chopped onion
⅔ cup chopped carrots
2 tsp finely chopped garlic
4 cups vegetable (or chicken) stock
1 cup peeled and chopped potato
¾ cup green split peas
¼ tsp salt
¼ tsp pepper

SPLIT PEA SOUP can be an entire meal if you'd like. It's such a hearty and filling soup that all you'll need is a green salad to accompany it. But it's also a great way to start off a meal. Having a soup like this is a great tool for weight management, since it's so nutritious and satisfying.

1. Combine the barley and the 2 cups of water in a large saucepan and bring to a boil. Reduce the heat and simmer, covered, for 25 minutes or until the barley is just tender. Drain any excess liquid. Set aside.
2. Lightly coat a large, nonstick pot with cooking spray, add the oil and set over medium heat. Add the onion and sauté for 5 minutes or until just softened. Add the carrots and garlic, and cook for another 5 minutes or until the carrots are slightly softened.
3. Stir in the 4 cups of stock and the potato, split peas, salt and pepper. Bring to a boil, then reduce the heat to low and simmer, covered, for 35 minutes or until the split peas are tender.
4. Purée 2 cups of the soup in a blender or food processor. Return the puréed soup to the saucepan and stir in the barley. Heat through and serve.

PER SERVING Calories 167 • Protein 11 g • Carbohydrates 24 g • Fiber 7.6 g • Total fat 3 g • Saturated fat 0.5 g • Cholesterol 0 mg • Sodium 487 mg • **PREP TIME** 15 minutes • **COOK TIME** 40 minutes (cook soup while cooking barley) • **MAKE AHEAD** Prepare up to a day ahead, but add the barley just before serving. Reheat gently. • **NUTRITION WATCH** Split peas are packed with insoluble fiber, which promotes digestive health and prevents constipation.

sweet pea and fennel soup { *Serves 6*

2 tsp vegetable oil
1 cup chopped onion
1½ cups chopped fennel
2 tsp finely chopped garlic
3 cups chicken (or vegetable) stock
1 cup peeled and diced potato
4 cups frozen green peas
pinch of salt and pepper
⅓ cup canned evaporated milk (2%)
3 Tbsp low-fat sour cream
3 Tbsp chopped fresh mint

FROZEN GREEN PEAS mean you can enjoy this recipe any time of year. In the summer try serving it cold. The fennel adds a hint of licorice flavor that goes well with the sweet peas.

1. Lightly coat a large, nonstick pot with cooking spray, add the oil and set over medium heat. Add the onion, fennel and garlic. Sauté for 5 minutes or until the vegetables just begin to soften.
2. Add the stock and potato and 3½ cups of the green peas. Bring to a boil, reduce the heat and simmer, covered, for 20 minutes or until the potato is just tender.
3. Purée the soup in a blender or food processor in batches. Return the soup to the saucepan and add the milk and the remaining ½ cup of peas. Heat through. Serve the soup in bowls, and garnish with sour cream and fresh mint.

PER SERVING Calories 177 • Protein 10 g • Carbohydrates 28 g • Fiber 7.6 g • Total fat 3.1 g • Saturated fat 0.8 g • Cholesterol 4 mg • Sodium 489 mg • **PREP TIME** 15 minutes • **COOK TIME** 20 minutes • **MAKE AHEAD** Prepare up to a day in advance and reheat gently. • **NUTRITION WATCH** Green peas provide nutrients such as vitamin K, which is important for maintaining bone health.

white bean soup with grated parmesan { *Serves 6*

2 tsp vegetable oil
1½ cups chopped onion
2 tsp finely chopped garlic
2 cans (19 oz each) white kidney beans, drained and rinsed
1 cup peeled and diced potato
3 cups chicken stock
pinch of salt and pepper
⅓ cup canned evaporated milk (2%)
¼ cup grated Parmesan cheese
3 Tbsp chopped parsley

PURÉED WHITE BEANS create a creamy, thick, rich-tasting soup. The Parmesan can be substituted with another strong-tasting cheese such as Swiss or Asiago, or even blue cheese.

1. Lightly coat a large, nonstick pot with cooking spray, add the oil and set over medium heat. Add the onion and garlic and sauté for 5 minutes or until the onions are softened and just begin to brown.
2. Set aside ½ cup of the kidney beans and add the rest to the saucepan, along with the potato, stock, salt and pepper. Bring to a boil, then reduce the heat and simmer, covered, for 15 minutes.
3. Purée in a blender or food processor in batches. Return the soup to the saucepan and add the milk and the remaining kidney beans. Heat through. Serve the soup in bowls, and garnish with the Parmesan and parsley.

PER SERVING Calories 216 • Protein 12 g • Carbohydrates 34 g • Fiber 8.0 g • Total fat 3.9 g • Saturated fat 0.6 g • Cholesterol 2 mg • Sodium 539 mg • **PREP TIME** 10 minutes • **COOK TIME** 15 minutes • **MAKE AHEAD** Prepare the soup up to a day in advance and refrigerate. Reheat gently. Garnish just before serving. • **NUTRITION WATCH** The carbohydrate energy from potatoes will refuel muscles to help them recover after exercise. Potatoes are low in fat and packed full of vitamins and minerals.

black and white kidney bean soup { *Serves 6*

2 tsp vegetable oil
1 cup chopped onion
2 tsp finely chopped garlic
¾ cup finely chopped carrots
2¾ cups chicken stock
1½ cups canned white kidney beans, drained and rinsed
1½ cups canned black beans, drained and rinsed
½ tsp ground cumin
½ tsp hot chili sauce
pinch of salt and pepper
2 Tbsp low-fat sour cream
2 Tbsp chopped fresh cilantro or basil

I'VE ALWAYS PREPARED BLACK BEAN SOUPS and white bean soups separately. But when I combined the flavors the result was amazing. The black bean flavor is softened by the white beans.

1. Lightly coat a large, nonstick pot with cooking spray, add the oil and set over medium heat. Add the onion and garlic and sauté for 5 minutes or until softened. Add the carrots and cook for 5 more minutes or until the carrots are slightly softened.
2. Add the stock, 1¼ cups of both kinds of beans, cumin, chili sauce, salt and pepper. Bring to a boil, then reduce the heat to low and simmer, covered, and cook for 15 minutes.
3. Purée the soup in a blender or food processor in batches. Return the soup to the saucepan, add the remaining beans, and heat through. Serve the soup in bowls, and garnish with the sour cream and chopped cilantro or basil.

PER SERVING Calories 139 • Protein 8 g • Carbohydrates 23 g • Fiber 6.4 g • Total fat 2.8 g • Saturated fat 0.4 g • Cholesterol 2 mg • Sodium 629 mg • **PREP TIME** 10 minutes • **COOK TIME** 25 minutes • **MAKE AHEAD** Prepare up to a day in advance and reheat gently. • **NUTRITION WATCH** Black beans supply energy, while stabilizing blood sugar.

broccoli, white bean and cheddar soup { *Serves 6*

2 tsp vegetable oil
1½ cups chopped onion
2 tsp finely chopped garlic
3½ cups chicken (or vegetable) stock
1½ cups canned white kidney beans, drained and rinsed
1 cup peeled and diced potato
1¾ cups trimmed and chopped broccoli
pinch of salt and pepper
3 Tbsp grated Parmesan cheese
½ cup shredded aged cheddar cheese

THIS IS A HEARTY SOUP perfect for the colder weather. The broccoli and white beans go well with the aged cheddar garnish.

1. Lightly coat a large, nonstick pot with cooking spray, add the oil and set over medium heat. Add the onion and garlic and sauté for 5 minutes or until the onion is just tender.
2. Add the stock, white kidney beans and the potato. Bring to a boil, then reduce the heat to low and simmer, covered, for 10 minutes. Add the broccoli and return to a boil. Reduce the heat to low and simmer, covered, for another 5 minutes or until the potato and broccoli are just tender.
3. Add 2 cups of the soup to a blender or food processor and purée. Add this back to the pot, along with the salt and pepper and Parmesan cheese, and heat through. Serve the soup in bowls, and garnish with cheddar cheese.

PER SERVING Calories 189 • Protein 10 g • Carbohydrates 23 g • Fiber 5.4 g • Total fat 6.5 g • Saturated fat 2.8 g • Cholesterol 11 mg • Sodium 545 mg • **PREP TIME** 10 minutes • **COOK TIME** 20 minutes • **MAKE AHEAD** Prepare up to a day in advance and reheat gently. • **NUTRITION WATCH** Broccoli is a superfood—it contains vitamin C, vitamin A, folic acid, calcium and fiber. It may help in the control of high blood pressure, and it may work to prevent colon cancer.

meatball and egg noodle soup { *Serves 6*

MEATBALLS
6 oz lean ground beef
3 Tbsp seasoned dry breadcrumbs
2 Tbsp barbecue sauce
1 egg
1 tsp finely chopped garlic
½ tsp dried basil
2 Tbsp Parmesan cheese

SOUP
2 tsp vegetable oil
1 cup chopped onion
1½ tsp finely chopped garlic
½ cup chopped green bell pepper
½ cup chopped carrots
3½ cups beef (or chicken) stock
2 cups tomato sauce (see page 334) (or store-bought spaghetti sauce)
2 Tbsp tomato paste
1 tsp chili powder
1 cup dried egg noodles
¼ cup grated Parmesan cheese

THIS IS A GREAT SOUP FOR CHILDREN AND TEENS. It's a complete meal in a bowl. Try using ground chicken, turkey or pork instead of beef. (Add an extra 1 Tbsp of breadcrumbs if you're using chicken or turkey.)

1. To make the meatballs, combine the ground beef, breadcrumbs, barbecue sauce, egg, garlic, basil and 2 Tbsp of the Parmesan cheese. Form into 1-inch meatballs (you should have enough for about 24 meatballs). Lightly coat a large, nonstick skillet with cooking spray and set over medium heat. Cook the meatballs for about 5 minutes, turning occasionally or until they are browned on all sides. Set aside.
2. To make the soup, lightly coat a large, nonstick pot with cooking spray, add the oil and set over medium heat. Add the onion and garlic and sauté for 5 minutes or until just softened and browned. Stir in the green pepper and carrots and cook for 3 minutes. Stir in the stock, tomato sauce, tomato paste, chili powder and browned meatballs. Bring to a boil, then reduce the heat to low and simmer, covered, for 15 minutes.
3. Stir in the egg noodles and simmer for 5 minutes or until the noodles are tender. Serve the soup in bowls, and garnish with remaining ¼ cup Parmesan cheese.

PER SERVING Calories 187 • Protein 14 g • Carbohydrates 21 g • Fiber 3 g • Total fat 6.3 g • Saturated fat 1.7 g • Cholesterol 58 mg • Sodium 568 mg • **PREP TIME** 20 minutes • **COOK TIME** 28 minutes • **MAKE AHEAD** Prepare soup up to a day early, but add the noodles just before serving. • **NUTRITION WATCH** Egg noodles are an excellent source of selenium, thiamin and folate.

vegetable beef barley soup { *Serves 6*

6 oz sirloin beef (round or tip), diced
3 Tbsp all-purpose flour
1 Tbsp vegetable oil
2 tsp finely chopped garlic
1½ cups diced onion
¾ cup diced carrots
2 cups sliced button mushrooms
½ cup diced parsnip
½ cup diced potato
7 cups beef stock
¼ cup pearl barley
1 tsp dried thyme (optional)
pinch of salt and pepper
2 Tbsp chopped parsley

A WONDERFUL HEARTY SOUP during the cold weather. Be sure not to use stewing beef, which takes much longer to cook to become tender.

1. Put the beef and flour in a bowl and toss to coat. Lightly coat a skillet with cooking spray and set over medium heat. Sauté the beef until browned on all sides, about 3 minutes. Set aside.
2. Heat the oil in a large, nonstick pot and set over medium heat. Add the garlic, onion, carrots and mushrooms and sauté until tender, about 10 minutes.
3. Add the parsnip, potato, stock, barley, dried thyme (if using) and seared beef. Bring to a boil, then reduce the heat to low and simmer, covered, for about 35 to 40 minutes or until the barley and potato are tender.
4. Add more stock if the soup is too thick, and season with salt and pepper. Serve in bowls, and garnish with parsley.

PER SERVING Calories 166 • Protein 11 g • Carbohydrates 21 g • Fiber 3.5 g • Total fat 4.3 g • Saturated fat 0.7 g • Cholesterol 23 mg • Sodium 640 mg • **PREP TIME** 15 minutes • **COOK TIME** 50 minutes • **MAKE AHEAD** Prepare up to a day in advance and reheat gently before serving. • **NUTRITION WATCH** Parsley is a good source of folic acid, one of the most important B vitamins.

beef and barley chili { *Serves 6*

2 tsp vegetable oil
1 cup chopped onion
2 tsp chopped garlic
1 lb extra-lean ground beef
2 tsp chili powder (or to taste)
1½ tsp dried basil
1 tsp dried oregano
¼ cup pearl barley
2½ cups tomato sauce (see page 334) (or store-bought spaghetti sauce)
1 cup beef (or chicken) stock
1 can (19 oz) red kidney beans, drained and rinsed
¼ cup low-fat sour cream
¼ cup shredded light cheddar cheese
¼ cup chopped green onions
¼ cup chopped fresh basil or parsley

CHILI HAS TO BE one of the most versatile, healthy and easy foods to prepare. It's the perfect dish to make for your own family, but also works great for entertaining. The key to keeping it nutritious is to use extra-lean or lean ground beef. The addition of barley makes this a complete meal.

1. Lightly coat a large saucepan with cooking spray, add the oil and set over medium heat. Add the onion and garlic and sauté for 3 minutes. Add the beef, chili powder, basil and oregano and sauté for another 4 or 5 minutes or until the beef is no longer pink.
2. Add the barley, tomato sauce, stock and kidney beans. Cover and simmer for 40 minutes or until the barley is tender.
3. Serve in bowls, and garnish with sour cream, cheddar, green onions and basil or parsley.

PER SERVING Calories 321 • Protein 26 g • Carbohydrates 40 g • Fiber 10 g • Total fat 7.4 g • Saturated fat 2.2 g • Cholesterol 47 mg • Sodium 620 mg • **PREP TIME** about 10 minutes • **COOK TIME** 50 minutes • **MAKE AHEAD** Chili can be cooked up to a day in advance and gently reheated. • **NUTRITION WATCH** When using store-bought spaghetti sauces, it's best to purchase a vegetable-based one for less calories and fat. The beef and cheese varieties add excess sodium as well.

turkey and sautéed corn chili with white cheddar cheese { *Serves 6*

2 tsp vegetable oil
1½ cups chopped onion
1 cup canned corn, drained
2 tsp finely chopped garlic
½ lb ground turkey
1 can (19 oz) red kidney beans, drained and rinsed
2½ cups tomato sauce (see page 334) (or store-bought spaghetti sauce)
1 cup diced potato
½ cup chicken (or beef) stock
2 tsp chili powder
1½ tsp dried basil
1 tsp brown sugar
⅓ cup shredded aged white cheddar
¼ cup chopped cilantro or parsley

BROWNING THE CORN is what gives this chili its deliciously distinctive taste. Feel free to make it vegetarian by substituting ground soy for the turkey. Use fresh, finely chopped jalapeño peppers for more heat. For a beautiful presentation, serve the chili in bread bowls: Simply cut the tops off Kaiser rolls (or any large, firm rolls) and remove the soft interior, leaving the outer crust intact. Fill with chili and serve.

1. Lightly coat a nonstick pot with cooking spray, add the vegetable oil and place over medium heat. Add the onion and sauté until soft, stirring frequently, about 5 minutes. Stir in the corn and garlic. Cook and stir for 8 minutes or until the corn is browned. Stir in the turkey and cook for 5 minutes, until the turkey is browned.
2. Stir in the beans, tomato sauce, potato, stock, chili powder, basil and sugar. Bring to a boil, reduce the heat and cover. Simmer for 25 to 30 minutes or just until the potato is tender. Serve the chili in bowls, and garnish with cheddar and cilantro or parsley.

PER SERVING Calories 305 • Protein 19 g • Carbohydrates 45 g • Fiber 12 g • Total fat 7 g • Saturated fat 2.2 g • Cholesterol 27 mg • Sodium 480 mg • **PREP TIME** 15 minutes • **COOK TIME** 40 minutes • **MAKE AHEAD** Prepare up to a day in advance and reheat gently. • **NUTRITION WATCH** Ground turkey is leaner than ground chicken; a 4 oz serving of turkey has 9 g of fat compared to the 14 g in the same amount of ground chicken.

mediterranean chili { *Serves 6*

12 oz sirloin beef (tip), diced
1 Tbsp all-purpose flour
1 tsp vegetable oil
1 cup chopped onion
1 cup sliced mushrooms
2 tsp finely chopped garlic
1 cup chopped green bell pepper
2 cups chopped zucchini
1½ cups canned red kidney beans, drained and rinsed
2 cups tomato sauce (see page 334) (or store-bought spaghetti sauce)
¾ cup beef (or chicken) stock
⅓ cup sliced black olives
1 Tbsp chili powder
1 tsp brown sugar
2 tsp dried basil
1½ tsp dried oregano
⅓ cup crumbled feta cheese (about 1½ oz)
⅓ cup chopped cilantro or parsley

INSTEAD OF THE TYPICAL SOUTHWEST FLAVORS, I tried adding a Mediterranean twist to this chili. It's delicious and quite different.

1. Dust the beef with the flour. Lightly coat a large, nonstick saucepan with cooking spray and sauté the beef for 4 minutes, just until browned on all sides. Set aside. Wipe out the pan and respray.
2. Add, the oil and onion and cook, stirring frequently, for 3 minutes or until lightly browned. Add the mushrooms, garlic, green pepper and zucchini and sauté for 5 minutes or until the mushrooms are no longer wet. Add the reserved meat along with the beans, tomato sauce, stock, olives, chili powder, sugar, basil and oregano. Stir well and bring to a boil. Reduce the heat to low, cover and simmer for 30 minutes.
3. Serve in individual bowls, garnished with feta cheese and cilantro or parsley.

soups & chilis

PER SERVING Calories 277 • Carbohydrates 31 g • Fiber 9 g • Total fat 8.3 g • Saturated fat 2.6 g • Cholesterol 41 mg • Sodium 560 mg • **PREP TIME** 15 minutes • **COOK TIME** 40 minutes • **MAKE AHEAD** Prepare up to a day early. Reheat gently, adding the garnish just before serving. • **NUTRITION WATCH** Beans are rich in complex carbohydrates, high in fiber and low in fat. They are an excellent source of plant protein and they also contain calcium, iron, zinc, magnesium and B vitamins. They can help lower cholesterol levels and aid in the fight against cancer, diabetes and heart disease.

tex mex chili { *Serves 6*

12 oz skinless boneless chicken breasts (about 3 breasts), diced
¼ cup all-purpose flour
2 tsp vegetable oil
1½ cups chopped onion
1 cup canned corn, drained
2 tsp finely chopped garlic
1½ cups canned black beans, drained and rinsed
2½ cups tomato sauce (see page 334) (or store-bought spaghetti sauce)
¾ cup chicken (or beef) stock
1 Tbsp chili powder
1½ tsp dried basil
1 tsp dried oregano
1½ tsp seeded and finely chopped jalapeño pepper (or 1½ tsp hot chili sauce)
pinch of salt and pepper
¼ cup chopped cilantro or parsley
½ cup shredded aged light cheddar cheese
¼ cup low-fat sour cream

THIS IS A GREAT, LIGHTER CHILI typically served in the Southwest. Using chicken rather than beef reduces the calories and fat. Dusting the chicken with flour maintains the moisture. Aged cheddar is the perfect accompaniment. Add diced avocado to the list of garnishes if you like.

1. Place the chicken and flour in a bowl and toss to coat. Lightly coat a nonstick saucepan with cooking spray, add 1 tsp of the vegetable oil and set over medium heat. Sauté the chicken for 5 minutes or until it is lightly browned on all sides, but do not cook through. Set aside.
2. Respray the same saucepan, add the remaining vegetable oil and set over medium heat. Add the onion and cook until soft, stirring frequently, about 5 minutes. Stir in the corn and garlic and continue to cook and stir for 5 minutes or until the corn is browned.
3. Stir in the beans, tomato sauce, stock, chili powder, basil, oregano, jalapeño, salt and pepper. Bring to a boil, reduce the heat and cover. Simmer for 15 minutes. Add the diced chicken and simmer, uncovered, for 5 minutes or until the chicken is just cooked through and the chili thickens. Serve the chili in bowls, and garnish with cilantro, cheese and sour cream.

PER SERVING Calories 333 • Protein 27 g • Carbohydrates 33 g • Fiber 6 g • Total fat 11 g • Saturated fat 3.9 g • Cholesterol 68 mg • Sodium 550 mg • **PREP TIME** 15 minutes • **COOK TIME** 25 minutes • **MAKE AHEAD** Prepare up to a day in advance. Reheat gently and garnish just before serving. • **NUTRITION WATCH** Use low-fat sour cream, which is obviously lower in fat and calories than regular sour cream—3% to 5% milk fat compared to 14%.

{ *sandwiches & wraps* }

Whole wheat flour tortillas or pitas give you 3 times more fiber than white flour tortillas and pitas • Freeze leftover tortillas for up to 1 month. You can defrost, gently remove the number you need and refreeze • Wraps and sandwiches containing freshly chopped vegetables are best prepared as close to serving time as possible, to avoid having the wrap become soggy • Wraps and sandwiches that don't have large amounts of fresh vegetables can be prepared early in the day and refrigerated • To warm wraps, place them in a 350°F oven for 10 minutes or use a grill pan or panini press, which will give them a toasted texture and grill marks • Leftover chicken can be used for wraps calling for freshly cooked chicken breast

pear and blue cheese quesadillas with spinach and pecans { *Serves 8*

⅓ cup light ricotta (5%)
¼ cup crumbled blue cheese (about 1 oz)
2 Tbsp light cream cheese, softened
2 Tbsp light mayonnaise
1 Tbsp lemon juice
½ tsp finely chopped garlic
pinch of salt and pepper

1 large ripe pear, peeled, seeded and thinly sliced
2 tsp brown sugar
pinch of cinnamon
4 large flour tortillas
1 cup baby spinach leaves
¼ cup chopped toasted pecans

BLUE CHEESE AND PEARS work well together. You could always substitute feta or goat cheese if you don't like blue cheese.

1. In the bowl of a food processor, combine the ricotta, blue cheese, cream cheese, mayonnaise, lemon juice and garlic. Season with salt and pepper and purée until smooth. Set aside.
2. Lightly coat a small, nonstick skillet with cooking spray and set over medium heat. Sauté the pears, sugar and cinnamon for 4 minutes or until the pears are tender and glazed with the sugar.
3. Divide the cheese spread evenly among the 4 tortillas. Arrange the pears on one-half of each of the tortillas. Top with the spinach and pecans. Fold each tortilla in half.
4. Lightly coat a nonstick grill pan with cooking spray and set over medium-high heat. Grill the tortillas for 2 minutes per side or until hot all the way through. Cut in half and serve.

PER SERVING (½ QUESADILLA) Calories 203 • Protein 5.5 g • Carbohydrates 26 g • Fiber 2.5 g • Total fat 8.9 g • Saturated fat 2.3 g • Cholesterol 8 mg • Sodium 362 mg • **PREP TIME** 10 minutes • **COOK TIME** 8 minutes • **MAKE AHEAD** Can be prepared early in the day and warmed just before serving. • **NUTRITION WATCH** Blue cheese is high in calcium and phosphorous. Both nutrients help in promoting the health of your bones, but blue cheese is very high in saturated fat, so use it in moderation.

cobb salad wraps with tomatoes, avocado and black beans { *Serves 8*

8 oz skinless boneless chicken breasts (about 2 breasts)
½ cup diced plum tomatoes
½ cup diced red bell pepper
½ cup diced ripe avocado
⅓ cup canned black beans, drained and rinsed
¼ cup finely chopped green onions
¼ cup chopped parsley
4 tsp lemon juice
1 Tbsp low-fat sour cream
1 Tbsp olive oil
1 tsp finely chopped garlic
½ tsp hot chili sauce
pinch of salt and pepper
½ cup shredded aged light cheddar cheese
4 large whole wheat flour tortillas

A COBB SALAD traditionally has loads of chicken, blue cheese, bacon and heavy dressing. I've lightened up this classic and tossed the main ingredients into a wrap. It's delicious.

1. Lightly coat a nonstick grill pan with vegetable spray and set over medium heat. Grill the chicken for 4 minutes on each side or until no longer pink. Cool slightly, then slice thinly.
2. Combine the tomatoes, red pepper, avocado, black beans, green onions and parsley in a large bowl. Add the lemon juice, sour cream, olive oil, garlic, chili sauce, salt and pepper and mix well.
3. Spread one-half of each of the tortillas with some of the tomato mixture. Top with slices of chicken and the shredded cheese. Fold in 2 sides and roll up. Place the wraps in a clean grill pan and cook for 5 minutes, turning halfway, just enough to warm through. (Or heat in a 400°F oven for 5 minutes until warm.) Cut in half and serve.

PER SERVING (½ WRAP) Calories 132 • Protein 11 g • Carbohydrates 19 g • Fiber 2.4 g • Total fat 5.1 g • Saturated fat 1.2 g • Cholesterol 19 mg • Sodium 193 mg • **PREP TIME** 15 minutes • **COOK TIME** 12 minutes • **MAKE AHEAD** Wraps can be made early in the day. Grill just before serving. • **NUTRITION WATCH** If you eat chicken on a regular basis, try to use certified organic chicken as much as possible. These chickens aren't given any hormones to enhance their size nor any antibiotics, and they are fed grains that have been grown organically.

greek vegetarian wraps with feta and hummus { *Serves 8*

½ cup finely chopped red onion
½ cup chopped green bell pepper
½ cup chopped tomato
½ cup chopped cucumber
⅓ cup chopped roasted red pepper
⅓ cup crumbled feta cheese (about 1½ oz)
1 Tbsp olive oil
½ tsp finely chopped garlic
½ tsp hot chili sauce
½ tsp dried basil
½ cup hummus
4 large flour tortillas

ENJOY THIS VERSION of a Greek salad in a wrap spread with hummus. The combination is excellent.

1. Combine the red onion, green pepper, tomato, cucumber, roasted pepper, feta, olive oil, garlic, chili sauce and basil in a large bowl.
2. Divide the hummus evenly among the tortillas. Divide the vegetable mixture on top. Fold in the sides of each tortilla and roll. Cut in half and serve.

PER SERVING (½ WRAP) Calories 183 • Protein 5.6 g • Carbohydrates 24 g • Fiber 2.4 g • Total fat 7.5 g • Saturated fat 1.7 g • Cholesterol 2 mg • Sodium 351 mg • **PREP TIME** 15 minutes • **MAKE AHEAD** Prepare early in the day and keep refrigerated. • **NUTRITION WATCH** Hummus is a good source of vegetable protein as well as vitamin B6 and manganese. If your child is experimenting with a vegetarian diet, try adding hummus as a protein source in their diet.

mango curry chicken wraps { *Serves 8*

1½ cups cooked and diced skinless boneless chicken breast
⅔ cup diced ripe mango
¾ cup diced red bell pepper
¼ cup diced green bell pepper
¼ cup diced red onion
¼ cup light mayonnaise
3 Tbsp chopped cilantro
1 Tbsp low-fat sour cream
1 Tbsp lemon juice
1 tsp curry powder
pinch of salt and pepper
1 cup shredded lettuce
4 large flour tortillas

THIS IS A LIGHT, Indian-flavored wrap with just a hint of curry. The sweet mango goes well with the chicken and curry mayonnaise.

1. Combine the chicken, mango, red and green peppers, onion, mayonnaise, cilantro, sour cream, lemon juice, curry, salt and pepper in a large bowl.
2. Divide the lettuce evenly among the 4 tortillas and divide the chicken mixture over the top. Fold in the sides and roll. Cut each wrap in half and serve.

PER SERVING (½ WRAP) Calories 188 • Protein 10 g • Carbohydrates 23 g • Fiber 1.9 g • Total fat 6.1 g • Saturated fat 0.9 g • Cholesterol 21 mg • Sodium 347 mg • **PREP TIME** 15 minutes • **MAKE AHEAD** Prepare early in the day and refrigerate. • **NUTRITION WATCH** Some research shows that *curcumin*, which is in turmeric (one of the main ingredients in curry powder), may help prevent colon cancer.

chicken salad pitas with creamy goat cheese dressing { *Serves 8*

DRESSING

- ⅓ cup crumbled goat cheese (about 1½ oz)
- 2 Tbsp light cream cheese, softened
- 1 Tbsp water
- 2 tsp olive oil
- 2 tsp lemon juice
- ½ tsp finely chopped garlic
- 2 tsp finely chopped fresh dill or parsley

WRAPS

- 8 oz skinless boneless chicken breasts (about 2 breasts)
- ½ cup chopped red bell pepper
- ⅓ cup chopped green bell pepper
- ⅓ cup chopped green onions
- ⅓ cup chopped black olives
- 4 large pitas
- 1 cup baby spinach leaves

THE SMOOTH GOAT CHEESE dressing goes well over the delicate chicken breast. This dressing can be made ahead and refrigerated, then used over vegetables or as a dip, or spread over a sandwich.

1. To make the dressing, combine the goat cheese, cream cheese, water, olive oil, lemon juice and garlic in the bowl of a food processor and purée until smooth. Stir in the dill and set aside.
2. Lightly coat a nonstick skillet or grill pan with cooking spray and set over medium heat. Add the chicken and sauté until no longer pink, about 8 minutes. Cool slightly, then chop into bite-size pieces.
3. Combine the cooked chicken with the goat cheese dressing in a large bowl. Add the red and green peppers, onions and olives. Cut the pitas in half and line each one with some of the spinach leaves. Divide the chicken filling evenly among the pitas and serve.

sandwiches & wraps

PER SERVING (½ PITA) Calories 163 • Protein 10 g • Carbohydrates 20 g • Fiber 3.2 g • Total fat 5 g • Saturated fat 1.7 g • Cholesterol 20 mg • Sodium 276 mg • **PREP TIME** 15 minutes • **COOK TIME** 8 minutes • **MAKE AHEAD** Prepare all the various stages early in the day and stuff the pitas just before serving. • **NUTRITION WATCH** Chicken breast is high in niacin—this B vitamin works with other B vitamins to release energy from carbohydrates and aids in healthy nerves and beautiful skin.

italian grilled chicken sandwiches with pesto-cheese sauce { *Serves 6*

- 2 Tbsp pesto (see page 244)
- 2 Tbsp light mayonnaise
- ⅓ cup light ricotta (5%)
- 3 Tbsp light cream cheese, softened
- ⅓ cup crumbled goat cheese (about 1½ oz)
- 1 whole Italian round loaf of bread (about 1¼ lb; about 12 inches across)
- 8 oz skinless boneless chicken breasts (about 2 breasts), pounded flat
- 1 roasted red pepper, thinly sliced (see page 100)
- 2 cups shredded romaine lettuce
- 2 medium plum tomatoes, sliced and seeded
- ⅓ cup diced red onion
- ⅓ cup chopped black olives
- pinch of salt and pepper

I SAVE CALORIES IN THIS SANDWICH by removing the interior from the loaf of bread and leaving the crust intact. The filling of chicken with vegetables, pesto-cheese sauce and shredded lettuce makes this a unique and delicious sandwich.

1. To make the pesto-cheese sauce, combine the pesto, mayonnaise, ricotta, cream cheese and goat cheese in a food processor and purée until smooth.
2. Cut the loaf of bread in half horizontally and pull out as much of the bread as possible, leaving only the crust.
3. In a nonstick grill pan or skillet lightly coated with cooking spray, cook the chicken breast just until no longer pink, about 5 minutes. Cool, then slice thinly.
4. Spread the pesto-cheese sauce over both the bottom and the top half of the loaf. Layer the bottom half with the chicken, roasted red pepper strips, lettuce, tomatoes, onion, olives, salt and pepper. Top with the top half of the loaf and cut into 6 sandwiches.

PER SERVING (1 SANDWICH) Calories 345 • Protein 17 g • Carbohydrates 53 g • Fiber 4.5 g • Total fat 8.3 g • Saturated fat 3.7 g • Cholesterol 20 mg • Sodium 560 mg • **PREP TIME** 20 minutes • **COOK TIME** 5 minutes • **MAKE AHEAD** Prepare the sandwich early in the day, wrap tightly and refrigerate. Serve at room temperature. • **NUTRITION WATCH** If you hollow out the bread by 75%, you reduce the amount of calories and carbohydrates and have a different and unique new sandwich, one that's much healthier for you.

chicken shawarmas (middle eastern pitas) { *Makes 8 half-pitas*

SAUCE
¾ cup hummus
1½ Tbsp lemon juice
2 Tbsp low-fat sour cream
1 tsp finely chopped garlic
pinch of salt and pepper

CHICKEN
12 oz skinless boneless chicken breasts (about 3 breasts)
¼ cup all-purpose flour
2 tsp vegetable oil
1½ cups sliced onion

PITAS
4 large pitas
½ cup chopped tomatoes
½ cup chopped cucumber
¼ cup chopped cilantro

SHAWARMAS ARE A TRADITIONAL MIDDLE EASTERN MEAL. Often beef or pork is used as well as chicken. I like to flour the chicken to keep it moist.

1. Combine the hummus, lemon juice, sour cream, garlic, salt and pepper in a small bowl. Set aside.
2. Place the chicken between 2 pieces of waxed paper, pound it flat and cut into thin strips. Coat the chicken strips with the flour. Lightly coat a nonstick skillet with cooking spray and set over medium-high heat. Add the oil and onion and sauté for 5 minutes or just until browned. Add the chicken and sauté for 10 minutes, stirring constantly, until the chicken is no longer pink. Respray the pan if necessary.
3. Slice each pita in half. Divide the chicken and onion mixture among the half-pitas. Sprinkle with tomatoes, cucumber and cilantro and spoon the hummus sauce over the pitas.

PER SERVING (½ PITA) Calories 212 • Protein 14 g • Carbohydrates 25 g • Fiber 3.8 g • Total fat 6.7 g • Saturated fat 1.3 g • Cholesterol 25 mg • Sodium 240 mg • **PREP TIME** 20 minutes • **COOK TIME** 15 minutes • **MAKE AHEAD** Prepare the sauce up to a day in advance. • **NUTRITION WATCH** Shawarma is a wholesome meal if you add loads of vegetables for vitamins and minerals. Spoon hummus on the insides of the pita instead of mayonnaise and save on calories and fat.

greek salad pitas with grilled chicken { *Serves 6*

12 oz skinless boneless chicken thighs (or breasts) (about 4 thighs)
3 Tbsp all-purpose flour
1 cup cherry tomatoes, halved
¾ cup chopped cucumber
⅓ cup chopped green onion
¾ cup chopped black olives
2 Tbsp light mayonnaise
1 Tbsp olive oil
1 Tbsp lemon juice
1 tsp finely chopped garlic
pinch of salt and pepper
⅓ cup crumbled feta cheese (about 1½ oz)
½ tsp dried oregano
¼ cup chopped fresh mint
3 whole wheat pitas
1 cup baby spinach

HERE'S THE ESSENCE OF A GREEK SALAD IN A PITA BREAD. The light lemon-garlic mayonnaise goes well with the vegetables and chicken.

1. Dust the chicken with the flour. Lightly coat a nonstick pan with cooking spray and set over medium-high heat. Sauté the chicken thighs for about 7 minutes on each side or just until cooked through. Cool and slice thinly.
2. Combine the tomatoes, cucumber, green onion, black olives and chicken in a large bowl. Add the mayonnaise, olive oil, lemon juice, garlic, salt and pepper, feta and oregano. Toss to combine. Add the fresh mint.
3. Cut the pitas in half and line each half with baby spinach. Divide the chicken mixture evenly among the 6 pita halves and serve.

PER SERVING (½ PITA) Calories 189 • Protein 10 g • Carbohydrates 20 g • Fiber 3.1 g • Total fat 8.4 g • Saturated fat 1.7 g • Cholesterol 23 mg • Sodium 381 mg • **PREP TIME** 15 minutes • **COOK TIME** 14 minutes • **MAKE AHEAD** Prepare early in the day, but stuff just before serving. • **NUTRITION WATCH** Olives are packed with monounsaturated fats and are a good source of vitamin E. These nutrients are thought to prevent cell damage and inflammation. Eat in moderation since they do contain excess calories.

roast beef, hummus and avocado wraps { *Serves 8*

⅔ cup hummus
4 large flour tortillas
6 oz medium-rare roast beef
⅔ cup chopped ripe avocado
⅓ cup finely chopped red onion
¾ cup shredded aged cheddar cheese

FORGET THE ORDINARY DELI and salty roast beef sandwiches. I like to use the real thing. You can ask for homemade, quality roast beef at your supermarket, thinly sliced. This is what will make the sandwich outstanding. The combination of hummus and avocado is delicious. You can also substitute thinly sliced turkey or chicken breast.

1. Divide the hummus evenly among the 4 tortillas and spread over each one. Top with the roast beef, avocado, onion and shredded cheese. Fold in sides of each tortilla and roll.
2. Place the wraps in a heated nonstick grill pan lightly coated with cooking spray and cook for 2 minutes on each side or just until warmed through. Cut in half and serve.

PER SERVING (½ WRAP) Calories 226 • Protein 14 g • Carbohydrates 22 g • Fiber 2.3 g • Total fat 9 g • Saturated fat 2.5 g • Cholesterol 29 mg • Sodium 284 mg • **PREP TIME** 10 minutes • **COOK TIME** 4 minutes • **MAKE AHEAD** Prepare early in the day and grill just before serving. • **NUTRITION WATCH** Regular roast beef is lower in sodium (on average, it has 46 mg of sodium per food-guide serving) than deli-style roast beef (which has on average 600 mg of sodium per serving).

pizza quesadillas with ground beef and parmesan { *Serves 8*

2 tsp vegetable oil
2 tsp finely chopped garlic
½ cup finely chopped onion
½ cup finely chopped green bell pepper
½ cup finely chopped carrots
6 oz lean ground beef
1 cup tomato sauce (see page 334) (or store-bought spaghetti sauce)
4 large flour tortillas
1 cup shredded mozzarella cheese
2 Tbsp grated Parmesan cheese

NEXT TIME YOUR KIDS WANT PIZZA, make this great pizza quesadilla. It's a lot tastier and healthier.

1. Lightly coat a nonstick skillet with cooking spray, add the vegetable oil and set over medium heat. Add the garlic, onion and green pepper and sauté for 5 minutes or until vegetables have softened. Add the carrots and sauté another 5 minutes. Add the ground beef and cook for 3 to 4 minutes or until it is no longer pink. Remove from the heat and stir in the tomato sauce.
2. Divide the ground beef mixture evenly among the 4 tortillas, spreading it over one-half. Top with the cheeses and fold in half. Set a skillet or grill pan over medium heat and grill the quesadillas for 2 minutes per side or just until the cheese melts and the quesadilla is heated through. Cut each tortilla in half and serve.

PER SERVING (½ QUESADILLA) Calories 213 • Protein 12 g • Carbohydrates 24 g • Fiber 2.1 g • Total fat 7.8 g • Saturated fat 2.7 g • Cholesterol 19 mg • Sodium 346 mg • **PREP TIME** 10 minutes • **COOK TIME** 18 minutes • **MAKE AHEAD** Prepare early in the day and grill just before serving. • **NUTRITION WATCH** Mozzarella cheese is a good source of calcium, but is also high in sodium (a 118 g serving has 840 mg of sodium). Don't add excess salt if using larger amounts of cheese in your cooking.

shrimp, avocado and feta wraps { *Serves 8*

6 oz raw shrimp, peeled and deveined
1½ cups chopped plum tomatoes
½ cup chopped avocado
¼ cup chopped cilantro
2 Tbsp finely chopped red onion
⅓ cup crumbled light feta cheese (about 1½ oz)
1 Tbsp olive oil
2 Tbsp lemon juice
1 tsp finely chopped garlic
1 tsp finely chopped jalapeño pepper (or 1 tsp hot chili sauce)
pinch of salt and pepper
4 large whole lettuce leaves
4 large whole wheat flour tortillas

YOU CAN SUBSTITUTE BABY COCKTAIL SHRIMP if you don't have the larger ones. Be sure to seed the tomatoes first to avoid excess liquid. If you are serving these to guests, let them assemble these wraps themselves. Keeping some or all of the shrimp whole makes a lovely presentation. Corn kernels are a nice addition to the filling.

1. Lightly coat a nonstick skillet with vegetable spray and set over medium-high heat. Add the shrimp and grill just until no longer pink, about 3 minutes, turning halfway through. Remove from the heat and let cool slightly. Dice the shrimp and place in a large mixing bowl.
2. Add the tomatoes, avocado, cilantro, red onion, feta, olive oil, lemon juice, garlic, jalapeño, salt and pepper.
3. Place 1 lettuce leaf on each of the 4 tortillas and divide the shrimp mixture evenly among the tortillas, spreading it to about ¼ inch from the edges. Fold in the sides of the tortillas and roll up. Cut each in half and serve.

PER SERVING (½ WRAP) Calories 104 • Protein 7 g • Carbohydrates 13 g • Fiber 2.2 g • Total fat 4.3 g • Saturated fat 0.9 g • Cholesterol 33 mg • Sodium 233 mg • **PREP TIME** 15 minutes • **MAKE AHEAD** Prepare early in the day and refrigerate. • **NUTRITION WATCH** Red onion is a very good source of vitamin C, which is great for promoting a healthy immune system.

shrimp and tahini wraps { *Serves 8*

TAHINI SAUCE
2 Tbsp chicken stock
2 Tbsp light ricotta (5%)
1 Tbsp tahini (sesame seed paste)
1 Tbsp lemon juice
1 Tbsp light mayonnaise
1 tsp low-sodium soy sauce
1 tsp sesame oil
1 tsp finely chopped garlic
¼ tsp dried oregano

WRAPS
8 oz raw shrimp, peeled and deveined
½ cup diced red bell pepper
⅓ cup diced red onion
¼ cup chopped cilantro
4 large flour tortillas
4 large lettuce leaves

TAHINI SAUCE, which is a Middle Eastern favorite, is traditionally served with chicken. I tried it with shrimp and it is just as fantastic. You can always use chicken if you'd like.

1. Combine the stock, ricotta, tahini, lemon juice, mayonnaise, soy sauce, sesame oil, garlic and oregano in the bowl of a food processor and purée until smooth.
2. Lightly coat a nonstick skillet with vegetable spray and set over medium-high heat. Add shrimp and cook just until done, about 5 minutes. Remove from the heat and let cool slightly. Dice the shrimp and place in a large mixing bowl. Add the tahini sauce, red pepper, red onions and cilantro, and stir to combine.
3. Place 1 lettuce leaf on each of the tortillas. Divide the shrimp mixture evenly among the tortillas, spreading it to about ¼ inch from the edges. Fold in the sides of the tortillas and roll up. Cut each in half and serve.

PER SERVING (½ WRAP) Calories 169 • Protein 8.5 g • Carbohydrates 21 g • Fiber 1.6 g • Total fat 5.5 g • Saturated fat 1.1 g • Cholesterol 44 mg • Sodium 331 mg • **PREP TIME** 10 minutes • **COOK TIME** 5 minutes • **MAKE AHEAD** Prepare early in the day and refrigerate. • **NUTRITION WATCH** Cilantro aids in digestion and helps settle the stomach and prevent flatulence.

shrimp quesadillas with cheese and avocado { *Serves 8*

6 oz raw shrimp, peeled and deveined
1 cup shredded Monterey Jack (or havarti) cheese
½ cup diced avocado
¼ cup chopped cilantro
2 tsp lemon juice
1 tsp finely chopped jalapeño pepper (or 1 tsp hot chili sauce)
¼ cup green onions
1 tsp chopped garlic
pinch of pepper
4 medium flour tortillas

DIPPING SAUCE

¼ cup medium salsa
2 Tbsp light mayonnaise

SHRIMP, A MILD CHEESE AND AVOCADO are a great combination in this quesadilla. This can also be served as an appetizer. Boneless chicken breast can be used instead of shrimp.

1. Lightly coat a nonstick grill pan with cooking spray and set over medium-high heat. Grill the shrimp just until no longer pink, about 3 minutes, turning halfway through. Remove from the heat and let cool slightly. Dice the shrimp and place in a large mixing bowl.
2. Add the cheese, avocado, cilantro, lemon juice, jalapeño, green onions, garlic and pepper, and mix until well combined. Divide the mixture evenly among the tortillas. Fold in half and grill on a clean grill pan over medium heat for about 1 minute per side or until the cheese begins to melt and the wrap is heated through. Slice the quesadillas in half and serve.
3. To make the dipping sauce, combine the salsa and mayonnaise in a small bowl and serve with the quesadilla.

PER SERVING (½ QUESADILLA) Calories 200 • Protein 10 g • Carbohydrates 21 g • Fiber 2.0 g • Total fat 8.7 g • Saturated fat 2.7 g • Cholesterol 43 mg • Sodium 417 mg • **PREP TIME** 10 minutes • **COOK TIME** 5 minutes • **MAKE AHEAD** Can be prepared early in the day. Grill just before serving. • **NUTRITION WATCH** Salsa is a low-fat complement to your meal. On average, 100 g of salsa will only add 36 calories.

seared tuna wraps with wasabi mayonnaise { *Serves 8*

WASABI MAYONNAISE
1 tsp wasabi paste
¼ cup light mayonnaise

WRAPS
12 oz raw tuna
1 Tbsp low-sodium soy sauce
1½ tsp rice vinegar
2 tsp sesame oil
1½ tsp honey
1 tsp toasted sesame seeds
½ tsp finely chopped garlic
½ tsp finely chopped ginger
¾ cup thinly sliced red bell pepper
¾ cup thinly sliced baby cucumber (unpeeled)
4 large flour tortillas

BUY THE BEST RAW TUNA you can find. Sushi-grade ahi tuna is a great choice. Make sure it's fresh and do not overcook it. I like to sear my tuna and then place it immediately in the refrigerator for 5 minutes to stop the cooking process. I buy wasabi in a tube for convenience.

1. Combine the wasabi paste and mayonnaise in a small bowl. Set aside.
2. Lightly coat a nonstick skillet or grill pan with cooking spray and set over high heat. Sear the tuna for 2 minutes on each side, or until the outside is seared and cooked but the interior is still raw. Remove from the heat and allow to cool. Dice the tuna and place in a small bowl.
3. Add the soy sauce, rice vinegar, sesame oil, honey, sesame seeds, garlic and ginger to the tuna and let sit for 5 minutes.
4. Spread a thin layer of wasabi mayonnaise over each of the tortillas. Divide the red pepper and cucumber strips among the tortillas. Divide the seasoned tuna evenly among each of the tortillas. Fold in the sides of each tortilla and roll. Cut each wrap in half and serve.

PER SERVING (½ WRAP) Calories 193 • Protein 13 g • Carbohydrates 21 g • Fiber 1.4 g • Total fat 6.2 g • Saturated fat 0.9 g • Cholesterol 22 mg • Sodium 337 mg • **PREP TIME** 10 minutes • **COOK TIME** 4 minutes • **MAKE AHEAD** Prepare early in the day and refrigerate. • **NUTRITION WATCH** Cucumbers are good source of vitamin A, pantothenic acid, magnesium, phosphorus and manganese, and a very good source of vitamin C, vitamin K and potassium.

smoked salmon and egg salad pitas { *Serves 8*

3 large eggs
⅓ cup finely chopped green onion
⅓ cup diced celery
⅓ cup diced red bell pepper
2 Tbsp light mayonnaise
1 Tbsp low-fat sour cream
pinch of salt and pepper
4 large whole wheat pitas
2 cups baby spinach leaves
3 oz smoked salmon, cut into strips

WE'VE ALL HAD SMOKED SALMON OR EGG SALAD SANDWICHES, but when I tried them together they were incredible. I've stuffed them into a pita lined with spinach.

1. Place the eggs in a saucepan, cover with water and bring to a boil. Reduce the heat, but keep it at a rolling boil, and cook the eggs for 15 minutes. Drain and cool the eggs under cold running water. Peel, and mash in a large bowl. Add the green onion, celery, red pepper, mayonnaise, sour cream, salt and pepper.
2. Cut each of the pitas in half and stuff each with ¼ cup of the baby spinach. Divide the egg salad and smoked salmon among the pita halves.

PER SERVING (½ PITA) Calories 122 • Protein 7 g • Carbohydrates 14 g • Fiber 2.2 g • Total fat 4.5 g • Saturated fat 0.9 g • Cholesterol 84 mg • Sodium 306 mg • **PREP TIME** 10 minutes • **MAKE AHEAD** Prepare early in the day and refrigerate. • **NUTRITION WATCH** Celery contains potassium and sodium, the central minerals for regulating fluid balance and stimulating urine production, thereby helping to free the body of excess fluid.

{ vegetable side dishes }

Use fresh vegetables as often as possible. Frozen vegetables are still healthy, but they don't have the same texture and flavor. Do not use canned vegetables (except for canned corn). They lack flavor and contain excess sodium • If vegetables are to be cooked in advance, steam, microwave, blanch or boil them. Vegetables are done when they are tender-crisp and still retain their color. Drain and rinse with cold water to prevent overcooking. Overcooked vegetables are dull and soft, and most of the nutrients are lost • Leaving the skin on vegetables (do so if it's not discolored or bruised) increases the fiber content • A 10 oz bag of fresh spinach yields the same amount as a 10 oz frozen package, once cooked. After cooking, squeeze out excess moisture • When sautéing vegetables, use a nonstick skillet sprayed with cooking spray, and only the amount of oil in the recipe. If the vegetables begin to burn or stick, respray or add a little water to the skillet. Do not add extra oil or butter • Most of the vegetable dishes should be cooked or baked just before serving, to retain freshness • Roasted vegetables can be stored in the refrigerator for up to 2 days and reheated

roasted vegetable platter with olive oil and balsamic dressing { *Serves 10*

VEGETABLES

2 sweet potatoes, each cut into six ½-inch-thick slices
6 mini or fingerling potatoes, sliced in half
1 large red bell pepper, cored and cut into 6 wedges
1 large green bell pepper, cored and cut into 6 wedges
8 large asparagus spears, trimmed
1 large red onion cut into wedges
6 medium portobello mushrooms, each sliced into 4 wedges
1 head of garlic with the top sliced off, wrapped in foil
2 Tbsp olive oil
2 tsp balsamic vinegar
½ tsp honey
pinch of salt and pepper

GOAT CHEESE GARNISH (OPTIONAL)

¼ cup chopped fresh basil
2 Tbsp toasted pine nuts
¼ cup crumbled goat cheese (about 1 oz)

THESE ROASTED VEGETABLES are a beautiful centerpiece for the table, and will accompany virtually any main course. Feel free to substitute vegetables of your choice, keeping in mind that they may require different cooking times, so remove each vegetable as it becomes tender.

1. Preheat the oven to 425°F. Lightly coat 2 baking sheets with cooking spray.
2. Place the sweet potatoes, mini potatoes, red and green peppers, asparagus, onion, mushrooms and garlic on the prepared baking sheets and lightly coat with cooking spray. Bake on 2 separate racks in the oven. Remove the asparagus after 10 minutes of roasting. Turn the other vegetables after another 15 minutes. Continue to cook for 10 more minutes, just until the vegetables are tender and browned. Gently peel the skin from the garlic and squeeze out the cloves. Place vegetables and garlic on a serving platter.
3. To make the dressing, whisk together the oil, vinegar, honey, salt and pepper in a small bowl.
4. Pour the dressing over the vegetables and garnish with fresh basil and pine nuts and goat cheese, if using.

PER SERVING Calories 244 • Protein 6 g • Carbohydrates 45 g • Fiber 5 g • Total fat 5 g • Saturated fat 1.2 g • Cholesterol 2 mg • Sodium 78 mg • **PREP TIME** 15 minutes • **BAKE TIME** 35 minutes • **MAKE AHEAD** Cook the vegetables up to a day in advance. Reheat in a 350°F oven for 10 minutes or until warmed through. • **NUTRITION WATCH** Olive oil is a healthy, monounsaturated fat that helps reduce the risk of cardiovascular disease.

molasses-coated carrots with fresh mint { *Serves 6*

1 lb thin carrots (about 6 inches long), peeled and trimmed
2 Tbsp molasses
1½ tsp sherry wine vinegar or white balsamic vinegar
1 Tbsp olive oil
3 Tbsp chopped fresh mint

THIS IS A SURE WAY to liven up carrots. The mint and molasses are an unusual combination, but they really go well together.

1. Place the carrots in a large saucepan or skillet. Cover with water and boil for 10 minutes or until just tender. Drain well and return to the saucepan.
2. Whisk together the molasses, vinegar and olive oil in a small bowl. Add to the carrots and sauté over high heat for 5 minutes or until the sauce is heated through and the carrots are coated. Place on a platter, garnish with fresh mint and serve.

PER SERVING Calories 120 • Protein 2 g • Carbohydrates 13 g • Fiber 4.5 g • Total fat 3 g • Saturated fat 0.5 g • Cholesterol 0 mg • Sodium 60 mg • **PREP TIME** 10 minutes • **COOK TIME** 15 minutes • **MAKE AHEAD** This can be prepared early in the day and served at room temperature. • **NUTRITION WATCH** Molasses is a very good source of calcium, iron, magnesium, potassium, vitamin B6 and selenium.

stir-fried edamame with garlic and ginger { *Serves 6*

1 lb frozen shelled edamame
4 tsp low-sodium soy sauce
1½ tsp sesame oil
1½ tsp oyster sauce
1 tsp finely chopped garlic
1 tsp finely chopped ginger
½ tsp hot chili sauce
1 tsp sesame seeds

EDAMAME IN THE SHELL have been all the rage for a few years. But now you can find them shelled in the freezer section of your supermarket. As an alternative to just steaming them, try this recipe with a delicious Asian sauce.

1. Bring a large saucepan of water to a boil. Add the edamame and boil for 2 minutes. Drain and return to the saucepan.
2. Add the soy sauce, sesame oil, oyster sauce, garlic, ginger and chili sauce. Sauté for 1 minute. Garnish with sesame seeds and serve immediately.

PER SERVING Calories 118 • Protein 10 g • Carbohydrates 10 g • Fiber 1.1 g • Total fat 4 g • Saturated fat 0.2 g • Cholesterol 0 mg • Sodium 250 mg • **PREP TIME** 5 minutes • **COOK TIME** 3 minutes • **MAKE AHEAD** This can be prepared early in the day and served at room temperature. • **NUTRITION WATCH** Sesame oil is a source of vitamin E, and may help to lower your blood pressure.

southwest stuffed peppers { *Serves 4*

2 cups beef (or chicken) stock
½ cup brown rice
2 tsp vegetable oil
1 cup diced onion
1 cup canned corn, drained
½ lb lean ground beef
1½ cups canned red kidney beans, drained and rinsed
1½ tsp chili powder
½ tsp dried basil
½ tsp ground cumin
pinch of salt and pepper
½ cup medium salsa
¾ cup shredded aged cheddar cheese
⅓ cup low-fat sour cream
⅓ cup chopped cilantro or parsley
4 medium bell peppers (any color)

STUFFED PEPPERS have been around for decades. But I've made them a healthier, more delicious side dish or main course by using brown rice and lean beef and adding a Tex Mex flavor.

1. Preheat the oven to 375°F. Line a baking sheet with foil and lightly coat with cooking spray.
2. In a medium saucepan, bring the stock and rice to a boil. Reduce the heat to low, then cover and simmer for 25 minutes or until the rice is tender. Drain any excess stock.
3. Lightly coat a large saucepan with cooking spray, add the oil and set over medium-high heat. Add the onion and sauté for 3 minutes. Add the corn and sauté another 5 minutes or until the corn starts to brown. Add the ground beef and sauté until no longer pink, about 3 minutes.
4. Add the cooked rice, beans, chili powder, basil, cumin, salt, pepper and salsa and cook for 1 minute. Remove from the heat and add ½ cup of the cheese, along with the sour cream and cilantro or parsley.
5. Carefully remove and discard the top from each of the peppers. Remove the ribs and seeds and discard. Place the peppers on the baking sheet and fill them with the beef stuffing. Bake for 25 minutes.
6. Sprinkle with the remaining cheese. Bake for another 2 minutes or just until the cheese melts.

PER SERVING Calories 455 • Protein 28 g • Carbohydrates 58 g • Fiber 9.7 g • Total fat 13 g • Saturated fat 5.1 g • Cholesterol 49 mg • Sodium 790 mg • **PREP TIME** 15 minutes • **COOK TIME** 37 minutes • **MAKE AHEAD** Prepare the filling and stuff up to a day in advance. Bake just before serving. • **NUTRITION WATCH** Red kidney beans are a very good source of fiber. They contain 6 g per ⅓ cup.

green beans with dried apricots and almonds { *Serves 4*

1 lb green beans, trimmed and cut in half
2 tsp olive oil
½ tsp finely chopped garlic
½ tsp finely chopped ginger
¼ cup finely chopped dried apricots
3 Tbsp toasted slivered almonds
1 tsp orange zest

GREEN BEANS are a staple in most homes because they're so affordable and versatile. But instead of just steaming them, try this unique recipe. (Pictured on page 269.)

1. Steam or boil the green beans for 2 minutes or until bright green but still crisp. Drain well and place in a large skillet over medium heat.
2. Add the olive oil, garlic and ginger, and sauté over medium heat for 1 minute. Add the apricots, almonds and orange zest. Toss well and serve.

PER SERVING Calories 121 • Protein 3 g • Carbohydrates 15 g • Fiber 4.8 g • Total fat 5 g • Saturated fat 0.6 g • Cholesterol 0 mg • Sodium 7 mg • **PREP TIME** 5 minutes • **COOK TIME** 3 minutes • **NUTRITION WATCH** Green beans are a good source of calcium.

green beans with roasted tomatoes, garlic and kalamata olives { *Serves 6*

1 head of garlic
2 cups halved cherry tomatoes
1½ lb green beans, trimmed
⅓ cup chopped black olives
1 Tbsp olive oil
½ tsp dried basil
pinch of pepper

THIS IS A GREAT Mediterranean vegetable dish. You can substitute asparagus or broccoli for the green beans.

1. Preheat the oven to 450°F. Line a baking sheet with foil and lightly coat with cooking spray.
2. Slice the top off the head of garlic to expose the tops of the cloves. Rub with a little vegetable oil. Wrap in foil and place on the foil-covered baking sheet. Place the cherry tomato halves on the baking sheet and put in the oven. Bake for 10 minutes, then remove the tomatoes. Set aside. Leave the garlic to roast for another 10 minutes. Remove the garlic from the oven and squeeze out the cloves.
3. Steam or boil the green beans for 2 minutes or until bright green but still crisp. Drain and place in a large bowl. Add the roasted cherry tomatoes, olives, olive oil, basil, pepper and garlic cloves with the skin removed. Toss and serve.

PER SERVING Calories 87 • Protein 3 g • Carbohydrates 13 g • Fiber 4.6 g • Total fat 3.6 g • Saturated fat 0.5 g • Cholesterol 0 mg • Sodium 100 mg • **PREP TIME** 5 minutes • **COOK TIME** 20 minutes • **MAKE AHEAD** This can be prepared early in the day and served at room temperature. • **NUTRITION WATCH** Garlic is a very good source of vitamin B6 and a good source of calcium. Vitamin C in garlic may also help boost your immune system.

baby bok choy and oyster mushrooms with sesame sauce { *Serves 4*

SESAME SAUCE
1 Tbsp low-sodium soy sauce
2 tsp sesame oil
1½ tsp oyster sauce
1 Tbsp brown sugar
1 tsp finely chopped garlic
1 tsp finely chopped ginger
1 tsp hot chili sauce

VEGETABLES
2 tsp vegetable oil
8 oz whole oyster mushrooms
6 baby bok choy
1 tsp toasted sesame seeds

THE COMBINED FLAVORS OF BOK CHOY, mushroom and this sesame sauce is outstanding. I love to serve this alongside a fish or chicken dish. I use whole oyster mushrooms for appearance as well as texture. Feel free to substitute other mushrooms, but it is best to slice them in large pieces.

1. Combine the soy sauce, sesame oil, oyster sauce, sugar, garlic, ginger and chili sauce in a small bowl and set aside.
2. Lightly coat a large, nonstick skillet with cooking spray, add the oil and set over medium-high heat. Add the mushrooms and sauté for 5 minutes or until tender. Add the sauce and cook for 2 minutes, until slightly thickened.
3. Place a shallow layer of water in a large saucepan and bring to a boil. Place the bok choy in the saucepan, cover and cook for 2 minutes or just until it is bright green. Drain well and place on a serving dish. Top with the sautéed mushrooms and sesame sauce, sprinkle with sesame seeds and serve immediately.

PER SERVING Calories 91 • Protein 4 g • Carbohydrates 9 g • Fiber 3.7 g • Total fat 5 g • Saturated fat 0.5 g • Cholesterol 0 mg • Sodium 257 mg • **PREP TIME** 5 minutes • **COOK TIME** 9 minutes • **MAKE AHEAD** Prepare the sauce up to a day in advance. • **NUTRITION WATCH** Bok choy is high in fiber and vitamins A and C.

three-mushroom teriyaki stir-fry { *Serves 6*

TERIYAKI SAUCE
3 Tbsp packed brown sugar
2 Tbsp low-sodium soy sauce
3 Tbsp water (or vegetable stock)
2 Tbsp rice vinegar
2 tsp sesame oil
1 tsp cornstarch
1 tsp finely chopped garlic
½ tsp finely chopped ginger

MUSHROOMS
1 tsp vegetable oil
2 large portobello mushrooms, cut into large pieces
3 cups oyster mushrooms, cut into large pieces
3 cups button mushrooms, cut in half
3 Tbsp chopped parsley or cilantro
1 tsp toasted sesame seeds

SAUTÉED MUSHROOMS, especially when served with a chicken or beef dish, have always been a favorite of mine. I've added an Asian twist to these mushrooms, and they're perfect to accompany any main course.

1. Combine the brown sugar, soy sauce, water, rice vinegar, sesame oil, cornstarch, garlic and ginger in a small saucepan. Bring to a boil over medium-high heat, whisking constantly. Reduce the heat to a simmer and cook for 2 minutes or until the sauce has thickened slightly. Set aside.
2. Lightly coat a large, nonstick skillet with cooking spray, add the oil and set over medium-high heat. Add the mushrooms and sauté for 10 minutes or until they are just softened and browned and most of liquid has evaporated, stirring occasionally. Add the sauce and simmer for 1 minute or until the sauce is heated through and everything is slightly thickened.
3. Garnish with parsley or cilantro and sesame seeds and serve immediately.

PER SERVING Calories 103 • Protein 3.8 g • Carbohydrates 13 g • Fiber 2.9 g • Total fat 2.9 g • Saturated fat 0.3 g • Cholesterol 0 mg • Sodium 200 mg • **PREP TIME** 10 minutes • **COOK TIME** 13 minutes • **MAKE AHEAD** Prepare sauce up to a couple of days in advance. • **NUTRITION WATCH** One medium portobello mushroom has as much potassium as a medium banana.

mashed root vegetables with roasted garlic { *Serves 4*

8 cloves of garlic
3 cups peeled and cubed Yukon Gold potatoes
1½ cups peeled and cubed sweet potatoes
1½ cups peeled and cubed parsnips
2 tsp vegetable oil
2 cups finely chopped Vidalia onion
1½ tsp brown sugar
2 tsp finely chopped garlic
2 Tbsp olive oil
pinch of salt and pepper
3 Tbsp chopped parsley

I CREATED THIS RECIPE for the Pickle Barrel chain of restaurants in Toronto. We serve these with beef, fish and chicken entrées. It's a nice change from regular mashed potatoes.

1. Preheat the oven to 450°F. Wrap the garlic cloves in foil and bake for about 15 minutes or until tender. Allow to cool, remove the skin and set aside.
2. Place the potatoes, sweet potatoes and parsnips in 3 separate large pots with enough cold water to cover them. Boil the potatoes for about 10 to 15 minutes or until tender, the sweet potatoes for about 10 minutes or until tender and the parsnips for about 20 minutes or until tender. Drain and place in 1 large pot, cover and set aside.
3. Meanwhile, lightly coat a large skillet with cooking spray, add the oil and set over medium-low heat. Add the onion and sauté for 10 minutes or until softened and browned. Reduce the heat to low, add the brown sugar and garlic and continue cooking for 5 minutes.
4. Partially mash the potatoes, sweet potatoes and parsnips using a potato masher. Add the roasted garlic cloves, sautéed onion, olive oil, salt and pepper. Garnish with parsley and serve immediately.

PER SERVING Calories 271 • Protein 4.5 g • Carbohydrates 41 g • Fiber 5.1 g • Total fat 10 g • Saturated fat 1.2 g • Cholesterol 0 mg • Sodium 100 mg • **PREP TIME** 20 minutes • **COOK TIME** 40 minutes • **MAKE AHEAD** Prepare up to a day in advance and reheat gently on top of the stove until warm. • **NUTRITION WATCH** Potatoes are a good source of potassium and vitamins C and B6.

baked root vegetables with maple syrup and cinnamon { *Serves 6*

1 lb sweet potatoes, unpeeled and cut into wedges
1 lb Yukon Gold potatoes, unpeeled and cut into wedges
1 lb butternut squash, peeled and cut into 2-inch pieces
1 large sweet yellow onion, cut into 8 wedges
2 large peeled parsnips, cut into 2-inch pieces
2 peeled beets, cut into 1-inch pieces

DRESSING
1 Tbsp olive oil
1 Tbsp balsamic vinegar
2 Tbsp maple syrup
½ tsp cinnamon
¼ cup chopped parsley

BAKED ROOT VEGETABLES are a real comfort side dish during the colder months. Use other varieties of your favorite vegetables such as turnips or rutabagas. You may need to add a little more maple syrup since these vegetables tend to be less sweet. (Pictured on page 289.)

1. Preheat the oven to 425°F. Line 2 baking sheets with foil and lightly coat with cooking spray.
2. Arrange the sweet potatoes, potatoes, squash, onion, parsnips and beets in a single layer on the lined baking sheets. Lightly coat lightly with cooking spray. Bake in the center of the oven for about 25 to 30 minutes, turning after 20 minutes or just until browned and tender. If the trays are on separate racks, switch their positions halfway through the cooking time. Bake the beets an extra 10 minutes, or until fork tender. Place the vegetables on a large serving platter.
3. To make the dressing, whisk together the olive oil, vinegar, maple syrup and cinnamon in a small bowl. Pour the dressing over the roasted vegetables. Garnish with parsley and serve.

PER SERVING Calories 260 • Protein 5 g • Carbohydrates 56 g • Fiber 7.9 g • Total fat 3 g • Saturated fat 0.4 g • Cholesterol 0 mg • Sodium 36 mg • **PREP TIME** 20 minutes • **BAKE TIME** 35 minutes • **MAKE AHEAD** Prepare up to a day in advance and reheat in a 350°F oven for 10 minutes or until warm. • **NUTRITION WATCH** Beets are packed with the B vitamin choline, which helps reduce inflammation and helps boost your memory.

acorn squash maple-cinnamon wedges { *Serves 6*

1 large acorn squash
1 Tbsp maple syrup
1 Tbsp brown sugar
1 Tbsp olive oil
¼ tsp cinnamon
pinch of ground ginger
pinch of salt
3 Tbsp chopped parsley

SQUASH IS A SWEET, delicate vegetable that's perfect when served in wedges with a maple syrup sauce.

1. Preheat the oven to 400°F. Line a baking sheet with foil and lightly coat with cooking spray.
2. Use a strong knife to cut the squash in half. Scoop out the seeds and cut into 6 wedges, leaving the skin intact. Place the squash wedges on the baking sheet.
3. Whisk together the maple syrup, brown sugar, olive oil, cinnamon, ginger and salt in a small bowl. Brush over the squash wedges. Bake for 35 to 40 minutes or until the squash is tender. Garnish with parsley and serve.

PER SERVING Calories 66 • Protein 1 g • Carbohydrates 11 g • Fiber 1.2 g • Total fat 2.5 g • Saturated fat 0.4 g • Cholesterol 1 mg • Sodium 53 mg • **PREP TIME** 10 minutes • **BAKE TIME** 35 minutes • **MAKE AHEAD** Prepare up to a day in advance and reheat in a 350°F oven for 10 minutes or just until warm. • **NUTRITION WATCH** Acorn squash is good source of folate and plant-based omega-3 fatty acids. Folate prevents certain birth defects when taken by women before and during pregnancy.

parsnip fries { *Serves 6*

1½ lb parsnips (about 8 to 10 medium size)
2 Tbsp olive oil
2 Tbsp maple syrup
¼ tsp cinnamon
pinch of ground ginger
pinch of salt and pepper

FORGET REGULAR POTATO or even sweet potato fries. The newest rage is parsnip fries. Parsnips are sweet, and are wonderful when roasted. They take longer to cook, so be patient.

1. Preheat the oven to 400°F. Line a baking sheet with foil and lightly coat with cooking spray.
2. Wash and peel the parsnips. Cut into strips about 3 inches long and 1 inch wide. Place on the baking sheet.
3. Whisk together the olive oil, maple syrup, cinnamon, ginger, salt and pepper in a small bowl. Brush on the parsnips and bake for 40 minutes or until tender and browned, turning halfway through the baking time if necessary. Bake parsnips longer if you want these to be really crisp. Serve immediately.

PER SERVING Calories 145 • Protein 2 g • Carbohydrates 25 g • Fiber 4.4 g • Total fat 5 g • Saturated fat 0.7 g • Cholesterol 0 mg • Sodium 61 mg • **PREP TIME** 10 minutes • **BAKE TIME** 40 minutes • **MAKE AHEAD** Can be prepared up to a day in advance. Gently reheat in a 350°F oven for 10 minutes or until warmed through. • **NUTRITION WATCH** Zinc, a mineral found in maple syrup, may help support male reproductive health.

smashed potatoes with lemon, cumin and goat cheese { *Serves 6*

2 lb mini potatoes
2 Tbsp olive oil
1 Tbsp lemon juice
1 tsp lemon zest
¼ tsp ground cumin
pinch of salt and pepper
¼ cup crumbled goat cheese (about 1 oz)
3 Tbsp chopped fresh mint

I CREATED A SIMILAR RECIPE for my last cookbook, *The Complete Light Kitchen*, and also serve these through our catering company and at the Pickle Barrel. I added a Middle Eastern flavor to this great potato side dish.

1. Preheat the oven to 400°F. Line a baking sheet with foil and lightly coat with cooking spray.
2. Wash the potatoes and place them in a large pot. Add enough cold water to cover. Bring to a boil and cook for 15 minutes or until the potatoes are just tender but not overcooked. Drain and cool.
3. Meanwhile, whisk together the olive oil, lemon juice and zest, cumin, salt and pepper in a small bowl. Set aside.
4. Place the cooled potatoes on the baking sheet and, using the palm of your hand, gently press each of the potatoes to "smash" them. Brush the dressing over the smashed potatoes and bake for 20 minutes. Sprinkle the goat cheese over the potatoes and bake for another 2 minutes. Garnish with mint and serve.

PER SERVING Calories 166 • Protein 3.5 g • Carbohydrates 25 g • Fiber 2.7 g • Total fat 6 g • Saturated fat 1.4 g • Cholesterol 2 mg • Sodium 76 mg • **PREP TIME** 5 minutes • **COOK TIME** 35 minutes • **MAKE AHEAD** Can be made early in the day, but leave out the goat cheese. Reheat gently in a 350°F oven for 10 minutes, then garnish. • **NUTRITION WATCH** Cumin is a good source of iron, which is important for growing children and adolescents, who have increased needs for iron, as do women who are pregnant or lactating.

goat cheese mashed potatoes with sun-dried tomatoes { *Serves 4*

8 cloves of garlic
1 lb Yukon Gold potatoes, cut into quarters
¼ cup finely chopped rehydrated sun-dried tomatoes
2 Tbsp olive oil
¼ cup low-fat sour cream
2 Tbsp chicken stock
½ cup crumbled goat cheese (about 2 oz)
pinch of salt and pepper
¼ cup chopped fresh basil

I LOVE MASHED POTATOES, but those in restaurants are filled with excess cream and butter. I found a way to make them taste rich without the extra calories and fat. I've added goat cheese and sun-dried tomatoes—absolutely delicious.

1. Preheat the oven to 450°F. Wrap the garlic cloves in foil and bake for about 15 minutes, or until tender. Allow to cool, then squeeze the garlic out of the skin and set aside.
2. Place the potatoes in a large pot and add enough cold water to cover. Bring to a boil and cook the potatoes for 15 minutes or until tender. Drain well, return to the saucepan and cover to keep warm.
3. Add the sun-dried tomatoes, olive oil, sour cream, chicken stock, goat cheese, roasted garlic, salt and pepper. Mash with a potato masher until well combined. Garnish with the chopped basil and serve.

PER SERVING Calories 233 • Protein 7 g • Carbohydrates 25 g • Fiber 2 g • Total fat 11 g • Saturated fat 3.8 g • Cholesterol 12 mg • Sodium 231 mg • **PREP TIME** 10 minutes • **COOK TIME** 30 minutes • **MAKE AHEAD** Prepare up to a day in advance and reheat gently on top of the stove for 10 minutes or until warm. • **NUTRITION WATCH** Chicken stock can be high in sodium, close to 1,000 mg per cup. Use lower-sodium chicken stock, which has about half the amount.

yukon gold potato and white bean mash { *Serves 4*

1 head of garlic
1 lb Yukon Gold potatoes, peeled and quartered
1 tsp vegetable oil
1 cup chopped red onion
1 cup canned white kidney beans, drained and rinsed
3 Tbsp canned evaporated milk (2%)
2 Tbsp olive oil
¼ tsp salt
¼ tsp pepper
3 Tbsp chopped fresh parsley or basil

INSTEAD OF TRADITIONAL MASHED POTATOES I added puréed white kidney beans and roasted garlic to this potato dish. It's delicious and a nice change from the standard recipes. The evaporated milk substitutes for the butter or cream normally used.

1. Preheat the oven to 450°F. Slice the top off the head of garlic to expose the tops of the cloves. Rub with a little vegetable oil. Wrap the head in foil and bake for 20 minutes.
2. Place the potatoes in a large pot and add enough cold water to cover. Bring to a boil and cook for 15 minutes or until tender.
3. Meanwhile, lightly coat a nonstick skillet with cooking spray, add the oil and set over medium-high heat. Add the onion and sauté for 5 minutes or until tender.
4. Drain the cooked potatoes and return to the pot. Squeeze the roasted garlic out of the skins and add to the potatoes. Add the sautéed onion to the potatoes and mash with a potato masher.
5. Combine the kidney beans, evaporated milk, olive oil, salt and pepper in the bowl of a food processor. Purée, then add to the mashed potatoes. If desired, return the potato mixture to the stovetop and heat gently. Garnish with parsley and serve.

PER SERVING Calories 258 • Protein 7.5 g • Carbohydrates 37 g • Fiber 4.7 g • Total fat 9 g • Saturated fat 1.3 g • Cholesterol 2 mg • Sodium 189 mg • **PREP TIME** 5 minutes • **COOK TIME** 20 minutes (roast the garlic while making the remainder of the dish) • **MAKE AHEAD** Can be prepared up to a day in advance, then gently reheated on top of the stove. • **NUTRITION WATCH** White kidney beans are a very good source of thiamin (vitamin B1).

roasted mini potatoes parmesan { *Serves 6*

1½ lb mini red or white potatoes, cut in half
1 Tbsp olive oil
¼ tsp kosher salt
1 cup tomato sauce (see page 334) (or store-bought spaghetti sauce)
½ cup shredded mozzarella cheese
1 Tbsp grated Parmesan cheese

ROASTED POTATOES CAN GET PRETTY MUNDANE after you've had them time and time again, so I created this unusual but delicious recipe. Kids love these!

1. Preheat the oven to 400°F. Line a baking sheet with foil and lightly coat with cooking spray.
2. Place the potatoes flat side down on the baking sheet. Brush with half of the oil and sprinkle with half of the salt. Bake for 15 minutes. Turn over, brush with the remaining oil and sprinkle with the remaining salt. Bake for another 15 minutes or until the potatoes are just tender.
3. Pour ¾ cup of the tomato sauce in the bottom of a 9-inch-square baking dish. Place the roasted potatoes flat side up on top of the tomato sauce. Sprinkle both of the cheeses over the top, then drizzle with the remaining tomato sauce. Bake for 10 minutes or until the cheese melts.

PER SERVING Calories 156 • Protein 6 g • Carbohydrates 23 g • Fiber 1.7 g • Total fat 4 g • Saturated fat 1.4 g • Cholesterol 6 mg • Sodium 200 mg • **PREP TIME** 5 minutes • **BAKE TIME** 40 minutes • **MAKE AHEAD** Prepare up to a day in advance. Reheat in a 350°F oven for 10 minutes or until warm. • **NUTRITION WATCH** Nutritionally, kosher salt is no different from table salt, although kosher salt does not provide iodine. You tend to use less since the grains are larger, therefore reducing the sodium.

southwestern baked potato skins { *Serves 4*

4 russet potatoes
2 tsp vegetable oil
1 cup diced onion
½ cup diced red bell pepper
2 tsp finely chopped jalapeño pepper
1 tsp finely chopped garlic
1 cup canned black beans, drained and rinsed
¾ cup medium salsa
⅓ cup chopped green onions
¼ cup chopped cilantro
¾ cup shredded aged cheddar cheese
¼ cup low-fat sour cream

POTATO SKINS ARE OFTEN SERVED in restaurants and are loaded with fat and calories from the excess oil and cheese. Sometimes they are even deep fried. I created this Tex Mex recipe for the skins to make a filling side dish or even main dish.

1. Preheat the oven to 450°F.
2. Wrap the potatoes in foil and bake directly on the oven rack for 45 to 50 minutes. Alternatively, prick each potato with a fork several times and microwave on High for 10 minutes or until soft.
3. When the potatoes are cool enough to handle, carefully scoop out the flesh, leaving about ¼ inch of potato and the skin intact. Save the potato flesh for another purpose.
4. Lightly coat a small skillet with cooking spray, add the oil and set over medium heat. Add the onion and sauté for 5 minutes. Add the red pepper, jalapeño and garlic, and sauté for 3 minutes or just until soft. Transfer to a large mixing bowl.
5. Add the black beans, salsa, green onions and cilantro, and stir to combine. Fill the potato skins with the bean filling and sprinkle with the cheese. Bake for 10 minutes or just until heated through and the cheese is melted. Serve with sour cream.

PER SERVING Calories 317 • Protein 11 g • Carbohydrates 46 g • Fiber 8.9 g • Total fat 11 g • Saturated fat 5.4 g • Cholesterol 24 mg • Sodium 375 mg • **PREP TIME** 10 minutes • **BAKE TIME** 60 minutes • **MAKE AHEAD** Bake the potatoes up to a day in advance. Complete the recipe just before serving. • **NUTRITION WATCH** Potato skins are loaded with fiber and antioxidants that can help reduce the risk of heart disease and cancer. Even if I'm boiling potatoes I keep the skin on.

fingerling potatoes with olive oil and sea salt { *Serves 6 to 8*

2 lb fingerling or small roasting potatoes
2 Tbsp olive oil
1½ Tbsp chopped fresh rosemary
½ tsp sea salt
pinch of coarsely ground pepper
3 Tbsp chopped parsley

POTATOES ARE A STAPLE in many homes as a vegetable accompaniment. But these fingerling ones can become addictive! I've been enjoying experimenting with them lately. They're small but long, with golden flesh. Just delicious when roasted. Use small red or white roasting potatoes if you cannot find fingerling. (Pictured on page 297.)

1. Preheat the oven to 425°F. Line a baking sheet with foil and lightly coat with cooking spray.
2. Wash the potatoes well. Cut the potatoes in half lengthwise and place in a large bowl. Add the olive oil, rosemary, salt and pepper and toss to combine. Place the potatoes on the lined baking sheet and bake for 30 minutes, turning halfway through the baking time. Garnish with chopped parsley and serve.

PER SERVING (BASED ON 6 SERVINGS) Calories 172 • Protein 4 g • Carbohydrates 27 g • Fiber 2 g • Total fat 5 g • Saturated fat 0.7 g • Cholesterol 0 mg • Sodium 160 mg • **PREP TIME** 10 minutes • **BAKE TIME** 30 minutes • **MAKE AHEAD** Can be prepared early in the day and reheated in a 300°F oven for 20 minutes. • **NUTRITION WATCH** Sea salt and table salt have the same nutritional value. However, fine sea salt tastes saltier than table salt, and therefore you are able to use less of it.

{ *grains & pasta* }

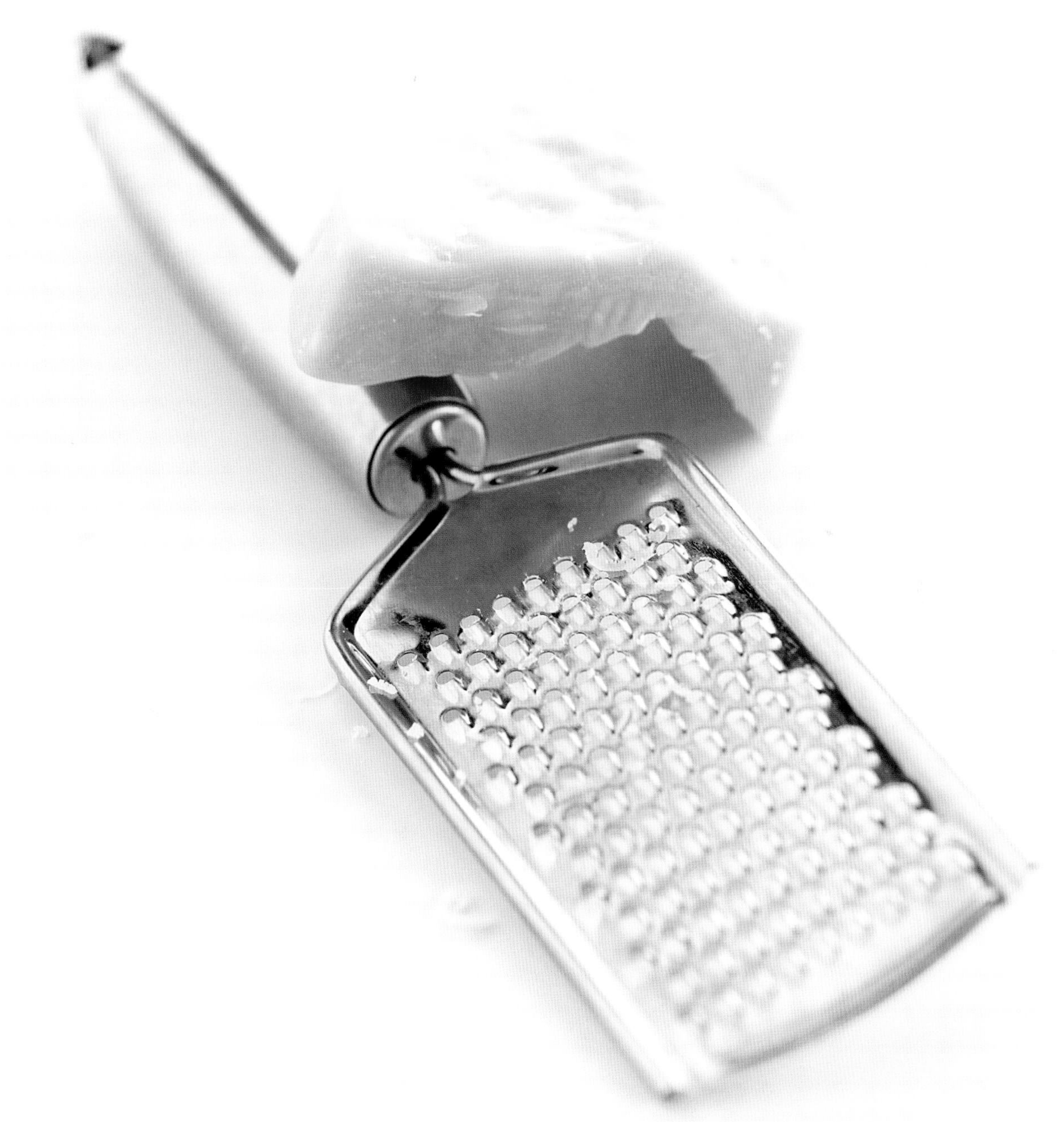

Cook pasta in a large pot of boiling water. Use 12 to 16 cups water for each pound of pasta. Add a little oil or vegetable spray to prevent pasta from sticking • Stir pasta occasionally while cooking • Cook pasta al dente, that is, firm to the bite • When cooking time is over, drain in a colander then transfer to a serving dish. Add sauce immediately and toss • Plan ahead so the sauce will be completed at the same time the pasta is cooked. Do not add sauce to pasta until you are ready to serve, or the pasta will absorb the sauce • You can prepare the pasta earlier in the day if necessary. Ensure the pasta does not stick to itself, by draining the cooked pasta, rinsing with cold water and adding 3 Tbsp of stock, the sauce or the water in which the pasta was cooked. Let sit at room temperature. Before serving, either warm slightly in a microwave for 1 minute at High (be careful not to overcook the pasta), or heat sauce thoroughly in a saucepan and pour over pasta • Do not overcook rice or other grains or they will become too soft. Wild rice begins to fall apart when overcooked • Grains are wonderfully versatile. By adding vegetables, cheese, meat, fish or poultry, these foods can become an entire meal. They can be served as salads, appetizers, main entrées or side dishes and can be eaten warm or cold

couscous with broccoli and sun-dried tomatoes { *Serves 4*

1 cup chicken (or vegetable) stock
1 cup couscous
1 cup chopped broccoli
⅓ cup diced rehydrated sun-dried tomatoes
1 cup diced Roma tomatoes
2 Tbsp olive oil
1 tsp finely chopped garlic
½ tsp hot chili sauce
⅓ cup crumbled goat cheese (about 1½ oz)
pinch of salt and pepper
¼ cup chopped fresh basil or cilantro

COUSCOUS HAS TO BE THE FASTEST FOOD to prepare—it only takes 5 minutes. The key is not to boil it, but rather to add it to boiling stock and then let it sit (off the heat) for 5 minutes. Look for whole wheat couscous, which is delicious and more nutritious. And instead of buying sun-dried tomatoes packed in oil, always purchase *dry* sun-dried tomatoes. Rehydrate them by simply placing them in boiling water for 10 minutes. Drain then chop.

1. Bring the chicken stock to a boil in a large saucepan. Add the couscous, stir and remove from the heat. Cover and let it sit for 5 minutes. Fluff with a fork and place in a serving bowl.
2. Steam or boil the broccoli for 3 minutes or until just tender. Drain and add to the couscous along with the sun-dried tomatoes, Roma tomatoes, olive oil, garlic, chili sauce, goat cheese, salt and pepper. Toss, garnish with the basil or cilantro and serve warm.

PER SERVING Calories 274 • Protein 9 g • Carbohydrates 39 g • Fiber 3.7 g • Total fat 9.1 g • Saturated fat 2.1 g • Cholesterol 3 mg • Sodium 318 mg • **PREP TIME** 10 minutes • **COOK TIME** 8 minutes • **MAKE AHEAD** Can be prepared the day before and gently reheated on top of the stove. • **NUTRITION WATCH** Couscous is a very good source of selenium. Whole wheat couscous is an excellent source of fiber, having 6 g per ¼ cup serving.

israeli couscous with roma tomatoes, three cheeses and basil { *Serves 4*

1 cup Israeli couscous
1 cup diced Roma tomatoes
¼ cup crumbled goat cheese (about 1 oz)
½ cup shredded havarti
⅓ cup chopped green onions
⅓ cup chopped fresh basil or parsley
2 Tbsp grated Parmesan (or Asiago) cheese
1 Tbsp olive oil
1 tsp finely chopped garlic
pinch of salt and pepper

ISRAELI COUSCOUS IS A SMALL, round semolina pasta, different from the tiny, yellow North African couscous. It's often referred to as pearl pasta because of its shape and texture. Although it is becoming more readily available, you may have to go to a specialty store to purchase it. You can substitute it with another very small-shaped pasta.

Bring a large pot of salted water to a boil and add the Israeli couscous. Boil for about 8 minutes or just until couscous is tender. Drain well and add to a serving bowl. Add the tomatoes, goat cheese, havarti, green onions, basil or parsley, Parmesan, olive oil, garlic, salt and pepper. Toss well and serve warm.

PER SERVING Calories 265 • Protein 12 g • Carbohydrates 34 g • Fiber 4.5 g • Total fat 11 g • Saturated fat 5.4 g • Cholesterol 19 mg • Sodium 300 mg • **PREP TIME** 15 minutes • **COOK TIME** 8 minutes • **MAKE AHEAD** Chop and combine all the ingredients except the couscous early in the day. Cook couscous and add to remaining ingredients just before serving. • **NUTRITION WATCH** One-third of a cup of Israeli couscous supplies 100% of the recommended intake for vitamin A. Vitamin A helps in promoting good eye health.

wheat berry pilaf with dried fruit and orange dressing { *Serves 4*

PILAF

1 cup wheat berries

3 cups vegetable (or chicken) stock

1 tsp vegetable oil

½ cup finely chopped onion

⅓ cup finely chopped red bell pepper

⅓ cup dried cranberries

⅓ cup chopped dried dates

⅓ cup chopped cilantro or parsley

¼ cup chopped toasted almonds

ORANGE DRESSING

1½ tsp olive oil

1½ tsp thawed orange juice concentrate

1½ tsp lemon juice

1 tsp low-sodium soy sauce

1 tsp balsamic vinegar

1 tsp sesame oil

½ tsp finely chopped garlic

WHEAT BERRY IS A HUSKED WHOLE KERNEL of wheat with its nutritious bran intact. It has a chewy, nutty texture. I buy it in bulk and keep it in my freezer.

1. Add the wheat berries and stock to a saucepan and bring to a boil. Reduce the heat to low, cover and cook for 45 to 50 minutes or until the wheat berries are tender but still chewy. Drain any excess liquid and place in a serving bowl.
2. Meanwhile, lightly coat a small nonstick skillet with cooking spray, add the oil and set over medium heat. Add the onion and sauté for 3 minutes or until just tender. Add the red pepper and sauté for 2 more minutes. Add to the serving bowl along with the cranberries, dates, cilantro or parsley and almonds.
3. To make the dressing, combine the olive oil, orange juice concentrate, lemon juice, soy sauce, balsamic vinegar, sesame oil and garlic. Pour the dressing over the wheat berry mixture, toss to coat and serve warm.

PER SERVING Calories 335 • Protein 12 g • Carbohydrates 58 g • Fiber 9 g • Total fat 8.5 g • Saturated fat 0.8 g • Cholesterol 0 mg • Sodium 400 mg • **PREP TIME** 20 minutes • **COOK TIME** 45 minutes • **MAKE AHEAD** Can be prepared a day in advance and reheated gently on top of the stove. • **NUTRITION WATCH** A cup of cooked wheat berries has about 300 calories and is packed with fiber, protein and iron.

wild mushroom risotto with parmesan and asparagus { *Serves 4*

2 tsp vegetable oil
1 cup finely chopped onion
2 tsp finely chopped garlic
4 cups chopped wild mushrooms (try oyster, shiitake and/or portobello)
1 cup arborio rice
3½ cups vegetable (or chicken) stock
1 cup chopped asparagus (cut into 1-inch pieces)
⅓ cup grated Parmesan cheese
pinch of salt and pepper
¼ cup chopped fresh basil

I LOVE RISOTTOS but the restaurant versions are loaded with butter, cream or cheese. This risotto is easy to make and has little fat and few calories by comparison. For a more elegant risotto try substituting truffle oil for the olive oil.

1. Lightly coat a saucepan with cooking spray, add the oil and set over medium-high heat. Add the onion and garlic, and sauté for 5 minutes or until the onions are just tender and lightly browned. Add the mushrooms and sauté for about 8 minutes or until the mushrooms are no longer wet.
2. Add the arborio rice and sauté for 1 minute. Add 1 cup of the stock and simmer until the stock has just been absorbed. Continue adding ½ cup stock at a time, stirring until absorbed; repeat until all the stock has been used (about 20 minutes in total). Add the chopped asparagus with the last ½ cup stock and cook until the asparagus is tender-crisp, about 3 minutes, and the liquid is absorbed.
3. Add all but 2 Tbsp of the grated Parmesan cheese and the salt and pepper and mix well. Garnish with the remaining Parmesan and the basil. Serve warm.

PER SERVING Calories 196 • Protein 11 g • Carbohydrates 29 g • Fiber 3 g • Total fat 4.9 g • Saturated fat 1.4 g • Cholesterol 5 mg • Sodium 450 mg • **PREP TIME** 10 minutes • **COOK TIME** about 35 minutes • **MAKE AHEAD** A classic risotto is always best made just before serving, but the onions and mushrooms can be prepared early in the day. • **NUTRITION WATCH** One cup of arborio rice is a good source of iron, which is important for providing active children with energy.

orzo with cherry tomatoes, olives and goat cheese { *Serves 4*

1 cup grape tomatoes, cut into quarters
⅓ cup finely chopped sweet yellow onion
⅓ cup sliced black olives
3 Tbsp grated Parmesan cheese
2 Tbsp olive oil
1½ Tbsp lemon juice
1½ tsp finely chopped garlic
½ tsp Dijon mustard
½ tsp hot chili sauce (or finely chopped jalapeño pepper)
½ cup crumbled goat cheese (about 2 oz)
2 anchovy fillets, diced
1⅓ cups orzo
½ cup chopped fresh basil

ORZO IS A RICE-SHAPED PASTA that cooks in about 8 minutes and makes for a quick, easy meal. It suits a tomato and cheese–based sauce.

1. Combine the tomatoes, onion, olives, Parmesan, olive oil, lemon juice, garlic, mustard, chili sauce, goat cheese and anchovies in a large bowl.
2. In a medium pot of boiling water, cook the orzo for 8 minutes or until just tender. Drain well and add to the tomato mixture. Toss well and garnish with fresh basil. Serve warm.

PER SERVING Calories 366 • Protein 14 g • Carbohydrates 47 g • Fiber 3 g • Total fat 14 g • Saturated fat 4.4 g • Cholesterol 12 mg • Sodium 341 mg • **PREP TIME** 15 minutes • **COOK TIME** 8 minutes • **MAKE AHEAD** Combine all the ingredients except for the orzo and basil early in the day. Cook orzo just before serving, add to the sauce and garnish with basil. • **NUTRITION WATCH** A ½ cup of plain, cooked orzo delivers 210 calories, 1 gram of fat, 41 g of carbohydrates and 7 g of protein.

soba noodles with creamy peanut-tahini dressing { *Serves 4*

PEANUT-TAHINI DRESSING

- 1 Tbsp tahini (sesame seed paste)
- 3 Tbsp natural peanut butter
- 3 Tbsp vegetable (or chicken) stock
- 1½ Tbsp low-sodium soy sauce
- 1 Tbsp rice vinegar
- 1 Tbsp honey
- 2 tsp sesame oil
- ½ tsp hot chili sauce
- 1 tsp finely chopped garlic
- 1 tsp finely chopped ginger

NOODLES

- ½ cup thinly sliced red pepper (about 1 small roasted red pepper) (see page 100)
- ½ cup thinly sliced yellow bell pepper
- 1 cup thinly sliced sugar snap peas
- 8 oz buckwheat noodles
- ¼ cup chopped green onions
- ⅓ cup chopped cilantro
- 2 Tbsp chopped toasted peanuts
- 1 tsp toasted sesame seeds

SOBA IS A TYPE OF THIN JAPANESE NOODLE made from buckwheat flour. It has a nutty flavor and firm texture and goes beautifully with this peanut-tahini sauce and sautéed vegetables.

1. To make the dressing, whisk together the tahini, peanut butter, stock, soy sauce, rice vinegar, honey, sesame oil, chili sauce, garlic and ginger in a small bowl. Set aside.
2. Lightly coat a nonstick skillet with cooking spray. Add the red and yellow peppers and sugar snap peas. Sauté for 2 minutes. Place in large serving bowl.
3. Cook the noodles according to the package directions. Drain well and add to the vegetables.
4. Pour the dressing over the noodles, toss and garnish with the green onions, cilantro, peanuts and sesame seeds. Serve warm or at room temperature.

PER SERVING Calories 400 • Protein 11 g • Carbohydrates 56 g • Fiber 2.6 g • Total fat 15 g • Saturated fat 1.9 g • Cholesterol 0 mg • Sodium 286 mg • **PREP TIME** 15 minutes • **COOK TIME** 10 minutes • **MAKE AHEAD** If you rinse the noodles with cold water you can prepare this dish up to a day in advance and serve at room temperature. • **NUTRITION WATCH** Soba noodles are low in calories, cholesterol and saturated fat and contain complex carbohydrates that are heart healthy.

shrimp fried rice with edamame { *Serves 6*

SAUCE

⅓ cup chicken stock
3 Tbsp low-sodium soy sauce
1 Tbsp sesame oil
1 tsp hot chili sauce

RICE

1½ cups white rice
1½ cups chicken stock
2 tsp vegetable oil
1 cup chopped onion
1½ tsp finely chopped garlic
1½ tsp finely chopped ginger
4 oz raw shrimp, peeled, deveined and diced (or kept whole)
1 cup frozen shelled edamame
½ cup grated carrots
½ cup chopped green onions

FRIED RICE IN ASIAN RESTAURANTS is often made with lard or excess oil, adding enormous amounts of calories and fat. In my recipe I use a stock-based sauce that only uses 1 Tbsp of flavored sesame oil. And instead of the traditional green peas, I have used edamame, which are Japanese soybeans.

1. To make the sauce, whisk together the chicken stock, soy sauce, sesame oil and chili sauce in a small bowl. Set aside.
2. Add the rice to the stock and bring to a boil. Reduce the heat to low, cover and simmer for 10 minutes. Remove from the heat and let sit for 10 minutes, covered.
3. Lightly coat a large, nonstick skillet or wok with cooking spray, add the oil and set over medium-high heat. Add the onion and sauté for 5 minutes or until it is softened. Add the garlic and ginger and sauté for 1 more minute. Add the shrimp and edamame and sauté for 3 minutes or until the shrimp just turns pink. Stir in the carrots and green onions.
4. Add the cooked rice to the shrimp mixture. Add the sauce and stir-fry for 2 minutes, or until everything is warmed through and the rice is coated with the sauce. Serve hot.

PER SERVING Calories 309 • Protein 12 g • Carbohydrates 52 g • Fiber 1.8 g • Total fat 5.4 g • Saturated fat 0.6 g • Cholesterol 28 mg • Sodium 459 mg • **PREP TIME** 15 minutes • **COOK TIME** 21 minutes • **MAKE AHEAD** Prepare up to a day in advance and reheat gently on top of the stove. • **NUTRITION WATCH** The vegetable oil I like to use is canola oil, which is very low in saturated fat and has a very high proportion of monounsaturated fat.

wild mushroom cannelloni with tomato sauce { *Serves 4*

8 cannelloni shells
2 tsp vegetable oil
1 cup finely chopped onion
2 tsp finely chopped garlic
2½ cups chopped wild mushrooms (try oyster, shiitake and/or portobello)
1 cup light ricotta (5%)
½ cup shredded low-fat mozzarella cheese
¼ cup + 1 Tbsp grated low-fat Parmesan cheese
1 large egg
2 Tbsp low-fat milk
pinch of salt and pepper
1½ cups tomato sauce (see page 334) (or store-bought spaghetti sauce)
3 Tbsp low-fat milk

CHEESE-STUFFED CANNELLONI are traditionally served in Italian restaurants. I took the basic idea, adding a variety of sautéed mushrooms. The dish, baked with a tomato sauce, is superb. Use any variety of mushrooms you prefer—just remember to sauté them until all the liquid evaporates.

1. Preheat the oven to 350°F.
2. In a large pot of boiling water, cook the cannelloni shells for 10 minutes or until just tender. Drain, rinse under cold running water and set aside.
3. Lightly coat a large, nonstick skillet with cooking spray, add the oil and set over medium-high heat. Add the onion and garlic, and sauté for 5 minutes. Add the mushrooms and continue to sauté over medium-high heat for 8 minutes or until softened. Place in a large mixing bowl. Set aside.
4. Place the ricotta, mozzarella and ¼ cup Parmesan cheese in the bowl of a food processor. Add the egg, milk, salt and pepper, and purée. Add the cheese mixture to the mushroom mixture and pulse on and off until chunky.
5. Cut 1 side of each cannelloni tube open, lay flat and place about 3 Tbsp of mushroom filling in the middle. Roll to close and repeat with the remaining shells.
6. To make the sauce, whisk together the tomato sauce and milk in a bowl, and pour about three-quarters of it over the bottom of a 9- × 13-inch casserole dish. Arrange the filled cannelloni (cut side down) in the casserole dish. Cover the cannelloni with the remaining sauce and sprinkle with the 1 Tbsp of Parmesan cheese.
7. Cover the dish with foil and bake in the preheated oven for about 20 minutes or until the dish is heated through. Serve hot.

• • • • • • •

PER SERVING Calories 389 • Protein 23 g • Carbohydrates 48 g • Fiber 3 g • Total fat 12 g • Saturated fat 5.2 g • Cholesterol 84 mg • Sodium 540 mg • **PREP TIME** 20 minutes • **COOK TIME** 45 minutes • **MAKE AHEAD** Prepare up to a day in advance and reheat in a 350°F oven for 15 minutes. • **NUTRITION WATCH** 1 oz of ricotta cheese has 39 calories and about 3 g of fat, whereas 1 oz of cream cheese has about 100 calories and 10 g of fat.

light fettuccine alfredo with sugar snap peas and red bell pepper { *Serves 4*

½ lb fettuccine
1 cup cold chicken (or vegetable) stock
¾ cup canned evaporated milk (2%)
½ tsp Dijon mustard
½ tsp pepper
1 tsp finely chopped garlic
2 Tbsp all-purpose flour
¼ cup light cream cheese (about 2 oz)
6 Tbsp grated Parmesan cheese
1 cup thinly sliced snow peas
1 cup thinly sliced red bell pepper
2 Tbsp chopped parsley

FETTUCCINE ALFREDO, better known as "heart attack on a plate," is definitely not recommended on a regular basis due to the amount of cheese and butter it contains. The sauce in this version, however, uses stock, evaporated milk and light cream cheese, and it's really delicious.

1. Bring a large pot of water to a boil. Add the fettuccine and cook for 8 to 10 minutes or until just tender. Drain and place in a large serving bowl. Cover to keep warm.
2. Meanwhile, in a saucepan off the heat, combine the stock, evaporated milk, mustard, pepper and garlic. Slowly whisk in the flour until smooth. Place the saucepan over medium heat and bring to a slight boil. Reduce the heat and simmer, whisking constantly, for 4 to 5 minutes or until slightly thickened. Remove from the heat and whisk in the cream cheese and 4 Tbsp of the Parmesan cheese, whisking just until the cheese is melted. Set aside.
3. Lightly coat a nonstick skillet with cooking spray and set over medium-high heat. Add the peas and bell pepper and sauté for 2 minutes or until warm but still crisp. Add to the cooked fettuccine, pour the sauce over the pasta and toss. Garnish with the remaining 2 Tbsp of Parmesan cheese and parsley. Serve immediately.

PER SERVING Calories 345 • Protein 18 g • Carbohydrates 55 g • Fiber 2.9 g • Total fat 6 g • Saturated fat 3.4 g • Cholesterol 15 mg • Sodium 244 mg • **PREP TIME** 10 minutes • **COOK TIME** 20 minutes • **MAKE AHEAD** Sauce can be made early in the day; reheat gently adding more stock if necessary. Prepare the vegetables and pasta just before serving. • **NUTRITION WATCH** Green peas are a very good source of thiamin (vitamin B1), as well as a good source of vitamin B6, riboflavin (vitamin B2) and niacin (vitamin B3). All of these vitamins are important for carbohydrate, protein and lipid metabolism.

traditional spaghetti and meatballs { *Serves 4*

1 lb lean ground beef
¼ cup seasoned dry breadcrumbs
¼ cup finely chopped green onions
¼ cup barbecue sauce
1 egg
2 tsp finely chopped garlic
1 tsp dried basil
3 cups tomato sauce (see page 334) (or store-bought spaghetti sauce)
½ lb spaghetti noodles
¼ cup grated Parmesan cheese
3 Tbsp chopped fresh basil

EVERYONE NEEDS A GREAT SPAGHETTI and meatball recipe. I love the flavor and simplicity of this dish. Try to use whole wheat spaghetti for the extra nutrients it offers.

1. Preheat the oven to 425°F. Line a baking sheet with foil lightly coated with cooking spray.
2. To make the meatballs, combine the ground beef, breadcrumbs, green onions, barbecue sauce, egg, garlic and dried basil. Form into about thirty 1-inch-round meatballs. Place on the baking sheet and bake for about 12 minutes, turning halfway through the cooking time.
3. Place the tomato sauce in a large saucepan and add the cooked meatballs. Bring to a boil over medium-high heat, reduce the heat and simmer, covered, for about 15 minutes, stirring occasionally.
4. Meanwhile, bring a large pot of water to a boil. Add the spaghetti and cook according to the package directions. Drain and serve immediately, with the meatballs and sauce spooned over the spaghetti. Garnish with Parmesan and fresh basil.

PER SERVING Calories 482 • Protein 39 g • Carbohydrates 64 g • Fiber 9.9 g • Total fat 9.2 g • Saturated fat 3.3 g • Cholesterol 119 mg • Sodium 510 mg • **PREP TIME** 15 minutes • **COOK TIME** 40 minutes • **MAKE AHEAD** Prepare the meatballs up to a day in advance. • **NUTRITION WATCH** 4 oz of extra-lean (95%) ground beef contains about 185 calories, 6.7 g of fat and 30 g of protein, whereas lean ground beef (85%) contains about 300 calories, 18 g of fat and 27 g of protein. The leaner the meat, the fewer the calories and fat it has, but the protein content stays relatively the same. Opt for extra-lean ground beef.

mushroom and spinach miniature lasagna rolls { *Serves 4*

8 lasagna noodles
2 tsp vegetable oil
1½ cups finely chopped onion
2 tsp finely chopped garlic
3 cups chopped mushrooms
4 cups fresh baby spinach
¾ cup light ricotta (5%)
⅔ cup shredded mozzarella cheese
⅓ cup grated Parmesan cheese
½ tsp Dijon mustard
pinch of salt and pepper
1⅓ cups tomato sauce (see page 334) (or store-bought spaghetti sauce)
3 Tbsp shredded mozzarella cheese

INSTEAD OF MAKING THE USUAL LASAGNA, in which leftovers often seem to go to waste, I opted for this version. I love the idea of rolling cooked lasagna sheets to make individual servings. This is a great vegetarian dish that has all the nutrients you need.

1. Preheat the oven to 400°F.
2. Bring a large pot of water to a boil. Add the lasagna noodles and cook for about 8 minutes or until the noodles are just tender, stirring often but carefully. Drain and rinse with cold water. Set aside.
3. Lightly coat a large, nonstick skillet with cooking spray, add the oil and set over medium-high heat. Add the onion and garlic and sauté for 5 minutes. Add the mushrooms and sauté for 5 more minutes or just until the mushrooms are no longer wet. Add the spinach and allow the spinach to wilt, about 3 minutes. Remove the skillet from the heat and add the ricotta, mozzarella and Parmesan cheeses, mustard, salt and pepper.
4. Place the mixture in the bowl of a food processor and pulse on and off until it is uniformly chopped.
5. Pour 1 cup of the tomato sauce into a 9- × 13-inch or 11- × 7-inch casserole dish. Spread about ¼ cup of the cheese mixture along the length of each sheet. Roll up each noodle and cut in half. Place in baking dish with the ruffled side of lasagna facing up. Pour the remaining ⅓ cup of the tomato sauce over and sprinkle with the grated mozzarella cheese. Cover with foil and bake for 20 to 25 minutes or just until heated through and the cheese is melted. Serve hot.

PER SERVING Calories 304 • Protein 18 g • Carbohydrates 40 g • Fiber 3.7 g • Total fat 9 g • Saturated fat 3.7 g • Cholesterol 22 mg • Sodium 500 mg • **PREP TIME** 20 minutes • **COOK TIME** 45 minutes • **MAKE AHEAD** Prepare up to a day in advance and reheat in a 350°F oven for 10 minutes or just until warmed through. • **NUTRITION WATCH** A carotenoid found in spinach may help combat prostate cancer.

sun-dried tomato and goat cheese lasagna { *Serves 6*

6 lasagna noodles

TOMATO SAUCE

⅔ cup chopped rehydrated sun-dried tomatoes
⅓ cup chicken (or vegetable) stock
2 Tbsp olive oil
2 Tbsp grated Parmesan cheese
2 Tbsp toasted pine nuts (or pecans)
1 tsp finely chopped garlic
½ cup chopped parsley

FILLING

1 cup light ricotta (5%)
¾ cup crumbled goat cheese (about 3 oz)
½ cup shredded mozzarella cheese
2 Tbsp grated Parmesan cheese
¼ cup low-fat milk
pinch of salt and pepper
⅓ cup diced black olives

WHITE SAUCE

⅔ cup chicken (or vegetable) stock
⅔ cup canned evaporated milk (2%)
1 tsp Dijon mustard
1½ Tbsp all-purpose flour
2 Tbsp grated Parmesan cheese

TOPPING

¼ cup chopped rehydrated sun-dried tomatoes
2 Tbsp crumbled goat cheese
¼ cup chopped parsley

THE COMBINATION OF SUN-DRIED TOMATOES and goat cheese never misses. I love this lasagna, which combines both flavors. This is a complete meal on its own along with a large salad.

1. Preheat oven to 375°F.
2. Bring a large pot of water to a boil. Add the lasagna noodles and cook for about 8 minutes or until tender. Drain and rinse with cold water. Set aside.
3. To make the sun-dried tomato sauce, combine the sun-dried tomatoes, chicken stock, olive oil, Parmesan, pine nuts, garlic and parsley in the bowl of small food processor. Purée until smooth and set aside. The mixture will be thick. (Add more stock if it's too thick.)
4. To make the cheese filling, combine the ricotta, goat, mozzarella and Parmesan cheeses, milk, salt and pepper in the bowl of a food processor. Purée until smooth and set aside. Fold in the olives.
5. To make the white sauce, combine the chicken stock, evaporated milk and Dijon in a saucepan. Whisk in the flour until smooth. Place the saucepan over medium heat and bring to a slight boil. Reduce the heat and simmer for 2 minutes or just until thickened, whisking constantly. Add the Parmesan and stir.
6. To assemble the lasagna, cut 2 noodles to fit the bottom of a 9-inch-square casserole dish. Top with one-third of the white sauce, one-half of the cheese filling and one-half of the sun-dried tomato sauce. Repeat the layers once. Top with the remaining noodles and remaining white sauce. Sprinkle with the chopped sun-dried tomatoes and goat cheese. Bake, covered, in the preheated oven for 20 minutes, and then uncovered for 10 minutes. Garnish with parsley and serve.

PER SERVING Calories 332 • Protein 19 g • Carbohydrates 25 g • Fiber 2.1 g • Total fat 18 g • Saturated fat 7 g • Cholesterol 31 mg • Sodium 589 mg • **PREP TIME** 25 minutes • **COOK TIME** 45 minutes • **MAKE AHEAD** Prepare up to a day in advance, but it's best to bake just before serving. • **NUTRITION WATCH** Pine nuts have fatty acids that may help stave off appetite.

creamy baked macaroni and cheese casserole { *Serves 6*

2 Tbsp all-purpose flour
¾ cup chicken (or vegetable) stock
¾ cup canned evaporated milk (2%)
¾ cup shredded aged light cheddar cheese
3 Tbsp grated Parmesan cheese
½ tsp Dijon mustard
1¾ cups elbow macaroni
¾ cup diced cooked chicken
¼ cup seasoned dry breadcrumbs
1 Tbsp grated Parmesan cheese
2 tsp olive oil
¼ cup shredded aged light cheddar cheese
3 Tbsp chopped parsley

ENJOY THIS CLASSIC COMFORT FOOD—without the guilt. I often make it and freeze individual servings in plastic containers, which are perfect for lunches. It's kids' favorite pasta dish, and when they prefer it to any of the boxed versions, you know their taste buds are tuned in to health! Feel free to add some vegetables—green peas, diced bell pepper or carrots look and taste great.

1. Preheat the oven to 425°F. Lightly coat a 9- × 13-inch casserole dish with cooking spray.
2. Whisk together the flour, stock and milk in a saucepan until smooth. Place over medium heat and cook, whisking constantly, for about 3 minutes or until the mixture is hot and thickened. Stir in the ¾ cup cheddar and Parmesan cheeses and the mustard. Cook until the cheese melts, about 1 minute. Remove from the heat.
3. Meanwhile, bring a large pot of water to a boil. Add the macaroni and cook for about 8 to 10 minutes, until tender but still firm. Drain well and place in the casserole dish. Add the cheese sauce and chicken and toss to combine.
4. To make the topping, combine the breadcrumbs, Parmesan and oil in a small bowl. Sprinkle evenly over the macaroni and top with the remaining ¼ cup cheddar cheese.
5. Bake in the center of the preheated oven for 10 to 15 minutes or until the filling is hot and the top is golden. Garnish with the parsley and serve.

PER SERVING Calories 321 • Protein 25 g • Carbohydrates 37 g • Fiber 1.6 g • Total fat 9 g • Saturated fat 3.9 g • Cholesterol 41 mg • Sodium 390 mg • **PREP TIME** 15 minutes • **COOK TIME** 25 minutes • **MAKE AHEAD** Prepare the entire dish a day in advance and refrigerate. Add 10 minutes to the cooking time, and garnish just before serving. • **NUTRITION WATCH** If you don't take the skin off the chicken, it will add 60 calories and 5.5 g of fat—mostly saturated.

small-shell pasta beefaroni { *Serves 6*

8 oz small-shell pasta

MEAT SAUCE

1 tsp vegetable oil
⅔ cup finely chopped onion
1½ tsp finely chopped garlic
8 oz lean ground beef
1 cup tomato sauce (see page 334) (or store-bought spaghetti sauce)

CHEESE SAUCE

1¼ cups canned evaporated milk (2%)
¾ cup beef (or chicken) stock
½ tsp Dijon mustard
2 Tbsp all-purpose flour
½ cup shredded aged cheddar cheese
2 Tbsp grated Parmesan cheese
2 Tbsp chopped parsley

BETTER THAN ANY PACKAGED version of beef and pasta. The combination of the meat and cheese sauce is fantastic.

1. Preheat the oven to 425°F. Lightly coat a 9- × 13-inch casserole dish with cooking spray.
2. Bring a large pot of water to a boil. Add the pasta and cook for 8 to 10 minutes or until tender but still firm. Drain and place in the casserole dish.
3. To make the meat sauce, heat the vegetable oil in a large skillet over medium heat. Add the onion and garlic and sauté for 4 minutes or until softened. Add the ground beef and cook, stirring to break up the meat, for 4 minutes or until no longer pink. Stir in the tomato sauce, cover and cook for about 5 minutes. Set aside.
4. To make the cheese sauce, combine the milk, stock and mustard in a saucepan. Slowly whisk in the flour. Place over medium heat and stir until the mixture begins to boil. Reduce the heat to low and simmer, stirring occasionally, for 5 minutes or until the sauce is slightly thickened. Stir in the cheddar cheese and half the Parmesan cheese and stir until melted. Remove from the heat and add to the meat sauce.
5. Pour the sauce over the cooked pasta and stir to combine. Sprinkle with the remaining Parmesan and bake in the preheated oven for 10 to 15 minutes or until completely heated through. Garnish with parsley.

PER SERVING Calories 320 • Protein 20 g • Carbohydrates 42 g • Fiber 2.1 g • Total fat 7.8 g • Saturated fat 3.7 g • Cholesterol 34 mg • Sodium 290 mg • **PREP TIME** 15 minutes • **COOK TIME** 40 minutes • **MAKE AHEAD** Make up to a day in advance and reheat in a 350°F in oven for 10 minutes. • **NUTRITION WATCH** The mustard seeds used in Dijon mustard are a very good source of omega-3 fatty acids as well as iron, calcium and zinc.

three-cheese beef lasagna { *Serves 10*

9 lasagna noodles

MEAT AND TOMATO SAUCE

- 8 oz lean ground beef
- 6 oz spicy sausage (casing removed, chopped)
- 2 tsp vegetable oil
- 1½ cups chopped onion
- 3 cloves of garlic, finely chopped
- 2 tsp dried basil, crumbled
- 1½ tsp dried oregano, crumbled
- pinch of salt and pepper
- 2 bay leaves
- 1 tsp granulated sugar
- 1½ cans (28 oz) Italian plum tomatoes, drained and puréed (42 oz altogether)
- ⅓ cup tomato paste
- 5 Tbsp grated Parmesan cheese

CHEESE FILLING

- 2 cups light ricotta (5%)
- 1 cup shredded aged white cheddar cheese
- 1 egg
- ⅓ cup canned evaporated milk (2%)
- ½ cup grated Parmesan cheese
- salt and pepper

TOPPING

- ½ cup shredded mozzarella cheese
- 2 Tbsp Parmesan cheese
- 3 Tbsp chopped fresh basil or parsley

I LOVE A GOOD OLD TRADITIONAL beef lasagna. But often the fat and calories are enormous due to the fat in the meat, the tons of cheese and the béchamel (white cream sauce). I use lean ground beef and drain both the beef and sausage fat. In the cheese layer I depend on more ricotta and evaporated milk so I don't need a béchamel sauce. If you don't have time to make the tomato sauce, replace with 6 cups of store-bought spaghetti sauce (with meat).

1. Preheat the oven to 350°F. Lightly coat a 9-×13-inch glass casserole dish with cooking spray.
2. Cook the lasagna noodles in boiling water just until tender to the bite, about 12 minutes. Drain and set aside.
3. To make the meat and tomato sauce, lightly coat a large nonstick skillet with the cooking spray. Add the ground beef and sausage and cook until brown, breaking up with fork, about 3 minutes. Using a slotted spoon, transfer the meat to a plate. Set aside.
4. Respray the pan. Add the oil, onion and garlic to skillet and sauté until the onion is tender, about 5 minutes. Return the beef and sausage to the skillet. Add the dried basil, oregano, salt, pepper, basil leaves, sugar, puréed tomatoes and tomato paste. Bring to a boil. Reduce the heat to medium-low. Cover and simmer until the sauce is thick, about 30 minutes. Add the Parmesan. Place in the bowl of a food processor and pulse on and off just until still crumbly. Do not purée.
5. To make the cheese filling, stir the ricotta, cheddar, egg, milk, Parmesan, salt and pepper together in a bowl.
6. Spread 1½ cups of the meat and tomato sauce over the bottom of the prepared casserole dish. Top with 3 noodles. Spread half of the cheese filling over the noodles. Add another 1½ cups of the meat and tomato sauce, 3 noodles and the remaining half of the filling. Add another 1½ cups sauce and the remaining 3 noodles. Finish with the remaining meat sauce. Top with the grated mozzarella and Parmesan.
7. Cover the pan tightly with foil. Bake in the center of the oven for 20 minutes, then another 15 minutes uncovered. Garnish with the basil.

PER SERVING Calories 343 • Protein 23 g • Carbohydrates 25 g • Fiber 3.0 g • Total fat 15 g • Saturated fat 7.4 g • Cholesterol 71 mg • Sodium 690 mg • **PREP TIME** 25 minutes • **COOK TIME** 65 minutes • **MAKE AHEAD** Bake the day before and reheat in a 300°F oven for 20 minutes. • **NUTRITION WATCH** One serving of traditional lasagna may have up to 700 calories, 40 g of fat and 1,130 mg of sodium. Try this lighter version instead.

{ vegetarian main dishes }

If you are planning on grilling tofu, make sure to purchase firm tofu • It's best to marinate tofu for at least 2 hours before cooking, to enhance the flavor • To ensure you're obtaining enough protein combine a grain and legume • Quinoa is the only grain that is a complete protein • Use whole wheat tortillas to get extra fiber • If there is a lot of cheese in the recipe you want to make, use lower-fat cheeses • Add beans or lentils to your soups, salads and wraps to add extra protein and fiber • Ground soy is an excellent substitute for ground beef. Use in lasagnas, pasta sauces, chilis, stews and soups

grilled tofu triangles with maple–soy sauce glaze { *Serves 4*

one 12 oz package firm tofu
3 Tbsp low-sodium soy sauce
3 Tbsp maple syrup
2 tsp cornstarch
1 tsp sesame seeds
3 Tbsp chopped cilantro or parsley

TOFU IS A SOFT, white food made of curdled soybean milk. It is delicious when sautéed and served with a flavorful sauce.

1. Cut the tofu into 2½-inch squares that are 1 inch thick.
2. Lightly coat a nonstick skillet with cooking spray and set over medium-high heat. Sauté the tofu for 4 minutes per side or until lightly browned. Place on a serving dish and keep warm.
3. To make the glaze, combine the soy sauce, maple syrup and cornstarch in a small saucepan. Whisk together until the cornstarch dissolves. Bring to a boil, then reduce the heat to low and whisk constantly for 2 minutes or until slightly thickened. Pour over the tofu and garnish with sesame seeds and cilantro.

PER SERVING Calories 115 • Protein 7 g • Carbohydrates 15 g • Fiber 0.3 g • Total fat 3.6 g • Saturated fat 0.5 g • Cholesterol 0 mg • Sodium 434 mg • **PREP TIME** 10 minutes • **COOK TIME** 10 minutes • **MAKE AHEAD** The glaze can be made up to a day in advance. • **NUTRITION WATCH** Tofu is a very good source of protein, specifically soy protein.

apricot-glazed tofu { *Serves 4*

one 12 oz package firm tofu
3 Tbsp apricot jam
1 Tbsp maple syrup
1 tsp Dijon mustard
2 tsp apple cider vinegar
2 Tbsp chopped cilantro
2 Tbsp chopped dried apricots

THIS IS A SWEET SAUCE that works well with tofu. Serve this dish over rice with some steamed bok choy.

1. Cut the tofu into 8 rectangles.
2. Lightly coat a nonstick skillet or grill pan with vegetable oil and set over medium heat. Grill the tofu until lightly browned, about 4 minutes per side.
3. To make the glaze, combine the apricot jam, maple syrup, mustard and apple cider vinegar in a small saucepan. Set over medium heat and simmer just until warm, about 2 minutes.
4. Serve the tofu drizzled with the glaze and garnished with the cilantro and apricots.

PER SERVING Calories 148 • Protein 15 g • Carbohydrates 19 g • Fiber 1.0 g • Total fat 2.3 g • Saturated fat 0.4 g • Cholesterol 0 mg • Sodium 53 mg • **PREP TIME** 10 minutes • **COOK TIME** 10 minutes • **MAKE AHEAD** The glaze can be made up to a day in advance. • **NUTRITION WATCH** Apricots are a rich source of the carotenoid lycopene, which helps fight prostate cancer.

polenta squares with roasted vegetables and goat cheese { *Serves 4*

3 cups vegetable stock
1 cup cornmeal
1 Tbsp grated Parmesan cheese
1 small head of garlic
½ medium red bell pepper
½ medium yellow bell pepper
½ medium red onion, cut into ½-inch rings
1 small zucchini, cut in half lengthwise
1 Tbsp olive oil
1 tsp balsamic vinegar
⅓ cup crumbled goat cheese (about 1½ oz)

THESE SQUARES ARE A COMPLETE MEAL in themselves, or they can be served as a side grain and vegetable dish. Substitute the vegetables and cheese of your choice.

1. Preheat the oven to 425°F.
2. Bring the stock to a boil in a large saucepan set over medium-high heat. Reduce the heat to low and gradually whisk in the cornmeal and Parmesan cheese. Cook, stirring, for about 5 minutes or until the mixture is thick and bubbly.
3. Lightly coat an 8-inch-square casserole dish with vegetable oil. Pour the polenta into the dish and smooth the top. Cover and let set while roasting the vegetables.
4. Line a large baking sheet with foil and lightly coat it with cooking spray. Cut the top off the head of the garlic so that all the cloves are exposed. Wrap in foil. Place the wrapped garlic on the baking sheet along with the bell peppers, onion rings and zucchini. Lightly coat with vegetable oil and roast in the preheated oven, turning occasionally, for 30 minutes or until tender.
5. Remove from the oven and allow to cool slightly. Squeeze the garlic cloves out of the skin and place in a large bowl. Chop the roasted vegetables and add to the bowl. Drizzle with the olive oil and balsamic vinegar.
6. Cut the set polenta into 4 squares (4 × 4 inch). Lightly coat a large, nonstick skillet with vegetable oil and set over medium-high heat. Add the polenta squares and sauté for 3 minutes or until golden. Turn and cook for 1 minute. Place the polenta onto serving plates. Top with the vegetable mixture and sprinkle with goat cheese.

PER SERVING Calories 250 • Protein 8 g • Carbohydrates 39 g • Fiber 4 g • Total fat 7.4 g • Saturated fat 2.5 g • Cholesterol 6 mg • Sodium 420 mg • **PREP TIME** 15 minutes • **COOK TIME** 40 minutes • **MAKE AHEAD** The entire dish can be prepared up to a day in advance and reheated in a 350°F oven for 10 minutes. • **NUTRITION WATCH** Cornmeal is a healthier grain than white flour or rice. It has four times the fiber of white rice.

tomatoes stuffed with barley and pesto { *Serves 6*

6 large field tomatoes
3 cups vegetable stock
1 cup pearl barley
⅔ cup diced carrots
⅔ cup diced red bell pepper
⅓ cup pesto (see page 244)
½ cup crumbled goat cheese (about 2 oz)

THIS IS A GREAT WAY to get your vegetables and grains in one dish. You can substitute tomatoes for the bell pepper as well.

1. Preheat the oven to 425°F.
2. Carefully cut the tops off the tomatoes and scoop out the flesh and seeds. Discard the flesh and seeds (or toss into a salad or stew).
3. Bring the stock to a boil in a large saucepan and add the barley. Cover, reduce the heat and simmer for about 25 minutes. Add the carrots during the last 5 minutes. Cook just until the barley is tender and the stock is completely absorbed. Place in a large bowl.
4. Add the red pepper and pesto and mix well. Stuff the tomatoes with the barley mixture. Place the stuffed tomatoes on a baking sheet and sprinkle with the goat cheese. Bake for 15 minutes or until the cheese is slightly browned and the tomatoes are heated through.

PER SERVING Calories 204 • Protein 8 g • Carbohydrates 32 g • Fiber 7 g • Total fat 6 g • Saturated fat 2.8 g • Cholesterol 6 mg • Sodium 366 mg • **PREP TIME** 15 minutes • **COOK TIME** 40 minutes • **MAKE AHEAD** Bake up to a day in advance and reheat in a 350°F oven for 10 minutes. • **NUTRITION WATCH** Barley is a good source of selenium, thiamin and fiber.

eggplant roulade { *Serves 4*

2 tsp vegetable oil
1 large eggplant
⅓ cup thinly sliced carrots (2-inch julienne)
⅓ cup thinly sliced snow peas (2-inch julienne)
⅓ cup thinly sliced red bell pepper (2-inch julienne)
¾ cup light ricotta (5%)
¼ cup crumbled goat cheese (about 1 oz)
¼ cup shredded Swiss cheese
pinch of salt and pepper
¾ cup tomato sauce (see page 334) (or store-bought spaghetti sauce)

THIS IS A VEGETARIAN DISH that we offer through Rose Reisman Catering as well as our fresh food delivery service called Personal Gourmet. It's a hit for those who want a break from meat or fish. It's also a great side dish.

1. Preheat the oven to 425°F. Lightly coat an 8-inch-square casserole dish with vegetable oil and set aside.
2. Slice the eggplant lengthwise into 8 slices, about ⅛ inch thick. Lightly coat a large, nonstick skillet or grill pan with cooking spray, add the oil and set over medium heat. Sauté the eggplant slices for about 3 minutes on each side, working in batches. Respray the pan after each batch.
3. Steam or boil the carrots for 3 minutes. Add the snow peas and red pepper during the last minute. The vegetables should be just tender. Drain and set aside in a bowl.
4. Combine the ricotta, goat cheese, Swiss cheese and salt and pepper in a separate bowl and mix well.
5. Working with the eggplant slices one at a time, spread some of the cheese mixture over each slice. Place some of the cooked mixed vegetables horizontally at the end of each slice and roll up.
6. Pour ½ cup tomato sauce in the casserole dish and place the rolled eggplant slices in the sauce, seam side down. Pour the remaining tomato sauce over the eggplant. Cover and bake for 15 minutes or until completely heated through. Serve immediately.

PER SERVING Calories 175 • Protein 11 g • Carbohydrates 16 g • Fiber 6 g • Total fat 8.2 g • Saturated fat 3.8 g • Cholesterol 21 mg • Sodium 300 mg • **PREP TIME** 20 minutes • **COOK TIME** 30 minutes • **MAKE AHEAD** Can be prepared up to a day in advance and reheated in a 350°F oven for 10 minutes. • **NUTRITION WATCH** Eggplant contains an anthocyanin phytonutrient called nasunin, an antioxidant that has been shown to protect cell membranes from damage, meaning that it helps support brain function.

mushroom barley burgers { *Serves 4*

BURGERS
- 2 cups vegetable stock (or water)
- ½ cup pearl barley
- 4 tsp vegetable oil
- 1 cup diced onion
- ½ cup diced carrots
- 2 cups diced mushrooms (any variety)
- ¾ cup seasoned dry breadcrumbs
- 1 egg
- 1½ tsp crushed garlic
- 1 tsp hot chili sauce or to taste
- ⅓ cup chopped cilantro
- 1 tsp low-sodium soy sauce
- pinch of salt and pepper

TAHINI SAUCE
- 1 Tbsp tahini (sesame seed paste)
- 1 Tbsp light mayonnaise
- ¼ cup low-fat plain yogurt
- ½ tsp crushed garlic
- 1 tsp low-sodium soy sauce
- 3 Tbsp chopped cilantro

I'VE BEEN LOOKING FOR A RECIPE for really delicious veggie burgers, and I know that this is the one. The cooked barley, mushrooms and tahini sauce are the perfect combination.

1. Bring the stock and barley to a boil, cover and simmer for 30 minutes. Drain and set aside.
2. Lightly coat a large, nonstick skillet with cooking spray and set over medium heat. Add 2 tsp of the oil and the onion and sauté for 5 minutes. Add the carrots and sauté for 3 minutes. Add the mushrooms and sauté for 8 minutes or until the vegetables are tender and no liquid remains.
3. Add the barley and vegetable mixture to the bowl of a food processor. Add the breadcrumbs, egg, garlic, chili sauce, cilantro, soy sauce and salt and pepper. Process just until still slightly coarse. Form the mixture into 4 burgers.
4. Lightly coat a large, nonstick skillet with cooking spray and set over medium-high heat. Add the remaining oil, then cook burgers for 3 minutes per side.
5. To make the sauce, whisk the tahini, mayonnaise, yogurt, garlic, soy sauce and cilantro together in a small bowl and serve with the burgers.

PER SERVING Calories 322 • Protein 10 g • Carbohydrates 46 g • Fiber 6.5 g • Total fat 11 g • Saturated fat 1.8 g • Cholesterol 55 mg • Sodium 490 mg • **PREP TIME** 15 minutes • **COOK TIME** 50 minutes • **MAKE AHEAD** Make these the day before and reheat in a 350°F oven for 10 minutes. • **NUTRITION WATCH** 1 Tbsp of regular soy sauce has 900 mg of sodium, almost an entire day's worth, while 1 Tbsp of low-sodium soy sauce has 600 mg of sodium. However, I still recommend you use the lower sodium version in moderation.

roasted vegetable wrap with artichoke and asiago spread { *Serves 8*

1 medium red bell pepper
1 medium green bell pepper
2 slices sweet onion (about ½-inch thick)
1 medium zucchini, unpeeled and cut lengthwise into 4 slices
½ cup shredded havarti
¼ cup shredded low-fat mozzarella cheese
¼ cup shredded Asiago (or Parmesan) cheese
3 Tbsp light mayonnaise
½ tsp finely chopped garlic
4 canned artichokes, drained and diced
1 Tbsp chopped parsley
4 large flour tortillas

THE ROASTED VEGETABLES go well with this intense-flavored spread. This is delicious served warm or at room temperature.

1. Preheat the oven to 425°F. Line a baking sheet with foil and lightly coat with cooking spray.
2. Place the red and green peppers and onion and zucchini slices on the baking sheet and bake for 25 minutes in the preheated oven. Turn over and bake another 10 minutes or just until tender and browned, turning occasionally. Chop the vegetables coarsely and set aside.
3. Meanwhile, prepare the spread by combining half of the havarti with the mozzarella, Asiago, mayonnaise, garlic and artichokes in the bowl of a food processor. Process until smooth. Stir in the chopped parsley and set aside.
4. Spread 2 Tbsp of the artichoke and Asiago spread over each tortilla. Place some of the roasted vegetables on each tortilla and sprinkle with the remaining havarti. Fold in the sides of each tortilla and roll up.
5. In a nonstick skillet or grill pan, warm the tortillas on medium heat for 2 minutes per side. Cut each tortilla in half and serve.

PER SERVING (½ QUESADILLA) Calories 252 • Protein 12 g • Carbohydrates 31 g • Fiber 4.2 g • Total fat 12 g • Saturated fat 5 g • Cholesterol 26 mg • Sodium 420 mg • **PREP TIME** 20 minutes • **COOK TIME** 45 minutes • **MAKE AHEAD** Can be prepared early in the day and cooked just before serving. • **NUTRITION WATCH** A large artichoke would add 6 g of dietary fiber to your diet. Add it to your salads or grain dishes.

creamy tomato manicotti with three cheeses and pesto { *Serves 4*

8 manicotti shells
1 cup light ricotta (5%)
¼ cup grated Parmesan cheese
¼ cup crumbled goat cheese (about 1 oz)
3 Tbsp pesto (see page 224)
1 large egg
1½ cups tomato sauce (see page 334) (or store-bought spaghetti sauce)
3 Tbsp canned evaporated milk (2%)
1 tsp dried basil
⅓ cup shredded low-fat mozzarella cheese
3 Tbsp chopped fresh basil or parsley

STUFFED PASTA SHELLS WITH A CREAMY CHEESE mixture are a comfort meal. You can also use jumbo pasta shells. You will need approximately 18 to 20 shells.

1. Preheat the oven to 350°F. Lightly coat a 9- × 13-inch ovenproof casserole dish with vegetable oil.
2. Bring a large pot of water to a boil. Add the manicotti shells and cook for about 8 minutes or until just tender. Drain and rinse with cold water.
3. Combine the ricotta, Parmesan, goat cheese, pesto and egg in the bowl of a food processor and process until well combined.
4. Make a lengthwise split to open up each manicotti. Lay flat and place 3 Tbsp of cheese filling in the middle. Close and repeat with the remaining manicotti.
5. Combine the tomato sauce, milk and dried basil in a bowl. Pour about half into the prepared casserole dish. Place the manicotti overtop, seam side down. Pour the remaining sauce overtop the manicotti and top with mozzarella cheese. Bake uncovered for 20 minutes or until completely heated through and the cheese is melted and bubbling. Garnish with fresh basil or parsley and serve.

PER SERVING Calories 345 • Protein 21 g • Carbohydrates 37 g • Fiber 2.7 g • Total fat 13 g • Saturated fat 6.4 g • Cholesterol 86 mg • Sodium 400 mg • **PREP TIME** 10 minutes • **COOK TIME** 30 minutes • **MAKE AHEAD** Can be baked the day before and reheated in a 350°F oven for 15 minutes. • **NUTRITION WATCH** Mozzarella is very high in saturated fat, but it is also a good source of vitamin B12. Select lower-fat mozzarella and use in moderation.

mushroom, spinach and goat cheese phyllo pie { *Serves 6*

2 tsp vegetable oil
1 cup finely chopped onion
2 tsp finely chopped garlic
3 cups sliced button mushrooms
½ package frozen spinach, thawed, drained, chopped and squeezed dry (about 5 oz)
½ tsp dried basil
¼ tsp salt
¼ tsp pepper
½ cup crumbled goat cheese (about 2 oz)
½ cup shredded low-fat mozzarella cheese
⅓ cup chopped fresh dill or parsley
⅓ cup chopped green onions
⅓ cup chopped black olives
2 Tbsp seasoned dry breadcrumbs
1 egg
6 sheets phyllo pastry

THIS IS SIMILAR TO SPANIKOPITA but is made in a pie pan. It's a wonderful main course and works equally well as a side dish. Serve it with a mesclun salad.

1. Preheat the oven to 350°F. Lightly coat a 9-inch pie pan with cooking spray.
2. To make the filling, lightly coat a nonstick skillet with cooking spray. Add the oil and set over medium heat. Add the onion and sauté for 5 minutes or just until the onion begins to brown. Add the garlic and mushrooms and sauté for 6 minutes or until mushrooms are no longer wet. Stir in the spinach, basil and salt and pepper. Cook for 3 minutes. Remove from the heat.
3. Stir in the goat cheese and mozzarella and the dill, green onions, olives, breadcrumbs and egg. Stir until all the ingredients are well combined.
4. Layer 2 sheets of phyllo in the prepared pie pan, keeping the remaining phyllo sheets covered with a damp tea towel to prevent them from drying out. Leave the edges of the phyllo sheets hanging over the edge of the pan. Lightly coat with vegetable oil. Layer the remaining sheets on top, spraying every other sheet. Carefully spoon the filling into the pie pan. Fold the phyllo sheets overtop to enclose and lightly coat with cooking spray.
5. Bake in the preheated oven for 25 minutes, or until the phyllo is golden and the filling is completely heated through.

PER SERVING Calories 189 • Protein 8.7 g • Carbohydrates 20.2 g • Fiber 3.2 g • Total fat 8.2 g • Saturated fat 3.2 g • Cholesterol 49 mg • Sodium 350 mg • **PREP TIME** 15 minutes • **COOK TIME** 40 minutes • **MAKE AHEAD** The filling can be prepared up to 2 days in advance. It's best to bake just before serving to keep the phyllo crisp. Reheat by placing in a 350°F oven for 10 minutes. • **NUTRITION WATCH** Vitamin E and the monounsaturated fats in black olives are associated with lower rates of colon cancer.

mushroom and ground soy lasagna with three cheeses { *Serves 6*

6 lasagna noodles

SAUCE
1 tsp vegetable oil
¾ cup finely chopped onion
1 tsp finely chopped garlic
3 cup finely chopped mushrooms
2½ cups tomato sauce (see page 334) (or store-bought spaghetti sauce)
1 tsp dried basil
8 oz soy-based ground-beef substitute

FILLING
¼ cup light ricotta (5%)
½ cup shredded low-fat mozzarella
3 Tbsp low-fat milk
3 Tbsp grated Parmesan cheese

GARNISH
3 Tbsp shredded low-fat mozzarella cheese
3 Tbsp chopped fresh basil or parsley

THIS LASAGNA IS SO FABULOUS that nobody will ever suspect there's no meat in it. Ground soy tastes like ground beef or chicken, but the healthy components of soy are known to help in the fight against heart disease and cancer. If you want a spicier flavor, try the Mexican-flavored ground soy or add 1 tsp of hot sauce. I have used a smaller casserole dish since extra lasagna so often goes to waste. You just have to trim the cooked lasagna sheets to fit the pan. If you'd like to increase the yield, use a regular 9- × 13-inch dish, double the recipe and cook nine lasagna noodles.

1. Preheat the oven to 350°F. Lightly coat a 9-inch-square casserole dish with cooking spray.
2. Bring a large pot of water to a boil. Add the lasagna noodles and cook for 12 to 14 minutes or until tender. Drain and rinse under cold running water and drain again. Set aside. Cut the noodles to fit the casserole dish.
3. To prepare the sauce, lightly coat a nonstick saucepan with cooking spray, add the oil and set over medium-high heat. Add the onion and garlic and sauté, stirring frequently, until browned, about 5 minutes. Add the mushrooms and sauté for 5 minutes or until no longer wet.
4. Stir in the tomato sauce and dried basil. Bring to a boil, then reduce the heat. Cover and simmer for 12 to 15 minutes or until slightly thickened. Stir in the ground soy and simmer for 5 more minutes. Set aside.
5. To prepare the filling, combine the ricotta, mozzarella, milk and the Parmesan together in a bowl.
6. To assemble, spread one-quarter of the tomato sauce mixture over the bottom of the casserole dish. Top with 2 lasagna noodles, trimming to fit the pan. Spread half of the cheese mixture over the noodles. Top with another one-quarter of the tomato sauce. Top with 2 noodles. Spread the remaining cheese mixture over the noodles. Top with another one-quarter of the tomato sauce. Top with the last 2 noodles. Spread the remaining tomato sauce overtop. Sprinkle with the mozzarella cheese.
7. Bake in the center of the oven for 20 to 25 minutes or until hot. Garnish with the basil or parsley.

PER SERVING Calories 240 • Protein 20 g • Carbohydrates 26 g • Fiber 3.9 g • Total fat 6 g • Saturated fat 3 g • Cholesterol 20 mg • Sodium 334 mg • **PREP TIME** 15 minutes • **COOK TIME** 50 minutes • **MAKE AHEAD** Can be baked up to a day in advance. Reheat in a 350°F oven for 15 minutes. • **NUTRITION WATCH** Soy has been shown to be helpful in alleviating the symptoms associated with menopause.

vegetable and tofu ratatouille with kidney beans and aged cheddar { *Serves 4*

2 tsp vegetable oil
1 cup chopped onion
2 tsp chopped garlic
1 cup sliced mushrooms
1 cup chopped red bell pepper
¾ cup cubed firm tofu (about 3 oz)
1½ cups chopped zucchini
1½ cups chopped eggplant
2 cups tomato sauce (see page 334) (or store-bought spaghetti sauce)
⅔ cup vegetable stock
1 cup canned red kidney beans, drained and rinsed
2 tsp dried basil
1 tsp dried oregano
1 tsp hot chili sauce (or 1 tsp minced jalapeño pepper)
⅓ cup shredded aged cheddar cheese
3 Tbsp chopped parsley

THIS HAS A SIMILAR FLAVOR AND TEXTURE to a chili or stew but with more vegetables. I like to serve this over soft-cooked polenta or brown rice.

1. Preheat the oven to broil.
2. Lightly coat a large nonstick skillet with cooking spray, add the oil and set over medium heat. Add the onion and garlic and sauté for 5 minutes or until softened. Add the mushrooms and sauté for another 8 minutes until browned and no longer wet. Add the red pepper and tofu and sauté for 3 more minutes or until soft. Add the zucchini and eggplant and cook for another 8 minutes. Finally, add the tomato sauce, stock, beans, basil, oregano and chili sauce. Cover and simmer for 15 minutes.
3. Pour the mixture into an ovenproof casserole dish and sprinkle with the cheese. Broil for 1 minute or until the cheese melts. Garnish with parsley and serve.

PER SERVING Calories 236 • Protein 13 g • Carbohydrates 36 g • Fiber 11 g • Total fat 6.3 g • Saturated fat 1.5 g • Cholesterol 5 mg • Sodium 400 mg • **PREP TIME** 20 minutes • **COOK TIME** 40 minutes • **MAKE AHEAD** Can be made up to 2 days in advance and reheated in a skillet. • **NUTRITION WATCH** The soy protein in tofu may act as a protective against heart disease.

corn, brown rice and black bean casserole { *Serves 6*

2 tsp vegetable oil
2 tsp chopped garlic
1 cup chopped onion
1 cup canned corn, drained
¾ cup chopped green bell pepper
2½ cups vegetable stock
¾ cup brown rice
2 tsp minced jalapeño pepper
1 tsp chili powder
1 tsp dried basil
½ tsp dried oregano
1 cup black beans, drained and rinsed
½ cup tomato sauce (see page 334) (or store-bought spaghetti sauce)
¼ cup chopped cilantro
⅓ cup shredded aged cheddar cheese

THIS IS A VEGETARIAN DELIGHT. With the vegetables, beans and grains you have a complete nutritious meal in one pot. Serve this with a green salad or soup to start.

1. Preheat the oven to 400°F.
2. Lightly coat a large nonstick saucepan with cooking spray, add the oil and set over medium heat. Add the garlic and onion and sauté for 5 minutes or until the onion is softened. Add the corn and sauté for 8 minutes or just until the corn begins to brown. Add the green pepper and sauté for 3 more minutes.
3. Add the stock, brown rice, jalapeño, chili powder, basil, oregano, black beans and tomato sauce. Cover and simmer for 30 to 35 minutes or until the rice is cooked. Stir in the cilantro.
4. Pour into an ovenproof casserole dish and sprinkle with the cheddar cheese. Bake for 10 minutes or until the cheese melts and the dish is completely heated through.

PER SERVING Calories 226 • Protein 7 g • Carbohydrates 38 g • Fiber 5 g • Total fat 5.3 g • Saturated fat 1.8 g • Cholesterol 6 mg • Sodium 480 mg • **PREP TIME** 15 minutes • **COOK TIME** 45 minutes • **MAKE AHEAD** Can be made up to a day in advance. Reheat for 10 minutes in a skillet. • **NUTRITION WATCH** Jalapeños are a good source of potassium, which helps regulate heart function and blood pressure.

layered tortilla, chickpea, tomato and cheese lasagna { *Serves 8*

1 cup canned corn, drained
2 tsp vegetable oil
½ cup chopped onion
2 tsp finely chopped garlic
½ cup chopped red bell pepper
½ cup chopped green bell pepper
2 cups tomato sauce (see page 334) (or store-bought spaghetti sauce)
1½ tsp dried basil
1 tsp chili powder
½ tsp ground cumin
2 cups canned chickpeas, drained and rinsed

FILLING

1 cup light ricotta (5%)
1 cup shredded low-fat mozzarella cheese
¾ cup shredded light cheddar cheese
3 Tbsp low-fat milk
pinch of salt and pepper
2 Tbsp grated Parmesan cheese

5 large flour tortillas

THIS IS ONE OF THE MOST BEAUTIFUL and delicious recipes to serve. Use a variety of colored tortillas to make it even more spectacular. When this dish is cut open to expose the tomato sauce, vegetables and cheese it looks amazing. I often prepare a couple of these to freeze, so I can bake them when I need them.

continued on page 234

layered tortilla, chickpea, tomato and cheese lasagna *continued*

1. Preheat the oven to 350°F. Lightly coat a 9-inch springform pan with cooking spray.
2. Lightly coat a nonstick saucepan with vegetable oil and set over medium heat. Add the corn and sauté, stirring often, for about 8 minutes or until slightly charred. Set aside.
3. Add the oil to the saucepan and keep over medium heat. Add the onion and garlic and cook for 4 minutes, stirring occasionally. Stir in the red and green peppers. Cook for 3 minutes, stirring occasionally. Stir in the tomato sauce, charred corn, basil, chili powder and cumin. Cover and cook over medium heat, stirring occasionally, for 10 minutes or until slightly thickened. Remove from the heat.
4. Place the chickpeas in a bowl and mash them roughly with a fork. Add to the vegetable mixture and stir to combine.
5. In a separate bowl, combine the ricotta, mozzarella and cheddar cheeses (but reserve ¼ cup of the cheddar for garnish). Add the milk and salt and pepper and stir until well combined.
6. Place a tortilla in the prepared springform pan. Spread with one-quarter of the vegetable-chickpea mixture. Sprinkle with one-quarter of the cheese mixture. Repeat the layers 3 times. Top with the final tortilla and sprinkle with the remaining cheddar cheese and the Parmesan cheese. Cover the pan tightly with foil.
7. Bake for 20 minutes in the preheated oven, then uncovered for 10 minutes or until it is completely heated through and the cheese has melted. Cut into 8 wedges with a sharp knife.

PER SERVING Calories 280 • Protein 14 g • Carbohydrates 39 g • Fiber 5 g • Total fat 8.5 g • Saturated fat 3.1 g • Cholesterol 22 mg • Sodium 710 mg • **PREP TIME** 20 minutes • **COOK TIME** 55 minutes • **MAKE AHEAD** Can be baked up to a day in advance. Reheat in 350°F oven for 10 minutes. • **NUTRITION WATCH** Choose lower-fat cheddar cheese more often (1 oz of regular fat cheddar cheese has 6 g of saturated fat; 1 oz of lighter cheese has less than 4 g of saturated fat).

two-bean chili with ground soy { *Serves 4*

2 tsp vegetable oil
1½ cups chopped onion
1 cup canned corn, drained
2 tsp crushed garlic
8 oz soy-based ground beef substitute
1 cup canned red kidney beans, drained and rinsed
1 cup canned chickpeas, drained and rinsed
2 cups tomato sauce (see page 334) (or store-bought spaghetti sauce)
1 cup vegetable stock
2 tsp chili powder
1½ tsp dried basil
1 tsp granulated sugar
½ tsp ground cumin
½ cup shredded aged cheddar cheese
¼ cup low-fat sour cream
3 Tbsp chopped fresh basil

USING TWO VARIETIES OF BEANS makes this dish full-bodied. I like to eat this on its own or serve it over some brown rice or a baked potato.

1. Lightly coat a nonstick skillet with cooking spray, add the oil and set over medium heat. Add the onion and sauté for 3 minutes or until soft. Stir in the corn and garlic and cook for another 5 minutes, or until the corn is browned, stirring occasionally. Add the ground soy and sauté for 2 more minutes.
2. Add the kidney beans, chickpeas, tomato sauce, stock, chili powder, dried basil, sugar and cumin. Bring to a boil, cover and reduce the heat. Simmer for 20 minutes or just until mixture is thickened.
3. Garnish with cheese, sour cream and fresh basil.

PER SERVING Calories 439 • Protein 28 g • Carbohydrates 60 g • Fiber 16 g • Total fat 9.6 g • Saturated fat 4 g • Cholesterol 18 mg • Sodium 500 mg • **PREP TIME** 10 minutes • **COOK TIME** 30 minutes • **MAKE AHEAD** Can be made up to 2 days in advance. Reheat in a saucepan until warmed through. • **NUTRITION WATCH** Use low-fat sour cream—1 Tbsp of regular sour cream has 4.5 g of fat, whereas 1 Tbsp of low-fat sour cream has 1.5 g of fat.

chickpea, corn and carrot loaf { *Serves 8*

LOAF
½ cup canned corn, drained
1 can (19 oz) chickpeas, drained and rinsed
1 cup coarsely grated carrots
⅓ cup chopped fresh cilantro or basil
1 egg
3 Tbsp tahini (sesame seed paste)
2 Tbsp lemon juice
3 Tbsp seasoned dry breadcrumbs
¼ cup chopped green onions
1½ tsp finely chopped garlic
pinch of salt and pepper

SAUCE
¼ cup light ricotta (5%)
2 Tbsp tahini
2 Tbsp light mayonnaise
1 Tbsp olive oil
1 Tbsp low-sodium soy sauce
1 Tbsp lemon juice
3 Tbsp chopped cilantro
1 tsp finely chopped garlic

I ORIGINALLY USED THIS RECIPE to make great veggie burgers, but then I tried it in a loaf pan and it was sensational! This is perfect as a holiday entrée for a vegetarian crowd or for anyone who wants a great meatless side dish.

1. Preheat the oven to 350°F. Lightly coat an 8- × 4-inch loaf pan with cooking spray, and line the bottom with parchment paper.
2. Lightly coat a small, nonstick skillet with cooking spray and set over medium heat. Add the corn and sauté for 5 minutes or until lightly browned.
3. Place the grilled corn in the bowl of a food processor. Add the chickpeas, carrot, cilantro or basil, egg, tahini, lemon juice, breadcrumbs, green onions, garlic, salt and pepper. Process lightly or just until the mixture comes together. Do not purée.
4. Put the mixture into the prepared loaf pan and pat down. Cover with parchment paper to prevent the loaf from drying out. Place the loaf pan in a larger pan and add water until it comes halfway up the loaf pan. Bake for 25 to 30 minutes or until heated through and feels firm to the touch. Remove from the pan of water, allow to cool slightly and remove the parchment, then either slice in the pan or carefully invert onto a serving platter before slicing.
5. Meanwhile, make the sauce by combining the ricotta, tahini, mayonnaise, olive oil, soy sauce, lemon juice, cilantro and garlic in the bowl of a food processor. Process until smooth.
6. Serve by pouring the sauce overtop the slices.

PER SERVING Calories 160 • Protein 6 g • Carbohydrates 15 g • Fiber 3 g • Total fat 6 g • Saturated fat 1 g • Cholesterol 35 mg • Sodium 250 mg • **PREP TIME** 20 minutes • **COOK TIME** 30 minutes • **MAKE AHEAD** Can be prepared up to a day in advance. Reheat in a 350°F oven for 10 minutes. • **NUTRITION WATCH** Choose fresh corn when it's in season, frozen and canned corn when it's not. The carotenoids found in corn increase with freezing.

zucchini, carrot and mushroom loaf { *Serves 8*

1 tsp vegetable oil
2 tsp finely chopped garlic
1 cup chopped onion
½ cup finely chopped carrots
1 cup chopped zucchini
1 cup chopped mushrooms
1 cup canned chickpeas, drained and rinsed
1 cup canned white kidney beans, drained and rinsed
¼ cup seasoned dry breadcrumbs
3 Tbsp grated Parmesan cheese
1 egg
1 tsp dried basil
½ tsp dried oregano
pinch of salt and pepper
½ cup tomato sauce (see page 334) (or store-bought spaghetti sauce)
1 Tbsp canned evaporated milk (2%) (or regular milk (2% or low-fat))

VEGETARIAN LOAVES take the place of a standard meatloaf but with greater flavor and texture and more nutrients. Substitute vegetables and beans of your choice.

1. Preheat oven to 350°F. Lightly coat an 8- × 4-inch loaf pan with cooking spray.
2. In a nonstick frying pan, heat the oil over medium-high heat. Add the garlic and onion and cook for 4 minutes. Add the carrots, zucchini and mushrooms and cook for 8 minutes or until the vegetables are softened.
3. In a food processor, combine the zucchini mixture, chickpeas, beans, breadcrumbs, Parmesan, egg, basil, oregano, salt and pepper. Pulse on and off until finely chopped and well combined. Press into the prepared loaf pan.
4. Bake, uncovered, for about 30 minutes or until a tester inserted in the center of the loaf comes out clean. Let cool slightly, then slice loaf into 8 pieces.
5. Whisk the tomato sauce and milk together in a small saucepan over medium-high heat. Serve drizzled over the sliced loaf.

PER SERVING Calories 190 • Protein 11 g • Carbohydrates 30 g • Fiber 8 g • Total fat 4 g • Saturated fat 1 g • Cholesterol 55 mg • Sodium 200 mg • **PREP TIME** 20 minutes • **COOK TIME** 45 minutes • **MAKE AHEAD** Can be made the day before and reheated in a 350°F oven for 10 minutes. • **NUTRITION WATCH** Homemade breadcrumbs are lower in sodium than the store-bought ones, and they have no preservatives. Use bread that has been left out to dry. Do not use stale bread. Bake bread in a 300°F oven for 15 minutes, until dry. Process in a food processor.

{ *fish & seafood* }

steamed salmon with fennel, pear and onion tartar sauce { *Serves 6*

1½ lb salmon fillet
pinch of salt and pepper

SAUCE
½ cup finely chopped fennel bulb
½ cup finely chopped peeled and cored ripe pear
⅓ cup finely chopped red onion
3 Tbsp light mayonnaise
2 Tbsp low-fat plain yogurt (2%)
3 Tbsp chopped fresh dill
2 tsp lemon juice
½ tsp finely chopped garlic

I HAVE ALWAYS LIKED POACHED SALMON, but I've found it's difficult to cook perfectly. This steamed recipe is quick and guarantees great flavor and texture. (You can also bake salmon in a 425°F oven for 10 minutes per inch of thickness.) The fresh fennel and pear sauce is a nice change from regular tartar sauce.

1. Sprinkle salmon with salt and pepper. Steam the salmon by placing 1 or 2 inches of water in a large pot and setting a rack or steamer into the pan (making sure the fish will sit above the water). Bring the water to a boil. Place the salmon on the rack, cover and reduce the heat to medium-low. Steam for about 10 minutes per inch of thickness. Remove the salmon and chill in the refrigerator. This dish can also be served at room temperature.
2. Combine the fennel, pear, red onion, mayonnaise, yogurt, dill, lemon juice and garlic in a bowl.
3. Spoon the sauce over the salmon before serving.

PER SERVING Calories 226 • Protein 26 g • Carbohydrates 7 g • Fiber 1.3 g • Total fat 10 g • Saturated fat 1.3 g • Cholesterol 74 mg • Sodium 159 mg • **PREP TIME** 15 minutes • **COOK TIME** 12 minutes • **MAKE AHEAD** Prepare the sauce and fish early in the day and refrigerate. • **NUTRITION WATCH** There is lots of controversy over regular (farmed) salmon. Farmed salmon is usually fattier than wild salmon and can contain more contaminants such as PCBs and mercury.

baked salmon with teriyaki hoisin sauce { *Serves 6*

1½ lb salmon fillet

TERIYAKI HOISIN SAUCE

3 Tbsp packed brown sugar
2 Tbsp low-sodium soy sauce
1 Tbsp rice vinegar
1 Tbsp hoisin sauce
1 Tbsp water
2 tsp sesame oil
2 tsp cornstarch
1 tsp finely chopped garlic
1 tsp finely chopped ginger
1 tsp sesame seeds
3 Tbsp chopped cilantro or parsley

SALMON AND ASIAN SAUCES always go well together. This hoisin sauce can be made ahead and kept refrigerated and used for other fish, chicken or beef dishes.

1. Preheat the oven to 425°F. Line a rimmed baking sheet with foil and lightly coat it with cooking spray.
2. Combine the brown sugar, soy sauce, rice vinegar, hoisin sauce, water, oil, cornstarch, garlic and ginger in a small saucepan. Bring to a boil, reduce the heat and simmer for 2 minutes or just until the mixture thickens.
3. Place the salmon on the prepared baking sheet and pour half the sauce over it. Bake for 10 minutes per inch of thickness or until the fish just flakes when tested with a fork.
4. Gently reheat the remaining sauce and serve over the baked salmon. Garnish with the sesame seeds and cilantro or parsley before serving.

PER SERVING Calories 233 • Protein 26 g • Carbohydrates 7 g • Fiber 0.2 g • Total fat 10 g • Saturated fat 1.5 g • Cholesterol 72 mg • Sodium 281 mg • **PREP TIME** 5 minutes • **COOK TIME** 15 minutes • **MAKE AHEAD** Prepare the sauce up to 3 days in advance and keep refrigerated. • **NUTRITION WATCH** Sesame oil is a source of calcium, which helps prevent osteoporosis, migraines and premenstrual syndrome.

salmon with pesto and cream cheese { *Serves 6*

1½ lb salmon fillet, cut into 6 fillets (about 4 oz each)

¼ cup low-fat cream cheese (about 2 oz), softened
2 Tbsp pesto
2 Tbsp toasted pine nuts (or chopped toasted almonds)

PESTO
1 cup packed fresh basil leaves
2 Tbsp grated Parmesan cheese
1 Tbsp toasted pine nuts
2 Tbsp light cream cheese, softened
1 tsp finely chopped garlic
3 Tbsp chicken stock (or vegetable stock or water)
2 Tbsp olive oil

THIS IS AN EASY AND DELICIOUS WAY to serve salmon. I prefer to use homemade pesto, which has fewer calories and less fat than store-bought pesto. This pesto recipe makes more than what you will use for the salmon; keep it refrigerated or freeze it for later use. To toast the pine nuts or almonds, just place a dry skillet over high heat, add the nuts and stir often for about 3 minutes or until they are lightly browned.

1. Preheat the oven to 425°F. Line a rimmed baking sheet with foil and lightly coat with cooking spray.
2. For the pesto, place all the ingredients in the bowl of a food processor and purée until smooth. Add more water if too thick.
3. Combine the cream cheese and pesto in a small bowl until smooth.
4. Make a small vertical slit on the top of each salmon fillet to within ¼ inch of each end and about ½ inch deep. Stuff each fillet by dividing the pesto filling between the 6 fillets.
5. Place on the prepared baking sheet and bake for 10 minutes per inch of thickness.
6. Garnish with toasted nuts before serving.

SALMON: PER SERVING Calories 241 • Protein 27 g • Carbohydrates 1 g • Fiber 0.2 g • Total fat 13 g • Saturated fat 2.8 g • Cholesterol 77 mg • Sodium 108 mg • **PREP TIME** 5 minutes • **COOK TIME** 12 minutes • **MAKE AHEAD** Make the stuffing up to 2 days in advance. • **NUTRITION WATCH** Make store-bought pesto lighter by adding some mayonnaise or sour cream or thin the pesto using stock.

PESTO: PER SERVING (1 TBSP) Calories 41 • Protein 1 g • Carbohydrates 0.6 g • Fiber 0.2 g • Total fat 3.9 g • Saturated fat 0.9 g • Cholesterol 2 mg • Sodium 22 mg

grilled halibut with roasted red pepper sauce { *Serves 6*

1½ lb halibut (or other firm white fish)
pinch of salt and pepper

SAUCE
2 red bell peppers, cored and cut in half
1 Tbsp light mayonnaise
1 Tbsp olive oil
2 Tbsp toasted pine nuts (or almonds)
2 Tbsp grated Parmesan cheese
pinch of salt and pepper
3 Tbsp chopped fresh basil

THIS TASTY ROASTED RED PEPPER SAUCE suits a mild-flavored white fish. You can also use cod, tilapia or sea bass. Try orange or yellow bell peppers for a change.

1. Preheat the oven to 425°F. See page 100 for instructions on how to roast red peppers. After roasting, keep the oven at 425°F.
2. Cool and peel the roasted red peppers and place in the bowl of a food processor along with the mayonnaise, oil, pine nuts, Parmesan, salt and pepper. Purée until smooth.
3. Line a rimmed baking pan with foil and lightly coat with cooking spray. Sprinkle the fish with salt and pepper and bake the halibut, cooking for 10 minutes per inch thickness of fish or until the fish flakes easily when tested with a fork, about 15 minutes.
4. When the fish is cooked through, serve it hot with the roasted red pepper sauce spooned over it. Garnish with basil.

PER SERVING Calories 192 • Protein 26 g • Carbohydrates 3.5 g • Fiber 1.2 g • Total fat 8.1 g • Saturated fat 1.2 g • Cholesterol 39 mg • Sodium 133 mg • **PREP TIME** 10 minutes • **COOK TIME** 40 minutes • **MAKE AHEAD** Prepare the sauce up to a day in advance. • **NUTRITION WATCH** Halibut, like most fish, has heart-healthy omega-3 fatty acids. These essential fats can lower your triglyceride levels.

seared ahi tuna with jicama, fennel and mango slaw { *Serves 4*

1 lb raw ahi tuna fillets
pinch of salt and pepper
1 tsp sesame seeds

SLAW
½ cup thinly sliced mango
1 cup thinly sliced fennel
1 cup thinly sliced jicama
1 cup thinly sliced red bell pepper
½ cup thinly sliced green bell pepper
½ cup thinly sliced carrots
¼ cup sliced green onions
¼ cup chopped cilantro
1 Tbsp olive oil
2 tsp lemon juice
1 tsp rice vinegar
1 tsp toasted sesame seeds
1 tsp finely chopped garlic
½ tsp hot chili sauce (or finely chopped jalapeño pepper)

GLAZE (OPTIONAL)
2 Tbsp low-sodium soy sauce
2 Tbsp maple syrup
1 tsp cornstarch

BE SURE TO ONLY BUY THE FRESHEST TUNA you can from a reputable fishmonger. If available, ahi tuna is the best quality. Served with this slaw, it makes for a very sophisticated dish. Jicama is a white-fleshed root vegetable, also known as a Mexican potato. It is crunchy and sweet, and can be eaten either raw or cooked. It's usually available from May to November; if unavailable, use canned sliced water chestnuts.

1. Make the slaw by combining the mango, fennel, jicama, red and green peppers, carrot, green onions and cilantro in a medium bowl. In a separate bowl, whisk together the olive oil, lemon juice, rice vinegar, 1 tsp sesame seeds, garlic and chili sauce. Pour over the slaw and toss to combine. Place on a serving platter.
2. Lightly coat a nonstick grill pan with cooking spray and set over high heat. Sprinkle the tuna with salt and pepper and sear for about 2 minutes per side; the center should still be raw. Remove from the heat. Slice thinly and top with the slaw.
3. Prepare glaze if desired. Combine the soy sauce, maple syrup and cornstarch in a small saucepan. Bring to a boil, reduce the heat and simmer, whisking, until the cornstarch is dissolved and the mixture is slightly thickened. Pour over the tuna. Garnish with 1 tsp sesame seeds before serving.

PER SERVING Calories 246 • Protein 27 g • Carbohydrates 21 g • Fiber 4.1 g • Total fat 5.8 g • Saturated fat 0.9 g • Cholesterol 53 mg • Sodium 129 mg • **PREP TIME** 20 minutes • **COOK TIME** 4 minutes • **MAKE AHEAD** Prepare the salsa early in the day, keeping refrigerated. • **NUTRITION WATCH** A cup of jicama has almost 6 g of fiber and only 50 calories. It is also high in vitamin C, potassium and folate.

seared tuna with orange and fennel salsa { *Serves 6*

1½ lb raw tuna fillets
1 Tbsp sesame seeds

SALSA
½ medium orange, peeled and finely diced
¾ cup finely diced fennel bulb
1 Tbsp orange juice concentrate
¼ cup chopped fresh mint
2 Tbsp finely diced green onions
2 tsp olive oil
1 tsp honey
pinch of salt and pepper

TO SEAR TUNA PERFECTLY, heat the skillet to a high temperature, then grill or sauté for only 1 or 2 minutes per side, depending upon the thickness. If not serving it immediately, stop the cooking process by placing it in the refrigerator for 5 minutes. This way, you'll be guaranteed tuna that's beautifully seared on the outside and rare on the inside.

1. Prepare the salsa by combining the orange, fennel, orange juice concentrate, mint, green onions, olive oil, honey, salt and pepper. Set aside.
2. Lightly coat a nonstick skillet with cooking spray and set over high heat. Sprinkle the tuna fillets with sesame seeds on both sides. Sear for 2 minutes on each side; the center should still be raw. Remove from the heat.
3. Slice the tuna into thin slices and serve with the salsa.

PER SERVING Calories 170 • Protein 27 g • Carbohydrates 7 g • Fiber 1.4 g • Total fat 3.6 g • Saturated fat 0.6 g • Cholesterol 53 mg • Sodium 109 mg • **PREP TIME** 10 minutes • **COOK TIME** 4 minutes • **MAKE AHEAD** Prepare salsa early in the day and refrigerate. • **NUTRITION WATCH** Tuna (fresh or canned) is low in fat and cholesterol and rich in protein, vitamins and omega-3 fatty acids.

sole stuffed with olives and sun-dried tomatoes { *Serves 4*

1 lb sole, cut into about four 4 oz fillets

FILLING

¼ cup finely chopped black olives

¼ cup finely chopped green olives

¼ cup finely chopped rehydrated sun-dried tomatoes

3 Tbsp seasoned dry breadcrumbs

1 Tbsp olive oil

1 tsp finely chopped garlic

1 tsp Dijon mustard

FOR THE FISH

1 egg

2 Tbsp low-fat milk

½ cup seasoned dry breadcrumbs

2 tsp vegetable oil

SOLE IS AN INEXPENSIVE FISH THAT TENDS TO TAKE ON the flavor of whatever you prepare with it. This savory olive and sun-dried tomato filling suits it beautifully. Rehydrate the sun-dried tomatoes by soaking them in boiling water until they are softened, about 10 minutes.

1. Preheat the oven to 400°F. Lightly coat a 9- × 13-inch baking dish with cooking spray.
2. Combine the black and green olives, sun-dried tomatoes, breadcrumbs, olive oil, garlic and mustard in the bowl of food processor. Pulse until finely chopped and all the ingredients are well combined but still thick, crumbly and chunky.
3. Prepare the coating by combining the egg and milk in a small bowl. Place the breadcrumbs on a shallow plate.
4. Lay the sole fillets flat and place some of the olive mixture down the middle of each fillet. Roll each fillet up tightly. Dip each fillet in the egg and milk mixture, then roll in the breadcrumbs. Secure with a toothpick and set on a plate.
5. Lightly coat a large, nonstick skillet with cooking spray, add the oil and set over medium-high heat. Add the fillets and sauté for about 5 minutes or just until browned on all sides. Place the fillets in the prepared baking dish and bake for 10 to 15 minutes in the preheated oven or just until the fish is cooked. The fish should flake easily when tested with a fork.

PER SERVING Calories 275 • Protein 24 g • Carbohydrates 17 g • Fiber 1.7 g • Total fat 12 g • Saturated fat 2 g • Cholesterol 108 mg • Sodium 510 mg • **PREP TIME** 15 minutes • **COOK TIME** 15 minutes • **MAKE AHEAD** Prepare the fish early in the day. Bake just before serving. • **NUTRITION WATCH** In addition to healthy omega-3 fats, sole is packed with phosphorus and selenium. Phosphorus is essential for normal heart and kidney function, and selenium is a great antioxidant.

tiger shrimp with spinach pesto and grilled corn salad { *Serves 4*

1 lb large shrimp, peeled and deveined

PESTO

1 cup tightly packed baby spinach leaves
2 Tbsp toasted pine nuts
1 Tbsp lemon juice
1 tsp lemon zest
3 Tbsp olive oil
½ tsp finely chopped garlic
3 Tbsp grated Parmesan cheese

SALAD

3 fresh cobs of corn
½ cup diced roasted red pepper (about 1 small roasted red pepper) (see page 100)
½ cup diced red onion
1 tsp chopped garlic
1½ tsp chopped jalapeño pepper
1 Tbsp apple cider vinegar
2 Tbsp olive oil
½ tsp honey (optional)
½ cup chopped fresh basil leaves
pinch of salt and pepper

TIGER SHRIMP ARE QUITE AFFORDABLE today compared to what they cost a few years ago. If you can't find them, you can use smaller shrimp. This spinach pesto is a good example of how you can use different ingredients to make variations on classic basil pesto. If you don't have fresh corn, sauté 2 cups canned or frozen corn until lightly charred.

1. Make the spinach pesto by combining the spinach, pine nuts, lemon juice and zest, olive oil, garlic and Parmesan in the bowl of a food processor. Purée until smooth. Set aside.
2. To prepare the salad, lightly coat the cobs of corn with cooking spray and grill on a barbecue for 5 minutes or just until charred, turning to avoid burning. Alternatively, you can bake the corn in an oven preheated to 450°F for 5 minutes, also turning to prevent burning. Let the corn cool slightly and cut the kernels off the cob with a sharp knife. Place in a bowl along with the red pepper, red onion, garlic, jalapeño, cider vinegar, olive oil, honey (if using), fresh basil, salt and pepper. Toss to combine.
3. Lightly coat a nonstick skillet or grill pan with cooking spray and set over medium high heat. Add the shrimp and sauté until they just turn pink, about 3 minutes.
4. Place the corn salad on a serving plate, top with the shrimp and garnish with the pesto.

PER SERVING Calories 408 • Protein 25 g • Carbohydrates 19 g • Fiber 3.7 g • Total fat 26 g • Saturated fat 4.4 g • Cholesterol 172 mg • Sodium 378 mg • **PREP TIME** 15 minutes • **COOK TIME** 10 minutes • **MAKE AHEAD** Prepare the pesto and the salad early in the day. Cook the shrimp just before serving. • **NUTRITION WATCH** Shrimp is low in fat but high in protein. It is also a good source of vitamin D, which has a host of health benefits—it fights cancer and supports the immune system.

white fish with black bean sauce and oyster mushrooms { *Serves 6*

1½ lb firm white fish (such as tilapia, halibut or pickerel)
1 tsp vegetable oil
4 cups sliced oyster mushrooms

SAUCE
1 Tbsp brown sugar
2 Tbsp sweet chili sauce (or ketchup)
2 Tbsp black bean sauce
3 Tbsp water
2 tsp rice vinegar
2 tsp sesame oil
1 tsp finely chopped ginger
1 tsp finely chopped garlic

GARNISH
3 Tbsp chopped green onions
2 Tbsp chopped cilantro

ANY FIRM WHITE FISH goes beautifully with this black bean sauce and mushrooms. Feel free to substitute any kind of mushroom; just remember to cook them on medium-high heat to avoid excess moisture. Black bean sauce is a Chinese sauce made from fermented soy beans, wheat flour and spices. You can find it in the Asian section of your supermarket.

1. Preheat the oven to 425°F. Line a rimmed baking sheet with foil and lightly coat with cooking spray.
2. Lightly coat a large, nonstick skillet with cooking spray, add the oil and set over medium-high heat. Add the mushrooms and sauté for 8 minutes or until the mushrooms are no longer wet, stirring often.
3. Meanwhile, make the sauce by combining the sugar, chili sauce, black bean sauce, water, vinegar, sesame oil, ginger and garlic in a small bowl. When the mushrooms are finished cooking, add the sauce to the mushrooms and sauté for 1 more minute.
4. Place the fish fillet on the prepared baking sheet and top with the mushroom mixture. Bake for 12 to 15 minutes or until the fish just starts to flake.
5. Garnish with the green onions and cilantro and serve.

PER SERVING Calories 203 • Protein 23 g • Carbohydrates 5 g • Fiber 0.7 g • Total fat 10 g • Saturated fat 1.4 g • Cholesterol 68 mg • Sodium 268 mg • **PREP TIME** 15 minutes • **COOK TIME** 20 minutes • **MAKE AHEAD** Sauté the mushrooms and prepare the sauce up to a day in advance. Cook the fish just before serving. • **NUTRITION WATCH** Black bean sauce, like most Asian sauces, is high in sodium. Use it in moderation, especially if you are watching your blood pressure. You can always dilute it by 50% with water.

roasted prosciutto-wrapped white fish with pesto { *Serves 6*

1½ lb firm white fish (such as halibut, sea bass or black cod), cut into six 4 oz fillets
6 thin slices prosciutto (about 3 oz in total)
pinch of pepper

PESTO

⅔ cup fresh basil leaves
⅔ cup fresh parsley leaves
¼ cup toasted pine nuts (or almonds)
2 Tbsp grated Parmesan cheese
2 Tbsp olive oil
½ tsp finely chopped garlic
pinch of salt and pepper

I HAD A VERSION of this in a restaurant recently and I had to re-create it. Prosciutto used sparingly is fine in your diet. You can experiment with different herbs and nuts to make the pesto.

1. Preheat the oven to 400°F. Line a rimmed baking pan with foil and lightly coat with cooking spray.
2. To make the pesto, combine the basil, parsley, pine nuts, Parmesan, olive oil, garlic and salt and pepper in the bowl of a food processor and process until all the ingredients are finely chopped and well combined. Do not purée.
3. Place the prosciutto slices horizontally on a flat surface. Spread the pesto down the middle of each slice. Place a fish fillet vertically on each slice and wrap the prosciutto around the fish.
4. Lightly coat a nonstick skillet with cooking spray and set over medium-high heat. Add the fish and sauté on each side for 1 minute or until the prosciutto begins to get crisp.
5. Place the fish on the prepared baking pan and bake for 10 minutes or until the fish just flakes when tested with a fork.

PER SERVING Calories 277 • Protein 28 g • Carbohydrates 3 g • Fiber 1.3 g • Total fat 17 g • Saturated fat 2.5 g • Cholesterol 79 mg • Sodium 442 mg • **PREP TIME** 15 minutes • **COOK TIME** 10 minutes • **MAKE AHEAD** Prepare the fish early in the day. Bake just before serving. • **NUTRITION WATCH** Prosciutto is higher in fat and sodium than other meats. I use it only to highlight a dish. Eat it in moderation.

pineapple scallop stir-fry with coconut hoisin sauce { *Serves 4*

SAUCE
½ cup light coconut milk
¼ cup hoisin sauce
2 Tbsp oyster sauce
1 Tbsp natural peanut butter
1 tsp cornstarch
1½ tsp finely chopped garlic
1 tsp finely chopped ginger
1 tsp hot chili sauce
1 Tbsp brown sugar

STIR-FRY
12 oz large scallops
1½ cups chopped broccoli (including stems)
2 cups sliced red bell pepper
½ cup diced fresh or canned pineapple
¼ cup chopped cilantro
3 Tbsp chopped green onions

I PREFER BUYING LARGE SCALLOPS for a stir-fry. The key is not to overcook them, or they become dry and chewy. Make sure to buy light coconut milk, which is much healthier for you than regular coconut milk. Serve over rice or noodles.

1. Make the coconut hoisin sauce by whisking together the coconut milk, hoisin sauce, oyster sauce, peanut butter, cornstarch, garlic, ginger, chili sauce and brown sugar in a small bowl until smooth. Set aside.
2. Lightly coat a nonstick grill pan (or wok) with cooking spray and set over medium-high heat. Add the scallops and sauté until the flesh is opaque and center is slightly translucent, about 3 minutes. Remove from the pan and set aside.
3. Steam or boil the broccoli for 2 minutes just until tender. Drain well. Respray the pan (or wok) and reduce the heat to medium. Add the broccoli and the red bell pepper and stir-fry for 2 minutes.
4. Add the sauce and scallops and stir-fry for another 2 minutes or until the sauce thickens and all the ingredients are heated through. Transfer to a serving platter and sprinkle with pineapple, cilantro and green onions.

PER SERVING Calories 226 • Protein 16 g • Carbohydrates 21 g • Fiber 2.7 g • Total fat 8.6 g • Saturated fat 0.7 g • Cholesterol 127 mg • Sodium 528 mg • **PREP TIME** 20 minutes • **COOK TIME** 10 minutes • **MAKE AHEAD** Prepare the sauce early in the day. • **NUTRITION WATCH** Oyster sauce is very high in sodium—1 Tbsp contains 500 mg of sodium. Use in moderation or use half water.

lake trout with spinach, cilantro and almond pesto { *Serves 6*

1½ lb lake trout (or tilapia)
¼ cup all-purpose flour
2 tsp vegetable oil

PESTO
¾ cup tightly packed baby spinach leaves
⅓ cup chopped cilantro
2 Tbsp chopped toasted almonds
2 Tbsp olive oil
2 Tbsp grated Parmesan cheese
1 tsp lemon juice
½ tsp finely chopped garlic

THIS UNIQUE, FLAVORFUL PESTO goes well over a mild-tasting fish like trout. Any firm white fish will work, as will shrimp. If you want to experiment, you can substitute herbs and nuts of your choice for a totally different pesto.

1. Lightly coat a large, nonstick skillet with cooking spray, add the oil and set over medium-high heat. Dust fish with flour and sauté for about 8 minutes, turning halfway through, or just until the fish flakes when tested with a fork.
2. Meanwhile, prepare the pesto by combining the spinach, cilantro, almonds, olive oil, Parmesan, lemon juice and garlic in the bowl of a food processor. Pulse until the ingredients are all finely chopped and well combined. If the mixture is too dry, add 1 or 2 Tbsp of water.
3. Serve the fish hot, with the pesto spooned over the top.

PER SERVING Calories 220 • Protein 21 g • Carbohydrates 5 g • Fiber 0.4 g • Total fat 12 g • Saturated fat 2.1 g • Cholesterol 66 mg • Sodium 60 mg • **PREP TIME** 5 minutes • **COOK TIME** 10 minutes • **MAKE AHEAD** Prepare pesto early in the day. • **NUTRITION WATCH** Almonds appear to decrease blood sugar after you eat, thereby helping prevent the risk of diabetes. Almonds are high in good fatty acids, but keep in mind that they are also high in calories and unsaturated fats.

lake trout with pear, pistachio and dried apricot salsa { *Serves 6*

1½ lb lake trout (or tilapia)
¼ cup all-purpose flour
2 tsp vegetable oil
3 Tbsp chopped fresh mint or basil

SALSA

1 large ripe pear, peeled, cored and diced (about 1 cup)
1 Tbsp brown sugar
½ tsp cinnamon
⅔ cup finely chopped dried apricots
⅓ cup finely chopped red onion
⅓ cup finely chopped roasted red pepper (see page 100)
¼ cup chopped toasted pistachio nuts
1 Tbsp olive oil
1 Tbsp lemon juice
1 Tbsp maple syrup
½ tsp finely chopped garlic
3 Tbsp chopped fresh mint or basil

RIPE CARAMELIZED PEARS and dried apricots with pistachios make a wonderful salsa, perfect for any mild fish or chicken dish. Feel free to substitute dried fruits and nuts of your choice.

1. For the salsa, lightly coat a small, nonstick skillet with cooking spray and set over medium heat. Add the pear, brown sugar and cinnamon. Sauté for about 3 minutes or until the pear is softened and begins to caramelize. Place in a small mixing bowl.
2. Add the dried apricots, onion, red pepper, pistachio nuts, olive oil, lemon juice, maple syrup and garlic. Stir to combine and set aside.
3. Dust fish with flour. Lightly coat a nonstick skillet with cooking spray, add the oil and sauté fish for about 8 minutes or just until cooked, turning halfway through.
4. Place on a serving platter, spoon the salsa over the fish and garnish with mint or basil.

PER SERVING Calories 310 • Protein 22 g • Carbohydrates 27 g • Fiber 2.9 g • Total fat 12 g • Saturated fat 2.1 g • Cholesterol 60 mg • Sodium 80 mg • **PREP TIME** 15 minutes • **COOK TIME** 11 minutes • **MAKE AHEAD** Prepare the salsa early in the day. • **NUTRITION WATCH** Pistachios are an excellent source of copper and manganese as well as a good source of phosphorus. Pistachios are the only nuts that have a high amount of the carotenoids lutein and zeaxanthin. Intake of these nutrients has been associated with a reduced risk of age-related macular degeneration, which can cause irreversible blindness in those over 65 years of age.

lake trout with cherry tomato, leek and fennel salsa { *Serves 6*

1½ lb lake trout (or tilapia)
¼ cup all-purpose flour
2 tsp vegetable oil

SALSA
2 tsp vegetable oil
1 cup thinly sliced fennel bulb
1 cup thinly sliced leeks
2 cups cherry tomatoes, sliced in half
⅓ cup chopped black olives
6 rehydrated sun-dried tomatoes, chopped
2 Tbsp olive oil
1 tsp finely chopped garlic
½ tsp dried basil
¼ tsp dried oregano
pinch of pepper
¼ cup chopped fresh basil

LAKE TROUT is a mild yet flavorful fish that goes well with a savory sauce and these Mediterranean vegetables.

1. For the salsa, lightly coat a nonstick skillet with cooking spray, add the oil and set over medium heat. Add the fennel, turn the heat to low and sauté for 15 minutes or until softened. Add the leeks and sauté 5 more minutes. Add the cherry tomatoes and sauté for 3 minutes or until just softened. Add the olives, sun-dried tomatoes, olive oil, garlic, dried basil, oregano and pepper and heat for 1 minute. Set aside.
2. Dust the fish with flour. Lightly coat a nonstick skillet with cooking spray, add the oil and sauté fish on medium-high heat for about 8 minutes, turning halfway through or until the fish just starts to flake.
3. Spoon the salsa over the fish and garnish with the fresh basil.

PER SERVING Calories 268 • Protein 22 g • Carbohydrates 14 g • Fiber 2.5 g • Total fat 14 g • Saturated fat 2.3 g • Cholesterol 60 mg • Sodium 230 mg • **PREP TIME** 20 minutes • **COOK TIME** 30 minutes • **MAKE AHEAD** Prepare the salsa early in the day. • **NUTRITION WATCH** The omega-3 fatty acids found in trout may help relieve the symptoms of rheumatoid arthritis.

{ chicken & turkey }

To store raw chicken, remove the wrapping and wash the chicken with cold water. Wrap chicken loosely in foil and place in the coldest part of the refrigerator for up to 48 hours. If freezing, wrap chicken in a plastic freezer bag and freeze for up to 4 months • Thaw poultry in the refrigerator (5 hours per pound), in a bowl of cold water (1 hour per pound) or in a microwave. Do not defrost at room temperature; harmful bacteria may develop. Never refreeze raw chicken after thawing • Raw chicken contains bacteria that can cause illness. After working with raw chicken, wash your hands, cutting board and utensils with hot water and soap. Never place cooked chicken on a plate that you've used for raw chicken • Pounding boneless chicken breasts makes them easier to stuff, and the breasts cook more quickly. You can ask your butcher to pound them for you. If you don't pound them, allow a longer cooking time • Always cook chicken until it is no longer pink and juices run clear, around 165°F. It must never be served rare, since harmful bacteria may remain • Boneless pounded chicken breasts can be replaced with turkey, veal or pork scaloppini in these recipes • Try not to overcook chicken, as it will become dry • If you are using the marinade as a sauce, boil the remaining marinade for at least 5 minutes; this will eliminate harmful bacteria that may remain from the raw chicken

chicken stuffed with sun-dried tomatoes, aged cheddar and olives { *Serves 6*

1½ lb skinless boneless chicken breasts (about 4 to 6 chicken breasts)
½ cup finely chopped rehydrated sun-dried tomatoes
½ cup shredded aged white cheddar cheese
¼ cup finely chopped black olives
2 tsp olive oil
½ tsp dried basil
1 egg
2 Tbsp low-fat milk
¾ cup seasoned dry breadcrumbs
2 tsp vegetable oil
3 Tbsp chopped fresh basil

A STUFFED BONELESS CHICKEN BREAST is moist and can be served sliced in medallions to show off the attractive interior. I like to use a white aged cheddar rather than orange. If white cheddar is unavailable, try using another stronger tasting hard white cheese.

1. Preheat the oven to 425°F. Lightly coat a 9- × 13-inch casserole dish with cooking spray.
2. Working with one at a time, place a chicken breast between 2 sheets of waxed paper and pound to an even ½-inch thickness. Set aside.
3. Combine the sun-dried tomatoes, cheddar cheese, olives, olive oil and dried basil in a small bowl. Divide tomato mixture equally among the chicken breasts. Roll each one up and close with a toothpick.
4. Whisk together the egg and milk in shallow dish. Place the breadcrumbs in another bowl. Carefully dip each chicken breast into the egg mixture and then into the breadcrumbs.
5. Lightly coat a large, nonstick skillet with cooking spray, add the vegetable oil and sauté for 2 minutes per side or just until browned on all sides. Place in a casserole dish. Bake for 10 minutes or just until cooked (the chicken is done when it has reached an internal temperature of 165°F). Serve garnished with fresh basil.

PER SERVING Calories 273 • Protein 29 g • Carbohydrates 13 g • Fiber 1.5 g • Total fat 11 g • Saturated fat 3.5 g • Cholesterol 109 mg • Sodium 373 mg • **PREP TIME** 15 minutes • **COOK TIME** 12 minutes • **MAKE AHEAD** Bake up to a day in advance and reheat gently in a 350°F oven for 10 minutes or until warmed through. • **NUTRITION WATCH** Sun-dried tomatoes retain, for the most part, most of their vitamins and minerals.

havarti and roasted red pepper layered chicken loaf { *Serves 6*

1½ lb ground chicken
½ cup seasoned dry breadcrumbs
1½ tsp finely chopped garlic
1 large egg
¼ cup finely chopped yellow onion
¼ cup ketchup
½ tsp dried basil
pinch of salt and pepper
⅓ cup finely diced green onions
2 oz roasted red pepper, chopped (about ½ whole red bell pepper) (see page 100)
¼ diced rehydrated sun-dried tomatoes
½ cup shredded havarti

THIS IS A HEALTHIER ALTERNATIVE to a regular meatloaf. The layered effect, using roasted red peppers, sun-dried tomatoes and havarti, not only adds flavor but is beautiful when sliced.

1. Preheat the oven to 375°F. Line the bottom and sides of a 9- × 5-inch loaf pan with foil or parchment paper.
2. In a bowl, combine the ground chicken, breadcrumbs, garlic, egg, onion, ketchup, dried basil, salt and pepper until well mixed. Pat half of the chicken mixture into the prepared loaf pan. Sprinkle with the green onions, red pepper, sun-dried tomatoes and all but 2 Tbsp of the havarti. Pat the remaining chicken mixture over the filling. Bake for 40 minutes or until the interior temperature reaches 165°F. Sprinkle with the remaining cheese and bake for 2 minutes or until the cheese melts. Let stand for 10 minutes, then slice and serve.

PER SERVING Calories 280 • Protein 22 g • Carbohydrates 13 g • Fiber 1.8 g • Total fat 14.3 g • Saturated fat 4.9 g • Cholesterol 130 mg • Sodium 420 mg • **PREP TIME** 15 minutes • **COOK TIME** 40 minutes • **MAKE AHEAD** Can be baked the day before and reheated in a 350°F oven for 10 minutes or until warm. • **NUTRITION WATCH** Ketchup is a tomato-based product and, as such, has lycopene, a cancer-fighting antioxidant. Experts say that processed tomato products are higher in lycopene than fresh tomatoes. Keep in mind that ketchup is high in sodium (1 Tbsp = 150 mg).

teriyaki chicken stir-fry { *Serves 4*

SAUCE

¾ cup beef (or chicken) stock

3 Tbsp packed brown sugar

2 Tbsp low-sodium soy sauce

2 Tbsp rice vinegar

2 tsp sesame oil

1 Tbsp cornstarch

2 tsp finely chopped garlic

1½ tsp finely chopped ginger

½ tsp hot chili sauce

STIR-FRY

12 oz skinless boneless chicken thighs (about 3 thighs), diced

3 Tbsp all-purpose flour

2 tsp vegetable oil

1 cup sliced onion

1 cup thinly sliced red bell pepper

1 cup snow peas, cut in half

GARNISH

¼ cup chopped cilantro or parsley

¼ cup chopped green onions

2 Tbsp chopped toasted cashews (optional)

HERE'S MY TRADITIONAL TERIYAKI-BASED STIR-FRY. This sauce can be used over beef or fish as well, and is great served with rice or rice noodles. To toast your cashews, just place them in a dry skillet over high heat for about 2 minutes, or until lightly browned.

1. To make the sauce, whisk the stock, brown sugar, soy sauce, vinegar, sesame oil, cornstarch, garlic, ginger and chili sauce in a bowl. Set aside.
2. Coat the chicken with flour. Lightly coat a large, nonstick skillet with cooking spray, add the oil and chicken and sauté for 3 minutes until browned. Do not cook through. Remove from pan.
3. Wipe the pan and respray. Add the onion and stir-fry for 3 minutes or until softened. Add the red bell pepper and snow peas and stir-fry for 2 minutes. Add the sauce to the vegetables along with the chicken. Cook on high heat until the sauce thickens and the chicken is cooked, about 2 minutes.
4. Place on a serving platter and garnish with cilantro, green onions and cashews (if using).

PER SERVING Calories 313 • Protein 19 g • Carbohydrates 29 g • Fiber 2.0 g • Total fat 14 g • Saturated fat 2.7 g • Cholesterol 56 mg • Sodium 435 mg • **PREP TIME** 20 minutes • **COOK TIME** 10 minutes • **MAKE AHEAD** Prepare the sauce and keep refrigerated for up to 2 days. • **NUTRITION WATCH** Studies suggest that the short-term use of ginger can safely relieve pregnancy-related nausea and vomiting.

hoisin chicken with mushrooms and red bell pepper { *Serves 6*

1½ lb skinless boneless chicken thighs (about 6 thighs)
¼ cup all-purpose flour
4 tsp vegetable oil
1½ cups sliced onion
4 cups thickly sliced oyster mushrooms
1⅓ cups sliced red bell pepper
1½ Tbsp low-sodium soy sauce
1½ Tbsp hoisin sauce
1 Tbsp water
2 tsp finely chopped garlic
2 tsp finely chopped ginger
1 Tbsp sesame oil
2 tsp rice vinegar
3 Tbsp chopped cilantro
1 tsp toasted sesame seeds

OYSTER MUSHROOMS go well with chicken and a hoisin sauce. Feel free to substitute another mushroom of your choice—just be sure to sauté long enough that no excess moisture remains.

1. Preheat the oven to 425°F. Lightly coat a 9- × 13-inch casserole dish with vegetable spray.
2. Dust the chicken with the flour. In a large, nonstick skillet lightly coated with cooking spray, add 2 tsp of the vegetable oil and set over medium heat. Add the chicken and sauté for about 8 minutes or until browned on all sides. Place in the casserole dish and set aside.
3. Wipe and respray the skillet, add the remaining 2 tsp of vegetable oil and set over medium heat. Add the onion and sauté for 5 minutes. Add the mushrooms and sauté for 8 minutes or until the mushrooms are no longer wet. Add the red bell pepper and sauté for 4 minutes.
4. Whisk together the soy sauce, hoisin sauce, water, garlic, ginger, sesame oil and rice vinegar in a small bowl. Add to the vegetables and cook for 1 minute. Pour over the chicken and bake for 10 to 15 minutes, or until the chicken is done (reaches an internal temperature of 165°F). Garnish with cilantro and sesame seeds.

PER SERVING Calories 264 • Protein 23 g • Carbohydrates 10 g • Fiber 1.2 g • Total fat 14.6 g • Saturated fat 3.0 g • Cholesterol 74 mg • Sodium 270 mg • **PREP TIME** 15 minutes • **COOK TIME** 35 minutes • **MAKE AHEAD** Bake the chicken up to a day in advance and reheat gently at 350°F for 10 minutes or until warm. • **NUTRITION WATCH** Although chicken thighs have twice the amount of fat as chicken breasts, they are high in niacin as well as selenium, which promotes men's reproductive health.

sesame-coated chicken fingers { *Serves 4*

1 lb skinless boneless chicken breasts (about 4 breasts)
½ cup all-purpose flour
1 tsp garlic powder
pinch of salt and pepper
1 egg
2 Tbsp low-fat milk
¾ cup seasoned dry breadcrumbs
5 Tbsp sesame seeds

AFTER HAVING HOMEMADE baked chicken fingers you'll wonder why you ever ate those deep-fried ones with all the fat and calories. Dip these in some honey or plum sauce.

1. Preheat the oven to 375°F. Line a baking sheet with foil and lightly coat with cooking spray.
2. Cut the chicken into strips about 6 inches long and 1 inch wide.
3. Combine the flour, garlic powder, salt and pepper and place in a shallow bowl. Whisk together the egg and milk in another bowl. Combine the breadcrumbs and sesame seeds in another bowl.
4. Dip the chicken strips in the flour mixture, followed by the egg mixture, then the breadcrumb mixture. Place the strips on the prepared baking sheet. Lightly coat with cooking spray and bake for about 10 minutes, until just cooked.

PER SERVING Calories 343 • Protein 31 g • Carbohydrates 29 g • Fiber 2.5 g • Total fat 10 g • Saturated fat 1.4 g • Cholesterol 116 mg • Sodium 314 mg • **PREP TIME** 10 minutes • **COOK TIME** 10 minutes • **MAKE AHEAD** Although these can be breaded up to a day in advance, they are best when baked just before you serve them. • **NUTRITION WATCH** One serving of fried chicken fingers will cost you about 873 calories, 58 g of fat and 1,100 mg of sodium.

chicken with plum tomatoes and three cheeses { *Serves 6*

1½ lb skinless boneless chicken breasts (about 4 to 6 breasts)
1 egg
2 Tbsp low-fat milk
¾ cup seasoned dry breadcrumbs
2 tsp vegetable oil
1⅓ cups diced plum tomatoes
½ cup shredded havarti
¼ cup crumbled goat cheese (about 1 oz)
2 Tbsp grated Parmesan cheese
¼ cup finely chopped black olives
1 tsp finely chopped garlic
1 tsp dried basil
3 Tbsp chopped fresh basil or parsley

I INITIALLY CREATED THIS RECIPE for white fish; I then tried the delicious topping over a grain. Now I've found it works well with chicken. Use a variety of cheeses of your choice, but be sure to include a couple of stronger-tasting ones.

1. Preheat the oven to 425°F. Lightly coat a 9- × 13-inch casserole dish with cooking spray.
2. Working with one at a time, place a chicken breast between 2 sheets of waxed paper and pound to an even ½-inch thickness.
3. Beat the egg and milk together in a shallow bowl. Place the breadcrumbs on a separate plate or shallow dish.
4. Lightly coat a large, nonstick skillet with cooking spray, add the oil and place over medium-high heat. Dip each flattened chicken breast into the egg mixture, then coat in the breadcrumbs. Cook for 3 minutes per side or until browned and almost cooked through. Transfer to the prepared casserole dish.
5. Combine the tomatoes, havarti, goat and Parmesan cheeses, olives, garlic and dried basil in a bowl. Spoon over the chicken breasts. Cover and bake for 10 minutes or until the cheese melts and the chicken is done (has reached an internal temperature of 165°F). Garnish with fresh basil or parsley and serve.

PER SERVING Calories 315 • Protein 32 g • Carbohydrates 13 g • Fiber 1.5 g • Total fat 13 g • Saturated fat 5.7 g • Cholesterol 116 mg • Sodium 379 mg • **PREP TIME** 15 minutes • **COOK TIME** 15 minutes • **MAKE AHEAD** Prepare the chicken up to a day in advance. Sauté and bake just before serving. • **NUTRITION WATCH** If you are pregnant, it is better to use hard cheeses instead of soft ones. Soft cheese tends to be contaminated more often and may be unpasteurized. It is safe for adults but may be a concern for pregnant women.

Served with *Green Beans with Dried Apricots and Almonds* (page 178)

pecan and panko–crusted chicken with orange and apricot glaze { *Serves 6*

CHICKEN

- 1½ lb skinless boneless chicken breasts (about 4 to 6 breasts)
- 1 egg
- 2 Tbsp low-fat milk
- ¾ finely chopped toasted pecans
- ⅓ cup panko crumbs (or seasoned dry breadcrumbs)
- ½ tsp garlic powder
- 2 tsp vegetable oil

GLAZE

- 2 tsp brown sugar
- 2½ Tbsp orange marmalade
- 2½ Tbsp apricot jam
- 1 tsp Dijon mustard
- 1½ Tbsp water
- 1 Tbsp lemon juice
- 2 Tbsp chopped toasted pecans
- 3 Tbsp chopped cilantro
- 3 Tbsp chopped dried apricots

SINCE I'VE DISCOVERED PANKO CRUMBS (Japanese-style breadcrumbs), I want to use them in everything where I had previously used regular breadcrumbs. They have a wonderfully different flavor and texture. If you can't find them, you can use regular or seasoned breadcrumbs. If you like, substitute any nuts of your choice for the pecans.

1. Working with one at a time, place a chicken breast between 2 sheets of waxed paper and pound to an even ½-inch thickness. Set aside. Whisk together the egg and milk and pour into in a shallow dish. Set aside. In the bowl of a food processor, combine the toasted pecans, crumbs and garlic powder. Set aside.
2. Lightly coat a large, nonstick skillet with cooking spray, add the oil and set over medium-high heat. Dip the pounded chicken breasts in the egg mixture, then into the pecan mixture. Sauté for 2 minutes per side or just until browned on both sides. Place in a casserole dish and bake for 5 minutes or until the chicken is no longer pink.
3. In the meantime, make the glaze by whisking together the brown sugar, marmalade, jam, Dijon, water and lemon juice in a small saucepan. Bring to a boil, reduce the heat and simmer for 1 minute. Pour over the cooked chicken. Garnish with the pecans, cilantro and dried apricots and serve immediately.

PER SERVING Calories 380 • Protein 28 g • Carbohydrates 25 g • Fiber 1.8 g • Total fat 17 g • Saturated fat 2.5 g • Cholesterol 99 mg • Sodium 128 mg • **PREP TIME** 20 minutes • **COOK TIME** 10 minutes • **MAKE AHEAD** Bread the chicken and prepare the glaze early in the day. Bake just before serving. • **NUTRITION WATCH** Panko or Japanese breadcrumbs contain only 100 calories per ½ cup and contain no fat. Traditional breadcrumbs contain 220 calories per ½ cup and have 3 g of fat.

grilled chicken with pineapple salsa { *Serves 6*

1½ lb skinless boneless chicken breasts (about 4 to 6 breasts)
1 cup diced fresh pineapple
⅓ cup diced red bell pepper
⅓ cup diced ripe avocado
¼ cup chopped fresh cilantro or basil
1 tsp lemon juice
1 tsp honey
½ tsp lemon zest
2 tsp olive oil
1½ tsp low-sodium soy sauce
½ tsp finely chopped garlic

THIS IS A QUICK AND DELICIOUS CHICKEN RECIPE when fresh fruit is in season. Substitute mango or papaya for the pineapple if you wish.

1. Working with one at a time, place a chicken breast between 2 sheets of waxed paper and pound to an even ½-inch thickness. Set aside.
2. Prepare the salsa by combining the pineapple, red bell pepper, avocado, cilantro, lemon juice, honey and zest, olive oil, soy sauce and garlic in a bowl.
3. Preheat a barbecue to medium-high heat or lightly coat a large, nonstick grill pan with cooking spray and set over medium-high heat. Grill the chicken for 3 minutes per side or until no longer pink. Serve the salsa on the grilled chicken.

PER SERVING Calories 167 • Protein 23 g • Carbohydrates 5 g • Fiber 0.8 g • Total fat 5.7 g • Saturated fat 1.2 g • Cholesterol 63 mg • Sodium 120 mg • **PREP TIME** 15 minutes • **COOK TIME** 6 minutes • **MAKE AHEAD** Prepare salsa early in the day. • **NUTRITION WATCH** Pineapple is a very good source of fiber and, like citrus fruits, is high in vitamin C.

chicken stuffed with dried apricots, goat cheese and pecans { *Serves 6*

CHICKEN

1½ lb skinless boneless chicken breasts (about 4 to 6 breasts)

1 egg

2 Tbsp low-fat milk

¾ cup seasoned dry breadcrumbs

2 tsp vegetable oil

STUFFING

½ cup finely chopped dried apricots

¼ cup chopped toasted pecans

½ tsp cinnamon

pinch of ground cloves

2 tsp olive oil

¼ cup diced green onions

2 tsp brown sugar

¼ cup crumbled goat cheese (about 1 oz)

3 Tbsp chopped fresh basil or parsley

GLAZE (OPTIONAL)

3 Tbsp apricot jam

1 Tbsp maple syrup

½ tsp Dijon mustard

2 tsp apple cider vinegar

THESE CHICKEN BREASTS can be served either whole, or sliced in medallions to show off the interior. The color and texture of the stuffing is outstanding, and really livens up plain chicken breast. Try a variety of different dried fruits, cheese and nuts. The glaze is optional but offers a nice finishing touch.

1. Preheat the oven to 425°F. Lightly coat a 9- × 13-inch casserole dish with cooking spray.
2. Working with one at a time, place a chicken breast between 2 sheets of waxed paper and pound to an even ½-inch thickness. Set aside. Whisk together the egg and milk and pour into in a shallow dish. Set aside. Place the breadcrumbs on a separate shallow dish or plate.
3. Make the stuffing by combining the dried apricots, pecans, cinnamon, ground cloves, olive oil, green onions, brown sugar and goat cheese in a small bowl. Divide the mixture evenly among the chicken breasts. Roll up the breasts tightly and secure with a toothpick.
4. Lightly coat a large, nonstick skillet with cooking spray, add the vegetable oil and set over medium-high heat. Dip each stuffed breast into the egg mixture, then into the breadcrumbs. Sauté the chicken breasts for about 5 minutes or just until browned on all sides. Place in the casserole dish and bake for 10 minutes or just until the chicken is no longer pink. Slice into medallions, garnish with basil or parsley and serve.
5. If making the glaze, combine the jam, syrup, mustard and vinegar in a small saucepan over medium-low heat. Simmer for 3 minutes, or until slightly thickened. Serve spooned over the chicken medallions.

PER SERVING Calories 298 • Protein 27 g • Carbohydrates 19 g • Fiber 2.0 g • Total fat 12 g • Saturated fat 2.6 g • Cholesterol 101 mg • Sodium 192 mg • **PREP TIME** 15 minutes • **COOK TIME** 15 minutes • **MAKE AHEAD** Stuff the breasts up to a day in advance. Sauté and bake just before serving. • **NUTRITION WATCH** Use dried fruit in moderation as it has more calories and sugar per gram than fresh fruit.

roasted chicken and vegetables with mediterranean sauce { *Serves 8*

CHICKEN

1 roasting chicken (about 3 lb) with skin

1 tsp olive oil

pinch of salt and pepper

¼ tsp paprika

VEGETABLES

6 plum tomatoes cut into wedges

1 large onion cut into wedges

1 large green bell pepper, cut into wedges

1 head of garlic (top sliced off and wrapped with foil)

SAUCE

¾ cup chicken stock

¾ cup tomato sauce (see page 334) (or store-bought spaghetti sauce)

1½ tsp cornstarch

2 tsp olive oil

½ tsp dried basil

¼ tsp dried oregano

GARNISH (OPTIONAL)

¼ cup chopped fresh basil

¼ cup crumbled light feta cheese (about 1 oz)

WHEN YOU FIND A GOOD ROASTED CHICKEN RECIPE, you keep it on hand for years. This is one of those recipes. Although it requires a few more steps than just a basic roasted chicken—with the roasted vegetables and tomato-based sauce—you'll find that the end result is outstanding.

1. Preheat the oven to 425°F. Lightly coat a 9-inch-square casserole dish (large enough for the chicken) with cooking spray. Place the chicken in the casserole dish breast side up. Rub with 1 tsp olive oil, salt, pepper and paprika.
2. Line a baking sheet with foil and lightly coat with cooking spray. Place the cut tomatoes, onion and green bell pepper on the prepared baking sheet and lightly coat with cooking spray. Place the wrapped head of garlic on the baking sheet as well.
3. Place the vegetables and the chicken in the oven. After 25 minutes, remove just the tomatoes and place in a large bowl. Turn the other vegetables over and continue roasting for another 15 minutes. Remove the tray of vegetables, and set the head of garlic aside to cool. Add the roasted onion and bell pepper to the roasted tomatoes. Set aside.
4. Reduce the heat to 350°F and continue roasting the chicken for another 40 minutes, basting with juice from the chicken every 15 minutes. Cook until the chicken temperature reaches 165°F or juices from the thigh run clear. Remove from the oven and let sit 10 minutes before carving. Drain the fat.
5. In a small pot, combine the chicken stock, tomato sauce, cornstarch, olive oil and dried basil and oregano. Whisk until the cornstarch dissolves. Bring to a slow boil, then simmer for 3 minutes or until slightly thickened.
6. Squeeze the roasted garlic out of the cloves and add to the roasted vegetables. Reheat the vegetables either in the microwave or in the casserole dish in oven.
7. Carve the chicken into 8 pieces and remove the skin before serving. Place on a serving dish with the cooked vegetables and serve the sauce on the side. Garnish with fresh basil and feta, if using.

PER SERVING Calories 274 • Protein 29 g • Carbohydrates 12 g • Fiber 3 g • Total fat 12 g • Saturated fat 2.7 g • Cholesterol 84 mg • Sodium 293 mg • **PREP TIME** 15 minutes • **COOK TIME** 85 minutes • **MAKE AHEAD** Roast the chicken and the vegetables up to a day in advance. Cut up and reheat in 350°F oven for 10 minutes or until warm. • **NUTRITION WATCH** A 3 oz chicken breast *without* the skin has 140 calories and 3 g of fat, whereas a 3 oz chicken breast *with* the skin has 180 calories and 7 g of fat!

tortilla chip–crusted chicken with guacamole and salsa { *Serves 6*

GUACAMOLE

- ½ cup mashed ripe avocado
- 2 Tbsp chopped cilantro
- 1 Tbsp light mayonnaise
- 1 tsp finely chopped jalapeño pepper (or ½ tsp hot chili sauce)
- ½ tsp finely chopped garlic
- 2 tsp lemon or lime juice
- pinch of salt and pepper

CHICKEN

- 1½ lb skinless boneless chicken breasts (about 4 to 6 breasts)
- 1 egg
- 2 Tbsp low-fat milk
- 2½ cups baked tortilla chips
- ⅓ cup seasoned dry breadcrumbs
- ¼ tsp chili powder
- 2 tsp vegetable oil

TO SERVE

- ⅓ cup medium salsa
- ¼ cup canned black beans, drained and rinsed
- ½ cup shredded aged white cheddar cheese

THE TORTILLA CHIP CRUST IS CRUNCHIER than a regular bread-crumb crust and gives the chicken a different texture. This is my version of a Southwest chicken dish, and has much less fat and fewer calories than the traditional Mexican version. If you can't find baked tortilla chips use regular, but the number of calories and amount of fat will be slightly higher.

continued on page 278

Pictured with *Fresh Corn Salad* (page 105)

tortilla chip–crusted chicken with guacamole and salsa *continued*

1. Preheat the oven to 400°F. Lightly coat a baking sheet lined with foil with cooking spray.
2. To make the guacamole, combine the avocado, cilantro, mayonnaise, jalapeño, garlic, lemon juice, salt and pepper in a small bowl. Cover and set aside.
3. Working with one at a time, place a chicken breast between 2 sheets of waxed paper and pound to an even ½-inch thickness. Set aside. Whisk together the egg and milk and pour into in a shallow dish. Set aside. In the bowl of a food processor, combine the tortilla chips, breadcrumbs and chili powder. Process until crumbly. Dip the pounded chicken breasts in the egg and milk mixture, then into the tortilla crumb mixture.
4. Lightly coat a large, nonstick skillet with cooking spray, add the oil and sauté the chicken breasts for about 3 minutes per side or until browned. Place the chicken on the prepared baking sheet.
5. Divide the salsa over the chicken. Top with the beans and cheese. Bake for 10 minutes or until the chicken is just cooked. Serve with the guacamole.

PER SERVING Calories 425 • Protein 33 g • Carbohydrates 37 g • Fiber 4.5 g • Total fat 16 g • Saturated fat 4.7 g • Cholesterol 114 mg • Sodium 334 mg • **PREP TIME** 25 minutes • **COOK TIME** 15 minutes • **MAKE AHEAD** Prepare the chicken and guacamole early in the day. Bake just before serving. • **NUTRITION WATCH** Canned beans can have a high amount of sodium, from 140 to 500 mg for a ½-cup serving, so consider rinsing them thoroughly with cold water before using in a recipe.

chicken breast stuffed with asparagus, roasted red pepper and brie { *Serves 6*

CHICKEN

1½ lb skinless boneless chicken breasts (about 4 to 6 breasts)

1 egg

2 Tbsp low-fat milk (or water)

⅔ cup seasoned dry breadcrumbs or panko crumbs

2 tsp vegetable oil

STUFFING

12 small (or 4 large) asparagus spears (about ¼ lb), trimmed

¼ cup diced brie

¼ cup chopped roasted red pepper (about ½ small roasted red pepper) (see page 100)

½ tsp dried basil

3 Tbsp chopped fresh basil

THIS IS A SIMPLE AND ELEGANT RECIPE for a boneless chicken breast. I like to serve this sliced to show the attractive interior. If you want a stronger flavor, use a sharp cheese such as Swiss or Asiago, instead of the brie. You could even try blue cheese.

1. Preheat the oven to 400°F. Lightly coat a 9- × 13-inch casserole dish with cooking spray.
2. Working with one at a time, place a chicken breast between 2 sheets of waxed paper and pound to an even ½-inch thickness. Set aside.
3. For the stuffing, boil or steam the asparagus until just tender, about 2 minutes. Drain and rinse with cold water. Dice and place in a bowl. Add the brie, red pepper and dried basil.
4. Lay the chicken breasts flat and divide the stuffing equally among them. Roll up and secure with a toothpick. Whisk together the egg and milk and place in a shallow bowl. Place the breadcrumbs in another shallow bowl or plate.
5. Lightly coat a large, nonstick skillet with cooking spray, add the oil and set over medium-high heat. Dip the rolled chicken into the egg mixture and then into the breadcrumbs. Sauté the rolled chicken just until browned on all sides, about 5 minutes.
6. Place in the prepared casserole dish and bake another 10 to 15 minutes or until the chicken is no longer pink (or reaches an internal temperature of 165°F). Slice in half or into medallions to serve. Garnish with fresh basil.

PER SERVING Calories 222 • Protein 27 g • Fiber 1.3 g • Total fat 7.2 g • Saturated fat 2.1 g • Cholesterol 104 mg • Sodium 221 mg • **PREP TIME** 15 minutes • **COOK TIME** 17 minutes • **MAKE AHEAD** Roll and refrigerate up to a day in advance. Sauté and bake just before serving. • **NUTRITION WATCH** 1 oz of brie has 95 calories and is packed with calcium, which your body needs to build strong bones. Always eat higher-fat cheeses such as brie in moderation.

chicken supreme stuffed with cranberries, almonds and havarti { *Serves 4*

CHICKEN
4 chicken supreme (with skin on)

STUFFING
½ cup dried cranberries
¼ cup toasted almonds
½ tsp cinnamon
2 tsp olive oil
½ cup shredded havarti

SAUCE
¼ cup maple syrup
¼ cup thawed orange juice concentrate
1 Tbsp honey
1 Tbsp low-sodium soy sauce
2 tsp sesame oil
1½ tsp Dijon mustard
1 tsp finely chopped garlic
1½ tsp cornstarch

GARNISH
3 Tbsp chopped parsley

CHICKEN SUPREME is a boneless breast of chicken with the wing tip attached, and is often served at more formal dinners. If your butcher doesn't carry it, just use a 6-ounce boneless breast with the skin on. The skin adds flavor while cooking, but remove it before eating to save on calories. Use any variety of dried fruits, nuts or cheese in this delicious stuffing.

1. Preheat the oven to 400°F. Line a rimmed baking sheet with foil and lightly coat with cooking spray.
2. Make a horizontal slit in each piece of chicken to form a pocket for the stuffing, making sure not to cut all the way through.
3. To make the stuffing, finely chop the dried cranberries and almonds and place in a bowl. Add the cinnamon, olive oil and havarti. You can also use a small food processor. Stuff into the pockets of the chicken and secure with a toothpick.
4. Lightly coat a large, nonstick skillet with cooking spray and set over medium-high heat. Sauté the supremes for about 2 minutes per side or until just browned. Place on the prepared baking sheet and bake for 25 to 30 minutes or until no longer pink inside (until the internal temperature reaches 165°F).
5. Meanwhile, prepare the sauce by whisking together the maple syrup, orange juice concentrate, honey, soy sauce, sesame oil, Dijon, garlic and cornstarch in a small saucepan. Bring to a boil, reduce the heat and simmer for 1 minute or just until slightly thickened. Pour over the cooked chicken and garnish with chopped parsley. Serve immediately.

PER SERVING Calories 524 • Protein 35 g • Carbohydrates 46 g • Fiber 5.8 g • Total fat 23 g • Saturated fat 7.0 g • Cholesterol 96 mg • Sodium 314 mg • **PREP TIME** 15 minutes • **COOK TIME** 30 minutes • **MAKE AHEAD** Prepare the Supremes and sauce early in the day and refrigerate. Sauté and bake just before serving. • **NUTRITION WATCH** Cinnamon may help those with diabetes control their blood-sugar levels.

turkey scaloppini with creamy tomato sauce and mozzarella cheese { *Serves 4*

- 1 lb turkey breast
- 1 egg
- 2 Tbsp low-fat milk
- 1 cup seasoned dry breadcrumbs
- 2 tsp vegetable oil
- 1⅓ cups tomato sauce (see page 334) (or store-bought spaghetti sauce)
- 2 Tbsp canned evaporated milk (2%)
- ¾ cup shredded mozzarella cheese
- 3 Tbsp chopped fresh basil

IF YOU WANT A CHANGE OF PACE from Chicken Parmesan, in addition to fewer calories and less fat, try this. The turkey has a different flavor and texture, and goes well with the cheese and tomato sauce.

1. Preheat the oven to 425°F. Lightly coat a 13- × 9-inch casserole dish with cooking spray.
2. Place the turkey between 2 pieces of wax paper and pound until ¼-inch thickness. Set aside. Whisk together the egg and milk in a shallow dish. Place the breadcrumbs in a separate shallow dish or plate.
3. Lightly coat a large, nonstick skillet with cooking spray, add the oil and set over medium-high heat. Dip the turkey in the egg, and then into the breadcrumbs. Sauté the scaloppini just until almost cooked, about 5 minutes. Respray pan if necessary. Set aside.
4. Combine the tomato sauce and milk. Add 1 cup of the tomato mixture to the bottom of the casserole dish. Add the turkey scaloppini, pour the remaining sauce over the turkey and sprinkle with cheese. Bake for 10 minutes or until the cheese melts. Garnish with basil.

PER SERVING Calories 372 • Protein 39 g • Carbohydrates 28 g • Fiber 2.5 g • Total fat 11 g • Saturated fat 3.7 g • Cholesterol 147 mg • Sodium 432 mg • **PREP TIME** 10 minutes • **COOK TIME** 15 minutes • **MAKE AHEAD** Prepare the entire dish and refrigerate until ready to bake. • **NUTRITION WATCH** A 5 oz serving of turkey provides almost half of the recommended daily allowance of folic acid, and is a good source of the vitamins B, B1 and B6, zinc and potassium, which are great for keeping blood cholesterol down.

turkey scaloppini with cranberry sauce and pistachios { *Serves 4*

TURKEY

1 lb turkey scaloppini
1 egg
2 Tbsp low-fat milk
1 cup seasoned dry breadcrumbs
2 tsp vegetable oil

SAUCE

½ cup canned whole-cranberry sauce
1½ Tbsp low-sodium soy sauce
1 Tbsp orange juice concentrate
1½ tsp sesame oil
1½ tsp lemon juice
1 tsp brown sugar
1 tsp cornstarch
1 tsp finely chopped garlic
½ tsp finely chopped ginger

GARNISH

2 Tbsp chopped pistachios
¼ cup chopped parsley

TURKEY SCALOPPINI is boneless turkey breast that is sliced thinly and pounded. It's a wonderful alternative to chicken breast, with fewer calories and less fat and cholesterol. The cranberry sauce is a great addition to turkey, especially during the fall and winter seasons.

1. To prepare the sauce, whisk together the cranberry sauce, soy sauce, orange juice concentrate, sesame oil, lemon juice, brown sugar, cornstarch, garlic and ginger in a small saucepan. Bring to a boil, reduce the heat and simmer for 2 minutes or just until the cornstarch is dissolved and the sauce is slightly thickened. Keep warm.
2. Whisk together the egg and milk in a shallow dish or bowl. Place the breadcrumbs in another shallow dish or bowl.
3. Lightly coat a large, nonstick skillet with cooking spray, add the oil and set over medium-high heat. Dip the turkey scaloppini into the egg mixture, then into the breadcrumbs. Sauté for 2 to 3 minutes per side or just until cooked through. Keep warm.
4. Serve the sauce over the turkey scaloppini and garnish with the pistachios and parsley.

PER SERVING Calories 394 • Protein 33 g • Carbohydrates 38 g • Fiber 2.3 g • Total fat 12 g • Saturated fat 2.2 g • Cholesterol 135 mg • Sodium 474 mg • **PREP TIME** 15 minutes • **COOK TIME** 10 minutes • **MAKE AHEAD** Bread the turkey scaloppini and prepare the sauce early in the day and refrigerate. Cook just before serving. • **NUTRITION WATCH** Cranberry sauce has zero fat and zero cholesterol with a minimum of sodium. Much healthier than gravy-type sauces.

{ *pork, beef & lamb* }

Tightly wrapped fresh pork, beef and lamb can be kept refrigerated for 2 days in a cold section of the refrigerator. Meat can be frozen for up to 6 months. Package well to avoid freezer burn or discoloration • Defrost meat in the refrigerator, or wrap in plastic and place in a bowl of cold water to quicken defrosting. An even faster method is to defrost in the microwave. Rotate meat every few minutes to ensure even defrosting • Tender cuts of beef from the rib and sirloin areas contain a lot of fat and calories. Choose leaner cuts of meat such as flank, chuck or round, and trim all excess fat • To make lean cuts of meat tender, marinate them for at least 4 hours, or preferably overnight • It's not necessary to marinate cuts such as rib eye, sirloin, porterhouse or filet. These are the most tender. Remove visible fat before cooking • Pork can now be cooked to a medium doneness of 145°F without the risk of bacteria forming. Do not overcook, or the meat will become dry • Beef and lamb can be cooked to medium-rare. Cook to an internal temperature of 135°F for the best flavor and texture • If basting grilled or roasted meat with a sauce, remember to boil the remaining basting sauce for 5 minutes if you plan to serve it in the finished dish, to destroy harmful bacteria • You can use a grill pan or barbecue to cook your meats. Be sure to spray your grill and sear your meats on a high heat to retain the juices • Burgers must be cooked until no longer pink

pork tenderloin with peach glaze { *Serves 4*

PORK

1½ lb pork tenderloin

SAUCE

¼ cup peach (or apricot) jam

2 Tbsp apple juice concentrate

2 Tbsp apple cider vinegar

1 tsp chopped garlic

1 tsp Dijon mustard

½ tsp cornstarch

PEACHES

2 cups sliced fresh or frozen (and defrosted) peaches

1 Tbsp brown sugar

GARNISH

¼ cup chopped cilantro or parsley

THIS DISH GOES WELL with the peach jam sauce and freshly sliced peaches. You can refreeze the juice concentrate and use it when needed. Be sure not to overcook the pork or it will be dry.

1. Preheat the oven to 375°F. Line a 9- × 13-inch casserole dish with foil and lightly coat with cooking spray.
2. In a grill pan or sauté pan lightly coated with cooking spray, sear the pork on all sides over medium-high heat, about 2 or 3 minutes on each side. Place on the prepared baking sheet.
3. To make the sauce, combine the jam, juice concentrate, cider vinegar, garlic, Dijon and cornstarch by whisking together in a small bowl. Brush about 2 Tbsp of the sauce over the tenderloin. Bake for about 20 minutes or until cooked to medium (until the meat reaches an internal temperature of 145°F). Let the pork rest for 10 minutes before slicing.
4. Meanwhile, set a sauté pan over medium heat. Add the peaches and sugar and sauté for 2 minutes. Add the remaining peach jam sauce and cook over high heat for 1 minute or until the sauce is slightly thickened. Drizzle the sauce over the sliced pork. Garnish with cilantro or parsley.

PER SERVING Calories 301 • Protein 46 g • Carbohydrates 25 g • Fiber 1.3 g • Total fat 6.1 g • Saturated fat 1.9 g • Cholesterol 94 mg • Sodium 88 mg • **PREP TIME** About 5 minutes • **COOK TIME** 30 minutes • **MAKE AHEAD** Prepare the glaze up to 2 days in advance, cover and refrigerate. The dish can be baked up to a day in advance and reheated in a 350°F oven just until warm, about 10 minutes. • **NUTRITION WATCH** Peaches have vitamin A that may help fight the effects of aging.

orange-glazed pork tenderloin with cranberry and walnut stuffing { *Serves 6*

PORK

1½ lb pork tenderloin, butterflied

STUFFING

⅔ cup dried cranberries
⅓ cup toasted walnuts
½ tsp cinnamon
pinch of ground cloves
2 tsp walnut (or olive) oil
1 oz diced brie

GLAZE

2 Tbsp orange juice concentrate
2 Tbsp red currant or black currant jelly
1 tsp balsamic vinegar
1 tsp olive oil
1 tsp orange zest
½ tsp finely chopped garlic

GARNISH (OPTIONAL)

3 Tbsp chopped parsley

PORK TENDERLOIN IS A DELICIOUS and economical cut of meat. It's lean and, due to improved farming practices, you can now safely cook your pork to medium instead of well done, keeping the meat moist. To butterfly means to cut the pork down the center without cutting all the way through; then you can open and stuff the tenderloin. You can ask your butcher to do this if you prefer.

continued on page 290

Pictured with *Baked Root Vegetables with Maple Syrup and Cinnamon* (page 184)

1. Preheat the oven to 375°F. Line a baking sheet with foil lightly coated with cooking spray.
2. To make the stuffing, combine the cranberries, walnuts, cinnamon, cloves and walnut oil in the bowl of a small food processor. Pulse on and off until the mixture is crumbly. Add the diced brie and pulse once or twice, just to combine.
3. Open the pork loin like a book and stuff with the fruit and nut stuffing. (If you would like to make this easier to roll, first pound the pork to a ¼-inch thickness before stuffing.) Secure with either kitchen string or toothpicks. Set a large, nonstick grill pan or skillet lightly coated with cooking spray over medium-high heat and sear until browned on all sides, about 2 or 3 minutes on each side. Place on the baking sheet and bake for about 20 minutes or until cooked to medium (until the meat reaches an internal temperature of 145°F). Let rest for about 10 minutes before slicing.
4. Meanwhile, prepare the glaze by combining the orange juice concentrate, jelly, vinegar, olive oil, orange zest and garlic in a small saucepan. Set over medium heat for 1 minute and drizzle over the sliced pork. Garnish with parsley.

PER SERVING Calories 279 • Protein 25 g • Carbohydrates 20 g • Fiber 1.4 g • Total fat 11 g • Saturated fat 2.8 g • Cholesterol 68 mg • Sodium 77 mg • **PREP TIME** 15 minutes • **COOK TIME** 25 minutes • **MAKE AHEAD** Cook the pork up to a day in advance and reheat in a 350°F oven for 10 minutes, until warmed through. • **NUTRITION WATCH** Pork cuts such as tenderloin are low in calories, fat and cholesterol; a 3 oz serving has 145 calories, 5 g of fat and only 67 mg of cholesterol. Pork is also very high in B vitamins and zinc.

beef, bok choy and oyster mushroom stir-fry { *Serves 4*

SAUCE

1 cup chicken (or beef) stock
¼ cup hoisin sauce
2 Tbsp low-sodium soy sauce
5 tsp cornstarch
1 Tbsp brown sugar
2 tsp sesame oil
1½ tsp finely chopped garlic
1 tsp finely chopped ginger

STIR-FRY

12 oz grilling steak cut into 1-inch cubes
2 Tbsp all-purpose flour
2 tsp vegetable oil
2 cups chopped oyster mushrooms
2 small baby bok choy, sliced (or 2 cups sliced)
½ cup sliced water chestnuts

GARNISH

½ cup coarsely chopped cashews
1 large green onion, chopped
¼ cup chopped cilantro

THIS IS A GREAT STIR-FRY with its tender cut of beef, crisp bok choy and savory hoisin sauce. Feel free to substitute boneless chicken breast or shrimp for the beef.

1. To make the sauce, combine the stock, hoisin sauce, soy sauce, cornstarch, brown sugar, sesame oil, garlic and ginger in a small bowl. Whisk together until smooth.
2. Dust the steak pieces with flour. Lightly coat a large, nonstick skillet with cooking spray and set over medium-high heat and add the oil. Sauté the steak for 3 minutes or just until browned. Do not cook through. Set aside and wipe the pan clean.
3. Respray the pan and sauté the mushrooms for 5 minutes or until soft. Add the bok choy and sauté for 2 minutes or it begins to wilt. Add the sauce, water chestnuts and beef and stir-fry for 2 minutes or until the sauce thickens.
4. Place on a platter and garnish with cashews, green onions and cilantro.

PER SERVING Calories 314 • Protein 24 g • Carbohydrates 25 g • Fiber 3.3 g • Total fat 13 g • Saturated fat 3.1 g • Cholesterol 37 mg • Sodium 600 mg • **PREP TIME** 15 minutes • **COOK TIME** 12 minutes • **MAKE AHEAD** Prepare the sauce a day in advance and refrigerate. • **NUTRITION WATCH** Bok choy is a great source of vitamin C, calcium and vitamin A.

asian meatloaf with oyster mushrooms and red bell pepper { *Serves 6*

MEATLOAF

1½ lb ground beef
⅓ cup seasoned dry breadcrumbs
⅓ cup finely chopped green onions
¼ cup finely chopped cilantro
3 Tbsp hoisin sauce
1½ tsp finely chopped garlic
1 tsp finely chopped ginger
1 large egg

TOPPING

2 tsp vegetable oil
1 cup chopped onion
2 cups chopped oyster mushrooms
1 cup chopped red bell pepper
2 Tbsp low-sodium soy sauce
2 Tbsp hoisin sauce
1 Tbsp water
2 tsp finely chopped garlic
2 tsp finely chopped ginger
1 Tbsp sesame oil
2 tsp rice vinegar

GARNISH

3 Tbsp chopped cilantro or parsley

FORGET THE OLD, STANDARD SUNDAY NIGHT MEATLOAF and try this one instead. The sautéed mushrooms and bell pepper with hoisin sauce suit the beef perfectly. Use any variety of mushrooms you like, but be sure to sauté them until all the liquid evaporates.

1. Preheat oven to 375°F. Line the bottoms and sides of a 9- × 5-inch loaf pan with foil or parchment paper.
2. To make the meatloaf, combine the ground beef, breadcrumbs, green onions, cilantro, hoisin sauce, garlic, ginger and egg in a large bowl. Stir together or use your hands to combine the ingredients well. Pat the beef mixture into the prepared loaf pan. Bake for 40 minutes, or until the internal temperature of the meatloaf reaches 165°F.
3. While the meatloaf is baking, make the mushroom topping by heating the oil in a nonstick skillet lightly coated with cooking spray over medium-high heat. Add the onion and sauté for 3 minutes. Add the mushrooms and bell pepper and sauté for another 5 minutes. Add the soy sauce, hoisin sauce, water, garlic, ginger, sesame oil and rice vinegar and cook for 1 minute. Keep warm.
4. Remove the meatloaf from the oven and allow to sit in the pan for 10 minutes. Use the foil to help you remove the meatloaf from the pan. Slice and serve topped with the warmed mushroom sauce and garnished with cilantro or parsley.

PER SERVING Calories 267 • Protein 26 g • Carbohydrates 17 g • Fiber 2 g • Total fat 10 g • Saturated fat 2.4 g • Cholesterol 96 mg • Sodium 480 mg • **PREP TIME** 20 minutes • **COOK TIME** 50 minutes • **MAKE AHEAD** Prepare and bake the meatloaf a day in advance. Reheat in a 350°F oven for 10 minutes or until warm. Make the sauce ahead of time and warm before serving. • **NUTRITION WATCH** Ginger has always been known to relieve symptoms of gastrointestinal distress.

beef enchiladas with aged cheddar cheese sauce { *Serves 6*

BEEF FILLING

2 tsp vegetable oil
1½ cups diced onion
2 tsp finely chopped garlic
12 oz lean ground beef
1 cup diced green bell pepper
1 cup medium salsa
1 tsp finely chopped jalapeño pepper
⅓ cup chopped cilantro

SAUCE

1½ cups canned evaporated milk (2%)
1 cup chicken stock
3½ Tbsp all-purpose flour
1 tsp Dijon mustard
pinch of salt and pepper
1 cup shredded aged light cheddar cheese

ASSEMBLY

6 large flour tortillas
¼ cup shredded aged cheddar cheese
2 Tbsp chopped cilantro

TRADITIONAL ENCHILADAS in Mexican restaurants are loaded with fat, calories and cholesterol. The excess cheese and fatty cuts of beef that are usually used are to blame, as well as the deep-fried corn tortilla shells. You'll enjoy my light version. Feel free to try ground chicken or pork.

1. Preheat the oven to 425°F. Lightly coat a 9- × 13-inch casserole dish with cooking oil.
2. To make the filling, lightly coat a large, nonstick skillet with cooking spray. Add the oil and set over medium heat. Add the onion and garlic and sauté for 5 minutes or until the onion begins to brown. Add the ground beef and sauté for 5 minutes or until the beef is no longer pink. Add the green pepper and sauté for 3 more minutes. Add the salsa and jalapeño, cover and simmer for 5 minutes. Add the cilantro and set aside.
3. To make the sauce, place the evaporated milk, stock, flour, mustard, salt and pepper in a medium saucepan over medium-high heat. Bring to a boil while whisking together. Reduce the heat to medium and simmer until slightly thickened, about 3 minutes. Add the cheese and simmer, while whisking continuously, for another 2 minutes.
4. Add half the sauce to the beef filling and stir to combine.
5. Lay the tortillas on your work surface. Divide the filling-and-sauce mixture among the tortillas, spreading it along the center of each. Roll the tortillas up, leaving the ends open. Place in the casserole dish, seam side down, and pour the remaining sauce over the tortillas. Sprinkle with the ¼ cup cheese and bake uncovered for 12 to 15 minutes or until heated all the way through. Serve immediately, garnished with cilantro.

PER SERVING Calories 315 • Protein 26 g • Carbohydrates 38 g • Fiber 3.4 g • Total fat 9.7 g • Saturated fat 4.3 g • Cholesterol 47 mg • Sodium 724 mg • **PREP TIME** 20 minutes • **COOK TIME** 35 minutes • **MAKE AHEAD** You can prepare the enchiladas early in the day and refrigerate, but don't cover them with sauce. Add the sauce and bake just before serving, adding 10 minutes to the baking time. • **NUTRITION WATCH** Beef enchiladas are usually high in calories and fat, packing on average 750 calories and more than 45 g of fat! Try my version and save your waistline.

mediterranean burgers with feta cheese sauce { *Serves 4*

BURGERS

1 lb extra-lean ground beef
1 egg
1 tsp dried basil
½ tsp dried oregano
3 Tbsp seasoned dry breadcrumbs
3 Tbsp ketchup
2 tsp finely chopped garlic
¼ cup finely chopped onion
¼ cup crumbled feta cheese (about 1 oz)

SAUCE

¼ cup crumbled feta cheese (about 1 oz)
¼ cup light cream cheese (about 2 oz), softened
3 Tbsp low-fat plain yogurt (or sour cream)
½ tsp finely chopped garlic
1 Tbsp lemon juice
1 Tbsp water
½ tsp dried basil

GARNISH (OPIONAL)

3 Tbsp chopped fresh basil or parsley

I CREATED THIS RECIPE FOR A PROMOTION I DID with Scott paper towels. It was such a hit that I knew I had to include it here. The sauce is a must and totally completes this burger. No need for a bun.

1. To make the burgers, combine the ground beef, egg, dried basil and oregano, breadcrumbs, ketchup, garlic, onion and feta in a large bowl and shape into 4 burger patties. Grill or sauté in a pan lightly coated with cooking spray. Cook on 1 side for 7 minutes, then turn over and cook 3 to 5 more minutes or just until beef is done.
2. Combine all the sauce ingredients in a food processor and purée until smooth.
3. Serve the burgers with the sauce and garnish with fresh basil or parsley.

PER BURGER Calories 257 • Protein 29 g • Carbohydrates 11 g • Fiber 0.9 g • Total fat 11 g • Saturated fat 4.8 g • Cholesterol 126 mg • Sodium 370 mg • **PREP TIME** 15 minutes • **COOK TIME** 10 minutes • **MAKE AHEAD** Prepare the burgers up to 1 day in advance or freeze, separately wrapped, for up to 2 months. Grill without defrosting, just before serving. • **NUTRITION WATCH** Lean ground beef is a high quality protein, is a good source of B vitamins and iron and contains zinc.

Pictured with *Fingerling Potatoes with Olive Oil and Sea Salt* (page 191)

grilled flank steak with edamame salsa { *Serves 4*

BEEF

1½ lb flank steak

VINAIGRETTE MARINADE

½ cup balsamic vinegar

¼ cup vegetable oil

1 Tbsp lemon juice

1 Tbsp low-sodium soy sauce

2 tsp Dijon mustard

2 tsp finely chopped garlic

pinch of salt and pepper

SALSA

¼ cup low-sodium soy sauce

2 Tbsp rice vinegar

2 Tbsp olive oil

4 tsp sesame oil

2 tsp honey

1½ tsp finely chopped garlic

1 tsp finely chopped ginger

1½ tsp cornstarch

½ cup diced water chestnuts

⅓ cup diced red bell pepper

1 package (10 oz) frozen shelled edamame

GARNISH

⅓ cup cilantro

1 tsp sesame seeds

FLANK STEAK IS ONE OF THE LEANEST CUTS of beef. I like to marinate it in an oil and vinegar dressing to keep it moist. If you don't have time to make the vinaigrette marinade, you can use ¾ cup of a light bottled dressing. Or you can create your own marinade with herbs of your choice. Edamame is a healthy and delicious accompaniment to this beef, and packages of shelled edamame can be found in the freezer section of your supermarket.

1. Make the vinaigrette marinade by combining the balsamic vinegar, vegetable oil, lemon juice, soy sauce, mustard, garlic, salt and pepper in a large bowl.
2. Marinate the flank steak in the vinaigrette for at least 2 hours or, if time permits, overnight, turning once. Lightly coat a nonstick grill pan or barbecue with cooking spray and preheat to medium-high. Cook the beef for 5 to 8 minutes per side or until done to your liking.
3. Meanwhile, make the salsa by whisking together the soy sauce, rice vinegar, olive and sesame oils, honey, garlic, ginger and cornstarch in a medium saucepan over medium heat. Cook for 2 minutes or until slightly thickened, then add the water chestnuts, red bell pepper and edamame and cook for 2 more minutes.
4. Slice the steak against the grain into thin slices, arrange on a platter and pour the salsa over the steak. Garnish with cilantro and sesame seeds.

PER SERVING Calories 485 • Protein 44 g • Carbohydrates 17 g • Fiber 22 g • Total fat 26 g • Saturated fat 6 g • Cholesterol 67 mg • Sodium 500 mg • **PREP TIME** 15 minutes (not including the marinating time) • **COOK TIME** 15 minutes • **MAKE AHEAD** Edamame salsa can be prepared early in the day, and can be gently reheated before serving. • **NUTRITION WATCH** A food-guide serving of flank steak has 177 calories and 7 g of fat. Compare that to regular rib eye, which has 217 calories and 12 g of fat.

steak with mashed white kidney beans { *Serves 4*

BEEF

1½ lb grilling steak

CARAMELIZED ONIONS

1 tsp vegetable oil

2 cups finely diced onion

2 tsp finely chopped garlic

2 tsp brown sugar

MASH

3 cups canned white kidney beans, drained and rinsed

½ tsp finely chopped garlic

1½ Tbsp olive oil

1 Tbsp lemon juice

1 Tbsp water

1 tsp hot chili sauce

pinch of salt and pepper

GARNISH

¼ cup chopped fresh basil

INSTEAD OF MASHED POTATOES with steak, try this white bean mash. It's delicious and certainly more nutritious. The caramelized onions add a sweet and savory depth to the dish.

1. Prepare the caramelized onions by spraying a small, nonstick skillet with cooking spray and setting it over medium heat. Add the oil and onion and sauté for 5 minutes. Add the garlic and sugar and reduce to low heat. Sauté for 10 minutes, until the onion is browned. Take off the heat and remove half of the onions for the garnish, setting them aside in a bowl. Keep the other half in the skillet off the heat.
2. To make the mash, combine the beans, garlic, oil, lemon juice, water, chili sauce, salt and pepper. Purée until smooth. Add the bean mash to the remaining sautéed onions in the skillet. Cover to keep warm.
3. Lightly coat a nonstick grill pan or barbecue with cooking spray and sauté the steak until done to your preference, about 10 minutes, depending upon the thickness of the steak.
4. Place the bean mash on a serving plate, slice the steak and arrange on top of the mash. Garnish with the remaining onion and fresh basil, and serve.

PER SERVING Calories 492 • Protein 46 g • Carbohydrates 34 g • Fiber 8.5 g • Total fat 18 g • Saturated fat 4.6 g • Cholesterol 73 mg • Sodium 320 mg • **PREP TIME** 15 minutes • **COOK TIME** 25 minutes • **MAKE AHEAD** Prepare the caramelized onions and white bean mash up to a day ahead. Reheat gently on the stovetop. • **NUTRITION WATCH** Kidney beans are a good source of protein and manganese, providing energy and antioxidant defense.

calf's liver with balsamic-glazed onions { *Serves 6*

LIVER

1½ lb calf's liver

⅓ cup all-purpose flour

ONIONS

1 large Vidalia onion (or 2 medium onions)

4 tsp vegetable oil

1 Tbsp brown sugar

1 Tbsp balsamic vinegar

GARNISH

3 Tbsp chopped parsley

MANY OF US WOULDN'T PREPARE LIVER as a main meal in our homes, and would rather order it in restaurants. Try making calf's liver, which is more tender than beef liver, with these delicious sautéed onions. Just remember not to overcook the liver or it will be dry.

1. Cut the onions into ¼-inch separated rings.
2. In a large skillet lightly coated with cooking spray, add 1 tsp of the oil and the onion rings and sauté for 10 minutes on medium heat, just until the onions begin to soften, stirring often. Add the brown sugar and cook on low heat for 15 minutes, stirring often. Add the vinegar and sauté for another 2 minutes, until the liquid is absorbed.
3. Dust the liver with flour. In a nonstick skillet lightly coated with cooking spray, add the remaining 3 tsp of the oil and sauté the liver just until medium, about 3 minutes per side, or done to your preference. If the pan gets dry, respray.
4. Serve the onions over the liver and garnish with parsley.

PER SERVING Calories 207 • Protein 23 g • Carbohydrates 10 g • Fiber 0.6 g • Total fat 8 g • Saturated fat 0.2 g • Cholesterol 408 mg • Sodium 102 mg • **PREP TIME** 10 minutes • **COOK TIME** 35 minutes • **MAKE AHEAD** Prepare the onions early on the day you want to serve them. Reheat gently before serving with the liver. • **NUTRITION WATCH** Calf's liver is filled with vitamin A and zinc, which can support your immune system.

leg of lamb stuffed with mushrooms, spinach and goat cheese { *Serves 6*

LAMB

2 lb boneless leg of lamb, butterflied

vinaigrette marinade (see pages 298–99)

SAUCE

⅔ cup beef stock

½ cup red wine

2 tsp finely chopped garlic

STUFFING

2 tsp vegetable oil

1½ cups diced onion

1 Tbsp finely chopped garlic

4 cups finely diced oyster mushrooms

4 cups chopped fresh baby spinach

½ cup crumbled goat cheese (about 2 oz)

1 tsp dried basil

pinch of salt and pepper

GARNISH

3 Tbsp chopped fresh basil or parsley

THIS STUFFING SUITS THE LAMB FLAVOR so well that you don't even need any gravy. Use any variety of mushrooms you have, but be sure to cook them until all the moisture is evaporated. Ask your butcher to butterfly your leg of lamb.

1. Preheat the oven to 375°F. Lightly coat a large roasting pan with cooking spray.
2. Lay the lamb flat, open it like a book, cover with plastic wrap and pound until it is an even thickness. Pour the marinade over the lamb and refrigerate for at least 2 hours, but preferably overnight.
3. To make the sauce, combine the beef stock, red wine and garlic in a bowl. Set aside.
4. To make the stuffing, lightly coat a large, nonstick skillet with cooking spray and set over medium heat. Add the oil, onion and garlic and sauté for 5 minutes. Add the mushrooms and sauté for 10 minutes or until they are dry, stirring often. Add the spinach and sauté for 3 minutes or until the spinach is wilted. Add the goat cheese, dried basil, salt and pepper and cook for about 1 minute, stirring until well combined.
5. Place half of the stuffing down the middle of the marinated lamb. Fold the lamb in half. Secure with kitchen string or toothpicks to keep the stuffing in place. Place the remaining stuffing in a bowl and set aside.
6. Lightly coat a large, nonstick skillet or grill pan with cooking spray and set over medium-high heat. Sear the lamb for 2 to 3 minutes on each side. Place the lamb in the roasting pan on an oven rack. Pour the sauce into the bottom of the roasting pan. Roast the lamb for about 30 minutes, or until done to your liking (the lamb should be at an internal temperature of 135°F for medium-rare). If the liquid in the pan evaporates, add more wine or stock.
7. Let the lamb rest for 10 minutes, then slice thinly and serve with any of the pan juices (if desired). Garnish with fresh basil and serve with the remaining stuffing.

PER SERVING Calories 302 • Protein 32 g • Carbohydrates 10 g • Fiber 1.9 g • Total fat 13 g • Saturated fat 4.9 g • Cholesterol 96 mg • Sodium 237 mg • **PREP TIME** 15 minutes (not including the marinating time) • **COOK TIME** 55 minutes • **MAKE AHEAD** Prepare the lamb early in the day and bake just before serving. Reheat leftovers in a 350°F oven for 10 minutes or just until warmed through. • **NUTRITION WATCH** Lamb is a good source of zinc, which supports the function of your immune system.

grilled lamb burgers { *Serves 4*

BURGERS

2 tsp vegetable oil

1 cup finely chopped mushrooms

½ cup finely chopped onion

½ cup crumbled light feta cheese (about 2 oz)

1 lb lean ground lamb

¼ cup finely chopped fresh chives (or green onions)

1 tsp dried oregano

2 Tbsp barbecue sauce

3 Tbsp seasoned dry breadcrumbs

1 egg

2 tsp finely chopped garlic

3 Tbsp finely chopped black olives

pinch of salt and pepper

SAUCE

⅓ cup hummus

I CREATED THIS RECIPE FOR THE PICKLE BARREL restaurant chain in Toronto, and it was featured in their local market menu. Ground lamb has a distinct flavor that I prefer to beef. Serving it with hummus is the perfect accompaniment.

1. Preheat the grill or grill pan and lightly coat with cooking spray.
2. In a nonstick frying pan lightly coated with cooking spray, add the oil and cook the mushrooms and onion over medium-high heat for 6 minutes or until cooked and mushrooms are no longer wet. Remove from the heat. Stir in the feta and set aside.
3. In a bowl, stir together the lamb, chives, dried oregano, barbecue sauce, breadcrumbs, egg, garlic, black olives, salt and pepper. Stir in the onion mixture. Form into 4 patties.
4. Grill the patties over medium-high heat for 3 to 5 minutes per side or until cooked through. Serve with hummus.

PER SERVING Calories 305 • Protein 27 g • Carbohydrates 12 g • Fiber 2 g • Total fat 16 g • Saturated fat 4.3 g • Cholesterol 124 mg • Sodium 389 mg • **PREP TIME** 15 minutes • **COOK TIME** 12 minutes • **MAKE AHEAD** Prepare the patties early in the day and refrigerate until ready to grill. • **NUTRITION WATCH** Lamb is a good source of vitamin B12, which supports the production of red blood cells and prevents anemia. Keep your portions in moderation, since lamb does contain saturated fat.

{ *recipes for the slow cooker* }

Brown your meat and sauté your vegetables before adding to the slow cooker. This improves their flavor • Less tender cuts of meat should be cooked as slowly as possible on the low setting. A more tender cut can be cooked at the high setting • If cooking white meat, such as chicken or turkey, leave the skin on to make sure that the meat doesn't dry out • Certain foods such as zucchini, peas, snow peas, fish, seafood or milk should be added during the last 30 minutes of the cooking time • Thaw frozen food before adding to the slow cooker • Do not lift the lid, as it will take 20 minutes to recover the lost heat • Do not reheat food in the slow cooker; instead use the oven, top of the stove or microwave

minestrone with diced chicken and brown rice { *Serves 8*

4 oz skinless boneless chicken breast (about 1 breast), diced
1 Tbsp all-purpose flour
2 tsp vegetable oil
2 tsp finely chopped garlic
1 cup chopped onion
1 cup chopped carrots
4½ cups beef (or chicken) stock
⅓ cup brown rice
1 cup canned chickpeas, drained and rinsed
1 can (19 oz) whole tomatoes (with juice), cut into quarters
2 bay leaves
2 Tbsp tomato paste
1½ tsp dried basil
½ tsp dried oregano
pinch of salt and pepper
2 cups chopped bok choy
3 Tbsp grated Parmesan cheese

IT'S SO WONDERFUL TO COME HOME TO A HOT SOUP just waiting for you in the slow cooker. To make it a complete meal, serve with a salad.

1. Dust the chicken with the flour. Lightly coat a large saucepan with cooking spray, add the oil and set over medium-high heat. Add the chicken and sauté just until browned, about 4 minutes. Remove the chicken from the saucepan and set aside.
2. Respray the same saucepan and keep over medium-high heat. Add the oil, garlic, onion and carrots and cook for 5 minutes or until the onion and carrot are softened.
3. Add the stock, rice, chickpeas, tomatoes and juice, bay leaves, tomato paste, dried basil and oregano, salt, pepper and the browned chicken. Bring to a boil, then add to your slow cooker. Cook on the high setting for 3 hours or on the low setting for 6 hours or until the rice is cooked. Add the bok choy during the last 10 minutes of cooking on the high setting and the last 20 minutes on the low setting. Garnish with the Parmesan cheese and serve.

PER SERVING Calories 185 • Protein 14 g • Carbohydrates 18 g • Fiber 4.8 g • Total fat 4.1 g • Saturated fat 1.2 g • Cholesterol 21 mg • Sodium 470 mg • **PREP TIME** 15 minutes • **COOK TIME** 3 hours (high) or 6 hours (low) • **NUTRITION WATCH** In addition to its high levels of fiber, brown rice is an excellent source of manganese (which is great for boosting energy), selenium (which fights cancer) and magnesium (which helps to maintain bones).

chicken with rice, green olives and tomato sauce { *Serves 6*

3 tsp vegetable oil
6 medium chicken thighs with bone and skin (about 1½ lb)
¼ cup all-purpose flour
2 tsp finely chopped garlic
1½ cups chopped onion
1½ cups chopped green bell pepper
1 cup brown rice
1 can (19 oz) whole tomatoes, puréed
3¼ cups chicken stock
½ cup sliced stuffed green olives
1 Tbsp drained capers
2 tsp chili powder
2 tsp dried basil
1½ tsp dried oregano
1 bay leaf
pinch of salt and pepper
¼ cup chopped parsley or cilantro

I'VE FOUND THAT COOKING WHITE RICE in the slow cooker is quite tricky—it gets either overcooked or not cooked enough. Here I've used brown rice, which seems to retain its texture better. In this recipe, I like to use canned, whole plum tomatoes that I've run through the food processor—I prefer this to canned crushed tomatoes. Also, remember to remove the skin from the chicken before eating to cut back on calories and fat.

1. Lightly coat a large, nonstick skillet with cooking spray and place over medium heat. Add 2 tsp of the vegetable oil. Dust the chicken with the flour and brown on all sides, about 6 minutes. Set aside.
2. Remove the fat from the skillet, wipe it clean and again lightly coat with cooking spray. Heat the remaining 1 tsp oil over medium heat. Add the garlic, onion and green pepper and cook, stirring frequently, for 4 minutes or until softened. Stir in the rice, puréed tomatoes, stock, olives, capers, chili powder, dried basil and oregano, bay leaf, salt and pepper. Add the chicken, bring to a boil and cook for 1 minute. Pour everything into the slow cooker and cook on the high setting for 3 hours, stirring once halfway through cooking time, or on the low setting for 4½ to 5 hours. Check to see if the chicken is cooked through and cook longer if necessary. Garnish with parsley or cilantro.

PER SERVING Calories 406 • Protein 22 g • Carbohydrates 44 g • Fiber 5.2 g • Total fat 11 g • Saturated fat 3.0 g • Cholesterol 58 mg • Sodium 650 mg • **PREP TIME** 15 minutes • **COOK TIME** 3 hours (high) or 4½ hours (low) • **NUTRITION WATCH** One chicken thigh with skin has 169 calories and 11 g of fat; one chicken thigh without skin has 124 calories and 5 g of fat per serving. Go ahead and cook chicken with the skin on because it adds so much flavor; just be sure you don't eat the skin.

chicken chili with barley and black beans { *Serves 6*

2 tsp vegetable oil
1 cup chopped onion
2 tsp finely chopped garlic
1 lb ground chicken
2 cups tomato sauce (see page 334) (or store-bought spaghetti sauce)
2 cups chicken stock
⅓ cup pearl barley
1 Tbsp seeded and finely chopped jalapeño pepper
1 tsp chili powder
2 tsp dried basil
1 tsp dried oregano
2 bay leaves
1 cup canned black beans, drained and rinsed
2 Tbsp tomato paste
pinch of salt and pepper
¼ cup chopped cilantro
⅓ cup shredded aged light cheddar cheese
¼ cup low-fat sour cream

CHILI IS A WONDERFUL MEAL to come home to, especially during the cooler months. Serve this with a slice of whole-grain baguette or cornbread and a large salad.

1. Lightly coat a large, nonstick skillet with cooking spray, add the oil and place over medium heat. Add the onion and garlic and sauté until browned, about 5 minutes.
2. Add the ground chicken and sauté until it's no longer pink, about 5 minutes, breaking it up into bite-size pieces with the back of a wooden spoon. Add the tomato sauce, stock, barley, jalapeño, chili powder, dried basil and oregano, bay leaves, beans, tomato paste, salt and pepper. Bring to a boil. Pour into the slow cooker and cook on the high setting for 2½ hours or on the low setting for 5 hours. Garnish each serving with cilantro, cheese and sour cream.

PER SERVING Calories 359 • Protein 27 g • Carbohydrates 28 g • Fiber 9.5 g • Total fat 8 g • Saturated fat 2.6 g • Cholesterol 67 mg • Sodium 365 mg • **PREP TIME** 15 minutes • **COOK TIME** 2½ hours (high) or 5 hours (low) • **NUTRITION WATCH** Barley is a nutritional powerhouse. It is packed with fiber, vitamins and minerals, low in fat and, like all plant products, cholesterol free.

chicken paella with sausage, shrimp and mussels { *Serves 6*

12 oz skinless boneless chicken breasts (about 3 breasts)
3 Tbsp all-purpose flour
2 tsp vegetable oil
6 oz mild Italian sausage, cut into ½-inch pieces
1 cup chopped onion
2 tsp finely chopped garlic
1 cup chopped red bell pepper
1 cup chopped green bell pepper
1 cup brown rice
3 cups chicken stock
3 cups chopped plum tomatoes
2 tsp dried basil
1 tsp dried oregano
1 bay leaf
½ tsp crumbled saffron threads (optional)
pinch of salt and pepper
8 oz raw shrimp, peeled and deveined
12 mussels, scrubbed and debearded
¼ cup chopped parsley

I LOVE PAELLA but I find it takes too long to cook, especially if I've just walked in the door and want something on the table in a hurry. The slow cooker is the perfect solution—all you have to do is add the seafood about 30 minutes before you're ready to eat.

1. Cube the chicken and dust with flour. Lightly coat a large, nonstick skillet with cooking spray and set over medium-high heat. Add the oil. Brown the chicken on all sides, for about 3 minutes or just until cooked. Remove from the pan and set aside.
2. Again lightly coat the pan with cooking spray. Add the sausage and cook over medium-high heat for 5 minutes or until cooked through. Remove from the pan with a slotted spoon, draining as much of the fat as possible. Set aside.
3. Wipe out the pan and respray it. Cook the onion and garlic over medium-high heat for 4 minutes or until softened. Stir in the red and green peppers and cook for 3 minutes. Stir in the rice and cook for 1 minute. Add the chicken, sausage, chicken stock, tomatoes, basil, oregano, bay leaf, saffron (if using), salt and pepper. Bring to a boil.
4. Place everything in the slow cooker and cook on the high setting for 3 hours or on the low setting for 5 hours. Add the shrimp and mussels during the last 30 minutes if the slow cooker is on the high setting, or during the last 60 minutes if on low. Serve garnished with parsley.

PER SERVING Calories 367 • Protein 31 g • Carbohydrates 43 g • Fiber 3 g • Total fat 7.6 g • Saturated fat 2.1 g • Cholesterol 92 mg • Sodium 490 mg • **PREP TIME** 25 minutes • **COOK TIME** 3 hours (high) or 5 hours (low) • **NUTRITION WATCH** 2½ oz of Italian sausage is high in calories (258), fat (20 g) and sodium (905 mg). Use it in moderation or use a leaner sausage.

turkey breast with sesame ginger sauce { *Serves 8*

SAUCE
⅔ cup chicken stock
3 Tbsp vegetable oil
¼ cup low-sodium soy sauce
2 Tbsp oyster sauce
1½ Tbsp sesame oil
2 tsp finely chopped garlic
2 tsp finely chopped ginger

TURKEY
3½ lb whole boneless turkey breast with skin on
⅓ cup chopped green onions
3 Tbsp chopped cilantro or parsley
1 tsp toasted sesame seeds

THIS RECIPE WILL FEED AN ENTIRE FAMILY and it is so easy to prepare. Serve alongside some rice or pasta. The Asian-inspired sauce complements the turkey nicely. A whole boneless turkey breast is available at most supermarkets or at your butcher.

1. To make the sauce, whisk together the stock, vegetable oil, soy sauce, oyster sauce, sesame oil, garlic and ginger in a bowl.
2. Place the turkey breast in a slow cooker and pour half the sauce over the turkey. Cook on the high setting for about 2½ hours or on the low setting for 5 hours or until the internal temperature of the turkey reaches 160°F. Do not overcook or turkey will dry out. Add the chopped green onions during the last 20 minutes of cooking. Remove the skin before serving. Serve garnished with cilantro, sesame seeds and the remaining sauce.

PER SERVING Calories 301 • Protein 46 g • Carbohydrates 1.5 g • Fiber 0.3 g • Total fat 10 g • Saturated fat 1.2 g • Cholesterol 130 mg • Sodium 400 mg • **PREP TIME** 5 minutes • **COOK TIME** 2½ hours (high) or 5 hours (low) • **NUTRITION WATCH** Turkey contains the amino acid tryptophan. Tryptophan helps the body produce the B vitamin niacin, which helps the body produce serotonin, a chemical that acts as a calming agent in the brain and plays a key role in sleep.

meatloaf with roasted red pepper and goat cheese { *Serves 6*

MEATLOAF

1½ lb lean ground beef
½ cup seasoned dry breadcrumbs
2 tsp finely chopped garlic
1½ tsp dried basil
1 large egg
¼ cup finely chopped green onions
¼ cup barbecue sauce

FILLING

⅓ cup finely chopped roasted red pepper (see page 100)
⅓ cup crumbled goat cheese (about 1½ oz)

GARNISH

¼ cup chopped fresh basil or parsley

I NEVER THOUGHT MEATLOAF COULD BE MADE IN A SLOW COOKER, but this one is even more moist than the oven-baked version. I layer the meatloaf with roasted pepper, goat cheese and green onions to give it a more sophisticated appearance and flavor.

1. Place the ground beef, breadcrumbs, garlic, basil, egg, green onions and 3 Tbsp of the barbecue sauce in a large bowl and stir until all the ingredients are well combined.
2. Roll out 2 feet of foil and fold in half. Line the container of the slow cooker with the foil, allowing it to come up the sides. Lightly coat with cooking spray. Place half of the beef mixture in the foil-lined slow cooker and form into a 6-inch square. Top with the roasted pepper and goat cheese. Pat the remaining beef mixture over the filling, enclosing the loaf. Spread the remaining barbecue sauce on the top of the beef mixture.
3. Cook on the high setting for 2 hours or on the low setting for 4 hours or until the internal temperature reaches 160°F. Garnish with fresh basil or parsley and serve.

PER SERVING Calories 196 • Protein 20 g • Carbohydrates 8.6 g • Fiber 0.8 g • Total fat 9.3 g • Saturated fat 3.8 g • Cholesterol 80 mg • Sodium 478 mg • **PREP TIME** 15 minutes • **COOK TIME** 2 hours (high) or 4 hours (low) • **NUTRITION WATCH** Goat cheese is lower in fat, calories and cholesterol than hard cheeses. It also provides more calcium and fewer carbohydrates than cream cheese.

curried beef casserole with sweet potatoes and parsnips { *Serves 4*

1 lb stewing beef, cut into ¾-inch cubes
3 Tbsp all-purpose flour
4 tsp vegetable oil
2 tsp finely chopped garlic
1 cup chopped onion
4 cups sliced mushrooms (about ½ lb)
1 cup peeled and diced carrots
1 cup peeled and diced parsnips
1 cup peeled and diced sweet potato
2 cups beef (or chicken) stock
⅓ cup red wine
3 Tbsp tomato paste
2 tsp curry powder
1½ tsp brown sugar
1 tsp hot chili sauce (or finely chopped jalapeño pepper)
pinch of salt and pepper
⅓ cup chopped cilantro or parsley

A BEEF CASSEROLE IS THE PERFECT DINNER during the colder months, but you would never have enough time to cook this in the traditional way on a typical evening. The slow cooker is a great solution. I love to serve this over mashed potatoes (pages 187, 318 or 344), which can be started when you come home from work.

1. Dust the beef with the flour and set aside. Lightly coat a large, nonstick Dutch oven with cooking spray. Heat 2 tsp of the oil over medium-high heat and sauté the beef for 3 minutes or just until seared and browned all over, stirring frequently. Remove the beef and set aside. Wipe out the pan.
2. Respray the pan, heat the remaining 2 tsp oil over medium-high heat and add the garlic and onion. Sauté for 3 minutes, or until just softened. Add the mushrooms and sauté for 5 minutes or until the liquid is evaporated. Add the carrots, parsnips, sweet potato, stock, wine, tomato paste, curry powder, sugar, chili sauce, salt and pepper and beef. Cover and bring to a boil. Add to the slow cooker and cook on the high setting for 3 hours or on the low setting for 5 hours. Garnish with cilantro or parsley just before serving.

PER SERVING Calories 296 • Protein 22 g • Carbohydrates 30 g • Fiber 5 g • Total fat 8 g • Saturated fat 3 g • Cholesterol 75 mg • Sodium 296 mg • **PREP TIME** 20 minutes • **COOK TIME** 3 hours (high) or 5 hours (low) • **NUTRITION WATCH** Lean cuts of beef are comparable to chicken and fish in fat content. For example, 3½ oz of beef eye round has 3.3 g of fat, whereas the same amount of chicken thigh has 7 g of fat. The same amount of farmed Atlantic salmon has 12.4 g of fat, but the fat in fish is healthier, since it's unsaturated and contains omega-3 fatty acids.

moroccan stew with pearl onions and baby carrots { *Serves 6*

1 lb boneless lamb leg, cut into 1-inch (2.5 cm) cubes
2 Tbsp all-purpose flour
2 tsp vegetable oil
1 cup pearl onions
1 cup chopped onion
2 tsp finely chopped garlic
2 cups peeled and diced sweet potato
1 cup baby carrots
1 cup canned chickpeas, drained and rinsed
1 cup beef (or chicken) stock
½ cup white wine
¾ cup raisins
1 Tbsp orange zest
3 Tbsp thawed orange juice concentrate
2 tsp finely chopped jalapeño pepper
1 tsp ground cumin
½ tsp cinnamon
¼ tsp salt
¼ tsp freshly ground black pepper
1 Tbsp cornstarch
1 Tbsp water
⅓ cup chopped cilantro or parsley

LAMB IS ONE OF MY FAVORITE MEATS. The leg is tender and perfect in a stew alongside the Moroccan flavors. Serve this over couscous or mashed potatoes (pages 187, 318 or 344).

1. Dust the lamb cubes with flour and set aside. Lightly coat a large, nonstick saucepan with cooking spray, add the oil and set over medium-high heat. Sear the lamb for 5 minutes or until browned on all sides. Remove the lamb from the pan.
2. Blanch the pearl onions in a pot of boiling water for 1 minute. Refresh in cold water and drain. Peel and set aside.
3. Respray the pan. Cook the chopped onion and garlic over medium-high heat for 3 minutes. Stir in the pearl onions, sweet potato, carrots, chickpeas, stock, wine, raisins, orange zest, orange juice concentrate, jalapeño, cumin, cinnamon, salt and pepper and browned lamb. Mix the cornstarch with water until smooth and add. Bring to a boil. Add to the slow cooker and cook on the high setting for 3 hours or on the low setting for 5 hours. Serve garnished with cilantro or parsley.

PER SERVING Calories 316 • Protein 21 g • Carbohydrates 41 g • Fiber 5 g • Total fat 7.3 g • Saturated fat 2.0 g • Cholesterol 55 mg • Sodium 250 mg • **PREP TIME** 25 minutes • **COOK TIME** 3 hours (high) or 5 hours (low) • **NUTRITION WATCH** On average, a 3 oz serving of lamb has only 175 calories. Lamb is an excellent source of protein, vitamin B12, niacin, zinc and selenium, and a good source of iron and riboflavin.

lamb vegetable stew over garlic mashed potatoes { *Serves 6*

STEW

one 1 lb boneless leg of lamb, visible fat removed, cut into cubes
3 Tbsp all-purpose flour
3 tsp vegetable oil
1 cup pearl onions
2 tsp finely chopped garlic
1½ cups sliced mushrooms
1½ cups chopped leeks
1 cup chopped green or yellow bell pepper
¾ cup chopped zucchini
1 cup chopped carrots
2 Tbsp tomato paste
⅓ cup red or white wine
2 cups chopped tomatoes
2 cups beef (or chicken) stock
1½ tsp hot chili sauce
2 tsp dried rosemary
1 bay leaf
pinch of salt and pepper
2 Tbsp cornstarch
2 Tbsp water

MASHED POTATOES

1½ lb potatoes, peeled and quartered
2 tsp vegetable oil
1 cup chopped onion
1 Tbsp finely chopped garlic
¼ cup canned evaporated milk (2%)
1 Tbsp olive oil
pinch of salt and pepper

GARNISH

¼ cup chopped parsley

THIS IS A TRADITIONAL MEAT STEW that uses lamb instead of beef, and is a perfect dish for the slow cooker. It's delicious served over these mashed potatoes, which are creamy but contain no cream or butter. I use olive oil and evaporated milk, or low-fat sour cream, as a substitute. Feel free to use any vegetables of your choice.

1. Dust the lamb cubes in the flour and set aside. In large, nonstick saucepan, heat 2 tsp of the oil over medium-high heat. Add the lamb cubes. Cook for 5 minutes or until well browned on all sides. Remove the lamb from the saucepan.
2. Blanch the pearl onions in a pot of boiling water for 1 minute. Refresh in cold water and drain. Peel and set aside.
3. In the same saucepan, heat the remaining 1 tsp of oil over medium heat. Add the garlic and mushrooms and sauté for 5 minutes, until the mushrooms are no longer wet. Add the leeks, bell pepper and zucchini and sauté for another 5 minutes.
4. Add the carrots, tomato paste, wine, tomatoes, stock, chili sauce, rosemary, bay leaf, salt and pepper along with the lamb and pearl onions. Combine the cornstarch and water until smooth and add to the stew. Bring to a boil, then add to the slow cooker and cook on the high setting for 3 hours or the low setting for 6 hours or until the lamb is tender.
5. Meanwhile, put the potatoes in a saucepan with water to cover. Bring to a boil and cook for 15 minutes or until tender when pierced with the tip of a knife.
6. In a nonstick skillet, add the oil, onions and garlic and cook for 4 minutes or until softened. Drain the cooked potatoes and mash with the milk, olive oil, salt and pepper and the onion mixture. Place the potato mixture on a large serving platter and top with the stew. Garnish with fresh parsley and serve.

PER SERVING Calories 343 • Protein 19 g • Carbohydrates 51 g • Fiber 7 g • Total fat 8 g • Saturated fat 3 g • Cholesterol 50 mg • Sodium 380 mg • **PREP TIME** 25 minutes • **COOK TIME** 3 hours (high) or 6 hours (low) • **NUTRITION WATCH** Potatoes are a nutrient-dense food. They are high in potassium and have no fat or cholesterol. The potassium in potatoes plays a role in lowering blood pressure, as part of a healthy, low-salt diet.

{ *children's favorites* }

Children like tasty, simple food. Don't use too many spices or ingredients that are foreign to their taste buds • Children have a natural sweet tooth. Satisfy it by giving them the dessert recipes in this book that have fewer calories and lower cholesterol. Over time they will crave fewer commercial baked goods • Foods that represent "fast food" to children—such as tortillas, chili, macaroni and cheese and "beefaroni-type" dishes—are always a sure way to get them to eat with a smile on their faces • Converting children and teenagers to eating better is easier than you may think. Do it slowly by introducing healthier versions of "fast foods." Once they start to enjoy these home-prepared foods, gradually introduce more sophisticated dishes. Over time, their taste for fatty foods will diminish as these new, tasty foods enter their repertoire • When preparing fajitas, quesadillas or wraps, try to use whole wheat tortillas to increase fiber intake • If you have really picky eaters, add extra-finely chopped vegetables to pasta sauce or chilis so they can't tell what they're eating

chicken fingers { *Serves 3*

8 oz skinless boneless chicken breasts (about 2 breasts or 1 large breast), pounded
1 egg
1 Tbsp water (or low-fat milk)
½ cup seasoned dry breadcrumbs
1 Tbsp grated Parmesan cheese
pinch of paprika

I DON'T KNOW A CHILD OR A TEEN that doesn't love their greasy deep-fried chicken fingers. Try this healthier and more delicious version at home. Dip the fingers in sweet and sour sauce, plum sauce or honey.

1. Place the chicken breast between 2 sheets of wax paper and pound to about ¾-inch thickness. Cut the chicken breast into long strips (about 4 × 1 inches; you should get about 6 strips in total).
2. Whisk the egg and water together in a bowl. In another bowl, combine the breadcrumbs, cheese and paprika. Dip the chicken fingers into the egg mixture and then the crumb mixture.
3. Lightly coat a large, nonstick skillet with cooking spray and set over medium-high heat. Sauté the chicken fingers for about 3 minutes per side or until no longer pink. Respray the pan if necessary.

PER SERVING (2 FINGERS) Calories 216 • Protein 20 g • Carbohydrates 7.5 g • Fiber 0.8 g • Total fat 8 g • Saturated fat 1.8 g • Cholesterol 114 mg • Sodium 180 mg • **PREP TIME** 10 minutes • **COOK TIME** 6 minutes • **MAKE AHEAD** Prepare up to a day in advance and bake just before serving. • **NUTRITION WATCH** These baked chicken strips have half the fat of the regular fried chicken strips or nuggets you'll find at fast-food restaurants, which often contain 12 g of fat and 600 mg of sodium per 3 oz serving. These ones are healthier, with all the flavor your kids will love.

pizza quesadillas { *Makes 4 quesadillas*

- 2 tsp vegetable oil
- 2 tsp finely chopped garlic
- ½ cup finely chopped onion
- ½ cup finely chopped green bell pepper
- ½ cup finely chopped carrots
- 6 oz lean ground beef
- 1 cup tomato sauce (see page 334) (or store-bought spaghetti sauce)
- 4 large flour tortillas
- 1 cup shredded mozzarella cheese
- 2 Tbsp grated Parmesan cheese

IMAGINE YOUR FAVORITE PIZZA topping inside a thin quesadilla. This is a great way to eliminate the heavy bread of pizza crusts and the excess cheese that's traditionally served on pizza. Cut into smaller pieces, these are also great appetizers. I serve them with a salad and my children have a complete meal.

1. Lightly coat a nonstick skillet with cooking spray and set over medium heat. Add the oil. Add the garlic, onion and pepper and sauté for 5 minutes or until the vegetables have softened. Add the carrots and sauté for another 5 minutes. Add the beef and cook for 2 minutes, stirring to break it up or until it is no longer pink. Remove from the heat and stir in the tomato sauce.
2. Divide the mixture among the 4 tortillas and spread to cover one-half of each tortilla. Sprinkle with the cheeses and fold in half.
3. In a large skillet or grill pan, heat for 2 minutes per side, just until hot. Cut each tortilla in half and serve hot.

PER SERVING (½ QUESADILLA) Calories 213 • Protein 13 g • Carbohydrates 24 g • Fiber 1.9 g • Total fat 7.5 g • Saturated fat 2.6 g • Cholesterol 20 mg • Sodium 580 mg • **PREP TIME** 10 minutes • **COOK TIME** 15 minutes • **MAKE AHEAD** Prepare up to a day in advance and keep refrigerated. Grill just before serving. • **NUTRITION WATCH** Flour tortillas, especially whole wheat ones, are loaded with B vitamins, which are important for children's health. They are lower in calories than a regular pizza crust, but taste just as good.

pesto chicken quesadillas { *Serves 6*

8 oz skinless boneless chicken breasts (about 2 breasts)
2 tsp vegetable oil
1 cup chopped onion
2 tsp crushed garlic
¼ cup pesto (store-bought, or see page 244)
½ cup shredded part-skim mozzarella cheese
4 large flour tortillas

PESTO AND CHICKEN are two foods most children like. Just add a little cheese, and you have a winner! These make a great appetizer or main meal. I always like to use my own recipe for pesto (see page 244), since it has a lot fewer calories and less fat than the store-bought type. In late summer, when basil is abundant, I make pesto in large batches and freeze it in small containers.

1. Lightly coat a nonstick skillet or grill pan with oil and place over medium-high heat. Sauté the chicken just until cooked, about 6 minutes per side. Dice the chicken and set aside.
2. Wipe out the skillet and respray. Heat the oil in a skillet over medium-high heat. Sauté the onion and garlic for 5 minutes or until the onions are tender and browned. Stir in the pesto and cheese. Add the chicken to the skillet.
3. Divide the mixture among the tortillas, placing it on half of each tortilla. Fold the tortillas in half. Heat on a grill pan or in a large skillet for 2 minutes on each side. Cut each tortilla into 3 wedges, making 12 wedges in total.

PER SERVING (2 WEDGES) Calories 203 • Protein 15 g • Carbohydrates 16 g • Fiber 2.1 g • Total fat 8.7 g • Saturated fat 2.5 g • Cholesterol 31 mg • Sodium 400 mg • **PREP TIME** 10 minutes • **COOK TIME** 20 minutes • **MAKE AHEAD** Make the quesadillas up to a day in advance. Cover and refrigerate. Grill just before eating. • **NUTRITION WATCH** Whole wheat tortillas are a source of iron, to give your children more energy, and are a good source of fiber, to keep their bowels regular and healthy. One whole wheat tortilla has 2.5 g of fiber.

chicken fajitas { *Serves 6*

8 oz skinless boneless chicken breasts (about 2 breasts)
2 tsp vegetable oil
1½ cups thinly sliced white onion
1½ tsp finely chopped garlic
1½ cups red bell pepper, cut into strips
¼ cup chopped parsley or cilantro
3 Tbsp chopped green onions
6 small (6-inch) flour tortillas
½ cup shredded light cheddar cheese
⅓ cup medium salsa
¼ cup low-fat sour cream

TEX MEX FOOD IS AN ALL-TIME KIDS' FAVORITE. These fajitas are creamy and rich tasting but without the fat of regular fajitas, which are loaded with a lot of cheese, sour cream, guacamole and beef. My version has plenty of vegetables, along with some light cheese and sour cream. Easy to make, and the whole family loves them.

1. Preheat the oven to 425°F. Line a baking sheet with foil and lightly coat with cooking spray.
2. Lightly coat a nonstick skillet with cooking spray and place over medium-high heat. Cook the chicken for about 8 minutes or until cooked and no longer pink. Let rest for 10 minutes, then slice thinly. Wipe out pan.
3. Add the oil to the pan and brown the onion and garlic, about 4 minutes. Reduce the heat to medium. Stir in the red pepper strips and cook until softened, about 5 minutes. Remove the pan from the heat. Stir in the parsley or cilantro, green onions and cooked chicken.
4. Divide the mixture among the tortillas. Top with the cheese, salsa and sour cream. Roll up.
5. Place on the prepared baking sheet. Bake in the center of the oven for 5 minutes or until the fajitas are heated through and the cheese has melted. Cut in half and serve immediately.

PER SERVING (1 FAJITA) Calories 220 • Protein 14 g • Carbohydrates 23 g • Fiber 2.1 g • Total fat 7.5 g • Saturated fat 2.5 g • Cholesterol 29 mg • Sodium 340 mg • **PREP TIME** 20 minutes • **COOK TIME** 20 minutes • **MAKE AHEAD** Prepare the filling up to a day in advance and refrigerate. Add 5 minutes to the baking time. • **NUTRITION WATCH** The average restaurant fajita has about 600 calories, 35 g of fat and about 2,500 mg of sodium (just over the maximum recommended amount of sodium in one meal). Make your own fajitas and avoid the excess fat and sodium.

grilled chicken caesar salad { *Serves 6*

4 oz skinless boneless chicken breast (about 1 breast)
2 cups cubed Italian bread (1-inch cubes)
4 Tbsp grated Parmesan cheese
2 Tbsp light mayonnaise
3 Tbsp olive oil
1 Tbsp water
2 tsp lemon juice
½ tsp finely chopped garlic
½ tsp Dijon mustard
8 cups torn romaine lettuce

THE KEY TO MAKING CAESAR SALAD healthy is twofold—reduce the amount of high-fat dressing and add nutrition. This dressing is lighter than the traditional one and by adding chicken you've got a protein, which will help make this a more filling and nutritious salad.

1. Preheat the oven to 400°F. Line a baking sheet with foil.
2. Lightly coat a grill or nonstick grill pan with cooking spray and heat to medium-high. Cook the chicken for 6 minutes per side or until cooked through and no longer pink in the center. Slice thinly.
3. To make the croutons, place the bread cubes on a baking sheet. Lightly coat with vegetable spray and bake for 8 to 10 minutes or until golden.
4. Combine 2 Tbsp of the Parmesan cheese, mayonnaise, oil, water, lemon juice, garlic and mustard either in a small food processor or by hand until smooth.
5. Toss the chicken, croutons and romaine in a large serving bowl. Pour the dressing over the top and toss to coat. Sprinkle with the remaining 2 Tbsp Parmesan cheese.

PER SERVING Calories 186 • Protein 8 g • Carbohydrates 13 g • Fiber 2.7 g • Total fat 11 g • Saturated fat 2.1 g • Cholesterol 15 mg • Sodium 173 mg • **PREP TIME** 15 minutes • **COOK TIME** 20 minutes • **MAKE AHEAD** The dressing can be made up to 2 days in advance and refrigerated. • **NUTRITION WATCH** Regular Caesar salad is packed with high-fat creamy dressing. On average, this means 400 to 600 calories, 30 to 50 g of fat and about 2,000 mg of sodium!

quick 'n easy pizzas { *Serves 4*

¾ cup tomato sauce (see page 334) (or store-bought spaghetti sauce)
4 flour tortillas
8 small mushrooms, thinly sliced
¼ cup diced red or green bell pepper
½ tsp dried oregano
1 cup shredded mozzarella cheese
¼ cup crumbled feta cheese (about 1 oz) (optional)
2 Tbsp chopped fresh basil

HERE'S A GREAT WAY to get the kids involved in cooking—they can come up with their own creations using the vegetables and cheeses that they like.

1. Preheat the oven to 400°F.
2. Divide the tomato sauce among the 4 tortillas and spread evenly. Top with the mushrooms, bell pepper and dried oregano. Sprinkle with the cheeses. Bake for 12 minutes or until crisp and the cheese is melted.
3. Garnish with basil and serve.

PER SERVING Calories 235 • Protein 13 g • Carbohydrates 42 g • Fiber 2.9 g • Total fat 8 g • Saturated fat 2.7 g • Cholesterol 14 mg • Sodium 540 mg • **PREP TIME** 5 minutes • **COOK TIME** 12 minutes • **MAKE AHEAD** Prepare the pizzas early in the day and refrigerate. Bake just before serving. • **NUTRITION WATCH** Tortilla pizza has a thin crust and is lower in calories than regular pizza. Using pitas or tortillas rather than the usual white flour pizza dough reduces the calories, fat and cholesterol by over 50%. And if you use whole wheat, you also get 3 times the fiber.

grilled two-cheese sandwich with tomatoes

{ *Serves 4*

2 oz aged light cheddar cheese, thinly sliced
1 oz light mozzarella cheese, thinly sliced
4 slices plum tomato
4 slices whole wheat bread

ANOTHER CLASSIC RECIPE FOR KIDS. Traditional grilled cheese is soaked with butter and oil and loaded with excess cheese. Instead, I use flavorful cheeses and lightly coat the bread with cooking spray. Serve this with my homemade tomato soup (next recipe).

1. Divide the cheddar and mozzarella between 2 slices of bread. Top with the sliced tomatoes. Cover with the remaining 2 slices of bread. Lightly coat both sides of each sandwich with cooking spray.
2. Lightly coat a nonstick skillet with cooking spray and place over medium heat. Grill the sandwiches for about 4 minutes per side, being careful not to burn them.

PER SERVING (½ SANDWICH) Calories 128 • Protein 9 g • Carbohydrates 14 g • Fiber 2.2 g • Total fat 4.8 g • Saturated fat 2.4 g • Cholesterol 11 mg • Sodium 285 mg • **PREP TIME** 10 minutes • **COOK TIME** 8 minutes • **MAKE AHEAD** Prepare sandwiches early in the day but grill just before serving. • **NUTRITION WATCH** A regular grilled cheese sandwich made with processed cheese will add 400 calories, 30 g of fat and 77 mg of cholesterol to your child's day. Make your own by using nonprocessed cheese, and make sure they're getting a healthy dose of protein.

homemade tomato alphabet soup { *Serves 4*

2 tsp vegetable oil
¾ cup chopped onion
1½ tsp finely chopped garlic
4 cups chopped ripe plum tomatoes
2 cups chicken (or vegetable) stock
1½ Tbsp tomato paste
2 tsp granulated sugar
pinch of salt and pepper
¼ cup dry alphabet pasta (or any small, shaped pasta)
2 Tbsp chopped fresh basil

FORGET THE CANNED VERSIONS—there is no comparison to a good homemade soup. Remember that the sodium levels are out of control in canned soups. I use ripe plum tomatoes in this recipe, and the addition of the alphabet pasta makes this a winner for children.

1. In a saucepan lightly coated with cooking spray, add the oil, onion and garlic. Sauté for 3 minutes. Add the tomatoes, stock, tomato paste, sugar and salt and pepper. Bring to a boil, cover and simmer for 15 minutes.
2. Meanwhile, bring a small pot of water to a boil, add the pasta and cook for 5 minutes or until the pasta is tender. Drain and set aside.
3. Purée the soup in a blender or food processor and pour back into the saucepan. Add the pasta and reheat.
4. Garnish with the fresh basil.

PER SERVING Calories 125 • Protein 5 g • Carbohydrates 20 g • Fiber 3.2 g • Total fat 3.2 g • Saturated fat 0.3 g • Cholesterol 0 mg • Sodium 300 mg • **PREP TIME** 10 minutes • **COOK TIME** 20 minutes • **MAKE AHEAD** Prepare up to a day in advance. Add the pasta just before reheating. • **NUTRITION WATCH** Cream-based soups are loaded with calories, fat and sodium. Try tomato- or broth-based soups to reduce the calories, fat and sodium for you and your children.

creamy chicken salad pitas { *Serves 4*

6 oz skinless boneless chicken breast (about 1 large breast)
¾ cup diced green bell pepper
⅓ cup diced red bell pepper
⅓ cup chopped green onions
3 Tbsp low-fat sour cream
2 Tbsp light mayonnaise
1½ tsp lemon juice
½ tsp finely chopped garlic
pinch of salt and pepper
2 large pitas
4 small lettuce leaves

I TEND TO AVOID CHICKEN SALAD when I go to restaurants because it's loaded with mayonnaise, which gives the innocent-seeming salad an abundance of calories and fat. This pita sandwich incorporates lots of diced vegetables and a light dressing, which give plenty of flavor without the fat.

1. Preheat the grill or grill pan to medium-high and lightly coat with cooking spray. Grill the chicken, turning once, until cooked through and no longer pink in the center, about 12 minutes. Remove from the grill, cool and dice.
2. Stir the chicken, green and red peppers, green onions, sour cream, mayonnaise, lemon juice, garlic and salt and pepper in a bowl.
3. Cut the pita breads in half and line the pockets with lettuce leaves. Divide the filling among the pitas.

PER SERVING (½ PITA) Calories 188 • Protein 13 g • Carbohydrates 23 g • Fiber 3.6 g • Total fat 5.5 g • Saturated fat 1 g • Cholesterol 30 mg • Sodium 341 mg • **PREP TIME** 15 minutes • **COOK TIME** 12 minutes • **MAKE AHEAD** Prepare the salad a day in advance. Fill the pitas just before serving. • **NUTRITION WATCH** A regular chicken salad sandwich or pita may have anywhere from 300 to 600 calories, with over 20 g of fat. Try this lighter version instead.

egg salad wraps { *Serves 4*

2 eggs
¼ cup finely diced celery
¼ cup finely diced red bell pepper
3 Tbsp finely diced green onions
2 Tbsp light mayonnaise
pinch of salt and pepper
4 small romaine lettuce leaves
2 large flour tortillas

EGG SALAD IS ANOTHER FAVORITE of many children. But the amount of mayonnaise added to chopped eggs dramatically increases the unnecessary calories, fat and cholesterol.

1. Boil the eggs for about 15 minutes. Drain and rinse with cold water. Peel the eggs. Mash and add the celery, red pepper, green onions, mayonnaise and salt and pepper.
2. Divide the lettuce leaves between the 2 tortillas and place in the center of each. Divide the egg mixture and add. Fold in the sides and roll. Cut in half.

PER SERVING (½ WRAP) Calories 185 • Protein 6 g • Carbohydrates 21 g • Fiber 1.8 g • Total fat 8.1 g • Saturated fat 1.5 g • Cholesterol 109 mg • Sodium 380 mg • **PREP TIME** 10 minutes • **COOK TIME** 15 minutes • **MAKE AHEAD** Prepare the salad up to a day in advance and keep refrigerated. • **NUTRITION WATCH** Traditional egg salad sandwiches and wraps may contain about 700 calories, 49 g of fat, 500 mg of cholesterol and over 1,000 mg of sodium. Watch the amount of cholesterol your kids get in a week to prevent future heart disease.

chicken and cheese tortellini with pesto { *Serves 4*

4 oz boneless chicken breast (about 1 breast)

12 oz tortellini

⅓ cup pesto (store-bought, or see page 244)

2 Tbsp grated Parmesan cheese

TORTELLINI IS A FAVORITE for even the pickiest of children. The chicken gives them the protein they need, and most kids like pesto especially if you add extra Parmesan cheese. Pack this in a Thermos food jar for their lunches.

1. In a small, nonstick skillet lightly coated with cooking spray, add the chicken and sauté for 4 minutes per side or just until no longer pink. Let cool, then dice.
2. Meanwhile, boil the tortellini for 8 minutes or until just tender. Drain and place in a serving bowl. Add the chicken, pesto and Parmesan cheese and toss well.

PER SERVING Calories 354 • Protein 20 g • Carbohydrates 41 g • Fiber 1.8 g • Total fat 12 g • Saturated fat 4.9 g • Cholesterol 56 mg • Sodium 548 mg • **PREP TIME** 5 minutes • **COOK TIME** 15 minutes • **MAKE AHEAD** Sauté the chicken up to a day in advance and keep refrigerated. • **NUTRITION WATCH** Pesto sauce is high in calcium and very high in vitamin A, an antioxidant that helps fight cancer.

thick and rich tomato pasta sauce { *Makes about 3½ cups*

2 tsp vegetable oil
2 tsp crushed garlic
½ cup chopped onion
½ cup chopped green bell pepper
½ cup chopped carrots
1 can (28 oz) crushed tomatoes
¾ cup chicken stock
¼ cup red wine
2 Tbsp tomato paste
1 bay leaf
1 Tbsp granulated sugar
1 tsp dried basil
½ tsp dried oregano
pinch of salt and pepper

GARNISH
¼ cup chopped fresh basil

THIS IS A PLEASING PASTA SAUCE without beef. The longer you let the sauce simmer, the sweeter it becomes. If a meat sauce is desired, sauté ½ lb lean ground beef, veal or chicken, breaking up the meat until it is no longer pink. Pour off the fat and add the meat to the sauce before simmering it for the 30 minutes. Serve over any kind of pasta.

1. Heat the oil in a large, nonstick saucepan. Sauté the garlic, onion, green pepper and carrots until softened, about 10 minutes.
2. Add the tomatoes, stock, wine, tomato paste, bay leaf, sugar, dried basil and oregano, salt and pepper. Cover and simmer for about 30 minutes, stirring occasionally. Discard the bay leaf. Purée until smooth. If too thick, add more stock. Garnish with fresh basil.

PER SERVING (¼ CUP) Calories 30 • Protein 0.8 g • Carbohydrates 4.6 g • Fiber 0.9 g • Total fat 0.1 g • Saturated fat 0.1 g • Cholesterol 0 mg • Sodium 102 mg • **PREP TIME** 15 minutes • **COOK TIME** 40 minutes • **MAKE AHEAD** Make the day before and keep refrigerated or freeze for up to 6 weeks. If it's too thin when reheated, add 2 Tbsp of tomato paste. • **NUTRITION WATCH** Homemade tomato sauce has much less sodium than the store-bought product, which has over 300 mg per ¼ cup.

fettuccine alfredo with green peas { *Serves 6*

12 oz fettuccine
1 cup cold chicken stock
1 cup canned evaporated milk (2%)
3 Tbsp all-purpose flour
1 tsp finely chopped garlic
pinch of salt and freshly ground black pepper
½ cup frozen green peas
¼ cup light cream cheese (about 2 oz), diced
⅓ cup grated Parmesan cheese
¼ cup chopped parsley

THE EXCESS BUTTER, CHEESE AND CREAM in fettuccine alfredo make it a pasta dish with little nutrition and loads of fat and calories. Let's not clog our children's arteries! Try my lightened-up, kid-friendly version. The key is to serve the pasta immediately after you've tossed it with the sauce.

1. Bring a large pot of water to a boil and cook the fettuccine for 8 to 10 minutes, until tender but firm. Drain.
2. While the pasta cooks, prepare the sauce. Combine the stock, milk, flour, garlic and salt and pepper in a large skillet and whisk until the flour is dissolved. Bring to a slow boil, then simmer until thickened, about 3 minutes, whisking constantly.
3. Stir in the peas, the cream cheese and half the Parmesan cheese and simmer for 1 minute or until the cheese is melted. Add the sauce to the drained pasta and toss.
4. Place on a serving platter. Garnish with the remaining Parmesan and the parsley.

PER SERVING Calories 339 • Protein 21 g • Carbohydrates 51.5 g • Fiber 2.7 g • Total fat 5.7 g • Saturated fat 2.4 g • Cholesterol 16 mg • Sodium 345 mg • **PREP TIME** 10 minutes • **COOK TIME** 15 minutes • **MAKE AHEAD** Prepare the sauce up to a day in advance, and reheat gently adding more stock to thin. • **NUTRITION WATCH** The creamy fettuccine alfredo in your favorite restaurant may cost you over 600 calories, 50 g of fat and over 1,000 mg of sodium. Make your own version with lighter sauce and add some fresh sautéed or grilled vegetables to boost the nutrients.

pasta shells with three cheeses { *Serves 4*

12 jumbo pasta shells (or 6 manicotti shells)
1¼ cups light ricotta (5%)
⅓ cup shredded cheddar cheese
3 Tbsp grated Parmesan cheese
¼ cup finely chopped fresh chives (or green onions)
2 Tbsp low-fat milk
1 egg
¾ cup tomato sauce (see page 334) (or store-bought spaghetti sauce)
¼ cup canned evaporated milk (2%)
⅓ cup shredded cheddar cheese

I LIKE USING JUMBO PASTA SHELLS rather than manicotti pasta since they hold less filling, and children are more likely to eat them. This cheesy filling goes very nicely with the creamy tomato sauce, and if you want the cheese filling to be smoother, use a food processor.

1. Preheat the oven to 375°F. Lightly coat an 8-inch-square baking dish with cooking spray.
2. Cook the shells in boiling water according to the package instructions or until firm to the bite. Drain, cover and set aside.
3. In a medium bowl, combine the ricotta, ⅓ cup cheddar and Parmesan cheeses. Add the chives, milk and egg and mix until well combined. Fill the pasta shells with approximately 2 Tbsp of the filling.
4. In a small bowl, combine the tomato sauce and evaporated milk until smooth. Pour half of the tomato mixture in the bottom of a large baking dish. Place the stuffed shells in the baking dish and pour the remaining sauce over the shells. Sprinkle with the ⅓ cup cheddar cheese. Cover and bake for 20 minutes or until heated all the way through.

PER SERVING Calories 298 • Protein 20 g • Carbohydrates 29 g • Fiber 1.8 g • Total fat 11 g • Saturated fat 6.6 g • Cholesterol 91 mg • Sodium 325 mg • **PREP TIME** 15 minutes • **COOK TIME** 30 minutes • **MAKE AHEAD** Prepare the stuffed shells up to a day ahead with sauce poured over. Do not bake until ready to serve. • **NUTRITION WATCH** Regular ricotta is high in calories and fat—¼ cup is about 100 calories, 8 g of fat and 5 g of saturated fat. Compare that to light ricotta (5%), which has only 60 calories, 2.5 g of fat and 1.5 g of saturated fat.

mac 'n cheese { *Serves 4*

8 oz dried macaroni shells
¾ cup chicken (or vegetable) stock
1 cup canned evaporated milk (2%)
2 Tbsp all-purpose flour
pinch of salt and pepper
3 Tbsp grated Parmesan cheese
¾ cup shredded cheddar cheese

PLEASE FORGET THE BOXED VERSIONS. They can stay on your shelves for years! Making your own macaroni and cheese is so delicious and nutritious. Add some sautéed vegetables or diced boneless chicken breast to boost the nutrition.

1. Bring a large pot of water to a boil and add the macaroni. Boil until just tender, about 10 minutes. Drain and place in a serving bowl.
2. Meanwhile, in a small saucepan, add the stock, milk and flour. Whisk until the flour is dissolved. Bring to a slow boil, then turn the heat down and simmer for 3 minutes or until slightly thickened. Add the salt and pepper, the Parmesan and three-quarters of the cheddar cheese. Cook for 1 minute.
3. Pour over the macaroni, mix well and garnish with the remaining cheddar.

PER SERVING Calories 368 • Protein 18 g • Carbohydrates 53 g • Fiber 1.9 g • Total fat 8.9 g • Saturated fat 5.4 g • Cholesterol 30 mg • Sodium 386 mg • **PREP TIME** 5 minutes • **COOK TIME** 15 minutes • **MAKE AHEAD** Prepare the dish a day in advance, but bake just before serving. • **NUTRITION WATCH** Kraft macaroni and cheese has close to 1,000 mg of sodium in only a quarter of the package. The cheese is also processed. Excess sodium is unhealthy for children and sets the stage for high blood pressure.

tuna cheddar melt { *Serves 4*

1 can (6 oz) flaked white tuna (packed in water), drained
¼ cup finely diced celery
¼ cup finely diced red bell pepper
2 Tbsp finely diced green onions
2 Tbsp light mayonnaise
1 Tbsp low-fat sour cream
1½ tsp lemon juice
pinch of salt and pepper
2 whole wheat English muffins, sliced in half and toasted
⅓ cup shredded cheddar cheese

GOOD QUALITY TUNA SALAD with melted cheddar over an English muffin is a treat for those children who love tuna. Let the kids get involved in the preparation. Make sure you buy tuna packed in water, not oil, to save unnecessary calories and fat.

1. Preheat the oven to broil. Line a baking sheet with foil.
2. In a small bowl, combine the tuna, celery, red pepper, green onions, mayonnaise, sour cream, lemon juice and salt and pepper until mixed.
3. Divide the filling over the English muffin halves and place on the baking sheet. Sprinkle with the cheese. Broil for 1 to 2 minutes or until the cheese is melted.

PER SERVING Calories 164 • Protein 13 g • Carbohydrates 16 g • Fiber 2.7 g • Total fat 6 g • Saturated fat 1.5 g • Cholesterol 21 mg • Sodium 525 mg • **PREP TIME** 10 minutes • **COOK TIME** 1 minute • **MAKE AHEAD** Prepare the tuna salad up to a day in advance and refrigerate. • **NUTRITION WATCH** Your children don't need the extra calories and fat from tuna that's packed in oil, so simply use tuna packed in water. White tuna packed in water is only 130 calories and 0.9 g fat per 4 oz can. Compare it with tuna packed in oil, which has 224 calories and 9 g of fat!

hamburgers stuffed with cheese and onions { *Serves 5*

1 lb lean ground beef
2 tsp crushed garlic
¼ cup finely chopped green onions
2 Tbsp ketchup
1 egg
2 Tbsp seasoned dry breadcrumbs
pinch of salt and pepper
¾ cup finely chopped onion
1 tsp vegetable oil
⅓ cup shredded cheddar cheese

A HEALTHY BURGER is not something you can easily find in fast-food restaurants today. This one has all the elements of an amazing burger while maintaining great nutritional value. The surprise is the cheese and sautéed onion pocket in the burger.

1. Preheat the oven to 400°F or preheat a grill or barbecue to medium-high.
2. In a bowl, mix together the beef, garlic, green onions, ketchup, egg and breadcrumbs, and salt and pepper to taste, until well combined. Form into 5 hamburgers.
3. In small, nonstick skillet, sauté the onions in oil until softened. Make a pocket in each hamburger and evenly stuff with onions and cheese. Press the meat mixture around the opening to seal.
4. Lightly coat the grill with cooking spray and grill burgers for 10 to 15 minutes or until no longer pink inside, turning the patties once.

children's favorites

PER SERVING (PER BURGER) Calories 240 • Protein 21 g • Carbohydrates 5 g • Fiber 1 g • Total fat 13 g • Saturated fat 4.5 g • Cholesterol 102 mg • Sodium 181 mg • **PREP TIME** 10 minutes • **COOK TIME** 10 minutes • **MAKE AHEAD** Make the patties a day in advance. Grill just before serving. These can also be frozen for up to a month. • **NUTRITION WATCH** A McDonald's Big Mac has 260 calories, 29 g of fat and 1,050 mg of sodium. Why not make your own? Use the freshest ingredients and end up with half the fat and sodium.

sweet 'n sour chicken meatballs with rice { *Serves 6*

12 oz ground chicken
¼ cup finely chopped onion
2 Tbsp ketchup
5 Tbsp seasoned dry breadcrumbs
1 egg
pinch of salt and pepper
2 tsp vegetable oil
2 tsp finely chopped garlic
½ cup chopped onion
½ cup diced red bell pepper
½ cup diced green bell pepper
1½ cups tomato juice
2 cups pineapple juice
½ cup sweet chili sauce (Heinz)
2 Tbsp brown sugar
1 Tbsp cornstarch
1 cup white rice
1 cup water
½ cup diced pineapple (fresh or canned)
3 Tbsp chopped parsley

CREATE YOUR OWN HEALTHY ASIAN FARE AT HOME. By using ground chicken, you reduce the calories, fat and cholesterol of regular ground beef, but feel free to substitute any meat of your choice for the chicken. I like to use the Heinz style of sweet chili sauce for this recipe, since it's not as spicy as Asian chili sauce.

1. In a bowl, combine the chicken, onion, ketchup, breadcrumbs, egg and salt and pepper and mix well. With wet hands, form the meatballs, using about 1 Tbsp of the mixture for each. Place on a plate and set aside.
2. In large saucepan, heat the vegetable oil over medium heat. Add the garlic and onion and cook just until softened, about 3 minutes. Add the bell peppers and cook for another 4 minutes. Add the tomato and pineapple juices, chili sauce, brown sugar, cornstarch and meatballs. Cover, reduce the heat and simmer for 25 minutes, or until the meatballs are cooked through.
3. Meanwhile, bring the rice and water to a boil, then cover and simmer for 10 minutes. Remove from the heat and let stand for 10 minutes, covered.
4. Serve the meatballs and sauce over the rice. Garnish with pineapple and parsley.

PER SERVING Calories 377 • Protein 15 g • Carbohydrates 61 g • Fiber 3 g • Total fat 7.7 g • Saturated fat 1.9 g • Cholesterol 73 mg • Sodium 429 mg • **PREP TIME** 20 minutes • **COOK TIME** 30 minutes • **MAKE AHEAD** Make the meatballs up to 2 days in advance and reheat gently on top of the stove. Can be frozen for up to 6 weeks. Great for leftovers. • **NUTRITION WATCH** Tomato juice is a source of the antioxidant lycopene, a cancer-fighting compound.

chicken parmesan { *Serves 4*

1 egg
1 Tbsp water (or low-fat milk)
⅓ cup seasoned dry breadcrumbs
1 Tbsp grated Parmesan cheese (optional)
1 lb skinless boneless chicken breasts (about 4 breasts)
2 tsp vegetable oil
1 cup tomato sauce (see page 334) (or store-bought spaghetti sauce)
½ cup shredded mozzarella cheese
2 Tbsp chopped fresh basil or parsley

THIS IS A REAL COMFORT MEAL for the whole family. Breaded chicken breast covered with mozzarella and baked with tomato sauce is simple to prepare and delicious. Complete the meal with a soup or large salad.

1. Preheat the oven to 400°F. Lightly coat an 8-inch-square baking dish with cooking spray.
2. In a bowl, mix the egg and water. In another bowl, combine the breadcrumbs and Parmesan cheese, if using.
3. Dip the chicken breasts in the egg mixture, then the breadcrumb mixture.
4. Lightly coat a large, nonstick skillet with cooking spray and place over medium-high heat. Add oil and sauté the chicken breasts for 2 minutes per side or just until browned.
5. Add half the tomato sauce to the baking dish. Place the chicken over the sauce, then pour the remaining tomato sauce over the chicken and sprinkle with the mozzarella cheese. Bake for 15 minutes or until the chicken is cooked through. Garnish with the basil or parsley.

PER SERVING Calories 258 • Protein 31 g • Carbohydrates 12 g • Fiber 1 g • Total fat 9 g • Saturated fat 2.9 g • Cholesterol 125 mg • Sodium 248 mg • **PREP TIME** 10 minutes • **COOK TIME** 20 minutes • **MAKE AHEAD** Prepare up to a day in advance. Bake just before serving. • **NUTRITION WATCH** Parmesan cheese is very high in calcium, which is good for your children's growing bones. But it's also high in saturated fat, so use it in moderation.

salmon teriyaki { *Serves 4*

¼ cup packed brown sugar
2 Tbsp low-sodium soy sauce
2 tbsp water
2 Tbsp rice vinegar
2 tsp sesame oil
2 tsp cornstarch
1 tsp finely chopped garlic
½ tsp finely chopped ginger
4 skin-on salmon fillets (4 oz each)
2 tsp sesame seeds
3 Tbsp chopped parsley or cilantro

WANT TO GET YOUR KIDS LOVING FISH? A good quality slice of salmon with this sweet Asian sauce is the way to go. This sauce can also go over chicken or Asian vegetables.

1. Preheat the oven to 425°F. Line a rimmed baking sheet with foil and lightly coat with cooking spray.
2. Whisk the brown sugar, soy sauce, water, vinegar, oil, cornstarch, garlic and ginger together in a small saucepan. Cook over medium heat until thickened and smooth, about 2 minutes. Remove from the heat.
3. Place the salmon fillets skin side down on the prepared baking sheet. Spoon half of the sauce over the fillets and sprinkle with the sesame seeds. Bake in the center of the oven for 10 minutes per inch of thickness, or until the fillet flakes easily when pierced with a fork.
4. Garnish with parsley or cilantro and serve with the remaining sauce on the side.

PER SERVING Calories 280 • Protein 24 g • Carbohydrates 20 g • Fiber 0.3 g • Total fat 11 g • Saturated fat 1.6 g • Cholesterol 64 mg • Sodium 590 mg • **PREP TIME** 5 minutes • **COOK TIME** 13 minutes • **MAKE AHEAD** Cook sauce up to 3 days in advance and refrigerate. Reheat in a small skillet over low heat just until warmed through. • **NUTRITION WATCH** Most store-bought Asian sauces, including teriyaki sauce, are loaded with almost a full day's recommended intake of sodium in 1 Tbsp, about 1,000 mg. Use low-sodium soy sauce in this recipe, which has half the sodium.

meatloaf with yukon gold mashed potatoes { *Serves 6*

MASHED POTATOES
- 1 lb medium Yukon Gold potatoes, peeled and cubed (about 1½ cups)
- 2 tsp vegetable oil
- 1 cup diced onion
- 1 tsp crushed garlic
- ¼ cup shredded cheddar cheese
- ¼ cup low-fat sour cream
- 1 Tbsp olive oil
- ¼ tsp salt
- pinch of pepper

MEATLOAF
- 12 oz extra-lean ground beef
- 1 egg
- ¼ cup barbecue sauce (or ketchup)
- ¼ cup seasoned dry breadcrumbs
- ¼ cup finely diced green onions
- 1½ tsp crushed garlic
- ½ tsp dried basil leaves
- pinch of salt and pepper

TOPPING
- 2 Tbsp shredded cheddar cheese
- 1 Tbsp grated Parmesan cheese

THE BEST WAY TO GET YOUR FAMILY eating meatloaf is to make it different and delicious. Here is the answer—a great-tasting meatloaf, baked along with mashed potatoes, which is something they'll all like.

1. Preheat the oven to 375°F. Line the bottom and sides of a 9- × 5-inch loaf pan with foil or parchment paper.
2. To make the mashed potatoes, add the potatoes to a large saucepan and cover with water. Boil for 15 minutes or just until tender. Drain and mash well.
3. Meanwhile, in a nonstick skillet lightly coated with cooking spray, heat the oil over medium heat. Cook the onion and garlic for 8 minutes or until browned. Stir into the mashed potatoes, along with the ¼ cup cheddar cheese. Add the sour cream, olive oil and salt and pepper, mixing just until combined.
4. To make the meatloaf, combine the ground beef, egg, barbecue sauce, breadcrumbs, green onions, garlic, basil and salt and pepper in a bowl. Pat into a loaf pan and bake for 20 minutes. Remove from the oven and spread the mashed potatoes over the meatloaf. Sprinkle with the 2 Tbsp cheddar cheese and Parmesan cheese. Bake another 10 minutes or until the internal temperature reaches 165°F. Let rest 10 minutes before slicing.

PER SERVING Calories 222 • Protein 14 g • Carbohydrates 19 g • Fiber 2.3 g • Total fat 9 g • Saturated fat 3 g • Cholesterol 50 mg • Sodium 200 mg • **PREP TIME** about 20 minutes • **COOK TIME** 55 minutes • **MAKE AHEAD** Prepare the entire meatloaf up to a day in advance. Bake just before serving. Leftovers are perfect. • **NUTRITION WATCH** Restaurant mashed potatoes are usually high in calories and fat because they're made with whole milk and butter. Try this recipe, which uses low-fat sour cream, for mashed potatoes that have a creamy texture yet are lower in calories and fat.

sloppy joes { *Serves 6*

1 cup finely diced onion
1½ tsp finely chopped garlic
1 tsp vegetable oil
12 oz extra-lean ground beef
4 oz spicy beef sausage, casings removed, diced
2 cups tomato sauce (see page 334) (or store-bought spaghetti sauce)
1½ tsp dried basil
1 tsp chili powder
2 Tbsp grated Parmesan cheese
2 Tbsp chopped fresh basil

SLOPPY JOES ARE MAKING A COMEBACK! The sauce is a thicker version of a meat sauce, and it becomes a sloppy joe when it's spooned over a hollowed-out bread roll, pasta, rice or even a baked potato.

1. In a medium saucepan lightly coated with cooking spray, add the onion, garlic and oil. Sauté for 5 minutes or until the onion begins to brown. Add the beef and sausage and cook for 5 minutes or until no longer pink, breaking apart the meat with a wooden spoon.
2. Add the tomato sauce, dried basil and chili powder. Cover and simmer for 15 minutes, stirring occasionally. Garnish with Parmesan cheese and fresh basil.

PER SERVING Calories 274 • Protein 25 g • Carbohydrates 14 g • Fiber 3 g • Total fat 14 g • Saturated fat 4.7 g • Cholesterol 69 mg • Sodium 256 mg • **PREP TIME** 10 minutes • **COOK TIME** 25 minutes • **MAKE AHEAD** Cook up to a day in advance and refrigerate. Reheat on top of the stove until warm. • **NUTRITION WATCH** Traditional sloppy joes are loaded with calories, saturated fat, cholesterol and sodium—a sandwich might have 635 calories, 27.1 g of fat and 48.0 g of carbohydrates. Reduce the calories by half by making this recipe.

asian beef with crisp vegetables { *Serves 4*

¾ cup beef (or chicken) stock
¼ cup packed brown sugar
2 Tbsp low-sodium soy sauce
2 Tbsp rice vinegar
2 tsp sesame oil
1 Tbsp cornstarch
2 tsp finely chopped garlic
1½ tsp finely chopped ginger
12 oz boneless grilling steak
2 tsp vegetable oil
1½ cups chopped broccoli
1½ cups thinly sliced red bell pepper
1½ cups snow peas
¼ cup chopped cilantro or parsley
¼ cup chopped green onions
2 Tbsp chopped toasted cashews (optional)

BEEF STIR-FRY IS AN ALL-TIME FAVORITE for the family, especially the kids. You can serve this over rice or rice noodles—one way I make sure my kids are getting their protein, vegetables and grains. The colors and textures of this dish give it great eye appeal. Be sure not to overcook the vegetables. Use the best quality steak, such as rib eye, sirloin, filet or New York.

1. To make the sauce, whisk the stock, brown sugar, soy sauce, vinegar, sesame oil, cornstarch, garlic and ginger in a bowl. Set aside.
2. Lightly coat a large, nonstick skillet with cooking spray and place over high heat. When the skillet is hot, brown the beef for 3 minutes, or until it's browned but still rare. Remove from the pan, let rest for 5 minutes, then slice thinly.
3. Respray the pan. Heat the vegetable oil, then add the broccoli, red pepper and snow peas. Cook for 3 minutes. Return the beef to the pan. Stir the sauce and add to the pan. Stir-fry for 2 minutes or until the sauce is thickened and bubbly and the beef is done to your liking. Be careful not to overcook.
4. Place on a serving platter and garnish with cilantro or parsley, green onions and cashews (if using).

PER SERVING Calories 161 • Protein 10 g • Carbohydrates 25 g • Fiber 3 g • Total fat 10 g • Saturated fat 2.5 g • Cholesterol 15 mg • Sodium 375 mg • **PREP TIME** 15 minutes • **COOK TIME** 8 minutes • **MAKE AHEAD** Prepare the sauce up to a day in advance and keep refrigerated. • **NUTRITION WATCH** Snow peas are full of nutrients (vitamins K and B6) that maintain bone health—important for your growing children.

shepherd's pie { *Serves 8*

2 tsp vegetable oil
1 cup finely diced onion
2 tsp crushed garlic
½ cup finely diced carrots
12 oz extra-lean ground beef
1 Tbsp all-purpose flour
1 Tbsp tomato paste
¼ cup beef (or chicken) stock
½ cup tomato sauce (see page 334) (or store-bought spaghetti sauce)
½ tsp dried basil leaves
pinch of salt and pepper
½ cup frozen green peas

1½ lb Yukon Gold potatoes, peeled and cubed
2 Tbsp olive oil
3 Tbsp canned evaporated milk (2%) (or regular milk (2% or low-fat))
3 Tbsp grated Parmesan cheese
¼ tsp salt
pinch of pepper
¾ cup shredded cheddar cheese

GARNISH

2 Tbsp chopped fresh basil (optional)

THIS IS A REAL CLASSIC that families still love to eat. For a change I sometimes use sweet potatoes instead.

1. Preheat the oven to 350°F. Lightly coat an 8-inch-square baking dish with cooking spray.
2. Place a large, nonstick skillet lightly coated with cooking spray over medium-high heat. Add the oil and onion and sauté for 3 minutes. Add the garlic and carrots and sauté for 3 minutes. Add the ground beef and sauté for 5 minutes or until no longer pink, breaking up the meat as it cooks.
3. Add the flour and cook for 1 minute. Add the tomato paste, stock, tomato sauce, basil leaves and salt and pepper. Cover and cook on low heat for 3 minutes or until thickened. Add the frozen peas. Place in a baking dish.
4. Meanwhile, cover the potatoes with water in a pot, and boil for 10 minutes or just until tender. Drain and add the olive oil, milk, Parmesan cheese and salt and pepper. Mash until smooth.
5. Spread the mashed potatoes over the beef mixture in the baking dish. Sprinkle with cheddar cheese and bake for 20 minutes or until hot. Garnish with fresh basil.

PER SERVING Calories 230 • Protein 230 g • Carbohydrates 15 g • Fiber 2.3 g • Total fat 8.9 g • Saturated fat 2.6 g • Cholesterol 30 mg • Sodium 214 mg • **PREP TIME** 20 minutes • **COOK TIME** 45 minutes • **MAKE AHEAD** Prepare the entire pie up to a day in advance and refrigerate. Bake just before serving. • **NUTRITION WATCH** Basil is an excellent source of vitamin K, which promotes good bone health. It is also a very good source of iron, calcium and vitamin A.

smashed potatoes { *Serves 4*

8 small red or white potatoes (about 1 lb), unpeeled
2 Tbsp olive oil
2 Tbsp grated Parmesan cheese
¼ tsp garlic powder
pinch of paprika
pinch of salt
3 Tbsp finely chopped parsley

WE ALL LOVE MASHED POTATOES, but if you've never had a "smashed" potato, you're in for a treat. (See page 186 for a version with a Middle Eastern flavor.) Seasoning and baking turns these flattened potatoes into a crispy, delicious dish. Let the kids prepare them.

1. Preheat the oven to 400°F. Line a baking sheet with foil and lightly coat with cooking spray.
2. Place the potatoes in a saucepan, cover with water and bring to a boil. Boil for 15 minutes or just until fork-tender. Drain and place on the prepared baking sheet. With the palm of your hand, press the potatoes flat, trying not to break them (cracks are normal). Brush with 1 Tbsp of the olive oil.
3. Combine the cheese, garlic powder, paprika and salt in a small bowl. Sprinkle half of the cheese mixture over the potatoes. Bake for 15 minutes. Turn the potatoes over, brush with the remaining olive oil and sprinkle with the remaining cheese mixture. Bake for another 15 minutes. Garnish with the parsley.

PER SERVING Calories 145 • Protein 3.1 g • Carbohydrates 15 g • Fiber 1.5 g • Total fat 7.9 g • Saturated fat 1.4 g • Cholesterol 2.5 mg • Sodium 82 mg • **PREP TIME** 5 minutes • **COOK TIME** 45 minutes • **MAKE AHEAD** Boil and flatten the potatoes up to a day ahead and refrigerate. • **NUTRITION WATCH** Potatoes are a very good source of vitamin C and a good source of vitamin B6, copper, potassium, manganese and dietary fiber.

sweet potato fries with cinnamon and maple syrup { *Serves 6*

2 large sweet potatoes (about 1½ lb), unpeeled and scrubbed
2 Tbsp vegetable oil
4 tsp maple syrup
¾ tsp cinnamon
¼ tsp ground ginger
pinch of nutmeg
3 Tbsp chopped parsley

SWEET POTATOES are the newest craze. They are more nutritious than regular potatoes and contain antioxidants that may help in the fight against cancer. Beware of those in restaurants, as they are usually deep fried.

1. Preheat the oven to 425°F. Lightly coat a rimmed baking sheet with cooking spray.
2. Cut the sweet potatoes in half lengthwise and then cut each half into 4 wedges. Lightly coat with cooking spray. Place on the prepared baking sheet.
3. Combine all the remaining ingredients except the parsley in a small bowl. Brush half the maple syrup mixture over the sweet potatoes.
4. Bake in the center of the oven for 20 minutes. Turn and brush with the remaining maple syrup mixture. Bake another 15 minutes or until tender. Sprinkle with the parsley.

PER SERVING Calories 170 • Protein 2.1 g • Carbohydrates 30 g • Fiber 3.9 g • Total fat 4.5 g • Saturated fat 0.2 g • Cholesterol 0 mg • Sodium 12 mg • **PREP TIME** 10 minutes • **COOK TIME** 35 minutes • **MAKE AHEAD** Prepare early in the day and reheat in a 350°F oven for 10 minutes or just until hot. • **NUTRITION WATCH** Sweet potatoes are an excellent source of vitamin A, which is beneficial for your eyes. They are also a very good source of vitamin C, to maintain your children's immune system.

potato wedges { *Serves 6*

3 large baking potatoes (about 2 lb), scrubbed
2 Tbsp olive oil
1 tsp finely chopped garlic
2 Tbsp grated Parmesan cheese
¼ tsp chili powder
3 Tbsp chopped parsley

THESE ARE THE BEST AND HEALTHIEST FRENCH FRIES you'll ever eat—forget deep-fried fast-food ones that can contain over 20 g of fat in a small serving. Experiment and use any seasonings you like. You can cut the potatoes early in the day, as long as you keep them in cold water so they won't turn brown.

1. Preheat the oven to 375°F. Lightly coat a rimmed baking sheet with cooking spray.
2. Cut each potato lengthwise into 8 wedges. Place on the prepared baking sheet. Combine the oil and garlic in a small bowl. Combine the cheese and chili powder in another small bowl. Brush the potato wedges with half of the oil mixture, then sprinkle with half of the cheese mixture.
3. Bake for 20 minutes. Turn the wedges and brush with the remaining oil mixture and sprinkle with the remaining cheese mixture. Bake for another 20 minutes or just until the potatoes are tender-crisp.

PER SERVING (4 WEDGES) Calories 156 • Protein 3 g • Carbohydrates 24 g • Fiber 2.3 g • Total fat 5.3 g • Saturated fat 1 g • Cholesterol 1.6 mg • Sodium 47 mg • **PREP TIME** 5 minutes • **COOK TIME** 40 minutes • **MAKE AHEAD** Prepare early in the day; keep refrigerated until ready to bake. • **NUTRITION WATCH** The deep-fried potato wedges that are served in restaurants have excess calories, fat and sodium. These homemade fries are delicious and much healthier.

{ *desserts* }

Different types of ovens and utensils can affect baking times. To be on the safe side, check cakes, muffins and loaves 5 to 10 minutes before the baking time is up. Stick a toothpick in several different points in the cake. If it comes out wet, continue baking. Brownies are the exception; when they are done, their center should still be wet • When mixing liquid and dry ingredients together for a cake batter, blend just until incorporated. Do not overmix • Cheesecakes should still be a little loose in the centre when you remove them from the oven. Do not bake until completely set—that is, until they appear firm—or cheesecake can dry out • Cookies can be baked longer than the recommended time to give them a crispy texture. Less baking time will give you a softer, chewier cookie • Cakes, cheesecakes and brownies can be frozen for up to 3 months if wrapped tightly • For cakes with fruit garnishes, freeze them without the garnish and add it just before serving • Whole wheat flour can replace up to half the white flour called for in a recipe. Do not add more, or the cake will be heavy and dense • Sifted icing sugar and cocoa can be sprinkled over the top of cakes for decoration. For a patterned effect, place a doily over the cake before sprinkling, then carefully remove it • Dessert batters can be mixed in a bowl with a whisk, in an electric mixer or in a food processor. If using a food processor, use the pulse feature (the quick on-and-off motion) so as not to overprocess.

pear crisp with cranberries and pecans { *Serves 12*

PEARS
6 medium-size pears, peeled, cored and sliced into ½-inch chunks (about 7 cups)
½ cup packed brown sugar
⅓ cup dried cranberries
2 Tbsp cornstarch
1 tsp cinnamon
1 Tbsp lemon juice

TOPPING
¾ cup all-purpose flour
¾ cup packed brown sugar
¾ cup large rolled oats
¼ cup chopped toasted pecans
¼ cup vegetable oil
2 Tbsp water
½ tsp cinnamon

THERE IS NOTHING EASIER AND MORE DELICIOUS than a crisp when you're using fruit that's in season. If they're more readily available, feel free to use apples, or combine them with the pears. For a large crowd, you can double or even triple the recipe.

1. Preheat the oven to 350°F. Lightly coat a 9- × 13-inch-square baking pan with cooking spray.
2. In a bowl, stir together the pears, ½ cup brown sugar, cranberries, cornstarch, cinnamon and lemon juice. Place in the pan.
3. In another bowl, stir together the flour, ¾ cup brown sugar, oats, pecans, oil, water and cinnamon and mix until the mixture is crumbly. Sprinkle over the pears.
4. Place the pan in the center of the oven and bake for 30 to 35 minutes or until the crisp is golden and pears are tender.

PER SERVING Calories 225 • Protein 2.1 g • Carbohydrates 43 g • Fiber 3.9 g • Total fat 5.2 g • Saturated fat 0.4 g • Cholesterol 0 mg • Sodium 7 mg • **PREP TIME** 15 minutes • **BAKE TIME** 30 minutes • **MAKE AHEAD** Can be baked a day in advance and reheated in a 350°F oven for 10 minutes. Best served warm. • **NUTRITION WATCH** Cranberries can protect against urinary tract and bladder infections.

lemon meringue custard pie { *Makes one 9-inch pie*

CRUST

1½ cups vanilla wafer crumbs (made from 3 cups vanilla wafers)
2 Tbsp water
1 Tbsp vegetable oil

FILLING

1 can (14 oz) + ⅔ cup low-fat sweetened condensed milk
1 Tbsp lemon zest
½ cup lemon juice (freshly squeezed)
3 egg yolks (save the whites)

MERINGUE

3 egg whites
⅔ cup granulated sugar
⅛ tsp cream of tartar
3 Tbsp water

THIS IS A TWIST on a lemon meringue pie—the filling has a creamier, custardlike texture. The meringue I have developed doesn't leak and holds its shape for at least 2 days in the fridge.

1. Preheat the oven to 350°F. Lightly coat a 9-inch pie pan with cooking spray.
2. To make the crust, combine the crumbs, water and oil a small bowl. Pat into the sides and bottom of the pie pan.
3. To make the filling, combine the sweetened condensed milk, lemon zest, lemon juice and egg yolks until well combined. Let sit for 10 minutes until thickened. Pour into the pie pan and bake for 20 minutes or just until the mixture is set.
4. Meanwhile, make the meringue. Combine the egg whites, sugar, cream of tartar and water in a clean bowl. With an electric beater, whip at the highest setting for about 6 to 8 minutes or until stiff peaks form. Spread over the lemon filling.
5. Increase the oven temperature to 375°F and bake for 10 minutes or until meringue is just lightly browned. Chill until cold and cut into 14 small slices.

PER SERVING (1 SLICE) Calories 257 • Protein 5.1 g • Carbohydrates 45 g • Fiber 0.3 g • Total fat 5 g • Saturated fat 1.9 g • Cholesterol 54 mg • Sodium 87 mg • **PREP TIME** 20 minutes • **BAKE TIME** 30 minutes • **MAKE AHEAD** Can be baked up to a day in advance and refrigerated. • **NUTRITION WATCH** Regular condensed milk is high in sugar and fat. Try a low-fat condensed milk instead. It has 50% less fat and carbohydrates.

orange cream pie { *Serves 12*

CRUST

1½ cups graham cracker crumbs
3 Tbsp granulated sugar
2 Tbsp water
1 Tbsp vegetable oil
1 tsp orange zest

FILLING

1 can (14 oz) low-fat sweetened condensed milk
½ cup light ricotta (5%)
½ cup light cream cheese (about 4 oz), softened
1 Tbsp orange zest
⅓ cup orange juice (freshly squeezed)
¼ cup granulated sugar

GARNISH

1 thin slice of orange

THIS IS A LIGHT TYPE OF CHEESECAKE, but it's still really creamy. The use of low-fat condensed milk gives this a dense, smooth texture without using whipping cream.

1. Preheat the oven to 375°F. Lightly coat a 9-inch pie pan with cooking spray.
2. To make the crust, stir together the crumbs, sugar, water, oil and orange zest in a bowl until mixed. Pat the mixture onto the bottom and up the side of the pan.
3. To make the filling, combine the condensed milk, ricotta, cream cheese, orange zest and juice, and sugar in a food processor. Purée the mixture until it is smooth. Pour it into the crust.
4. Place the pan in the center of the oven and bake for about 20 minutes or until the filling has just set. Let the pan cool on a wire rack.
5. Chill before serving and garnish with the orange slice.

PER SERVING Calories 277 • Protein 6.8 g • Carbohydrates 47 g • Fiber 0.5 g • Total fat 6.9 g • Saturated fat 3 g • Cholesterol 16 mg • Sodium 90 mg • **PREP TIME** 15 minutes • **BAKE TIME** 20 minutes • **MAKE AHEAD** Can be prepared a day in advance and refrigerated. • **NUTRITION WATCH** Orange juice is a excellent source of vitamin C, which boosts your immune system.

cheesecake phyllo pie with caramelized pears { *Serves 12*

FILLING
⅓ cup light cream cheese (about 3 oz), softened
¾ cup light ricotta (5%)
⅓ cup granulated sugar
3 Tbsp low-fat sour cream
1 large egg
1 Tbsp all-purpose flour
1 tsp vanilla extract

PEARS
2 tsp vegetable oil
3 cups peeled, sliced ripe pears (about 3 pears)
⅓ cup packed brown sugar
½ tsp cinnamon
6 sheets phyllo pastry

1. Preheat the oven to 350°F. Lightly coat a 9-inch springform pan with cooking spray.
2. In a food processor, combine the cream cheese, ricotta, sugar, sour cream, egg, flour and vanilla. Purée the mixture until it is smooth.
3. Place a large, nonstick skillet lightly coated with cooking spray over medium-high heat. Add the oil and sauté the pears for 1 minute. Add the brown sugar and cinnamon and sauté for another 2 minutes. Remove and drain the pears from the sauce, reserving the sauce.
4. Place 2 sheets of the phyllo in a prepared pan, letting the excess hang over the sides. Lightly coat with cooking spray. Place 2 more sheets in the pan, arranging them so that the corners of the phyllo sheets are staggered; the excess should fall over opposite sides of the pan from the first 2 sheets. Lightly coat with cooking spray. Place the last 2 sheets of the phyllo in the pan. Place the pears in the pan and pour the cream cheese filling over the pears. Fold the excess phyllo up and over the filling, leaving a little of the filling exposed. Lightly coat with cooking spray.
5. Bake for 35 to 40 minutes or until the phyllo is golden and the filling is set. Let cool on a wire rack. Drizzle the remaining pear sauce over the top, and serve.

PER SERVING Calories 138 • Protein 3.3 g • Carbohydrates 24 g • Fiber 1 g • Total fat 3.2 g • Saturated fat 1.6 g • Cholesterol 25 mg • Sodium 50 mg • **PREP TIME** 20 minutes • **BAKE TIME** 40 minutes • **MAKE AHEAD** Prepare both the pears and filling early in the day. Bake just before serving. • **NUTRITION WATCH** Cinnamon may help lower your blood pressure.

caramelized banana and coconut pie { *Serves 12*

CRUST

2 cups chocolate wafer crumbs

2 Tbsp water

1½ Tbsp vegetable oil

FILLING

2 tsp vegetable oil

2 ripe medium bananas, cut into ¼-inch slices

¼ cup packed brown sugar

TOPPING

¼ cup unsweetened coconut flakes

⅔ cup light ricotta (5%)

¼ cup light cream cheese (about 2 oz), softened

½ cup granulated sugar

⅔ cup low-fat plain yogurt

1½ tsp vanilla

2 tsp unflavored gelatin powder

3 Tbsp cold water

2 large egg whites

¼ tsp cream of tartar

¼ cup granulated sugar

BANANA CREAM PIE AND COCONUT CREAM PIE are both favorites of mine, so I decided to combine the flavors of both. Traditionally, cream pies are made with loads of whipping cream, which accounts for the excess fat and calories. I use a combination of light cream cheese, ricotta and whipped egg whites to get a delicious and light flavor and texture.

1. Lightly coat a 9-inch pie pan with cooking spray.
2. To make the crust, stir together the crumbs, water, and oil in a bowl. Pat the mixture onto the bottom and up the side of the pan.
3. To make the filling, lightly coat a nonstick skillet with cooking spray and place over medium heat. Add the oil and bananas and sauté for 1 minute. Add the brown sugar and sauté for 2 minutes, until the bananas begin to caramelize. Do not overcook. Pour the mixture evenly into the crust.
4. Place the coconut flakes in a small nonstick skillet and toast for 2 minutes or until just lightly browned. Set aside.
5. In a food processor, combine the ricotta, cream cheese, ½ cup granulated sugar, yogurt and vanilla until smooth. Add 2 Tbsp of the toasted coconut.
6. In a small, microwavable bowl, combine the gelatin and water and let sit for 2 minutes. Microwave on High for 20 seconds. Stir the mixture until it is dissolved. With the food processor running, add the gelatin through the feed tube. Transfer the mixture to a large bowl.
7. In another bowl, beat the egg whites with the cream of tartar until they are foamy. Gradually add ¼ cup sugar, beating until stiff peaks form. Stir one-quarter of the egg whites into the ricotta mixture. Gently fold in the remaining egg whites until just blended. Pour the mixture into the filling. Sprinkle with the remaining coconut. Chill for 2 hours or until set.

PER SERVING Calories 239 • Protein 5.2 g • Carbohydrates 39 g • Fiber 1.1 g • Total fat 6.9 g • Saturated fat 2.1 g • Cholesterol 7.7 mg • Sodium 95 mg • **PREP TIME** 20 minutes • **COOK TIME** 5 minutes • **MAKE AHEAD** Can be prepared the day before and refrigerated. • **NUTRITION WATCH** Coconut is a good source of manganese, which helps in maintaining your nervous system. But it is also very high in saturated fat.

miniature chocolate mud pies { *Serves 12*

1 cup chocolate wafer crumbs
1 Tbsp water
2 tsp vegetable oil
2 Tbsp semisweet chocolate chips
2 Tbsp hot water
1 tsp instant coffee
1 cup packed brown sugar
½ cup cocoa powder
2 Tbsp all-purpose flour
¼ cup + 1 Tbsp light cream cheese (about 2.5 oz), softened
2 large eggs
¼ cup low-fat sour cream
3 Tbsp corn syrup
1 tsp vanilla extract
icing sugar (to decorate)

THESE ARE THE BEST-SELLING DESSERTS at Rose Reisman Catering. They are so dense, they will put you into chocolate heaven. You will never believe they are lower fat. Drizzle with melted chocolate for an extra special touch.

1. Preheat the oven to 350°F. Lightly coat a 12-cup muffin tin with cooking spray.
2. In a small bowl, combine the crumbs, 1 Tbsp water and oil until mixed. Divide and pat into the bottom of the muffin tins.
3. In a small bowl, combine the chocolate chips, 2 Tbsp hot water and coffee. Microwave for 40 seconds on High or just until the chocolate begins to melt. Stir until smooth.
4. In the bowl of a food processor, add the sugar, cocoa powder, flour, cream cheese, eggs, sour cream, corn syrup and vanilla. Purée until smooth. Add the chocolate mixture and purée until smooth. Divide among the muffin cups and bake for 12 to 14 minutes or just until the centers are still slightly loose. Cool and chill at least 2 hours before serving. Carefully remove from the tin with a knife. Decorate with icing sugar.

PER SERVING Calories 220 • Protein 3.6 g • Carbohydrates 30 g • Fiber 1.5 g • Total fat 5.8 g • Saturated fat 2.1 g • Cholesterol 23 mg • Sodium 62 mg • **PREP TIME** 15 minutes • **BAKE TIME** 12 minutes • **MAKE AHEAD** Can be baked 2 days in advance and refrigerated. • **NUTRITION WATCH** There is increasing evidence that compounds in chocolate (dark chocolate) may beneficially affect cardiovascular health.

chocolate and cashew cream cheese pie { *Serves 12*

CRUST

1½ cups chocolate wafer crumbs

2 Tbsp water

1 Tbsp vegetable oil

CHEESECAKE FILLING

¾ cup light ricotta (5%)

⅓ cup granulated sugar

⅓ cup light cream cheese (about 3 oz), softened

¼ cup low-fat sour cream

1 large egg

1 Tbsp all-purpose flour

3 Tbsp cocoa powder

1 tsp vanilla extract

CASHEW FILLING

⅔ cup packed brown sugar

½ cup chopped toasted cashews

¼ cup semisweet chocolate chips

1 large egg

2 large egg whites

½ cup corn syrup

I DEVELOPED A PECAN CREAM CHEESE PIE in my book *Divine Indulgences,* and since I'm a chocoholic I had to remake this. This dessert tastes like a decadent pecan pie but is much lighter due to the cheesecake filling.

1. Preheat the oven to 350°F. Lightly coat a 9-inch pie pan with cooking spray.
2. To make the crust, mix the crumbs, water and oil together until the mixture holds together. Press into the bottom and sides of the pan.
3. To make the cheesecake filling, combine the ricotta, sugar, cream cheese, sour cream, egg, flour, cocoa powder and vanilla in a food processor until the mixture is smooth. Pour into the piecrust.
4. To make the cashew filling, whisk together the brown sugar, cashews, chocolate chips, egg, egg whites and corn syrup in a bowl. Pour carefully over the cheesecake layer.
5. Place the pan in the center of the oven and bake for about 35 to 40 minutes or until the filling is almost set.
6. Let the pan cool on a wire rack, then chill for at least 2 hours. Use a sharp knife when cutting.

PER SERVING Calories 286 • Protein 5.8 g • Carbohydrates 46 g • Fiber 1.2 g • Total fat 10 g • Saturated fat 3.4 g • Cholesterol 45 mg • Sodium 131 mg • **PREP TIME** 25 minutes • **BAKE TIME** 45 minutes • **MAKE AHEAD** Prepare a day in advance and refrigerate. • **NUTRITION WATCH** Brown sugar is not more nutritious than white; there are no significant nutritional differences between the two types. Brown sugar is composed of white sugar crystals that have been flavored and colored with small quantities of dark-sugar syrups (such as molasses).

banana-chocolate brownie cake { *Serves 16*

BROWNIE CAKE

⅔ cups granulated sugar
¼ cup vegetable oil
1 egg
1 tsp vanilla extract
⅓ cup unsweetened cocoa powder
⅓ cup all-purpose flour
1 tsp baking powder
¼ cup low-fat plain yogurt (or sour cream)
¼ cup semisweet chocolate chips

BANANA CAKE

½ cup granulated sugar
3 Tbsp vegetable oil
1 egg
1 tsp vanilla extract
1 large ripe banana, mashed (about ½ cup)
3 Tbsp low-fat plain yogurt (or sour cream)
¾ cup all-purpose flour
1 tsp baking powder
½ tsp baking soda

ICING

¼ cup light cream cheese (about 2 oz), softened
⅔ cup icing sugar
1½ tsp cocoa powder
1½ tsp water

I LOVE BANANA CAKE AND I LOVE BROWNIES. Well, take the elements of both and make a new dessert. These flavors have always gone well together. Use the ripest bananas you have. I always freeze my leftover ripe bananas in their skin and use them for baking.

1. Preheat the oven to 350°F. Lightly coat an 8-inch-square baking pan with cooking spray.
2. To make the brownie cake, combine the sugar, oil, egg and vanilla in a bowl until well mixed. Add the cocoa and mix well. Add the flour, baking powder, yogurt and chocolate chips, mixing just until combined and smooth. Don't overmix. Pour the batter into the pan.
3. To make the banana cake, combine the sugar, oil, egg, vanilla and banana in a bowl until well mixed. Add the yogurt, flour, baking powder and baking soda. Mix until just combined. Pour over the brownie cake.
4. Bake for 30 minutes or just until a tester comes out dry.
5. To make the icing, blend all the icing ingredients in a blender or food processor until smooth. Spread on the cake once cool, and serve.

PER SERVING Calories 213 • Protein 3.6 g • Carbohydrates 32 g • Fiber 1.5 g • Total fat 8.5 g • Saturated fat 1.8 g • Cholesterol 29 mg • Sodium 141 mg • **PREP TIME** 20 minutes • **BAKE TIME** 30 minutes • **MAKE AHEAD** Bake a day in advance and refrigerate. • **NUTRITION WATCH** Use light cream cheese, which has 25% less fat than regular.

milk chocolate fudge cake { *Serves 16*

CAKE

⅓ cup milk chocolate chips
¼ cup hot water
½ cup packed brown sugar
½ cup granulated sugar
⅓ cup vegetable oil
2 eggs
2 tsp vanilla extract
½ cup cocoa powder
¾ cup low-fat sour cream
¼ cup light mayonnaise
1 cup all-purpose flour
1½ tsp baking powder
½ tsp baking soda

ICING

¼ cup light cream cheese (about 2 oz), softened
⅔ cup icing sugar
2 tsp cocoa powder
2 tsp water

I DEVELOPED THIS RECIPE for a contest put on by the Scott paper towels company. It won for the best recipe in the series. This is similar to a devil's food cake, with half the calories and fat. The use of light mayonnaise gives it a dense and creamy texture.

1. Preheat the oven to 350°F. Lightly coat a 9-inch springform pan with cooking spray.
2. Combine the chocolate chips and hot water in a small bowl. Microwave on High for 30 seconds. Mix until smooth.
3. In a large mixing bowl, combine both sugars and the oil, eggs and vanilla with a whisk until smooth. Add the cocoa powder, sour cream, mayonnaise and melted chocolate. Mix until combined. Add the flour, baking powder and baking soda. Mix just until combined.
4. Pour into the pan and bake for 25 to 30 minutes or until a tester comes out dry. Let cool.
5. To make the icing, purée all the icing ingredients in the small bowl of a food processor until smooth. Ice the top of the cake.

PER SERVING Calories 202 • Protein 3.5 g • Carbohydrates 27.5 g • Fiber 1.2 g • Total fat 9.5 g • Saturated fat 2.2 g • Cholesterol 33 mg • Sodium 160 mg • **PREP TIME** 15 minutes • **BAKE TIME** 25 minutes • **MAKE AHEAD** Prepare the day before and refrigerate. • **NUTRITION WATCH** Unsweetened cocoa powder is one of the purest forms of chocolate you can eat and has less than 50% of the calories and fat of semisweet chocolate. Cocoa powder and dark chocolate contain many heart-healthy antioxidants. They contain a compound called flavonoid, which may lower bad cholesterol and raise good cholesterol.

chocolate carrot cake { *Serves 16*

CAKE

⅓ cup vegetable oil
1¼ cups granulated sugar
2 large eggs
1 tsp vanilla extract
1 large ripe banana, mashed (about ½ cup)
2 cups grated carrots
¼ cup canned crushed pineapple, drained
½ cup low-fat plain yogurt
1⅔ cups all-purpose flour
½ cup cocoa powder
1½ tsp baking powder
1 tsp baking soda
1½ tsp cinnamon
⅓ cup semisweet chocolate chips
1 Tbsp water

ICING

⅓ cup light cream cheese (about 3 oz), softened
⅔ cup icing sugar
1 Tbsp low-fat milk (or water)

EVERYONE LOVES CARROT CAKE, but add some chocolate to it and you have a totally new dessert. The key is adding cocoa powder and just a small amount of melted chocolate to keep the calories and fat under control.

1. Preheat the oven to 350°F. Lightly coat a 9-inch Bundt pan with cooking spray.
2. To make the cake, add the oil, sugar, eggs and vanilla to a large bowl and mix until smooth. Add the banana, carrots, pineapple, and yogurt. Stir until everything is well combined.
3. In another bowl, stir together the flour, cocoa powder, baking powder, baking soda and cinnamon until combined. Add to the cake mixture and mix until combined.
4. Place the chocolate chips and water in a small bowl and microwave on High for 30 seconds or just until the chocolate is beginning to melt. Stir until smooth. Add to the cake mixture, stirring just until everything is combined. Pour the mixture into the pan.
5. Place the pan in the center of the oven and bake for 35 to 40 minutes or until a tester inserted in the center comes out clean. Let the pan cool for 10 minutes before inverting the cake onto a serving plate.
6. To make the icing, beat together the cream cheese, icing sugar and milk in a bowl or food processor until the mixture is smooth. Drizzle over the cake. Decorate with grated carrots if desired.

PER SERVING Calories 237 • Protein 3.9 g • Carbohydrates 39 g • Fiber 2.2 g • Total fat 7.8 g • Saturated fat 1.9 g • Cholesterol 30 mg • Sodium 180 mg • **PREP TIME** 20 minutes • **BAKE TIME** 35 minutes • **MAKE AHEAD** Prepare up to 2 days in advance and refrigerate. • **NUTRITION WATCH** Pineapples have an enzyme called bromelain that has been shown to reduce inflammation and reduce certain types of swelling.

pumpkin molasses cake { *Serves 12*

CAKE

1 cup packed brown sugar
1 tsp cinnamon
½ tsp ground ginger
2 large eggs
½ cup low-fat plain yogurt
½ cup canned pumpkin purée
3 Tbsp molasses
¼ vegetable oil
1¼ cups all-purpose flour
1 tsp baking powder
½ tsp baking soda

ICING

¼ cup light cream cheese (about 2 oz), softened
½ cup icing sugar
2 tsp molasses
1½ tsp water

THIS CAKE HAS THE FLAVOR OF PUMPKIN PIE with a cream-cheese glaze. Be sure to use the canned pure pumpkin vegetable, not the canned pumpkin pie filling. You can freeze any remainder. This is a great seasonal dessert.

1. Preheat the oven to 350°F. Lightly coat a 9-inch Bundt pan with cooking spray.
2. To make the cake, use a whisk or electric mixer to beat the brown sugar, cinnamon, ginger, eggs, yogurt, pumpkin, molasses and oil in a large bowl.
3. In another bowl, stir together the flour, baking powder and baking soda. With a wooden spoon, stir the dry ingredients into the molasses mixture just until everything is combined. Pour the mixture into the pan.
4. Place the pan in the center of the oven and bake for 25 to 30 minutes or until a tester comes out dry.
5. Let the pan cool on a wire rack. Carefully invert onto a plate.
6. To make the icing, use a food processor or electric mixer to beat the cream cheese, icing sugar, molasses and water until the mixture is smooth. Drizzle over the cake.

PER SERVING Calories 219 • Protein 3.3 g • Carbohydrates 37 g • Fiber 0.5 g • Total fat 6.5 g • Saturated fat 1.2 g • Cholesterol 39 mg • Sodium 148 mg • **PREP TIME** 15 minutes • **BAKE TIME** 25 minutes • **MAKE AHEAD** Bake the day before and refrigerate. • **NUTRITION WATCH** Pumpkin has loads of antioxidants and beta-carotene, which strengthen the immune system. Pumpkins are also very low in fat and calories, and high in potassium.

lemon pudding cake { *Serves 12*

2 large eggs, separated
⅔ cup granulated sugar (for egg yolks)
1 cup low-fat plain yogurt
1 Tbsp lemon zest
¼ cup lemon juice (freshly squeezed)
¼ cup all-purpose flour
¼ tsp cream of tartar
3 Tbsp granulated sugar (for egg whites)

I LOVE ANY DESSERT WITH LEMON FLAVORING. This one has the texture of a soufflé but is slightly more dense. The pudding cake texture is unusual. During baking, the cake tends to separate. The top layer bakes as a cake and the bottom layer has a pudding consistency. It's incredibly moist.

1. Preheat the oven to 350°F. Lightly coat an 8-inch-square baking pan with cooking spray.
2. In a large bowl and using a whisk or electric beater, beat the egg yolks with ⅔ cup sugar until the mixture is thick and pale yellow. With a wooden spoon, stir in the yogurt, lemon zest, lemon juice and flour.
3. In another bowl and using clean beaters, beat the egg whites with the cream of tartar until they are foamy. Gradually add the 3 Tbsp sugar, continuing to beat until stiff peaks form. Fold the mixture into the batter just until blended. Pour it into the baking dish.
4. Set the baking dish into a larger baking dish. Pour in enough hot water to reach halfway up the side of the smaller dish. Bake for 25 to 30 minutes or until the cake is golden and the top is firm to the touch. Serve immediately.

PER SERVING Calories 93 • Protein 2.4 g • Carbohydrates 18 g • Fiber 0.1 g • Total fat 1.2 g • Saturated fat 0.5 g • Cholesterol 37 mg • Sodium 14 mg • **PREP TIME** 15 minutes • **BAKE TIME** 25 minutes • **MAKE AHEAD** You can bake this early in the day and eat it at room temperature or cold. But it is outstanding when served warm. • **NUTRITION WATCH** Lemons are an excellent source of vitamin C, but they start to lose their nutritional potency as soon as they're squeezed. They're also known to protect against arthritis.

mocha brownies { *Serves 12*

BROWNIES

⅔ cups granulated sugar
¼ cup vegetable oil
1 egg
1 tsp vanilla extract
1 Tbsp instant coffee
2 tsp hot water
½ cup unsweetened cocoa powder
⅓ cup all-purpose flour
1 tsp baking powder
⅓ cup low-fat plain yogurt (or sour cream)
¼ cup semisweet chocolate chips

ICING

¼ cup light cream cheese (about 2 oz), softened
¾ cup icing sugar
1½ tsp instant coffee
2 tsp hot water

I THINK I COULD CREATE A HUNDRED VARIATIONS on brownies. But coffee and chocolate ones are my favorites. These brownies have much less fat and fewer calories than regular ones, due to the use of vegetable oil, low-fat yogurt and cocoa powder. The key to keeping brownies moist is not to overbake them. They can be slightly unset in the center and they will be perfect.

1. Preheat the oven to 350°F. Lightly coat an 8-inch-square baking pan with cooking spray.
2. To make the brownies, combine the sugar, oil, egg and vanilla, and the coffee dissolved in hot water, in a bowl until well mixed. Add the cocoa and mix well. Add the flour, baking powder, yogurt and chocolate chips, mixing just until combined and smooth. Do not overmix.
3. Pour the batter into the pan and bake in the center of the oven for 15 to 18 minutes, just until set. Do not overbake. Cool.
4. To make the icing, blend the cream cheese and icing sugar, and coffee dissolved in hot water, in a blender or food processor until smooth. Spread over the brownies. Cut into squares.

PER SERVING Calories 175 • Protein 2.6 g • Carbohydrates 27 g • Fiber 1.5 g • Total fat 7.5 g • Saturated fat 2.0 g • Cholesterol 21 mg • Sodium 80 mg • **PREP TIME** 10 minutes • **BAKE TIME** 15 minutes • **MAKE AHEAD** Can be baked the day before and refrigerated. • **NUTRITION WATCH** Traditional store-bought brownies have 243 calories and 10 g of fat. My brownies have only 175 calories and 7.5 g of fat.

peanut-butter brownie cheesecake { *Serves 12*

BROWNIE LAYER

- ⅔ cup granulated sugar
- ¼ cup vegetable oil
- 1 large egg
- 1 tsp vanilla extract
- ⅓ cup all-purpose flour
- ⅓ cup unsweetened cocoa powder
- 1 tsp baking powder
- ¼ cup low-fat sour cream
- ¼ cup semisweet chocolate chips

CHEESECAKE LAYER

- 1½ cups light ricotta (5%)
- ¾ cup granulated sugar
- ½ cup light cream cheese (about 4 oz), softened
- ⅓ cup low-fat sour cream
- ⅓ cup smooth natural peanut butter
- 1 large egg
- 2 Tbsp all-purpose flour
- 1½ tsp vanilla extract
- icing sugar (to decorate)

PEANUT BUTTER, CHEESECAKE AND CHOCOLATE FLAVORS combine to make this an outstanding, decadent dessert. I keep the fat and calories down by using a combination of ricotta and light cream cheese, and more cocoa powder than chocolate.

1. Preheat the oven to 350°F. Lightly coat a 9-inch springform pan with cooking spray.
2. To make the brownie layer, beat together the sugar, oil, egg and vanilla in a bowl. In another bowl, stir together the flour, cocoa and baking powder. Stir the wet mixture into the dry mixture just until combined. Stir in the sour cream and chocolate chips. Pour the mixture into the pan.
3. To make the cheesecake layer, combine the ricotta, sugar, cream cheese, sour cream, peanut butter, egg, flour and vanilla in a food processor. Process until smooth. Pour the mixture on top of the brownie layer.
4. Bake the cheesecake in the center of the oven for 35 minutes. The brownie layer may rise slightly around the edges. Chill before serving. Decorate with icing sugar.

PER SERVING Calories 304 • Protein 8.1 g • Carbohydrates 36 g • Fiber 1.6 g • Total fat 14 g • Saturated fat 4.4 g • Cholesterol 53 mg • Sodium 171 mg • **PREP TIME** 15 minutes • **BAKE TIME** 35 minutes • **MAKE AHEAD** Bake the day before and refrigerate. • **NUTRITION WATCH** All-purpose flour is a good source of selenium. Selenium is incorporated into proteins to make *selenoproteins*, important antioxidant enzymes. The antioxidant properties of selenoproteins help prevent cellular damage from free radicals.

miniature lemon curd cheesecakes { *Serves 12*

CHEESECAKES
1½ cups light ricotta (5%)
½ cup light cream cheese (about 4 oz), softened
⅓ cup low-fat sour cream
1 large egg
¾ cup granulated sugar
3 Tbsp all-purpose flour
2 Tbsp lemon juice
1 Tbsp lemon zest

CURD
¼ cup granulated sugar
2 tsp cornstarch
½ cup water
1 tsp lemon zest
2 Tbsp lemon juice
1 egg yolk
12 sliced strawberry pieces

THIS WILL SATISFY ANYONE'S CRAVINGS, but especially those who love lemon desserts. The lemon curd is what makes this dessert so exceptional, and the miniature size is perfect for a sweet little ending to any meal.

1. Preheat the oven to 350°F. Line a 12-cup muffin tin with paper liners.
2. To make the cheesecakes, combine the ricotta, cream cheese, sour cream, egg, sugar, flour, lemon juice and zest in a food processor. Purée until smooth. Divide the mixture among the prepared muffin cups.
3. Set the muffin tin in a larger pan. Pour enough hot water into the pan to come halfway up the sides of the muffin cups. Bake in the center of the oven for 20 minutes or until almost set (it's okay if the centers are slightly loose).
4. Remove the muffin tin from its water bath. Let cool on a wire rack. Chill.
5. Meanwhile, prepare the curd by placing the sugar, cornstarch, water, lemon zest and juice in a small saucepan. Whisk until smooth. Place on medium heat, bring to a simmer and cook for 2 minutes, whisking constantly, until the mixture begins to thicken.
6. Beat the egg yolk in a separate bowl. Slowly add half of the lemon mixture to the yolk and whisk until combined. Pour back into the skillet and continue to cook on the lowest heat for 2 minutes, until smooth and slightly thickened, whisking constantly. Cool and serve over chilled cheesecakes. Decorate with strawberry slices.

PER SERVING Calories 150 • Protein 5.3 g • Carbohydrates 22 g • Fiber 0.2 g • Total fat 4.4 g • Saturated fat 2.5 g • Cholesterol 51 mg • Sodium 91 mg • **PREP TIME** 15 minutes • **BAKE TIME** 20 minutes • **MAKE AHEAD** Prepare the day before and refrigerate. If the curd is too thick, gently reheat in the microwave. • **NUTRITION WATCH** Sour cream is a source of calcium. Use the lower-fat varieties to reduce the fat, cholesterol and calories; they are just as delicious. Regular sour cream has 14% fat.

coconut cheesecake squares { *Makes 16 squares*

CRUST

½ cup granulated sugar

3 Tbsp unsweetened cocoa powder

2 Tbsp vegetable oil

1 large egg

½ tsp vanilla extract

⅔ cup all-purpose flour

FILLING

⅔ cup granulated sugar

2 Tbsp all-purpose flour

¾ cup light ricotta (5%)

⅓ cup light cream cheese (about 3 oz), softened

⅓ cup light coconut milk

1 large egg

½ tsp vanilla extract

4 Tbsp toasted unsweetened coconut flakes

COCONUT AND CHEESECAKE go so well together. To toast coconut flakes, just place them in a skillet over medium heat and brown for about 2 minutes, stirring constantly to prevent burning.

1. Preheat the oven to 350°F. Lightly coat an 8-inch-square baking pan with cooking spray.
2. To make the crust, stir together the sugar, cocoa, oil, egg and vanilla in a bowl. Stir in the flour just until combined. Pat the mixture into the bottom of the pan.
3. To make the filling, combine the sugar, flour, ricotta, cream cheese, coconut milk, egg and vanilla in a food processor. Purée until the mixture is smooth. Add 3 Tbsp of the toasted coconut. Spread the mixture over the crust.
4. Bake in the center of the oven for 25 to 30 minutes or until the center is still slightly loose. Decorate with the remaining coconut. Let the dish cool on a wire rack, then chill until cold.

PER SERVING Calories 145 • Protein 3.2 g • Carbohydrates 21 g • Fiber 0.6 g • Total fat 5.7 g • Saturated fat 2.7 g • Cholesterol 18 mg • Sodium 90 mg • **PREP TIME** 20 minutes • **BAKE TIME** 25 minutes • **MAKE AHEAD** Prepare the day before and refrigerate. • **NUTRITION WATCH** Use light coconut milk, which has over 50% less fat and fewer calories than regular coconut milk.

cappuccino rocky road cheesecake { *Serves 12*

1⅔ cups chocolate wafer crumbs
2 Tbsp water
1 Tbsp vegetable oil
1½ Tbsp instant coffee or espresso powder
1½ Tbsp hot water
2 cups light ricotta (5%)
½ cup light cream cheese (about 4 oz), cubed
1 large egg
¾ cup low-fat sour cream
1 cup granulated sugar
3 Tbsp all-purpose flour
⅓ cup miniature marshmallows
3 Tbsp semisweet chocolate chips
3 Tbsp slivered toasted almonds

A GREAT COMBINATION FOR A CHEESECAKE is coffee, chocolate chips, marshmallows and toasted almonds. This cheesecake is not only delicious but beautiful to present to your family and guests, especially if you drizzle it with more chocolate.

1. Preheat the oven to 350°F. Lightly coat a 9-inch springform pan with cooking spray.
2. In a small bowl, combine the crumbs, water and oil. Pat onto the bottom and partially up the sides of the pan.
3. Dissolve the coffee in the hot water. In the bowl of a food processor, add the ricotta and cream cheese, egg, sour cream, sugar, flour and dissolved coffee. Purée until smooth. Pour into the pan and bake for 35 minutes. Remove from the oven.
4. Sprinkle the marshmallows, chocolate chips and almonds over the cake and bake for another 5 minutes. Allow to cool, and chill before serving.

PER SERVING Calories 256 • Protein 7.3 g • Carbohydrates 35 g • Fiber 0.9 g • Total fat 9.5 g • Saturated fat 4.1 g • Cholesterol 38 mg • Sodium 179 mg • **PREP TIME** 15 minutes • **BAKE TIME** 35 minutes • **MAKE AHEAD** Bake the day before and refrigerate. • **NUTRITION WATCH** Some studies report that caffeine in coffee is a brain stimulant and can lead to temporary improvements in awareness, which may be useful at times of extreme exhaustion. But excess caffeine could overstimulate.

peanut-butter cappuccino-chip biscotti { *Makes 22 cookies*

1 Tbsp instant espresso powder or instant coffee granules
2 tsp hot water
½ cup granulated sugar
¼ cup packed brown sugar
1 Tbsp vegetable oil
3 Tbsp natural peanut butter
1 egg
1 tsp vanilla extract
1 cup all-purpose flour
1 tsp baking powder
¼ cup semisweet chocolate chips
¼ cup raisins

BISCOTTI ARE A GREAT LIGHT DESSERT or snack. They are lighter than most desserts yet seem to satisfy your sweet tooth. Be sure to use natural peanut butter without added sugar.

1. Preheat the oven to 350°F. Line a large baking sheet with foil and lightly coat with cooking spray.
2. Dissolve the instant espresso granules in the hot water. Combine the dissolved espresso, granulated and brown sugars, oil, peanut butter, egg and vanilla in a medium bowl, stirring until smooth. Add the flour, baking powder, chocolate chips and raisins. Mix only until the flour is combined. Form the batter into a 12- × 3-inch log.
3. Place on the baking sheet and bake for 20 minutes. Remove from the oven, let cool for 5 minutes, then slice into ¼-inch pieces. Place the pieces flat on the baking sheet. Return to the oven and bake for another 15 minutes or until crisp. Cool on a rack.

PER COOKIE Calories 82 • Protein 1.6 g • Carbohydrates 14 g • Fiber 0.5 g • Total fat 2 g • Saturated fat 0.7 g • Cholesterol 10 mg • Sodium 39 mg • **PREP TIME** 10 minutes • **BAKE TIME** 35 minutes • **MAKE AHEAD** Bake and keep stored in an airtight container for up to 3 days. • **NUTRITION WATCH** Raisins are a source of iron, for energy.

date and cranberry oatmeal squares { *Makes 12 squares*

1½ cups chopped dried dates
¾ cup dried cranberries
⅓ cup granulated sugar
1¼ cups water
1¼ cups large rolled oats
1 cup all-purpose flour
¾ cup packed brown sugar
¼ cup chopped toasted pecans
½ tsp cinnamon
⅓ cup vegetable oil
¼ cup water

INSTEAD OF JUST USING DATES I'VE ADDED DRIED CRANBERRIES, which give these squares a different and delicious flavor. I keep my dried fruits in the freezer so I always have some on hand. You can use scissors to cut your dates.

1. Preheat the oven to 350°F. Lightly coat a 9-inch-square baking pan with cooking spray.
2. In a saucepan, combine the dates, cranberries, sugar and water. Bring the mixture to a boil, then cover and simmer over medium heat for 15 minutes or until the dates and cranberries are soft and the liquid is absorbed. Mash the mixture and let it cool for 5 minutes.
3. In a bowl, stir together the oats, flour, brown sugar, pecans, cinnamon, oil and water until combined. Press half of the mixture onto the bottom of the pan to make a crust. Spread the date and cranberry mixture evenly over the crust. Sprinkle the remaining oat mixture over the filling.
4. Bake in the center of the oven for 25 minutes or until the squares are golden. Let cool on a wire rack.

PER SERVING Calories 290 • Protein 3.2 g • Carbohydrates 48 g • Fiber 3 g • Total fat 8.5 g • Saturated fat 0.6 g • Cholesterol 0 mg • Sodium 7 mg • **PREP TIME** 15 minutes • **BAKE TIME** 25 minutes • **MAKE AHEAD** Bake the day before and keep at room temperature. • **NUTRITION WATCH** Dried dates are loaded with both soluble and insoluble fiber. They keep your bowel habits regular and are an excellent source of potassium.

white and dark chocolate chip cookies { *Makes about 26 cookies*

⅓ cup granulated sugar
½ cup packed brown sugar
5 Tbsp margarine (or butter)
1 large egg
2 tsp vanilla extract
1⅓ cups all-purpose flour
½ tsp baking powder
pinch of salt
¼ cup miniature semisweet chocolate chips
¼ cup miniature white chocolate chips

A COMBINATION OF WHITE AND DARK CHOCOLATE CHIPS gives these lighter cookies a great flavor and appearance. I usually use vegetable oil for my fat in desserts, but the margarine keeps the cookie moister.

1. Preheat the oven to 350°F. Lightly coat 2 baking sheets with cooking spray.
2. In a large bowl, combine the granulated and brown sugar, margarine, egg and vanilla until well mixed.
3. In another bowl, stir together the flour, baking powder and salt. With a wooden spoon, stir the dry mixture into the wet ingredients until everything is combined. Stir in the chocolate chips.
4. Using a tablespoon, drop the batter onto the baking sheets. Bake for 12 minutes, for softer cookies.

PER COOKIE Calories 92 • Protein 1.2 g • Carbohydrates 13 g • Fiber 0.2 g • Total fat 3.7 g • Saturated fat 1.1 g • Cholesterol 9 mg • Sodium 45 mg • **PREP TIME** 10 minutes • **BAKE TIME** 12 minutes • **MAKE AHEAD** Prepare the day before and keep in an airtight container for up to 3 days. • **NUTRITION WATCH** The darker the chocolate, the more nutritional benefits it has. The amount of cocoa in the chocolate is indicated by percentages; for example, chocolate with 70% cocoa is better than 50% cocoa because it contains more antioxidants. In recent studies, cocoa has been shown to have heart-protective properties.

{ acknowledgments }

Thanks to:

Robert McCullough, publisher at Whitecap Books. You are truly the number one food publisher in this country. You're an inspiration to me, and I will always look to you for my next idea!

Taryn Boyd, Grace Yaginuma, Michelle Mayne and Mauve Pagé at Whitecap for their detailed work on the editing, design and format of this book.

Wendy Wong, CEO of Breakfast for Learning, a wonderful organization that ensures children in need are eating a nutritious breakfast at schools across Canada. This book is in support of them.

Ryan Szulc, the fantastic photographer who brought out the essence of my recipes, and who captured my family in action.

Roxanna Roberts for her intense and flawless work on the nutritional analyses.

Peter Higley, the inspiring president of the Pickle Barrel restaurants and owner of Glow Fresh Grill & Wine Bar, in Toronto. Thank you for believing in my work and implementing my philosophy in your restaurants. You've been a joy to work with.

To everyone at Rose Reisman Catering for keeping true to my recipes and communicating the message of eating well to our clients. Thanks to Stewart Webb, Charles Kerr, Ryan Rozella, Jennifer Droznika, Catherine Chalmers and Lauren Halloran.

To everyone at Personal Gourmet for making our fresh-food delivery service number one in Toronto. Thanks to Reagan Macklin, Miriam Farber and Bryan Birch.

Stokely Wilson, executive chef of the Pickle Barrel restaurants, and Barry Serrao, chef of Glow. Thanks for taking my recipes and making them your own works of art.

Maya Tchernina, my assistant at The Art of Living Well. Thanks for your daily research, and your assistance in editing the book and with all aspects of my work.

Parmjit Parmar, my publicist, who continues to manage my media campaign for my various ventures.

Kathy Kacer and Susan Gordin, my best buddies, who are always there for me ready to either walk through or taste recipe after recipe!

To my wonderful household assistants who helped test each and every recipe—Lily Lim, Dang Idala and Mila Doloricon.

{ index }

{ a

{ b

{C

{ d

{ e

{n

{o

{p

{q

{r

{s

{t

v

w

y

z

{ metric conversions }

{ VOLUME

⅛ tsp	0.5 mL
¼ tsp	1 mL
½ tsp	2 mL
¾ tsp	4 mL
1 tsp	5 mL
1½ tsp	7.5 mL
½ Tbsp	7.5 mL
2 tsp	10 mL
1 Tbsp	15 mL
4 tsp	20 mL
1½ Tbsp	22.5 mL
2 Tbsp	30 mL
3 Tbsp	45 mL
¼ cup	60 mL
4 Tbsp	60 mL
5 Tbsp	75 mL
⅓ cup	80 mL
½ cup	125 mL
⅔ cup	160 mL
¼ cup	185 mL
1 cup	250 mL
1¼ cups	310 mL
1½ cups	375 mL
1⅔ cups	410 mL
1¾ cups	435 mL
2 cups	500 mL
3 cups	750 mL
3½ cups	875 mL
4 cups	1 L
5 cups	1.25 L
6 cups	1.5 L
7 cups	1.75 L
8 cups	2 L

{ WEIGHT

1 oz	30 g
1½ oz	45 g
2 oz	60 g
2½ oz	75 g
3 oz	90 g
3½ oz	105 g
4 oz/¼ lb	125 g
5 oz	150 g
⅓ lb	170 g
6 oz	175 g
7 oz	200 g
8 oz/½ lb	250 g
9 oz	270 g
10 oz	300 g
⅔ lb	350 g
12 oz	375 g
1 lb/16 oz	500 g
1¼ lb	625 g
1⅓ lb	670 g
1½ lb	750 g
1¾ lb	875 g
2 lb	900 g
2½ lb	1.1 kg
3 lb	1.4 kg
3½ lb	1.6 kg
4 lb	1.8 kg

{ CAN SIZES

6 oz can (tuna)	170 g can
14 oz can	398 mL can
19 oz can	540 mL can
28 oz can	796 mL can

{ LENGTH

⅛ inch	3 mm
¼ inch	6 mm
½ inch	1 cm
¾ inch	2 cm
1 inch	2.5 cm
1½ inches	4 cm
2 inches	5 cm
2½ inches	6 cm
3 inches	8 cm
3½ inches	9 cm
4 inches	10 cm
4½ inches	11 cm
5 inches	12 cm
6 inches	15 cm
7 inches	18 cm
8 inches	20 cm
8½ inches	22 cm
9 inches	23 cm
10 inches	25 cm
11 inches	28 cm
12 inches	30 cm
13 inches	33 cm
14 inches	35 cm
2 feet	60 cm

{ TEMPERATURE

130°F	54°C
135°F	57°C
145°F	63°C
155°F	68°C
160°F	71°C
165°F	74°C
200°F	95°C
225°F	105°C
250°F	120°C
255°F	124°C
275°F	140°C
300°F	150°C
325°F	160°C
350°F	180°C
375°F	190°C
400°F	200°C
425°F	220°C
450°F	230°C
475°F	240°C
500°F	260°C

{ GLASS, PAN AND DISH SIZES

8 oz glasses	250 mL glasses
8-inch-square pan/dish	20 cm square (2 L) pan/dish
9-inch-square pan/dish	23 cm square (2.5 L) pan/dish
9- × 13-inch dish	23 cm × 33 cm (3.5 L) dish
11- × 7-inch dish	28 cm × 18 cm (2 L) dish
8- × 4-inch loaf pan	20 cm × 10 cm (1.5 L) loaf pan
9- × 5-inch loaf pan	23 cm × 12 cm (2 L) loaf pan
9-inch springform pan	23 cm (2.5 L) springform pan